TO THE
JEW
FIRST

TO THE
JEW
FIRST

THE CASE FOR JEWISH EVANGELISM
IN SCRIPTURE AND HISTORY

DARRELL L. BOCK AND MITCH GLASER

EDITORS

To the Jew First: The Case for Jewish Evangelism in Scripture and History

Published in 2008 by Kregel Publications, a division of Kregel, Inc., P.O. Box 2607, Grand Rapids, MI 49501.

Library of Congress Cataloging-in-Publication Data
    To the Jew first : the case for Jewish evangelism in Scripture and history / by Darrell L. Bock and Mitch Glaser, general editors.
        p.   cm.
Includes bibliographical references.
    1. Missions to Jews. I. Bock, Darrell L. II. Glaser, Mitchell.
BV2620.T58   2008
266.0088'296—dc22   2007048383

ISBN 978-0-8254-3658-1

Printed in the United States of America

08 09 10 11 12 / 5 4 3 2 1

Contents

Foreword

It has been a delight to work for several decades with my friend Dr. Mitch Glaser, president of Chosen People Ministries. Therefore, when I was invited to present a paper at the September 23–25, 2000, conference in New York City titled "To the Jew First in the New Millennium," I responded immediately. The results of that conference compose much of what is printed here and published for the first time by Kregel Publications in Grand Rapids, Michigan.

The significance of carrying the ancient message promised to Abraham, Isaac, Jacob, David, and Yeshua to the people descended from the patriarchs and the nation of Israel cannot be downplayed or underestimated in terms of the divine purpose for history and eternity. "To the Jew First" is more than a slogan or a cute way for the apostle Paul to introduce his message to the Jewish and Gentile believers in Rome (Rom. 1:16). Neither is the message of the gospel of Yeshua the Messiah one that must be aimed only at the Gentile audiences since there is allegedly another separate covenant that God has made with the Jewish people. On the contrary, the so-called Gentile church does not have any grounding if it does not find itself grafted into the roots of the patriarchal promises made in Genesis 12–50 and the trunk of the Olive Tree, which is Israel (Rom. 11:11–24).

A church cut off from Israel is a church that merely floats in the air with no past, no grounding, and no promises on which to build her present or her future. It simply is a figment of our imagination if it loses its grounding and support. Without these promises made to Israel in the Tanakh, there is no "good news" to be shared with anyone—including the Gentiles! The so-called "dual covenant," which allows for one way of salvation for Jewish people through the keeping of the Torah and another way of salvation for Gentiles through belief in Yeshua, will not work. The Jewish authors of the

New Testament and Yeshua himself deliberately claimed there are not two ways of salvation but only one unified plan of redemption that embraces all who put their trust in Messiah, whether they are Jewish or Gentile.

Some Christian interpreters have incorrectly argued that the promises made to Israel have now expired because of her unbelief and the church has been credited with receiving all those promises after Israel's default of unbelief. Such supersessionism (also called replacement theology) finds no biblical support in the text of either the Tanakh or the later testament. Moreover, if one is going to deed over the promises of blessing, then the curses of God's promise-plan ought to be inherited by the church as well. But there is no need for either transfer, for as the Jewish apostle Paul argued on behalf of a proper understanding of the Sovereign God's enduring blessing of Israel: "For the gifts and the calling of God are irrevocable" (Rom. 11:29 NASB).

Accordingly, there is good news for all Jewish people whether they currently live in Israel or in the Diaspora around the world: Messiah still is seeking all who will listen to the promises made in the Tanakh and repeated in the New Testament. Even if many Jewish people have given up hope, God has not given up and he declares that he has no plans to do so in the future—if only all (Jew and Gentile) will receive the good news, for it is the power of God to everyone who believes, to the Jew first and then to the Gentile.

The essays that follow are arranged in three sections titled Bible, Theology, and Mission. The fourteen chapters should open up a good basis for interacting not just with the great list of writers, but with the Scriptures themselves. May the Sovereign Lord himself grant a great blessing to the promised nation of Israel as well as to the wild branches of the Gentiles that have been so lately grafted into the same Olive Tree.

—WALTER C. KAISER JR.

Contributors

Richard E. Averbeck, Professor of Old Testament and Semitic Languages, Trinity Evangelical Divinity School

Craig A. Blaising, Executive Vice President, Provost, and Professor of Theology, The Southern Baptist Theological Seminary

Darrell L. Bock, Research Professor of New Testament Studies and Professor of Spiritual Development and Culture, Dallas Theological Seminary

J. Lanier Burns, Research Professor of Theological Studies and Senior Professor of Systematic Theology, Dallas Theological Seminary

Arnold G. Fruchtenbaum, Director, Ariel Ministries, San Antonio, Texas

Mitch Glaser, President, Chosen People Ministries, New York, New York

Arthur F. Glasser, Dean Emeritus of the School of World Mission, Fuller Theological Seminary

Walter C. Kaiser Jr., President Emeritus and Colman M. Mockler Distinguished Professor of Old Testament, Gordon-Conwell Theological Seminary

Kai Kjær-Hansen, International Coordinator, Lausanne Consultation on Jewish Evangelism, Denmark

Barry R. Leventhal, Dean, Professor of Church Ministry and Missions, and Director of Ministry Program, Southern Evangelical Seminary

Richard L. Pratt Jr., Professor of Old Testament, Reformed Theological Seminary, Orlando, Florida; President, Third Millennium Ministries, Fern Park, Florida

Michael Rydelnik, Professor of Jewish Studies, Moody Bible Institute

Mark A. Seifrid, Mildred and Ernest Hogan Professor of New Testament Interpretation, The Southern Baptist Theological Seminary

David L. Turner, Professor of New Testament, Grand Rapids Theological Seminary

Introduction

The mission of Chosen People Ministries is to reach the Jewish people around the world with the saving message of the gospel. Rabbi Leopold Cohn, our founder, established the mission with this purpose after first hearing about and then accepting Jesus as the Messiah on the lower east side of New York City. Since 1894, Chosen People Ministries, formerly called the American Board of Mission to the Jews, has practiced a two-pronged approach to bring the gospel message to God's chosen people.

The first prong is an unswerving commitment to Jewish evangelism. The staff and congregations of Chosen People Ministries are dedicated to bringing the message of our Messiah directly to the Jewish people in major Jewish population centers around the world. The second prong is to encourage and equip members of the church to do the same.

It is the second part of our ministry that gave birth to this book, which is designed to help the church develop a sound biblical and theological basis for Jewish evangelism. This volume is the product of two major conferences sponsored by Chosen People Ministries. The chapters are developed from articles that originated at the conferences and cover the theological, missiological, and practical issues facing the church as it brings the gospel to the Jewish people.

The theme of the two conferences, "To the Jew First in the New Millennium," is based upon Paul's striking statement in Romans 1:16 that the gospel is "to the Jew first" (NASB). This biblical text became the conference's point of departure for an exploration of the deeper theological truths that underlay Paul's teaching. It is the hope of Chosen People Ministries that, in this new millennium, Christians will take seriously the task of Jewish evangelism and prioritize outreach to the Jewish people.

The first conference was held in New York City, which boasts the largest Jewish population of any city in the world. The event took place over three days at the historic Calvary Baptist Church in the center of Manhattan, across the street from Carnegie Hall. The pastor of the church, David Epstein, himself a Jewish believer, hosted the conference, which closed with a large rally on Saturday night, featuring Messianic Jewish attorney Jay Sekulow giving his testimony; Dr. Paige Patterson, then the president of the Southern Baptist Convention, speaking; and Messianic musician Marty Goetz performing in concert. The conference was privileged to host some of the top evangelical scholars in the world, who spoke on various topics related to Jewish evangelism. Articles by such speakers as Dr. Walter Kaiser, Dr. Darrell Bock, and Dr. Richard Pratt appear as chapters in this book.

The conference was marked by controversy as Jewish evangelism is as much a "theological football" as any other issue deemed "politically incorrect" by some within the Christian and Jewish community. There were daily protests at the conference as well as numerous critical articles, which appeared in the *New York Times* and many Jewish publications at the time.

A second conference, "To the Jew First in the New Millennium," was held in southern Florida in 2000 and became the source for a number of chapters in this book. This event was hosted by two prominent churches in the area—the First Baptist Church of West Palm Beach, where Dr. Keith Thomas was the pastor, and by Christ Fellowship Church, led by Pastor Tim Mullins.

Some of the greatest theological minds and missions practitioners in the United States gathered again for this conference. The conference concluded with a message from Dr. Albert Moehler, president of The Southern Theological Baptist Seminary, as well as a concert with Messianic artist Paul Wilbur.

This second conference was also met by protests from within the Jewish community. One of the main reasons for this passionate opposition relates to the past. My people generally have a negative impression of Christianity based upon the terrible facts of history. The Crusades, pogroms, and the Holocaust have unfortunately resulted in a painful relationship between Jews and Christians.

There is still a great need for repentance on the part of those who love the Jewish Messiah—not that any of us can atone for the sins of those who lived before us. But Christians today can certainly do everything possible to let Jewish friends and neighbors know that the actions of "Christians" that have been so destructive to Jewish people in the past are not representative of the message we believe and teach. I use quotes above because it is clear to all faithful Christians that the teachings of Jesus have never promoted the persecution or mistreatment of others. In fact, all Christians are called to imitate Jesus' love for God's chosen people, the Jewish people.

The response of those involved with both conferences toward those who opposed the effort was nothing less than gracious and loving. It is our hope that the rest of the church would follow suit. Efforts to reach Jewish people for Jesus will, after all, for the very reasons explained above, be misunderstood by the Jewish community, opposed and demeaned by theological universalists, deemed politically incorrect in our current political-social context, and ultimately protested by some leaders within the Jewish community.

This, again, is unfortunate, but Christians faithful to Romans 1:16 should not think that the negative responses are in reality a reaction to their gospel proclamation. Some Jewish community leaders are protesting because they believe that Jewish evangelism will harm the Jewish people and that, eventually, Jews who believe in Jesus will become non-Jews. It is our expectation, though, that the church will love the Jewish people, affirm the Jewish identity of Jewish people who become followers of Jesus, pray for the Jewish people, and do all it can to support them—especially by bringing the gospel to God's chosen people.

These two conferences and this book are providing a new beginning that aims to transform the relationship between evangelicals and the Jewish people. There is no need to accept the notion that a Jewish or Gentile person who believes in Jesus needs to choose between loving and respecting Jewish people and bringing the gospel message to their Jewish family, friends, or neighbors. This is a false dichotomy and leads to a departure from the teaching and practice of the New Testament. The greatest act of love and respect for Jewish people—and for any and every person in our global community—is to bring them the message of eternal life through the Messiah of Israel, Jesus.

Anything less is unloving, disrespectful, and stands against the clear teaching of Scripture. Reaching Jewish people for Jesus in love is the Christian's response of obedience to God. The manner in which this task is accomplished, however, is critical, and this book will also cover practical concerns in bringing the gospel to Jewish people.

We look forward to the day when Jewish evangelism will become the concern of the entire church in this new millennium. We anticipate, too, that seminaries and Christian colleges will utilize this volume as a textbook. Every Christian will benefit from reading this book for deeper personal study in the vital area of missions and evangelism.

It is also our prayer that every Christian will develop a passion and heartbreaking burden for the salvation of Jewish people based upon the truth of Scripture. As a result, Christians will have the same heart of Jesus for his chosen people. The words of Jesus have the power to pierce our souls today as much as when he spoke,

> O Jerusalem, Jerusalem, the one who kills the proph-
> ets and stones those who are sent to her! How often
> I wanted to gather your children together, as a hen
> gathers her chicks under her wings, but you were
> not willing! (Matt. 23:37 NKJV)

Clearly the Savior had a broken heart for his people, weeping over Jerusalem, as Luke records:

> Now as He drew near, He saw the city and wept over
> it. (Luke 19:41 NKJV)

My hope is that Christians who read this book—the fruit of these two conferences—will respond with this same broken heart of Jesus to the need of the Jewish people to hear the gospel. My prayer for this book is that Christians will call out to God in the same way the apostle Paul did:

> Brethren, my heart's desire and prayer to God for
> Israel is that they may be saved. (Rom. 10:1 NKJV)

Underlying Beliefs

As the leader of a Jewish mission, I believe that all Jewish people need to accept Jesus in order to have a place in the age to come

(John 14:6; Acts 4:12). It is not possible for a Jewish person to keep the Law to the extent that their human efforts would in some way satisfy God's demands for righteousness, enabling the individual Jewish person to enter heaven on his or her own merit (Rom. 10:2–4ff.; Gal. 2:15–16; 3:23–25). Rather, saving faith involves an understanding of the gospel and the need to embrace Yeshua (Jesus) as the Messiah (John 3:16–17).

The way of salvation is also the same for non-Jews, even though, according to the argument of the apostle Paul in the early chapters of Romans (Rom. 2:12–16; 3:9–20), they are *judged* on a different basis than the Jewish people. Jews are judged by the written Law, while Gentiles are judged by natural law. Yet both Jew and Gentile are accepted by the same act of conscious faith in the Son of God, who died and rose for our sins (Rom. 10:9–12). These gospel truths are certainly not new but need to be reaffirmed, as these biblical tenets are currently being challenged.

Jewish people also need to be properly discipled so that they not only have a secured place in heaven but are able to make a contribution on earth as they grow in faith and serve the Messiah Yeshua. Proper discipleship will encourage Messianic Jews to maintain their Jewish identity as part of the visible remnant of Israel (Rom. 11:5ff.) as well as part of the church (Eph. 2:11–22; 4:4–6). Both Jews and Gentiles are individually baptized into the body of Messiah at the point of salvation and thereafter share a common spiritual life through the Spirit of God (1 Cor. 12:13).

Men and women as well as Jews and Gentiles are one in the body of Messiah, and yet as men and women have distinctive traits, so do Jews and Gentiles. Our unity does not demand uniformity of identity, duties, and responsibilities before God (Gal. 3:28). Messianic Jews should live as Jews, a visible expression of the remnant of Israel and a testimony to God's faithfulness (Gen. 12:1–3; Rom. 11:1–36).

Finally, it is a biblical mandate for Gentiles in the body of Messiah to reach Jewish people with the gospel message. According to Paul's statement in Romans 11:11, the Gentiles are called to make the Jewish people jealous of the Messiah who dwells within them. In fact, the Great Commission does not present Jewish evangelism as simply one aspect among many. It is a unique venture that is specifically addressed in Scripture. This mandate for Jewish evangelism and discipleship, which Paul gives the Gentiles in the body of Messiah, is based upon many different biblical texts. The two passages dealt with below, however, are the most prominent.

The Biblical Basis of Jewish Evangelism
Paul writes,

> For I am not ashamed of the gospel of Christ, for it is the power of God to salvation for everyone who believes, for the Jew first and also for the Greek. (Rom. 1:16 NKJV)

This critical passage of Romans reveals God's plan for world evangelism. The Gentile world is not to be ignored, but the first step in reaching the world is to reach God's chosen people. Even the word *first* clearly expresses that the Jewish people are to be viewed as a priority for evangelism. This is the divine strategy—*for it is the power of God to salvation for everyone who believes, for the Jew first . . .*

Paul is not suggesting, of course, that the Roman believers withhold the gospel from the Gentiles until every Jewish person in the world is reached. Neither is the apostle implying that the gospel has already come to the Jewish people first and, therefore, preaching the gospel "to the Jew first" no longer has any contemporary application. Romans 1:16 is written in the present tense and applicable to every generation. Follow the logic of the text: if the gospel is *still* the power of God "to" salvation and is *still* for "everyone who believes," then the gospel is *still* "for the Jew first" (NKJV).

The Greek word used by Paul and translated as *first* is προτον.[1] It implies a priority[2] rather than a sequential order of events.[3] The word is also used in the same sense when Jesus teaches, "Seek first the kingdom of God . . ." (Matt. 6:33 NKJV).

The kingdom of God should always be sought as a priority in our lives, even as we seek other things. In a similar way, reaching Jewish people with the gospel must be a priority for all who know Jesus as their Savior.

Paul, the Apostle to the Gentiles, focused his ministry on reaching non-Jews with the gospel message. But this did not lessen his concern for the salvation of Jewish people. Wherever Paul went in his ministry among the Gentiles, he also preached the gospel to the Jewish people living in that area. His custom was, in fact, to witness to the Jewish people of a particular city before he spoke to the Gentiles (Acts 13:13–52; 14:1–5; 18:7–11; 19:8–10). The salvation of the Jewish people was an ever present concern for Paul, and his actions recorded in Acts reveal his understanding of what he wrote in Romans 1:16.[4]

Too often, however, Jewish evangelism has become the "great omission" of the Great Commission. This is beginning to change, and some church bodies are taking Jewish evangelism more seriously than ever before. It is my hope that this positive development will continue.

A wonderful story tells about the relationship between John Wilkinson, a Gentile missionary who founded the Mildmay Mission to the Jews, and J. Hudson Taylor, founder of the China Inland Mission (now OMF). Every January, Taylor would send Wilkinson a check for a sum of money with a note attached, "To the Jew first." Wilkinson would then send the same amount back to Taylor with a note that read, "And also to the Gentiles."

This story characterizes the very real interdependence that the Jewish and Gentile missions have in Scripture. I would argue that it is impossible to effectively accomplish one without the other. At the same time, it is possible to prioritize the Jewish mission and ensure its success without negating the possibility of fulfilling the Gentile mission. We can prioritize reaching Jewish people because of God's choice of Abraham's seed according to the flesh, and still reach the world as commanded by our Messiah prior to his ascension.

Making Israel Jealous

God also specifically calls the Gentile members of the body of Messiah to make Jewish people spiritually jealous (Rom. 11:11). That jealousy ultimately would drive Israel to Yeshua as detailed in Romans 11:25–26. Nor can one avoid the evident link between the salvation of Israel and the return of the Messiah. A mystery perhaps, but linked nonetheless. This might even explain why Paul gladly accepted the mantle of Gentile apostleship, knowing that the salvation of the Gentiles would lead to the salvation of Israel. Paul also anticipated that the salvation of Israel and the nations would lead to the consummation of all things.

The implementation of these few teachings can transform the world. The Gentiles within the body of Messiah are called to reach Jewish people for Jesus, which, in turn, leads to the redemption of the world. Chosen People Ministries, as a twenty-first-century mission to the Jews, exists to help our brothers and sisters in accomplishing this great work. It is part of our organizational mission statement: "Chosen People Ministries exists to evangelize and disciple Jewish people and to empower and equip our brothers and sisters in the church to do the same." Chosen People Ministries has been accomplishing this mission of more than a century. We will continue to encourage, provide materials to, and build strategic bridges with the greater body of Messiah.

As followers of the one who opened the Scriptures to the two disciples on the road to Emmaus, our claim that Jesus is the Messiah is based upon the Word of God.

> Then He said to them, "O foolish ones, and slow of heart to believe in all that the prophets have spoken! Ought not the Christ to have suffered these things and to enter into His glory?" And beginning at Moses and all the Prophets, He expounded to them in all the Scriptures the things concerning Himself. (Luke 24:25–27 NKJV)

In this Word we base our faith and discover the will of God for how we must live in obedience to his will. It is the foundation for all we understand about God and what his expectations are for our lives. Therefore, if God says that we are called to bring the gospel to the Jewish people, then what choice do we have? We are compelled by the truth of Scripture to be involved with bringing the gospel to the Jew first and also to the Gentile. There is no doubt that this is part of God's will for us, personally and for the entire church.

Will a new generation of Christians take the Scriptures to heart? Although the idea of reaching Jewish people with the gospel may not be popular, I pray that we will nonetheless be obedient to God's Word.

This volume has come together through the efforts of many. Special thanks to those working behind the scenes who made the To the Jew First conferences and this book possible, especially Dr.

Rich Freeman, vice president of church ministries and conferences, and Eileen Baehr who assisted Dr. Freeman in coordinating these conferences. A very special thanks to Andrew Sparks, director of publications, who worked diligently with Kregel Publications. I am also thankful to Dr. Noel Rabinowitz, associate professor of New Testament at Talbot School of Theology and the Charles Feinberg Center, for his efforts and scholarship toward this writing project. Alan Shore, a Chosen People Ministries staff writer, was also instrumental in bringing this work to publication. Many others, including our contributors and the staff of Kregel Publications, made this book a reality.

It is with prayerful expectation that this book will bring glory to God and eternal good to his chosen people.

—Dr. Mitch Glaser
President of Chosen People Ministries
Rosh Hashanah, 2007

PART 1

BIBLE

Throughout the ages, men and women have listened to or read the words of the Bible. It has provided information about history and instruction for life. Great teachers and scholars have also pored over the Bible's texts in an attempt to solve the mysteries of life and to apply the meaning of God's Word.

Two questions have loomed large over the centuries. Put simply, are these books, individually and collectively, the Word of God? If so, how do they address us?

If the Bible is nothing more than a collection of historical artifacts, we need not concern ourselves overmuch with their contemporary application. The world from which it came is long past. But if the Creator of heaven and earth continues to speak to us today through its pages, then we ought to pay attention.

The scholars who wrote the papers that constitute the chapters contained in this first section have wrestled with the meaning and application of the Bible in regard to Israel and Jewish evangelism. Their work is presented here.

Chapter 1: "'For the Jew First': Paul's *Nota Bene* for His Gentile Readers," by Mark A. Seifrid

Dr. Seifrid asserts that Paul's phrase "to the Jew first" indicates that an ongoing witness to the Jewish people is an essential component of the hope of the gospel. If, then, the authenticity of the gospel's hope and power is rooted in Israel's salvation, we must not suppose Jewish evangelism to be an unfruitful or ineffective activity. Difficult though its outworking may be, whether in the first or twenty-first century, the good news "to the Jew first" testifies to the veracity of God's gospel. Dr. Seifrid also draws a connection between Jewish evangelism and the identity of the body of Messiah.

Chapter 2: "Jewish Evangelism in the New Millennium in Light of Israel's Future (Romans 9–11)," by Walter C. Kaiser Jr.

With arguments rooted in Romans 9–11, Dr. Kaiser makes a case for the continuing importance of Jewish evangelism. He also explains God's overarching plan of salvation for humanity contingent on a positive relationship between the Jewish people and the nations. His careful exegesis of the text offers an effective challenge to those who assert that the church has replaced Israel in God's unfolding will in history.

Chapter 3: "The Book of Acts and Jewish Evangelism: Three Approaches and One Common Thread," by Darrell L. Bock

Dr. Bock examines the three major speeches in Acts 2; 3; and 13 that address a Jewish audience and present Jesus as the one through whom the God of Israel has worked. Stressing the Jewish perspective of these speeches, Dr. Bock invites us to consider how our gospel message to the Jewish people might become more effective.

Chapter 4: "Jesus' Denunciation of the Jewish Leaders in Matthew 23, and Witness to Religious Jews Today," by David L. Turner

Dr. Turner tackles the questions raised by New Testament passages in which Jesus denounces some Jewish religious leaders. These passages have been misused by Christian leaders and scholars to denounce Judaism, and misinterpretation has led to Christian anti-Semitism. By placing such passages in the context of other Jewish writings, Dr. Turner counters the distortion and abuse of these passages. For Dr. Turner, Yeshua's teaching is not a "Gentile" critique of Judaism, but a critique of a segment of Jewish leadership arising from within Jewish life itself. The content and style of this (often heated) intrafamily discussion within Israel was typical of the time.

Chapter 5: "The Message of the Prophets and Jewish Evangelism," by Richard E. Averbeck

Dr. Averbeck scrutinizes the close relationship between the Holy Spirit and the institution of prophecy in the Hebrew Scriptures. He demonstrates how these spiritual realities relate to the new covenant, and he portrays evangelism as a prophetic activity for the church today.

Chapter 1

"For the Jew First"

Paul's *Nota Bene* for His Gentile Readers

MARK A. SEIFRID

The Gospel for the Jewish People Is Essential to Gentile Faith

Paul makes it quite clear to his Gentile readers in Rome that an ongoing witness to the gospel among Jews is essential to the hope of the gospel. If God's rejection of the nation has meant the reconciliation of the world to God, what will God's acceptance of them entail, after all, but life from the dead (Rom. 11:15)? This hope was not solely for readers in Paul's time; rather, this hope is fixed and bears implications for the present. The Apostle to the Gentiles sought through his ministry to provoke his own people to jealousy, so that he might save "some" of them (Rom. 11:14). Thus, the apostolic mission to the Gentiles turns out to serve a purpose quite apart from them. As the power of God for salvation, the gospel *remains,* then, "for the Jew first and also to the Greek" (see Rom. 1:16 NASB).

This qualification of the gospel as "for the Jew first," by which Paul introduces his gospel, is integral to it and is *not* overturned or reversed by the surprising work of God among the Gentiles.[1] Thus, although we as Gentile believers are children of the *uncircumcised* Abraham (Rom. 4:9–12), the gospel still retains a certain "otherness" as regards Gentiles, a *necessary* indication that our participation in it is a gift of the Creator.

The apostle underscores this otherness from the very start of his address to the Gentile house-churches in Rome. The gospel, which came to them, had been

> ... promised beforehand [by God], through his prophets, in Holy Scriptures, concerning his Son, who came to be of the seed of David according to the flesh. (Rom. 1:2–3)

The good news of salvation is, then, a gift to Gentiles as aliens, given through the one in David's royal lineage whom God had promised. In the closing of the letter, Paul hears this gift as being given to "others" also in the voice of the risen Messiah speaking in the words of the Psalms and the Torah (Rom. 15:9–11):

> I shall confess you among the nations and to your name I shall sing praise. (Ps. 18:49)

> Rejoice, o nations, with his people! (Deut. 32:43 LXX)

> Praise the LORD all you nations, and may all the peoples worship him! (Ps. 117:1)

According to Psalm 18:1–50 (cf. 2 Sam. 22:2–51), with which Paul introduces this series of citations, the nations enter into salvation only as conquered enemies, or aliens (Ps. 18:43–50). The same is expressed in the Isaianic text, which Paul also cites: the Gentiles now have come to place their hope in the new David, the scion of Jesse, who has arisen to rule them (Rom. 15:12; Isa. 11:10).

The above introductory and concluding remarks serve as brackets to the epistle, describing God's saving work in David's promised seed. As such they highlight the uncompromising particularity of the gospel as being for the Jew first, but which *nevertheless* encompasses the salvation of the Gentiles.

The entrance of Gentiles into salvation does not, however, result in an indiscriminate, and therefore bland, universalism in which all cultural distinctives are leveled. Rather, it represents a dramatic joining of highly fissile peoples, Jew and Gentile, who are held together solely by the risen Messiah. In him is overcome the differences of peoples, nations, and tongues that were initiated at Babel. It is for this reason that Paul is able to speak of their common worship "with one voice" as a sign of hope (Rom. 15:5–6 JNT). Had their cultural differences been leveled out and their earthly identities done away with, there would have been no cause to celebrate their union in Messiah (see Rom. 15:1–4).

The same dynamic appears in Romans 4, where, as we have noted, Paul underscores the continuity between Abraham and the Gentiles. Like Abraham, they have believed while uncircumcised (Rom. 4:11). Those who *are* circumcised cannot claim for themselves Abraham as their father from whom they have received circumcision unless they follow in his steps of faith (Rom. 4:12). This reversal of the place of Gentiles and Jews is not absolute, however, and all-encompassing. Paul in this passage underscores the priority of faith, which makes children of believing Gentiles and excludes unbelieving Jews. But this faith is only an answer to God's promise to Abraham, in which the priority of Israel remains, even as the Gentiles are included.

This priority of Israel is recognized implicitly, then, in Romans 4, and comes to concrete expression in Romans 11:28 ("according to election, they are beloved on account of the fathers"). The gospel, in which we Gentiles have believed, is nothing other than the promise given to Abraham come to fulfillment in the resurrection of Jesus from the dead (Rom. 4:23–25). This Jesus, who is risen Lord, is none other than the promised seed of David (Rom. 1:2–4), and in this seed, Jesus, particularity and universality meet without qualifying or reducing one another.

Thus, the promise to Abraham—that he would become the father of many nations—never comes to united fulfillment in the narrative of Genesis nor in the entire course of the story of Scripture (Rom. 4:17; Gen. 17:5). God's saving work transcends Babel but does not remove its mark on humanity. As we have seen already, Jew and Gentile are brought together not in their earthly identities but in Jesus the Messiah alone. Salvation is nothing other than recognizing and giving thanks to the One, who in Messiah has acted as the Creator, who "makes alive the dead, and calls the things which are not into being" (Rom. 4:17). Abraham's hope was a "hope against hope," contrary to human calculations *and* human capacities (Rom. 4:18 NASB). In other words, the joining of Jew and Gentile in Jesus *alone* is essential to Paul's gospel. The apostle's message challenges, therefore, all supersessionism.

His message challenges, too, all attempts to trace the Creator's dealings chronologically. According to the apostle, God's saving dealings with all humans encompasses all that we are as creatures, including our ethnic and cultural identity. In a corresponding way, our salvation in confessing God as our Creator through Jesus necessarily entails our recognition of our place and time as God's creatures. As regards Paul's Gentile readers, it is often overlooked that one of his fundamental aims in Romans 9–11 is to bring them to see this truth about themselves in relation to the people of Israel. In that light, the apostle's lament concerning the unbelief of his people should be regarded as a biblical lament, which arises from the unfulfilled promises of God (Rom. 9:1–5). Not only Paul's recounting of Israel's benefits (and his subsequent affirmation of them, Rom. 11:28), but also the echo of his lament—which he hears in the voice of the prophet Isaiah ("Isaiah cries out on behalf of Israel," Rom. 9:27–29)—anticipate his open affirmation of the salvation of ethnic Israel, which affirmation appears at the conclusion of his argument for a redeemed Israel (Rom. 11:25–27).

It is in this context that we ought to hear Paul's words of warning to his Gentile readers in the latter part of Romans 11. We Gentiles are not to imagine that we are the end of all things (Rom. 11:11–36). Israel and the nations are mere tools in the hands of God, which he uses in unexpected, unfathomable ways to effect his saving purposes. The salvation that has come to the Gentiles is intended to provoke Israel to jealousy and ultimately to save it (Rom. 11:11). As was noted at the outset of this discussion, the apostolic proclamation of the gospel to the nations appears here as an instrument to the greater end of Israel's salvation. The Gentiles are merely the branches of an uncultivated olive tree, which by the untraceable mercy of God have been engrafted into the stock and root of Israel (Rom. 11:17). The root is not dependent upon us; we are dependent on the root (Rom. 11:18). Unbelieving Israel, which was broken off like branches to make room for us, shall, in fact, again be engrafted by the hand of God into its own tree and share in the salvation promised to the patriarchs (Rom. 11:22–24, 25–32).

Here, in Romans 11, Paul is speaking of Israel primarily in corporate and therefore in ethnic and cultural terms: it is for this reason that he comes to address the Gentiles with the singular "you" and is able to speak in a transtemporal way of the severed branches of Israel being grafted again into their own olive tree (Rom. 11:18–24). He understands that as God's human creatures we are shaped fundamentally by ethnicity, culture, and the invisible bonds of national identity. Each of us has been given, through human means, our time and place by our Creator. Paul further recognizes that our cultural identity, while not wrong in itself, can easily become a threat to the gospel. It is for this reason that he issues his warning to us as Gentiles, and it is this warning that is the basic thrust of Romans 11—we have nothing about which to boast in our cultural, ethnic, or national identity.

Insofar as we stand, then, we stand by faith. We remain "in" the kindness of God only so long as we recognize it for what it is: unconditional, inexplicable kindness (Rom. 11:22). If we discard this faith, we Gentiles, like Israel before us, shall fall and be cut off from salvation (Rom. 11:22). Paul, in fact, indicates that there shall come a time when the Gentiles shall be cut off, that is to say, the mission to the Gentiles shall come to an end (Rom. 11:22). For in the divine purpose, Israel's no to the proclamation of the gospel has been God's yes to the nations. And the salvation of Israel, according to Paul, shall bring with it the resurrection of the dead and the end of this world (Rom. 11:15).

The hour of Israel's disobedience has therefore provided the hour for the extension of God's mercy to the Gentiles through the gospel. God has for a time not delivered the people of Israel, but he loves them yet on account of the promises he gave to their ancestors (Rom. 11:28–29). The final hour of this world will belong not to the nations, but to God, when through the risen Messiah he grants Israel the salvation that it has been promised.

The word of the gospel, which is a stumbling block to Jew and Gentile alike, is nothing other than the fulfillment of God's promises to Israel, which have determined the history of his relationship with that nation (1 Cor. 1:18–25; cf. 2 Cor. 1:20). Paul understood, like the prophets of Israel before him, that the salvation that God promised Israel through the prophets was not a deliverance *from* judgment but a deliverance *through,* and *by means of,* judgment.[2]

The past destruction and exile that the prophets of Israel and Judah had announced was the very vehicle by which God remembered mercy to his people.

In bringing the nation of Israel to nothing, however, God promised to create it anew. Israel was to be brought back to its beginning, to a new exodus and sojourn in the wilderness, from where it would again love and seek the Lord as it ought (Hos. 2:1–23). Jerusalem was to be purged of its evil by the refiner's fire (Isa. 1:1–31). The shoot of Jesse arises from the stump, which remains in the wake of divine judgment (Isa. 11:1; Rom. 15:12). This scion, who is the *new* David, replaces the earlier dynasty that had been removed. It is this prophetic theology of the "new creation" by divine mercy out of divine judgment that guides Paul's discussion of Israel in Romans 9–11. The divine word of judgment of which Isaiah spoke has come to fulfillment in Israel's rejection of the gospel. As a result of this judgment, had God not preserved a remnant, the nation would have been obliterated like Sodom and Gomorrah (Rom. 9:27–29; Isa. 1:9; 10:22; 28:22). Israel's past was repeated in the coming of the Messiah: it stumbled on the stone of offense, which God had placed in Zion (Rom. 9:33).

God does not, however, intend this stumbling to be Israel's final destruction, its "fall" (Rom. 11:11). As is especially clear in Isaianic theology, the preservation of a remnant implies the restoration of the nation (see e.g., Isa. 6:13; 10:20–23; 11:11–16; 37:30–32; 49:5–6, 14–21; 51:1–3).[3] God, as Moses foretold, now provokes Israel by a "non-people" in order to bring it to salvation (Rom. 10:19; 11:11, 14). He has not rejected his people, whom he foreknew (Rom. 11:1–2). Rather, the exile of the nation that the prophets foretold has been recapitulated eschatologically in its rejection of the gospel. Israel's present hardening, then, is the precursor to its salvation. As in Israel's past, the nation had to be reduced to nothing in order to receive salvation as it really is and in the only way that God gives it: Israel's salvation shall and must be the justification of the ungodly. Here we may cite Paul, as he, in turn, cites the prophets:

> The Deliverer shall come forth from Zion to turn
> aside ungodliness from Jacob. And this [promise]
> shall be my covenant with them, when I take away

their sins. (Rom. 11:26–27; cf. Isa. 27:9; 59:20; Jer. 31:33)

Salvation comes only through judgment. It is in this manner—through Israel's present, partial hardening—that all Israel shall be saved (Rom. 11:25–26).[4] It is the work of God the Creator, by which he again establishes his right as Creator over against his rebellious people. Paul summarizes his message in Romans in precisely these terms:

> [Israel] now is disobedient in the mercy given to you [Gentiles], in order that they now might be given mercy. God has shut up all [both Israel and the nations] under disobedience in order that he might have mercy upon all. (Rom. 11:31–32)

In this way and only in this way do fallen human beings, Jew and Gentile alike, come to a saving knowledge of God the Creator, whose judgments remain unsearchable and whose ways are inscrutable, "from whom and through whom, and unto whom are all things" (Rom. 11:36). Israel's path to salvation must necessarily pass, therefore, through judgment. Just as God justified the ungodly Abraham, Israel's forefather, God shall at the end of all things in the same way justify Abraham's seed according to the flesh (Rom. 4:5).

We should remind ourselves that Paul has the entire nation of Israel in view when he speaks in this manner. His longing for *all* his kin people, in fact, colors his lament, which opens this section of Romans, and moves his argument throughout these chapters. In much the same way as the prophet Isaiah, who announces divine judgment, "cries out on behalf of Israel," the apostle himself does, according to Paul's citation (Rom. 9:27; Isa. 10:22–23). The apostle draws a sharp distinction between the remnant that God has preserved (now, as in the past) and the nation as a whole:

> That which Israel seeks it has not gained. The remnant has gained it the rest have been hardened. (Rom. 11:7)

Paul's hope is set not merely upon the continuing preservation of a remnant, to which even his mission to the Gentiles contributes, but upon the salvation of the nation as a whole (Rom. 11:14–15). The figure of the olive tree presupposes this understanding, and for this reason Paul can speak of the severed branches as still being "holy" and of their future engrafting into the stock that is theirs by nature (Rom. 11:17–24).

Israel presently has been hardened in part. This national, ethnic Israel shall, however, finally be saved. Its salvation shall come about by the coming of the Redeemer from Zion, by a fresh and final act of God, and not by the proclamation of the gospel (Rom. 11:26). Like the apostle Paul, who describes himself elsewhere as a "premature birth," Israel shall be saved by the appearance of the risen Lord (1 Cor. 15:8). Paul, though, does not expect that every Jew from all time will enjoy salvation. His agonizing lament in Romans 9:1–5, and his endeavor to save "some" of his kin people, show his recognition that some of them would be lost. The time of the Messiah's coming remains incalculable, and thus there are no guarantees for any particular generation. Yet Paul expects the salvation of eschatological Israel.

I shall have more to say about this last matter. But first we return for a moment to our main point: Gentile faith rests on a gospel that belongs first to Jews. The apostle intends for Gentiles to look backward not only to Abraham and his faith, but also to the faith of the earliest Jewish believers in the gospel message in Jerusalem and to recognize our present indebtedness to them. He also intends for us to look forward to the salvation of Israel in which God's saving purposes for the world shall be consummated. And in the meantime, he surely intends us to join in whatever way possible in the continuing witness to the risen Messiah among the Jewish people.

None of Us Ought to Suppose That Jewish Evangelism Must Remain Basically Unfruitful

Coming as it does after Paul's discussion of the remnant, his stated desire to win "some" of his fellow Jews might seem to suggest that only a few of them will be won, that Jewish evangelism has been predestined to meager results (Rom. 11:14). That would be a misreading of the apostle; his words may well be taken to indicate precisely the opposite. His diminished expectations for the present must be measured against his astounding hope for the future. Against the background of the redemption of the *whole* of Israel at the coming of the Messiah, anything less is almost bound to look lamentable. But that does not at all mean that Jewish believers in Jesus will be numerically insignificant. Paul's appeal to the account of Elijah (Rom. 11:4) intimates that the "remnant" is larger than it may appear at times.[5] The prophet, it may be recalled, complains to the Lord that he alone out of all of Israel has remained faithful—and his life is in danger. But God is well in control of the situation and sees far beyond what the prophet can see: he has kept for himself seven thousand who have not bent the knee to Baal (1 Kings 19:9–18). Compared with the nation, the number is small; compared with the prophet's perspective, it is very large indeed.

Much the same can be said with respect to the reports of Paul's limited success among Jews in the book of Acts. Paul's concluding citation of Isaiah 6:9–10 ("Go and say to this people, you will listen and not understand . . .") is again drawn from the larger framework of the prophetic expectation of the restoration of the nation and must be understood against that background (Acts 28:26–28).[6] Luke indicates to us in no uncertain terms that this hope was common to the earliest church, a hope that the risen Lord implicitly affirms when the eleven ask him whether the time had come for the restoration of the kingdom to Israel. He replies only that it is not for them (or us) to know the times that the Father himself has set (Acts 1:6–7). The hope itself remains firm (see, too, Acts 3:19–21; 28:20; perhaps even 5:31).

Moreover, the narrative of Acts can hardly be taken to indicate that Jewish evangelism is doomed to failure. It is clear only that it will face resistance. In coming to this conclusion, we need not set aside the significance of Paul's vision in which the risen Jesus tells him to flee Jerusalem, "for they will not receive your witness concerning me" (Acts 22:17–21). On account of their rejection of Paul's testimony, he is sent to the Gentiles (Acts 22:21). Nevertheless, according to Luke, Paul again and again preaches to Jews in the synagogues. Only when the main body of a synagogue rejects his message does he turn to the Gentiles. Further, these words of Jesus' instruction to Paul appear within Paul's testimony to the Jews of Jerusalem! In Luke's perspective, Israel's rejection of the gospel takes place in repeated encounters with the gospel, not in a once-and-for-all decision on the part of the nation. By implication, the gospel must today be presented afresh to Jews, where it undoubtedly will meet with a similar response of partial acceptance and partial denial.

Here it should be remembered that according to Luke's report, Paul did not meet with unqualified success among Gentiles, either. Generally they participated in persecution against him, or were themselves the instigators of it (Acts 13:50; 14:5, 19–20; 19:21–41). It is likewise important to notice that the resistance Paul meets in the synagogues of Pisidian Antioch, Iconium, Thessalonica, Corinth, and Ephesus is more than balanced out by the successes of the gospel, which begins with the day of Pentecost and continues all the way to Paul's witness in Rome, where some Jews were convinced by what he had to say (Acts 28:24). The initial proclamation in Jerusalem not only led to acceptance by great numbers of persons, it extended into the priestly families and Pharisaic circles (Acts 6:7; 15:5).

Nor did the work of God end in Jerusalem when Luke shifts his focus elsewhere. When James greets Paul upon his arrival in Jerusalem, he announces to him, "how many *thousands* of believers there are among the Jews" (Acts 21:20). Paul himself finds considerable success within the synagogues, even where he meets opposition (Acts 13:43 ["many Jews and devout God-fearers"]; 14:1 ["a great number of Jews and Greeks believed"]). In Berea he seems to have, in fact, found an entirely receptive synagogue audience (Acts 17:11–12).

The incidental evidence of the New Testament writings likewise points to an ongoing and fruitful witness among Jews in the first century. At the very least it appears that the gospel according to Matthew, the epistle to the Hebrews, and the epistle of James were originally written to communities of believing Jews. The gospel may also have served as a witness to unbelieving Jews. The circles of churches that required such instruction and the need for an evangelistic tool such as the gospel testify to its impact among Jews in the first century.

In short, neither Paul's letters nor the broader witness of the New Testament provide us with any theological basis for supposing that Jews must remain basically unresponsive to the gospel. That is not to say that there are not now considerable obstacles to effective witness among Jews, chief among them being the reasonable fears of cultural assimilation, the remembrance of cruelties perpetrated in the name of Christ, and the Holocaust. Nevertheless, there is no reason why God might not perform a surprising work among Jews in our own time. And we ought not limit him in our thinking, our prayers, and our efforts.

The Common Worship of Jesus the Messiah by Believing Jews and Gentiles Is Fundamental to Our Witness

In our earlier discussion we left unexplored precisely how it is that Paul wishes to "provoke [his] kinspeople to jealousy and to save some of them" by means of his Gentile mission (Rom. 11:14). If God's ways are surprising and contrary to our expectations, the apostle's ways are equally so. Why not simply evangelize Jews, as Paul elsewhere indicates that he did, even within his calling as Apostle to the Gentiles (1 Cor. 9:19–20; see, too, Paul's synagogue testimonies in Acts 13:5, 13–43; 14:1; 17:1–4, 10–12, 17; 18:4–6)? Why choose this roundabout method of reaching Jews by evangelizing their Gentile neighbors? According to the reports of Acts, jealousy of Paul's success among Gentiles in the synagogues seems to have repelled a good number of Jews from the gospel rather than having attracted them to it (Acts 13:45). How is it, then, that Paul hoped to win "some" by means of his Gentile mission?

As we might expect, the answer is deeply rooted in Paul's gospel itself. We may recall that Paul's initial mention of the provocation to jealousy appears in Romans 10:19, where Paul applies the Song of Moses to Israel's failure to believe the gospel:

> I shall provoke you to jealousy by a non-nation, by
> a nation without understanding I shall antagonize
> you. (Rom. 10:19; Deut. 32:21)

In speaking of a "non-nation" Paul does not have in mind the Gentiles, i.e., "the nations," to which he *always* refers in the plural. His citation of Deuteronomy recalls his earlier citation of Hosea 1:10:[7]

I shall call "the-One-Who-Is-Not-My-People," "My-People"; and "the-One-Who-is-Not-Beloved," "Beloved." And it shall be in the place where it was said to them, "You are not my people," there they shall be called "Sons of the Living God." (Rom. 9:25–27)

As the immediately preceding context to this passage indicates, the "nonpeople" of which Paul speaks is the new people of God, Jews and Gentiles together, which has been created by the word of God. When he speaks in Romans 10:19 of this non-people as "a people without understanding," he is not describing Gentiles alone, but the ungodly who have been called by the gospel, Jew and Gentile alike. As he indicates in his citation of Scripture earlier in the letter,

There is no one who is righteous, not one. There is *no one* who understands. There is no one who seeks God. (Rom. 3:10–11; Ps. 14:1–2)

It is not a "Gentile church" that provokes Israel: Paul knows of no such entity. Rather, the eschatological people of God, who are already being called and created out of nothing by the gospel, are to stir Israel to jealousy. Naturally, the proclamation of the gospel among the Gentiles and its success stands at the fore of Paul's argument in Romans 9–11. The irony of Israel's failure in the face of the justification of the pagans is not lost on him (Rom. 9:30–33). But as we have seen, Paul regards the conversion of the Gentiles as their being incorporated into Israel. They do not form some sort of body of their own. That which is to provoke Israel to jealousy is the believing community of Jews and Gentiles, which constitutes the entrance of the age of salvation into the present time. Paul "glorifies" his ministry to the Gentiles by setting forth its significance as the fulfillment of Scripture (that is essentially what he does in Romans 9–11), and thereby seeks to save "some" of his flesh (Rom. 11:13–14).

Seen in this light, the difficulties of modern readers become resolved in regard to Paul's understanding of his mission to the Gentiles and its relationship to Jewish evangelism. The ingathering of the Gentiles represents the fulfillment of the divine promise to Abraham and of Israel's hope. It is the presence of the eschaton—the arrival of the hour of salvation, made manifest in a proleptic way through Paul's mission to the Gentiles—which is to make Israel jealous. The very manner in which Paul speaks of the provocation to jealousy displays, in fact, this tension between the "already" and the "not yet," which in various ways runs through Paul's letters and the entire New Testament. When in Romans 10:19 Paul cites the Song of Moses, he applies it to the entire nation. The Lord foretells that he shall provoke Israel as a *whole* to jealousy by means of a "non-people." When Paul speaks of the "provocation to jealousy" in relation to his own ministry, however, it appears in diminished dimensions, as we have already seen: he hopes to save "some" (Rom. 11:14). The distance between the two texts is that of the coming of the kingdom in its fullness and its presence here and now in the proclamation of the gospel and its effects.

The continuing remnant of Israel is essential to this "provocation," which is intended in the end to win the nation. By its very nature this remnant represents a sign of hope for Israel that "God has not rejected his people, whom he foreknew" (Rom. 11:1–2). As in God's past judgments upon Israel, he even now keeps for himself this remnant, which by its very presence announces that God has remembered mercy in judgment. The remnant, which exists in Paul's words, "by grace and not by works," emerges on the far side of the divine judgment, which has consigned Israel to apostasy (Rom. 11:6). It is a visible indication that God is not yet finished with Israel, and that his plans for it are welfare and not calamity, a future and a hope (cf. Jer. 29:11).

From the statements of Paul that we have already examined, it is clear that he is not interested in mere words or mere ideas about Jews and Gentiles. God has fulfilled his promises in Jesus the Messiah, not with words, but with mighty deeds, which themselves bear witness to and continue God's saving work in this world. The collection for the poor in Jerusalem gathered from converted Gentiles was not, after all, mere charity in Paul's mind. It was a tangible indication, recognized by the Gentiles themselves, that their conversion represented the fulfillment of God's promises to Israel. We as Gentiles remain indebted to believing Jews of all generations for the spiritual blessings that we have received, and that indebtedness must receive expression in concrete deeds in the real world (Rom. 15:16, 27).

In another way as well, Paul expects the ethnic dimension of his gospel to be displayed visibly in the world. Paul calls his Jewish and Gentile addressees in Rome to "with one voice glorify the God and Father of our Lord Jesus the Messiah" (Rom. 15:6). As we saw at the outset of our discussion, Paul understands this common worship by believing Jews and Gentiles to be the fulfillment of the promises of Scripture. Such works are both an expression of hope and a call to hope in the promise of God fulfilled in Jesus the Messiah, which is yet to be fulfilled in all creation (Rom. 15:13). In such worship God is glorified, because in such worship we implicitly confess that salvation is not of ourselves but that "Messiah has accepted us, to the glory of God" (Rom. 15:7). Paul expects a visible expression of the truth, which he articulates in Ephesians 2:11–22, that Jews and Gentiles have been made one with one another and with God through Messiah.

We must not fail to see that when Paul enjoins Jews and Gentiles in the Roman house-churches to be of one mind, to accept one another, and to worship God with one voice, he presupposes that each will retain their ethnic identities. God is glorified not in the homogenization of the believing community, but precisely in our recognition that our unity is found solely in the risen Messiah in whom we all believe—in him and nowhere else. Such unity is the work of God, not the work of human beings. Only in this way can the common worship of Jews and Gentiles be a sign of hope for Israel and the world. Paul offers no formula by which to negotiate the form this worship is to take, or what sort of cultural imprint it is to bear. Indeed, in some sense worship may even be countercultural to both Gentiles and Jews.

Paul does indicate, however, some of the implications of his summons to unity. On the one side, as is particularly evident in the letter to Rome where the Gentiles constituted an apparently large majority, he warns them against pushing aside those conservative Jewish believers who felt themselves bound to certain dietary restrictions (Rom. 14:1–23). In in his charge not "to judge one another" and in his insistence that we restrict our freedom for the sake of another's conscience, he defends the space necessary for the practices of these Jewish believers (Rom. 14:13–23). In other words, Paul makes sure that Jews are not pressured to assimilate to the larger Gentile culture, but in outward and visible ways maintain their identity as Jews while they believe in Jesus the Messiah.

If Paul here curbs the tendencies of the Gentile majority, he elsewhere makes it clear that a price is to be paid from the side of Jewish believers as well. The acceptance of believing Gentiles for common worship and table fellowship, including the Lord's Table, proved to be one of the most divisive issues of the earliest community of Jewish believers in Jesus the Messiah. At this point, the gospel itself is at stake, and with it, the church (of Jews and Gentiles!) stands or falls. This is so because acceptance of uncircumcised Gentiles—those who do not observe the law of Moses as brothers and sisters and full members of the people of God—is the necessary outward and visible expression of the truth of the gospel: all are set right with God, not by any works of our own, but by the work of God in his Son. Just as Paul calls Gentile believers to embrace Jewish believers without imposing their own Gentile culture on them, he calls Jewish believers to accept the scandal of open fellowship with these Gentiles.

Jewish Evangelism Requires Jewish Evangelists

Jewish believers having the right to maintain certain, distinctive practices is not incompatible, then, with the gospel. Their right to do so creates even greater reason to ensure that the gospel is presented to unbelieving Jews in a manner that makes clear that faith in Jesus as Messiah does not necessitate the loss of Jewish identity. That will mean, of course, that in many instances Jewish evangelism will require Jewish evangelists and Messianic congregations in which new believers may grow without the threat of assimilation to Gentile culture. I do not mean to underplay the ways in which God has used and continues to use a loving, considerate Gentile witness to Jews. God is certainly not limited in his work! And we must not fail to bear witness where we are able. Nevertheless, Paul's own example urges the indispensability of a Jewish witness to the Jewish people. Although he himself had found a new identity as what we might call "an eschatological Jew," and had lived among Gentiles for many years, he testifies in 1 Corinthians that,

> To the Jews I became as a Jew, that I might win Jews.
> To those under the Law, I became as one under the
> Law, although not myself being under the Law, that
> I might win those under the Law. (1 Cor. 9:19–21)

According to Luke's testimony, this flexibility on Paul's part, born out of genuine love for his own people, was characteristic of the Apostle to the Gentiles. Paul's commitment to Jewish practices appears so strikingly in Acts that critical scholarship has often concluded that Luke has misrepresented him. In reality, we find in Acts the outworking of the claim that Paul makes to his Corinthian congregation: he circumcises Timothy, whose mother was a Jewish believer (Acts 16:1–3); he apparently makes and keeps a Nazarite vow; he participates in another vow with others as a sign of his respect for the Law (Acts 18:18; 21:21–24; Num. 6:1–21). Paul makes himself a "slave to all, that he might win the many" (1 Cor. 9:19). In our own time, Gentiles have every reason to pray for, encourage, and materially support Jewish ministries and the witness of Jewish believers to Jesus the Messiah among the Jewish people. That commitment ought not keep us from bearing witness ourselves where God grants us opportunity.

Further, the increasing distance between American culture and Christian faith may yet provide to Gentiles opportunity for a hearing of the gospel among Jews that would not have been imaginable in the past. We *must* engage in this witness, since the gospel in which we believe is nothing other than the fulfillment of promises to Abraham, which shall yet come to fulfillment in the resurrection of the dead and the redemption of Israel. Nor in the meantime should our expectations for the progress of the gospel among the Jewish people remain small. God may yet grant great fruitfulness from the seed that is scattered in our generation. And we who are believing Jews and Gentiles must find times and places and ways to join in common worship of Jesus the Messiah. Such unity of worship and witness is a sign of hope for Israel and the world. In the words of the apostle Paul,

> May the God of hope fill us with all joy and peace
> in believing, that we might abound in hope by the
> power of the Holy Spirit. (Rom. 15:13)

Amen.

Chapter 2

Jewish Evangelism in the New Millennium in Light of Israel's Future
(Romans 9–11)

WALTER C. KAISER JR.

It is impossible to read and interpret the epistle to the Romans without confronting its central issue—the relation of the Jewish people to God's plan of salvation and evangelism. Throughout the entire apostolic ministry of Paul, we, in fact, find this "two-step missionary pattern":[1] "to the Jew first and also to the Greek" (Rom. 1:16; 2:10 RSV). Paul's custom, upon arrival in a city where he had not previously preached, was first to enter the synagogue to preach, then turn to preach to the Gentiles of that city.[2] This two-step pattern is a distinctive of the apostle's ministry and message: the Jew first and then to the Gentiles.

Nevertheless, even though all will agree on the correctness of this assessment, it has become commonplace among more recent theologians to regard the Christian church as the new successor and replacement for the Israel of Romans 9–11. Or alternatively,

Israel is treated as a parenthetical insertion into, or disruption to the Gentile evangelistic outreach of, the otherwise unified argument of the book of Romans.

Examples of the former mistake can be seen in a fairly large number of places. The second Vatican Council described the Christian church as "the new Israel."[3] A similar document titled "Report of the Joint Commission on Church Union of the Congregational, Methodist, and Presbyterian Churches of Australia" also identified the church with "the true Israel."[4] These citations are only a small representation of the reigning thought among many reformed and covenantal theologians today.

But just as troubling is another sentiment among many dispensational and nonreformed theologians. This perspective asserts that the doctrine of salvation in the book of Romans can be dealt with apart from the question of the Jewish people. It is thought that Romans 9–11 is merely a parenthetical insertion between Romans 1–8 and Romans 12–16, one that momentarily halts the discussion of the doctrine of salvation in the former passage and its practical implications in the latter. Even though this group correctly believes there is a future for ethnic Israel of the flesh, they do not clearly connect it with the everlasting plan of God, or with the present-day church. It is almost as if the plan of God for salvation changes as the days of the *eschaton* appear in the windup of the present period of history.

To counter such a belief, both of these positions must come in for some serious modification according to the biblical data. The task of this chapter, then, is not only to interpret the meaning of Romans 9–11 as faithful to the apostle's assertions, but also to show that Romans 9–11, with its message about Israel, is integral to the subject matter of the epistle as a whole with its single plan of the salvation of God.

The Ancient Covenant: A Troubling Question

Romans 9–11 is not, as Hendrikus Berkhof affirmed, some sort of "eccentric outburst, nor is it particularly difficult, as is suggested by the contradictory explanations."[5] Berkhof went on to correctly observe that this text becomes especially difficult only when we wish to make it say something it does not say.

Why, for example, does the apostle say, "I have great sorrow and unceasing anguish in my heart" (Rom. 9:2 NIV)? So strongly does Paul feel about this matter that he could wish himself personally accursed and cut off from Messiah if it would have the benefit of bringing his Jewish brethren to the light of the gospel in the Messiah (Rom. 9:3).

Surely, this is a noble and praiseworthy sentiment, but it does not explain why the area of Jewish acceptance of the gospel is so troubling for Paul. Only when we get to Romans 11:1 do we find out what is so troubling to the apostle: "Did God reject his people?" The question poses a potential problem not only about Israel, but a bigger problem about God. In short, how can the everlasting plan of God be trusted and believed in for the salvation of all peoples? If God—the same God, who, based on His word and his own life (Gen. 12; 22; Heb. 6:18)—once promised to Israel similar outcomes as those found in Romans 9–11, but has now rejected Israel and turned his back on them, what is left of the doctrine of the faithfulness and dependability of God? It is simply impossible for God to lie or to go back on what he promises. Therefore, the problem of Israel is the problem of God due to his eternal promise-plan.[6]

The answer Paul will give to his own question is that the rejection of Israel is not total or complete, but only temporary and partial at that. "It is not as though the word of God had failed; for not all who are descended from Israel are Israel" (Rom. 9:6 NIV). That is, there are many Israelites who are not lost, but are saved. This same divine discriminating policy has been observed from the very beginning. God chose Isaac, not Ishmael; Jacob, not Esau (Rom. 9:7–12). In so doing, Paul argues, God was not unjust. The marvel is that *anyone* experienced the mercy of God. The better question to ask is why God spared anyone at the time of the golden calf (Rom. 9:14–18). Furthermore, this divine sovereignty does not exempt human responsibility, for while this grace and mercy of God cannot be pursued by works, but only by faith (Rom. 9:31–32), mortals still are culpable for their own refusals of this grace of God.

But there is more to the answer: in Romans 10 Paul demonstrates that the rejection of so large a number in Israel is not arbitrary or out of character for God. Israel disregarded the righteousness that came from God and substituted instead a homemade righteousness that refused to submit to God's righteousness (Rom. 10:3). Most of Israel failed to "confess with their lips and believe in their hearts that Jesus is Lord and that God had raised Jesus from the dead" (Rom. 10:9). Thus, there is no way that any Israelite, who rejects God's way of salvation, can blame anyone other than themselves. Had not the prophet Isaiah cried out on God's behalf, "All day long I have held out my hands to an obstinate people, who walk in ways not good, pursuing their own imaginations" (Isa. 65:2 NIV)? Paul used in Romans 10:21 this very argument from the prophet Isaiah to show that many of the Jewish people must bear responsibility.

The rejection of the majority of Israel, however, is "neither absolute nor unqualified."[7] Romans 11:1–10 argues that God's dealings with the Jews and the Gentiles are closely interrelated. What may have seemed to be a divine rejection of the Jewish people was and is not such, for there has always been a remnant selected by grace who did believe and were saved (Rom. 11:5). Thus, the gospel had a twofold effect: some were saved and others were hardened by the same good news. This double effect mirrors that which the plagues of Egypt had on Pharaoh and the Egyptians. The plagues were meant to lead the Egyptians to repentance (Exod. 7:17; 8:22; 9:14, 29 *et passim*), but it hardened many of them. Some did believe (Exod. 12:38), but most, like Pharaoh, rejected all of God's evidences.

Israel: An Indefectible Destiny

It is clear that Paul focuses his attention on Israel in these three chapters, but what "Israel" is Paul thinking about? Nowhere else in Paul's writings has he expounded and used the term *Israel* so centrally and so insistently. Elsewhere in Paul's writings, *Israel* occurs only five times (NIV):

1. 1 Corinthians 10:18—"Consider the people of Israel," a passing allusion to the sacrificial order in the older testament;
2. 2 Corinthians 3:7, 13—"the Israelites," who were unable to look on Moses' face when he came down from Mount Sinai;
3. Ephesians 2:12—"excluded from citizenship in Israel," refers to Christians who were not part of the state of Israel;
4. Philippians 3:5—"of the people [stock] of Israel," describes Paul as being a legitimate Jew;
5. Galatians 6:16—"Israel of God," is a passage hotly contested both for and against an identification with Israel.

In Romans 9–11, however, the term *Israel* or *Israelites* occurs fourteen times. But this recurrence represents more than focus: Paul speaks from within, and on behalf, of Israel. We shall badly misunderstand Paul if we think that he has renounced his membership within Israel due to his faith in Jesus. The apostle never seceded from his Jewish heritage and his people, for what he taught was consistent with his Jewish faith taught in the Tenakh.

Paul proposes no new definition for Israel: for him there was only one Israel. C. F. D. Moule had thought that the name *Israel* had lost its original character, with Paul reserving the name *Jews* for those who are externally, or by birth, Jewish, and the term *Israel* being reserved for those who were part of the people of God, the religious community.[8] This cannot be sustained, however, in biblical usage. These two terms, *Jews* and *Israel*, are never contrasting terms, for when Paul wished to make that distinction, he spoke of those who were Jews "outwardly" versus those who were Jews "inwardly" (Rom. 2:28–29).

The real character and definition of Israel is set out in Romans 9:4–5. Their articles of incorporation, as it were, included "the adoption as sons," "the divine glory," "the covenants," "the receiving of the law," "the temple worship," "the promises," "the patriarchs," and "the human ancestry of Christ [the Messiah]" (NIV). But even more startling, this calling and these gifts were "irrevocable" (Rom. 11:29). God himself could not change his purpose and plan toward his people whom he had set as the object of his election (Rom. 11:2).

It is this simple but complex affirmation that makes Romans 9–11 so difficult for those who approach it with a different idea in mind. The Jewish people are forever loved by God because of the promise God had given to the patriarchs (Rom. 11:28). Moreover, the promise of Isaiah 45:17 was true: "Israel will be saved by the LORD with an everlasting salvation" (NIV). This would be fulfilled when "all Israel" would be saved (Rom. 11:26).

Therefore, we must not separate and set asunder an eschatological Israel of the promise from an ethnic-empirical Israel of history. The Israel that Paul refers to in these three chapters is the one that "descended from Jacob/Israel" (Rom. 9:6, 10). What is more, the salvation of the Gentiles is closely related to the salvation of Israel, two arms of the one and same divine purpose and plan of

God. That single plan for both is, in fact, the finale to the whole argument of the book of Romans. Paul concludes, "Messiah has become a minister of the circumcision [Jews] for the truth of God, that he might confirm the promises given to the patriarchs, and that the Gentiles might glorify God for his mercy" (Rom. 15:8–13). Accordingly, the salvation of the Gentiles rests on the promises given to the patriarchs just as much as did the salvation of the Jews. But that same salvation is the one now confirmed in the appearance of the Messiah, Yeshua/Jesus, who is also a minister to the Jewish people with the same message of salvation.

There is the marvel: even though the Gentiles lacked the covenant and the divine promises made with Israel, they can now enter into that same experience through faith without becoming Israelites. They are partners with Israel, but not Israel. As believers, Gentiles are "children of Abraham" (see Gal. 3:29), but that's not the same thing as saying they are "children of Israel."[9] Paul uses the former term, but he refrains from using the latter. Thus, the term of continuity between all believers, Jew and Gentiles, is "the people of God."[10] God may, and does, call other nations as "his." Egypt, for example, is called "my people" in that future day of the Lord (Isa. 19:25). He also took out of the Gentiles "a people for his name" (Acts 15:14), but in no case did the writers of Scripture ever thereby consider these new believers as the "new Israel" and to be equated with national Israel.

The One Olive Tree

The imagery of the olive tree[11] is developed to warn the new Gentile believers that they have not supplanted Israel or that the ancient promises made to the patriarchs have been rescinded. W. D. Davies[12] suggests that Paul may have purposely chosen the olive tree analogy over that of the vine, which is more natural to the Jews. The olive, Davies remarks, is a powerful symbol of Athens and the Greek culture. Paul's primary purpose, though, was to make his sharp contrast between the wild and cultivated olive trees. The wild olive (Gr. *agrielaios*) was unproductive and bore no useful fruit, thereby making it a perfect analogy for contrast between the Jewish culture as supplied by God and the Hellenistic culture of the Gentiles.

The olive tree analogy focuses on the root and the branches. The other symbols in Romans 11:16, that of the "firstfruits," the "dough," and the "whole batch," serve the same purpose as the root and the branches: the solidarity of the part with the whole. The apostle uses the Semitic concept of solidarity when he argues that the character of the root of a tree, or body, carries over into the whole plant or the branches themselves. It is impossible to force the root and the branches into two separate entities, for the quality of the source of nourishment inheres in the quality of the resulting branches.

But what is the "root"? Whether the root is Abraham, the blessings and promises given to Abraham, or Messiah himself, as he is the "seed of Abraham to whom the promises were made" (Gal. 3:16ff.), makes little difference here. The same covenantal promise of God is referred to in any event: the promised Messiah who would come through Abraham. It is this root that sustains all the branches, whether they are newly grafted in or are part of the original olive tree.

The branches, however, are a different story. The olive tree is rightly regarded as the Israelites' "own olive tree" (Rom. 11:24). But does the entire tree represent Israel? Yes, insofar as it represents the dependence of Israel on the Abrahamic blessing. "Certain," or "some" (Gr. *tines*), of the olive branches, however, have been lopped off (Rom. 11:17). So sensitive is Paul to the unbelief of his people that he uses the word "some," or a "certain" number, of branches have been cut off, thereby suggesting a minority, even though he perceives that it is a majority for the present time (cf. Rom. 3:3).

But from what have these natural branches been cut? They have not been severed from their ethnic entities, for they are still Jews regardless of their lack of belief. Moreover, Paul uses the passive verb (Gr. *exeklasthesan*—Rom. 11:17, 19–20) for the breaking off of the branches, indicating that it is the action of God himself. (If it is a middle voice, then the action is one that the branches have brought on themselves.) The branches have left the rootage spoken of in the promises that God gave to Abraham. It is not that these branches have been replaced, but branches from a wild olive have been grafted in—in and among those natural branches that still have their roots in the promise of Abraham. The salvation now enjoyed by the Gentiles is continuous with the root of Abraham. In this way, Gentiles share in what had originally been given to Israel, which "some," or "certain," of Israel now reject.

The Gentile believers are designated as a wild olive. It is not their "wildness" that is in view here, however, but that they are not "cultivated," "cultured." In and of themselves, the Gentiles will never produce olive oil. (Had Paul used a vine for his analogy, it wouldn't have worked because the wild grapevine does produce wild grapes.) Therefore, if the Gentiles are going to produce anything, they must be grafted into the people of God who spring from the root of Abraham. The Gentiles do not "support the root, but the root supports [them]" (Rom. 11:18 NIV). Without this root, Gentile Christians cannot live—nor can the church exist, for it would float in midair with no anchorage in the past or present.

Has God grown weary of Israel? Is that why some of the natural branches were lopped off? Paul meets this misconception in Romans 11:19. On the contrary, the Jews have chosen not to believe and thus were lopped off. The Gentiles have been grafted in not because of a superior virtue on their part; rather, it was solely because of their belief (Rom. 11:19–20). Jews who believe in Messiah do not need to be grafted into an alien root as do the Gentiles, who came from paganism (Rom. 11:23–24). Jews could be reengrafted into the olive tree all the more easily than the Gentiles were grafted in.

The ultimate acceptance of the Jews into those "in Christ" would be like "life from the dead" (Rom. 11:15 NIV). By this, Paul meant that more than merely untold spiritual blessings would result. The "acceptance" (Rom. 11:15—Gr. *prolempsis*) would be an act inaugurating the end of all things. The final act of history would rest upon the Jews. When these who were "in Abraham" would also be "in Christ," untold benefits would result, signaling the coming of the *eschaton* itself.

The Mystery of Romans 11:25

The "mystery" in Romans 11:25 does not hark back to the olive tree analogy so much as it does to the earlier statements in Romans 11:11–14, with its reference to "provoking to emulation," i.e., "arouse my own people to envy and save some of them" (Rom. 11:14 NIV). The mystery is not so much that "all Israel will be saved" as it is *how* all Israel will be saved.

So the mystery is not the fact of Israel's having "stumbled" (Gr. *proskoptein*). Note that Paul distinguishes between Greek *ptaiein*, "to stumble," and Greek *piptein*, "to fall." Israel has stumbled but not fallen. The question is *why* Israel stumbled and *how* they will be saved. The mystery, then, is the process that God is employing to bring about Israel's final redemption.

How, then, does the metaphor of "hardening" of Israel illustrate the mystery of how God is dealing with the nation that has rejected him? Paul has used the concepts of "stumbling," over the "stone that causes men to stumble" (see Rom. 9:32–33 NIV), and the branches that have "been broken off" (Rom. 11:17)—as well as the concept of "hardening" (Rom. 11:7)—to indicate the status of "the others" from the "remnant" (Rom. 11:7, 5). Mark D. Nanos comments that the word *hardening* (Gr. *porosis*) is derived from a medical group of words that refers to the hardened swelling of a bone that has been broken. It was used so frequently and so interchangeably with the Greek *paposis*, meaning "maiming," or "blinding," that there was often little or no distinction between the two terms.[13] This hardening is not final, but is a temporary division of Israel that will set up the final benefits that will come in the end times.

What, then, is the "partial hardening," or "hardening in part" (Gr. *apo merous*—Rom. 11:25) that has come over Israel? Some interpreters argue that only *a part* of the people were hardened while others argue that all Israel is hardened *partially*. But Paul is only concerned here with that part of Israel that has stumbled, not with all of Israel stumbling partially. Further, not all Israel has been hardened, even partially. There have always been a remnant and holy branches in the nation of Israel. But it is the hardened part in contrast to the remnant, that is in Paul's view, who will eventually see and believe along with the newly grafted-in Gentile believers.

When will this hardening that has come over a part of the Jewish people end? Not "until [Gr. *achri*, a conjunction followed by an untranslated relative pronoun *hou*, that gives a future, temporal sense] the fullness of the Gentiles has come in" (Rom. 11:25 NASB). Sometime during or after the "fulness of the Gentiles" (KJV) takes place, this hardening of part of Israel will end.

But what did Paul mean by "the fulness of the Gentiles"? The "fulness" (Gr. *pleroma*) usually takes on a numeric quality of that which brings to completion what had been planned or sought. The RSV translates the term "fulness" in Romans 11:12 as the "full inclusion," or "full number." Thus, God has in mind a full number of Israelites just as a full number of Gentiles. When the full number of the Gentiles is reached, it will be Israel's opportunity to experience their full number. The gathering of Gentiles goes on throughout all history, but there will come a time when this process will be wrapped up. That time is similar to Luke 21:24, where "Jerusalem shall be trodden down of the Gentiles, until the times of the Gentiles be fulfilled" (KJV). Upon that happening, Jesus' comment was, "You know that the kingdom of God is near" (Luke 21:31 NIV).

The benefits that God has bestowed on the Gentiles are but "the proleptic deposit of what God will bestow upon Israel at the culmination of salvation history."[14] That is the point of Paul's jealousy motif: Israel will one day realize that some Gentiles are enjoying what was originally promised to all Israel and thereby be provoked to jealousy to start emulating the faith that the Gentiles are exercising. Accordingly, the Gentiles are presently awaiting their full adoption as sons (Rom. 8:23), an adoption that Israel originally enjoyed (Rom. 9:4). These two adoptions come together, as we have already seen in Romans 15:2, where it is said that Gentiles share in the blessings of the Jews.

All Israel Will Be Saved

"All Israel" cannot refer to the church. Instead, the real goal of Paul's ministry could now be announced: it was the restoration of "all Israel" as God had promised (Rom. 11:26).

The "And so" (KJV Gr. *kai houtos*) that introduces verse 26 is descriptive of a process that plays off the earlier "until the full number of the gentiles has come in." As Nanos said, "This balance allows one to avoid the bifurcation most interpreters find necessary to support their larger reading of Paul's message here. Paul is telling his reader both *how* and *when* God is saving 'all Israel.'"[15]

Surely this will answer Anthony A. Hoekema's objection that Romans 11:26 does not say, "And *then* [implying the Greek word *tote* or *epeita*] all Israel will be saved," but it has (*kai*) *houtos* ("thus, so, in this manner"), a word describing *manner*, not temporal succession. "In other words, Paul is not saying, 'Israel has experienced a hardening in part until the full number of the Gentiles has come in, and *then* (after this has happened) all Israel will be saved.' But he is saying, 'Israel has experienced a hardening in part until the full number of the Gentiles has come in, and *in this way* all Israel will be saved.'"[16]

Hoekema's objection was dealt with more than a decade before Hoekema's time when Hendrikus Berkhof also connected the "And so" with "until the full number of the gentiles has come in." But a point that both Hoekema and Berkhof missed was that Romans 11:27 linked this "And so," with "this is my covenant with them when I take away their sins." That has to be a clear reference to the new covenant[17] that Jeremiah announced in 31:31–34 and that is seen in some sixteen other passages that refer to the "eternal covenant," "my covenant," or "the new heart and the new spirit." The contents of that new covenant are not only a replication of the promises made to Abraham and David but an expansion of them into the future.

The late Reformed theologian John Murray commented, after noting that Romans 11:26–27 is a quotation from Isaiah 59:20–21 and Jeremiah 31:34, "There should be no question but Paul regards these Old Testament passages as applicable to the restoration of Israel." He went on to say, "We cannot dissociate this covenantal assurance from the proposition in support of which the text is adduced or from that which follows in verse 28 ['on account of the patriarchs']. Thus the effect is that the future restoration of Israel is certified by nothing less than the certainty belonging to covenantal institution."[18]

It can be concluded, then, that while the "And so" may not be as fully temporal in its reference as some may desire, it is sequential in thought and consequential in that it ties the promises of the patriarchal-Davidic-new covenant with the coming in of the full number of Israel. Once this interconnectedness is admitted, the three elements—Messiah, the gospel, and the land—come back into play once again.

Hoekema also did not like limiting the "full inclusion" to the end times. But this too came from a refusal to see the past and present remnant of Israel as the foundation and guarantee that God would complete his work in a grand eschatological and climactic act. Had not the prophets of Israel depicted a remnant returning to the land (e.g., Isa. 10:20–23) and becoming prominent among the nations in the latter day (Isa. 2:2; Mic. 4:1)? Paul's phrase of "life from the dead" in Romans 11:15 takes on new force in light of Ezekiel's figure in 37:12, 14. There, Ezekiel intoned, "O my people. I am going to open your graves and bring you up from them; I will bring you back to the land of Israel. . . . I will put my Spirit in you and you will live, and I will settle you in your own land" (NIV).

But how many of Israel will be saved—"all"? Who does Paul point to when he says "all"? It cannot mean "true" or "spiritual" Israel, as some have alleged, as if the church had supplanted Israel. That was the very point Paul was arguing against.

The notion of the substitution of the church for Israel was a historical development that Richardson says first began with Justin Martyr around A.D. 160.[19] But this conclusion is not based on what Paul is claiming in this passage; it owes more to many having concluded that Israel has been rejected. Surprisingly, however, Paul claims the reverse: Israel has not been rejected. Indeed, the church is built on the shoulders of the ancient promises to Israel and the future restoration of all Israel.

So how many did "all Israel" involve? "All Israel," argued Dunn, was a common idiom for corporate or collective Israel as a whole. It referred to Israel as a people, even if not every person was necessarily meant.[20] The apostle has maintained a distinction between the "remnant" and "the others" in Israel. His goal was to "save some of them" (i.e., "the others," Rom. 11:14) who were among the hardened. In this way, he sees all Israel being saved.

How will the coming "Deliverer," who comes out of Zion, accomplish this task of restoring Israel and regathering the dispersed of Israel? Contrary to Mark Nanos, the Deliverer is a christological figure. He alone is able to "turn godlessness away from Jacob" (Rom. 11:26 NIV). If it is asked, "When shall this Deliverer do this?" the answer is "When [he] take[s] away their sins" (Rom. 11:27 NIV), as was promised in the covenant promises.

Thus the pendulum of history swung from Israel to the Gentiles, but it will swing back to Israel again. And that is but another way of stating the mystery of this passage. From the standpoint of Messiah, many of the Jewish people are enemies of the gospel, but from the standpoint of God, they are beloved for the sake of the patriarchs (Rom. 11:28).

Conclusion

It is possible that the Gentile Christian church has lost its root-age and connectedness with its past and the single plan of redemption that stretched from eternity to eternity. When many in the church denied a physical Israel as being a part of God's plan, it lost its missionary and evangelistic strategy for Jews, for it floated in the air without any antecedent history of, or connectivity to, the plan of God delivered in and through Israel.

The key objection to replacement or parenthetical theologies was made by Willis J. Beecher in his 1904 Stone Lectures at Princeton Seminary. He warned,

> If the Christian interpreter persists in excluding the ethical Israel from his conception of the fulfillment, or in regarding Israel's part in the matter as merely preparatory and not eternal, then he [*sic*] comes into conflict with the plain witness of both testaments. . . . Rightly interpreted, the biblical statements include in their fulfillment both Israel the race, with whom the covenant is eternal, and also the personal Christ and his mission, with the whole spiritual Israel of the redeemed in all ages.[21]

Jewish evangelism in the new millennium will need to take a full accounting of this marvelous book of Romans. God's plan of salvation cannot be announced without taking the promise of God given to Israel and her history into its purview. The two-step program of Paul appears to be more than a matter of personal strategy: it is a program to go to the Jew first and also to the Gentiles, and has a divine rationale behind it. It would be wise for the church to once again take another look at how she is carrying out the work of the kingdom and how she is regarding the nation of Israel. Otherwise we will have small victories here and there, but we will miss the full favor of our Lord, who calls us to a much higher biblical standard of performance for the sake of his excellent name and his Jewish people.

Chapter 3

The Book of Acts and Jewish Evangelism

Three Approaches and One Common Thread

DARRELL L. BOCK

My purpose here is twofold. First, it is to present an overview of how the promise of Scripture and how Jesus were addressed in the book of Acts. This overview surveys how the gospel was presented in three different messages, or passages, to three distinct Jewish audiences, and it will raise a theme that is central to Luke's presentation of the gospel in Acts. Then, I take a closer look at one of the messages—that of where Jesus is and what he does *now*. That message in Acts 2 develops the main point of the text, and is also shared by the three different passages in Acts that address a Jewish audience.

By way of introduction, though, let me set some context for these goals. Today, it is popular to present Jesus in a Jewish setting by appeals to Messianic prophecy. Lists of key texts are assembled to construct an understanding of Jesus. This is an effective approach. Often the stress is on the core of the gospel message, that is, the sacrifice of Jesus—and what his death has accomplished. We have inherited this emphasis on the core message from the tradition that was passed on to Paul (1 Cor. 15:3–5) and from Paul's own emphases on the centrality of Jesus' death (Rom. 3:21–26). Tucked away in Paul, however, and in the good news that the early church preached to Jews, is this other important emphasis. That emphasis was also a part of the manner in which Jesus was proclaimed in those early days, and it could also be a point of focus in the explanation of what God had done through Jesus.

A look at Romans 1:1–7 reveals, first, yet another Pauline capsule statement of the gospel. Note that verses 1–7 precede the passage Romans 1:16, where we get our theme verse for the "To the Jew First" conference. Paul's summary here in Romans 1, though, is both like and unlike the more frequently cited summary in 1 Corinthians 15, which also points to Jesus' death and resurrection. The Romans 1 summary, though, also contains a message that we shall see in Acts. This message is an emphasis that we need to reflect upon as we share God's good news of fulfilled promise.

Romans 1 emphasizes the person of Jesus as the one who fulfills what God "promised beforehand through his prophets" (v. 2 NIV). Here, Paul mentions Jesus, the Davidic Son, in his humanity. Paul also notes in Romans 1:4, however, a uniqueness to Jesus' sonship: God literally has "horizoned"—that is, marked out or designated—Jesus with power through the Spirit by his resurrection. This "marked out one" Paul called Jesus the Messiah, our Lord. It is true that Paul sees his mission as taking the gospel also to the nations, but my point in turning to this capsule of the gospel in Romans 1 is to underscore what the book of Acts will emphasize for us even more. The resurrection is important not just because it shows Jesus is alive. The resurrection is important not just because it shows there is life after death. The resurrection is important because of where it took Jesus and what that destination shows about him.

We will see this emphasis in the messages of Acts. As important as Jesus' death is in securing forgiveness and laying the foundation for the blessings of covenant, it is his resurrection that affirms he is alive and is active in our world *today*. This emphasis also needs to be prominent in our presentation of Jesus as the promised Messiah.

The Three Approaches

Three major speeches in Acts address a Jewish audience and present Jesus as the one through whom the God of Israel has worked.[1] These speeches are found in Acts 2; 3; and 13. Two of the speeches are tied to Peter and one belongs to Paul. Let's first look at them in overview before we more closely focus on Acts 2.

Acts 2 Overview

In this speech, Peter is responding to the distribution of the Spirit on the day of Pentecost. It is interesting that Pentecost, in the Judaism of the first century, was the day many Jews believed the Law had been given to Moses.[2] So, as we shall see, on the day often regarded as the day when God made the covenant with Israel through Moses, God is again at work on behalf of covenant promise.

The crowd is confused about what is taking place, thinking that the babbling in tongues they are hearing is an indication that these Jewish believers in Jesus have had too much to drink. So Peter gets up to address them. Peter's speech explains that excessive early drinking is not the cause. He gives his explanation of what is taking place by walking the crowd through four Jewish Scripture texts, citing three of them and alluding to one. They are (1) the promise in Joel 2:28–32 of the Spirit's distribution, (2) the promise in Psalm 16:8–11 of God's protection of his Holy One, (3) the promise in Psalm 132:11 that God would one day again place a Davidic descendant in rule on his behalf, an allusion to 2 Samuel 7:6–16, and (4) the promise in Psalm 110:1 that God would exalt this King and his kingship into a place of full authority.

Peter argues that the combination of these four texts explains what is happening and proves that Jesus is "both Lord and Christ," that is, Jesus is the one endowed with divine authority over salvation and is the promised Anointed One. Peter says that the proof of this is found in Jesus' ascension to the side of God and the evidence of the coming of the Spirit. If proof is in the pudding, then Peter claims the pudding of the divine Spirit is available for the tasting as a result of what God has done to and through Jesus. Now, note something about this speech as it presents the gospel. There is no word about how Jesus' death accomplished salvation. The entire stress is not on what Jesus did but what he is doing *now*. Salvation is focused here, not on a forgiveness provided for in the past but on a hope and enablement God makes in the present through Jesus.

By calling on the name of this exalted one through whom God is working, one receives forgiveness (although we are not given details here about how this provision is made). In addition, God gives the promised gift of the Spirit through this Jesus. The Spirit signals the arrival of the era of hope as Joel promised. The Spirit's bestowal is proof that Jesus is at the side of the Father by divine invitation. Thus, the gospel in this speech to Jewish listeners highlights how the resurrection-ascension revealed who Jesus is and, at the same time, makes the promise of the Spirit available to those who embrace what God has done through his chosen, Anointed One.

Acts 3 Overview

The second speech in Acts 3 is a response to a healing that Peter has performed. The healing pictures the very restorative character of Jesus' work, allowing a lame man to walk again. Here, Peter takes a different approach, walking through the great covenant promises of Israel. He announces, "The God of Abraham, Isaac, and Jacob, the God of our fathers [i.e., Israel's God of promise], glorified His Servant Jesus, whom you delivered up and denied in the presence of Pilate" (3:12–13 NKJV).

Peter describes Jesus as "the Holy and Righteous One" and the "Author of Life," while noting that by faith in his name this lame man has been made strong. Peter then notes that his listeners' rejection of Jesus was out of ignorance and had been foretold in the Prophets, specifically, that the Promised One would suffer. So he calls on this audience to repent and turn, so that times of refreshing (the promised days of renewal through the Spirit) could come and God might send the Anointed One from heaven, the One appointed for this very Jewish audience—Jesus! Heaven will hold him until God accomplishes all things he has already promised he would do in the Prophets.

Once again, it is an exalted, ascended Jesus who is preached. But here, instead of explaining what Jesus is doing, is an explanation of what Jesus will do still, despite his past ignominious, unjust death. It is here that Peter invokes promise as supporting his claim, looking to a passage from Torah. God's promise, given through Moses in Deuteronomy 18:15, is of a prophet like Moses. In the near context of Deuteronomy, this is likely a reference to Joshua, who will be a leader-prophet. The prophet *like Moses* is not, however, just a prophet, but also a leader-liberator-prophet who brings the deliverance of the nation with him as he shares God's revelation. This is what both Moses and Joshua did.

In the Judaism of the first century was an expectation that, in the days when God again would work to complete his promise, there would be another "prophet like Moses," a leader-liberator-prophet who would bring the promise to pass.[3] It is to this promised hope that Peter appeals. But if God raises up a true prophet, he also exacts accountability. So Peter warns that failure to heed this prophet leads the one who rejects him to be excluded from the people. In other words, thinking about Jesus is not like choosing a flavor of ice cream. In our postmodern world, it doesn't matter what model of religious piety we pick, as long as that model person is righteous and good. That is not the view of Scripture, no matter which testament we read. If God has sent a prophet, then he *must* be embraced, as Deuteronomy 18:19 makes clear—just as he should not be accepted if God did not send him (Deut. 18:20). Peter is telling his audience that accepting Jesus is not merely an option. He is arguing that Torah *compels* them to consider who Jesus is and respond to him. Do not be mistaken, Peter is telling his audience. This discussion about Jesus is a walk on divine, holy ground. One must seriously consider him and his claims.

Peter continues, claiming that "all the prophets from Samuel and those who came afterwards" (Acts 3:24 NIV) also proclaimed these days. Peter addresses his audience as sons of the prophets and of the covenant that God gave. They are the recipients of a promise God gave long ago, that "in your seed shall all the families of the earth be blessed" (v. 25 NIV). Thus, Peter preaches the raised Jesus from the Torah. It is Jesus in his exalted power and state to which his "raising" points. As Acts 3:26 says, in closing the speech, "God, having raised up his servant, sent him to you *first*, to bless you in turning every one of you from your wickedness" (ESV).

The gospel here is both an opportunity and a risk. If believed, it is an opportunity to enter into blessing; if rejected, it creates a risk. But note as well the thread here that ties to the speech in Acts 2—it is the resurrected exalted Jesus who is at work. It is his authority that is testified to by God through his right to offer salvation to the very nation that originally received God's wonderful promises. As a leader-prophet, Jesus delivers the people even as he reveals God's way and promise to them. But to receive the promise, one must embrace with faith the promise and the Promised One. There is no explanation in this message of how Jesus' death works forgiveness.

Rather, the focus of the message lies here: who Jesus *is* makes it imperative that one respond to him. He is the raised prophet like Moses, the second and greater Moses.

Acts 13 Overview

Paul makes this speech in a Jewish synagogue in Pisidia Antioch. In it, he first plods step by step through the history of Israel and then jets over a thousand-year span. Israel was chosen during the time of the fathers. God made them great while in Egypt. God led them out. God bore up with them for forty years. He gave them the land as an inheritance. He gave them judges. Then he gave them Saul when Israel asked for a king. Then God raised up David.

Here, Paul's speech is a Boeing 747 flight that cuts right through Israel's history. It is as if the narrative story between David and Paul's time did not count. In terms of the promised ruler for whom the nation looked, nothing in the intervening thousand years changed anything. But now, Paul argues, things are different. From David's seed "God has brought to Israel a Savior, Jesus, as he promised" (Acts 13:23 NIV).

Then Paul discusses John the Baptist. Paul reports how John, a prophet like those of old, said, "I am not he" (v. 25). In other words, he is not the Messiah. The remark alludes to Luke 3:15–17, where John told people he was not the Messiah, but that the Messiah would be known because he would baptize with the Spirit and fire. Does this sound familiar? It is the theme of Acts 2! And here in Acts 13 is an allusion to John the Baptist's clue to identifying when Messiah comes; you can know the Messiah has come when the Spirit comes.

Paul continues, preaching his gospel to his Jewish audience, "the message of this salvation" (v. 26). He reviews how Jesus was rejected and crucified. His rejection and death, even to the point of being taken down from the tree, fulfilled all that was written of him. But the tomb did not end Jesus' story. God raised him from the dead and he appeared to many people, from Galilee to Jerusalem. So Paul preaches the "good news" (v. 32) "that what God had promised to the fathers, this he has fulfilled to us his children" (vv. 32–33).

Paul builds his case, as did Peter, from the Jewish Scriptures, in this case three texts: (1) Psalm 2, a regal text that indicates that the

Promised One is God's Son (something 2 Sam. 7:14 also declared—"I will be his father, and he will be my son" [NIV]); (2) Isaiah 55:3, which points to the promise made to David ("the holy and sure blessings of David" [NASB]), and which is being given to *you all*. (The point is that the promises of God to his Messianic line will benefit those tied to him. Here Paul uses a good ol' Southern second person plural, a "you all" who get blessed. The promise of a redeeming king benefits the people of God); (3) Psalm 16:10, which also appeared in Acts 2.

As regards Psalm 16:10, God will not allow his Holy One to see corruption, so God raised him from the dead. Thus, Jesus' resurrection points to who he *is*—the Holy One—and where he has gone—to share in the divine rule from the side of God. Paul preaches resurrection to make a point about exaltation. This text is not about David, because David remained in his grave. The One who saw no corruption is the One whom God raised. So Israel is to know that through this Man, forgiveness of sins is proclaimed, and that everyone who believes is justified, which is something that the law of Moses could never accomplish. Just as Jeremiah had noted that a new covenant would come to do what the old could not, so Paul preaches in Acts 13 that Jesus brought the salvation that leads to forgiveness and to being declared righteous before God.

As in Acts 2 and Acts 3, *how* this is done—through the cross and through Jesus' taking our place, paying the penalty of our sin—is not mentioned. What is mentioned is who Jesus *is* and what he gives—the raised up Son who gives forgiveness and justification.

The speech then closes with a warning. Those who scoff will perish. Who are the scoffers? Scoffers look at a deed that God has done and do not believe, even after it is explained (declared). Paul is saying that Jesus is the promised exalted Son of God, Son of David. Jesus is the culmination of where Israel's history was going all along. The living Jesus is preached as the exalted Jesus. The One raised up to God's side lives to give divine blessing.

The preceding all-too-brief survey has highlighted how three messages to Jewish audiences were given. It is of interest that the stress is not on the sacrificial "hows" of Jesus' death and how it accomplished forgiveness. Rather, the point is to make clear who he is. But notice how the message works to explain Jesus' exalted position, not merely assume it. These speeches do not underscore how Jesus is God in an explicit manner. Rather, they explain that God marked out his Son and gave testimony to him by raising him up into God's very own presence and giving him authority to dispense God's blessing and salvation. In preaching to a Jewish audience, the exaltation of the Son is not assumed, but argued for—and the testimony is not in a verbal claim, even a claim of Scripture. The testimony is grounded in a historical act of God. This event is to be seen as God's speaking on Jesus' behalf, his vote for Jesus, pointing out by divine action who Jesus is.

As Paul said in Romans, Jesus was "horizoned" (marked out) as the unique Son in power through the resurrection. This qualifies him to be seen as Messiah and Lord. The gifts that he gives also show him to be the One God has marked out to bring salvation to God's people.

Taking now a closer look at the core portion of one of these speeches, Acts 2, I'll show exactly how the book of Acts makes this argument for Jesus. In the process we see the gospel according to the promise of the Hebrew Scripture.

Acts 2: A Closer Look at the Argument from Exaltation

This current chapter argues that the earliest evangelism to the Jewish community stressed God's exaltation of Jesus in resurrection to underscore God's elevation of him. Acts 2 highlights this point. God's exaltation of Jesus in resurrection not only served to vindicate his claims, but also revealed who he is and set the stage for dispensing great promises to God's people.

We've already noted that this speech given by Peter on Pentecost is built around four passages from the Jewish Scripture. I'll structure this examination accordingly and then point out the application of the speech in a fifth section.

The first passage, Joel 2:28–32, involves the promise of the Spirit in Joel. Four points are important to the use of Joel. The first is that the pouring out of the Spirit is evidence that the "last days" have come and is evidence of where Jesus has gone (Acts 2:16–17, 32). Key to this speech is the idea that the Spirit has been poured out, that this outpouring is associated with the last days, and that what the audience is seeing is the very thing Joel promised. Peter simply introduces these ideas here as an explanation of what is taking place on this special Pentecost. He will make the connections later.

The second point from Joel is that the presence of the Spirit in the last times must mean that the Messiah is also present (2:33). This implication will be developed in the rest of the speech.

Thirdly, the result of the Spirit's coming is that people are again giving prophecy about what God is doing (Acts 2:6–11, 17–18). Peter's preaching of the gospel here is called prophecy. If so, this is a message to be heeded (2:40).

The fourth point is the warning to escape the coming day of the Lord (Acts 2:20–21, 36–40). The way to do that is to call on "the name of the Lord" (2:21). At this point in Peter's address, any Jew hearing this message would conclude that the way to be delivered is by turning to Yahweh. How Peter develops this point about calling on the name of the Lord is the key to the speech.

The second passage used by Peter, Psalm 16:8–11, is preceded by a historical overview of what had just taken place days before in Jerusalem. Jesus, a man attested by God through his mighty works during his earthly ministry, was delivered up through lawless men according to God's plan. Some of those responsible are in Peter's current audience, so Peter speaks of "this Jesus . . . you crucified" (Acts 2:23).

But God raised this Jesus up. In other words, those responsible were on the wrong side in trying to remove Jesus. The resurrection is God's vote of support for Jesus. The hope of resurrection is, in fact, part of a promise made in Psalm 16, where David declared about the "Holy One" that God would not abandon his "soul to Hades" or let him "see corruption" (Acts 2:27). Thus, Psalm 16 promised that God would protect his Promised One and not let his body decay.

This psalm serves the purpose for Peter's pointing to the immediate physical resurrection of Jesus as something Scripture affirmed. It also serves as a bridge to the discussion on what that resurrection reveals about who Jesus is and what he is now doing. Peter continues, arguing that this psalm must ultimately be about Jesus and not David, because David's body still lies decayed in a grave.[4] Rather, David uttered these words as a prophet, delivering an oath uttered by God. The reference to the oath moves us from the second passage to the third.

The third text, Psalm 132:11, is a divine oath made to David that "one of your seed I will place on your throne." As a prophet,

David, when he spoke the psalm's words, knew about the divine
promise of protection for the body of his Holy One. So David spoke
about resurrection, about nonabandonment of the Holy One to
hades, and about no corruption for his flesh. The promise of Psalm
132 is for a ruler who sits with the authority of Davidic promise
and rules at God's discretion.

This promise, then, is realized when Jesus is raised up and exalted through resurrection. Just as the coming of the Spirit fulfills
Joel's prophecy and resurrection fulfills Psalm 16, so the exaltation
of Jesus fulfills the Davidic hope of a ruler sent by God as promised
in Psalm 132. Of this exaltation there can be no doubt, as Peter and
his circle of believers are witnesses of it, having seen it with their
own eyes (Acts 2:32).

But if Jesus is exalted, what does that tell us? That is the point
of Psalm 110:1, the fourth Jewish Scripture. For this last key point,
Peter gives the explanation and then cites Psalm 110:1. He says,
"Being therefore exalted at the right hand of God, and having
received from the Father the promise of the Holy Spirit, he has
poured out this which you see and hear" (Acts 2:33 RSV).

In other words, the resurrection-exaltation of Jesus was not
for show and vindication only. It did not just make Jesus alive or
show that we, too, one day will be resurrected. Resurrection had
a destination and a purpose, giving Jesus a throne and a home,
a permanent residing place at the side of God in heaven. From
this place, Jesus could administer the blessings of the new era and
its salvation. So Peter cites Psalm 110:1 as proof that resurrection
locates Jesus at the right hand of God, just as God had promised.
"The Lord said to my Lord, 'Sit at my right hand until I make your
enemies a footstool for your feet'" (NIV). Jesus went to the side of
God not simply to park and watch. No, he went there to share in
the distribution of Messianic benefits of new life in the new era. He
went to act as a divine vice-regent for God, welcome to sit in God's
very presence at his side in heaven.

To understand the implications of this speech, a Jewish perspective is required. Who gets to sit in God's presence in heaven?
I mean who sits permanently, not just to visit or be a part of his
counsel room? Think of the temple as the representation of God's
presence. Who dwells in God's presence there? No one is there but
God alone. Only the high priest, once a year, brings a sacrifice on

behalf of God's people, and stays for only a brief moment. He goes, makes sacrifice, and, according to the *Mishnah Yoma* 5.1, makes a short prayer once outside the Most Holy Place, lest the nation worry about him and his well-being.[5]

Other ancient Jewish literature, too, stresses the exclusive nature of God's throne. Two figures are portrayed as being able to sit on God's throne in his presence. One is Moses, in a work called *The Exagoge of Ezekiel*. In a dream, Moses pictures God as inviting him to sit on the thrones (plural) of God, an allusion to Daniel 7:9. The scene depicts Moses' authority during the time that God makes Moses, as Exodus 7:1 puts it, "God to Pharaoh." It is but a figurative picture, though, of divinely bestowed authority that operated through the plagues.

The second figure is the Son of Man—whether one looks at his riding the clouds in Daniel 7 to go and receive authority from God, or reads an apocalyptic work like 1 Enoch where he actually sits in God's presence to perform the final judgment of God.[6] The point is, someone who is invited to sit in God's presence, distribute his blessing, and exercise the final judgment is not a mere mortal. God gives him such a place because he is a special person. That is precisely Peter's meaning. To testify to Jesus' uniqueness, God has chosen to exalt his Chosen One and bring him to his side in heaven, to his right hand. Not only that, God has given to Jesus the task of distributing the blessing of the promised new era—the Spirit. Jesus shares in the divine task and in the divine presence because he is truly both Lord and Christ.

Read again Acts 2:33–36. Peter attributes to Jesus the exact privileges we just discussed: "Being therefore exalted at the right hand of God, and having received from the Father the promise of the Holy Spirit, he has poured out this which you see and hear. For David did not ascend into the heavens; but he himself says, 'The Lord said to my Lord, Sit at my right hand, till I make thy enemies a stool for thy feet.' Let all the house of Israel therefore know assuredly that God has made him both Lord and Christ, this Jesus whom you crucified" (RSV).

One final point needs noting. That point comes not from the use of Psalm 110:1 here in Acts 2, but from Jesus' earlier use of it in Matthew 22:41–45; Mark 12:35–37; and Luke 20:41–44. In that scene Jesus asks how David could call his own "son" his

Lord. Remember the verse: "The Lord [God] said to my Lord [i.e., David's Lord], 'Sit. . . .'" Jesus then asks, *If the Messiah is David's son, then why does David call him Lord?* This is a pregnant question. In a patriarchal culture the respect and authority go to the older person, not to the descendant. The question then becomes, *If the promised Messiah of Psalm 110:1 gets David's respect, then what does that say about who the Messiah is?* Jesus was pointing out there, as Peter does here, that the Messiah is Lord, even over the greatest of Israel's kings. His exaltation to God's side, distributing God's benefits of life from God's presence, shows just how unique and great Jesus is. And Peter makes the point that it was God who made it all take place. God did this to and for and through Jesus to show who Jesus is.

How do I know this is the point? Look at the application Peter makes when the crowd asks what they must do: "'Repent, and be baptized every one of you in the name of Jesus Christ for the forgiveness of your sins; and you shall receive the gift of the Holy Spirit. For the promise is to you and to your children and to all that are far off, everyone whom the Lord our God calls to him.' And he testified with many other words and exhorted them, 'Save yourselves from this crooked generation'" (vv. 38–40 rsv).

Did you notice what just happened? Earlier in Peter's speech, he told the crowd that the way to be saved was to call on the name of the Lord. Now, at the climactic point of the speech, Peter is saying that Jesus is both Messiah and Lord and that the rite of baptism, which pictures repentance, takes place in the name of the Messiah, that is, in the authority of the Messiah who is also Lord. The name called upon in turning to God is that of Jesus. One cannot have the blessing of one without also embracing the other. To call on the Lord God is to turn in belief to the Messiah Jesus. It is in the Lord Messiah Jesus' name and through this Jesus that forgiveness and the Spirit, the blessings of the new era, come from God the Father. The Father and Jesus act as one when it comes to salvation and the promises of old.

For Peter, this is the gospel and how to preach it to a Jewish audience. Stress who Jesus is, where he has gone, and what he makes available. Jesus' exaltation through resurrection reveals not only God's vindication of Jesus and that we, too, one day will be raised; it also reveals beyond all doubt whom God showed Jesus to be.

Conclusion

The preceding overview outlines three approaches that the early church used in reaching out to Jewish audiences. Each of these approaches starts in Scripture and promise, with the hope God gave of delivering his people. All three approaches have one common thread—Jesus' exaltation. Whether he is raised to be Messiah (Acts 2; 3), Lord (Acts 2), Servant (Acts 3), Holy One (Acts 2; 3; 13), the Author of Life (Acts 3), Leader-Prophet like Moses (Acts 3), Savior (Acts 13), Bearer of Davidic blessing to God's people (Acts 13), or Son (Acts 13), it is Jesus' exaltation in resurrection that tells us where he went, where he is, what he is doing, and, most especially, who he is.

The vividness of texts like Acts 2 in explaining what God has done through Jesus needs to become a key part of our outreach. Jesus' uniqueness, as Messianic congregations present him, initially seems strange to Jewish minds. Texts like Acts 2, however, and the explanation that comes with it, present with clarity and sensitivity why believers in Jesus view their Messiah with such majesty.

Remember Paul's word to us from Romans 1:1–7, how God had "horizoned" Jesus in power through the Spirit by the resurrection. Acts 2 explains to us exactly how God marked out Jesus as the unique and exalted bearer of the blessings of the new era. Acts 2 shows us how the early church preached it. We who have ears to hear, let us hear. If you know this message and truth, share it, even with your Jewish neighbors. It was for the Jew first.

If you do not know the truth of this message, then consider it seriously and reflect on what God did to mark out Jesus as the unique bearer of forgiveness and the Spirit. Come to him and find life. Know that the choice has consequences, for to reject the One through whom God worked is to reject God. To embrace God's work, however, is to receive life from the vindicated and exalted Author of Life.

Jesus' Denunciation of the Jewish Leaders in Matthew 23, and Witness to Religious Jews Today

DAVID L. TURNER

The ferocity of rhetoric in Jewish texts, and especially the volatile language of the Dead Sea Scrolls, shows that Matthew's polemic need not signal a break with Judaism. So far from that being the case, we indeed deny that Matthew is a Christian critique of Judaism. It is rather a Jewish-Christian critique of Jewish opponents—and therefore no more "anti-Semitic" than the Dead Sea Scrolls.[1]

David Gushee recently has addressed the estrangement of the synagogue and the church. He spoke of it as the church's "ultimate theological loose end."[2] He acknowledges that the largely Gentile church's spite against the Jews has historically fostered such activities as the repression of Jewish culture and the coercion of conversions. But can this sorry record of Christian anti-

Semitism be properly tied to Jesus himself, as he is portrayed in the canonical Gospels? No honest person—Christian, agnostic, Jew, Gentile, whatever—can deny that the language of Jesus, particularly in Matthew, is at times severe. Among such severe texts is the parable of the tenant farmers, with its conclusion that "the kingdom of God will be taken away from you and given to a nation producing the fruits of it" (21:33–46 RSV).[3] Another example of severe language is the eager acceptance of responsibility for Jesus' condemnation, as voiced by Jews witnessing his trial before Pilate: "his blood be on us and on our children" (27:25 NIV). In terms of sheer, sustained, caustic polemic directed against the Jewish leaders, however, Matthew 23 is arguably even more notable. The ironic imperative of Matthew 23:32 ("Fill up the measure of [the sins of] your ancestors [by killing me]") climaxes, in fact, a pericope already brimming with negativity.

Thus, Matthew 23 has been called "a unique, unparalleled specimen of invective."[4] It presents Jesus' disputes with the Jewish leaders in bold relief, and those disputes come to a head with Jesus' pronouncement of seven[5] woes against the Jewish leaders. These strident denunciations disturb many people today.

But heated rhetoric in the service of religious disputes was quite the norm in ancient times.[6] It can be argued that such rhetoric had, in fact, been in Jewish circles since the days of the biblical prophets, and that it continued to be used in the days of the second temple as various Jewish groups critiqued the religious establishment in Jerusalem. Jesus' polemical language in Matthew is rather typical, then, of second-temple Jewish disputes. Thus, Matthew should be viewed not as a Christian critic of the Jewish people but as a vigorous intramural dispute between one Jew and other Jews over the identity of the Jew Jesus.[7]

Matthew is not, then, attacking Jews or Judaism as a Gentile outsider who claims that his new religion has superseded the outdated religion of the Jews. This mistaken perception may be traced to the polemical writings of some of the early church fathers, but it is anachronistic to place it in Matthew on the lips of Jesus. To the contrary, Matthew presents the dispute of Jesus with the Jewish leaders as a thoroughly *Jewish* prophetic critique of the Jerusalem religious establishment, calling for a return to the values of the Torah. This assertion will be demonstrated by considering the seven woes of Matthew 23 in their Jewish context, first by an exposition of the chapter and second by a consideration of three key themes of the chapter. If the demonstration is valid and persuasive, religious Jews today, whether or not they believe Jesus to be their Messiah, can at least view his teaching as a valid expression of authentic Jewish spirituality. Perhaps a small step will have been taken thereby toward tying up the church's ultimate theological loose end.

The Seven Woes of Matthew 23

Introduction to Matthew 23

Matthew 23 culminates the running dispute of Jesus with the leaders of the Jerusalem religious establishment, which has been narrated since 21:12. Jesus argues successively with

1. the chief priests and scribes (21:12–17);[8]
2. the chief priests and elders of the people (21:23–22:14; according to 21:45 this included Pharisees);
3. certain disciples of the Pharisees and certain Herodians (22:15–22);
4. certain Sadducees (22:23–33);
5. a certain lawyer who was a Pharisee (22:34–46).

These arguments take the form of questions by the various religious leaders (21:16, 23; 22:17, 28, 36) and responses by Jesus, which include scriptural quotations (21:16, 33, 42; 22:32, 37, 39, 44), parables (21:28–30, 33–39; 22:1–14), and questions directed back at the leaders (21:16, 25, 28, 31, 40, 42; 22:18, 20, 42, 43, 45). Finally the disputes come to the point where no further dialogue is possible, and the indictments of Matthew 23 ensue.

Matthew 23 also serves as a sort of introduction to the eschatological discourse of Matthew 24–25. Jesus' disputes with the Jerusalem religious leaders end in an impasse (22:46), and Jesus then warns his followers against being like those leaders (23:1–12) upon whom he pronounces woes (23:13–36). He laments Jerusalem's fate, yet he holds out hope for its future (23:37–39). As Jesus departs the temple, perhaps reenacting the departure of the Shechinah (Ezek. 9:3; 10:4, 18–19; 11:22–23; 43:2), his disciples nervously point out to him the glorious architecture (24:1). At this point he speaks bluntly about the coming destruction of the temple, and the disciples respond with the question, "When will these things be and what will be the sign of your coming and of the end of the age?" (24:2–3 RSV). That question gives rise to the discourse about signs at the end of the age. Thus the judgment of Jerusalem, primarily its leaders and its temple, is justified in Matthew 23 before it is predicted in Matthew 24–25.

It seems best to view Matthew 23 as having three parts. First, Jesus addresses the multitudes and his disciples with concerns about the scribes and Pharisees and urges the disciples to adopt a different model of leadership (23:1–12). Then Jesus denounces the scribes and Pharisees with seven woes, which expose their hypocrisy in crucial matters (23:13–33). The seven woes conclude with the accusation that Israel's rejection of her own prophets culminates in Jerusalem's impending rejection of Jesus. The concluding section of the chapter (23:34–39) predicts the rejection of Jesus' future messengers to Israel, which can only exacerbate her guilt (23:34–36). Nevertheless, Jesus laments Jerusalem and holds out the hope that Israel's desolation will end when she finally acknowledges him with the words of Psalm 118:26 (23:37–39).[9]

This present section of our study focuses on the woes of 23:13–39. The goal is to show Jesus' expression of these woes as sharing continuity with not only the rebuke of the biblical prophets but also with the criticisms against the second-temple sectarians.

The First Two Woes
The Scribes and Pharisees Prevent Access to God (23:13)

The first two woes go right to the heart of the matter, charging that the scribes and Pharisees keep people out of the kingdom. The scribes and Pharisees "are not leaders but misleaders."[10] Not only do they not enter the kingdom—they prevent others from doing so. This language is similar to that of Jeremiah 23:2 and Ezekiel 34:2–8, which likens the wicked leaders of Israel to shepherds who feed themselves and scatter, rather than feed, their flock.

The Scribes and Pharisees Make Proselytes for Gehenna (23:15)

The second woe builds on the theme of the first. The efforts of the scribes and Pharisees to convert others[11] are tragically ironic. The description of the extent of their efforts ("sea and dry land") recalls Jonah 1:9 and Haggai 2:6, 21. Since they themselves are not entering the kingdom, their efforts only result in others not entering it. So far from their converts becoming sons of the kingdom (8:12; 18:3), they become sons of hell.[12]

The Third and Fourth Woes: Halakhic Matters
The Scribes and Pharisees Misguide the People Concerning Oaths (23:16–22)

While the first two woes deal with the general matter of preventing access to the kingdom, the next two speak of specific legal rulings or *halakhot*. The third woe addresses in some detail the matter of oaths. Although the scribes and Pharisees viewed some oaths as binding and others as nonbinding (23:16–19), Jesus teaches that this distinction is empty casuistry and that all oaths are valid (23:20–22). He totally rejects here their halakhic distinctions between valid and invalid oaths. Previously in this gospel, Jesus has flatly denied the need for any oaths at all (Matt. 5:33–37).[13]

The Scribes and Pharisees Neglect the Weightier Matters of the Torah (23:23–24)

The fourth woe addresses a second halakhic matter, that of weightier versus lighter matters of legal obligation. Here Jesus does not summarily reject the Pharisaic insistence on the tithing of spices. Rather, he contextualizes it as a relatively light matter when one considers the relatively heavy matters of justice, mercy, and faith. This reminds the reader of the citation of Hosea 6:6 in Matthew 9:13 and 12:7. Tithing is important, but it ought to be done with proper motives and in the context of one's weightier obligations. Here, Jesus teaches as did Micah (6:6–8) that justice, kindness, and humility, rather than religious rituals or duties, are essential. Such religious acts are valid only when they are done with the proper spirit and intention.

The Fifth and Sixth Woes: Internal vs. External Matters
The Inside and Outside of the Cup (23:25–26)

The fifth and sixth woes together address the matter of Pharisaic neglect of internal matters. In the fifth woe, the scribes and Pharisees are described metaphorically[14] as those who clean the outside of tableware but neglect the inside. Despite their zeal

for the Torah and their traditions, they remain people characterized by extortion and self-indulgence.

Whitewashed Tombs Full of Bones (23:27–28)

The sixth woe, like the fifth, addresses piety of heart as opposed
to mere outward piety. Jesus turns from the metaphor of cups and
dishes to the macabre simile of tombs. Tombs are made beautiful
on the outside, but on the inside they house only bones and decay-
ing corpses. Similarly, the scribes and Pharisees appear to men as
righteous, but their hearts are full of hypocrisy and lawlessness.

The Seventh Woe: A History of Rejection of the Prophets (23:29–31)

The simile of tombs from the sixth woe becomes the transi-
tional motif, linking it to the seventh. But here the tombs are those
of the prophets, which the Pharisees adorn while claiming that
they would never have taken part with their ancestors in killing
the prophets. But Jesus points out that they have unwittingly im-
plicated themselves in the guilt of their ancestors. Their attempt
to distance themselves from their ancestors contains an implicit
admission that they are the descendants of murderers. Figuratively,
to be a son (*ben*) of an entity is to be characterized by the ethical
traits associated with that entity.[15]

Key Themes in Matthew 23
Prophetic Oracles of Woe

It is well known that the prophets frequently cried "woe" against
Israel's sins.[16] These oracles spoke with a blend of anger, grief, and
alarm about the excruciating consequences that would come upon
Israel due to her sin. After the pronouncement of woe, such oracles
contain a description of the persons upon whom the woe will come.
This description amounts to the reason why the woe is merited.
Thus, a woe oracle states the conclusion before stating the premises
on which it is based. Woe oracles may have developed from covenant curses (Deut. 27:15) or even from funeral lamentations (Jer.
22:18).[17] The Greek translation of the Tanakh (LXX) usually uses
the same word also used in oracles of woe in the New Testament.[18]

It is important to note that a prophet's attitude in an oracle of
woe is not simply one of anger. Clearly, a prophet's anger at Israel's
sin is tempered at times by his grief and alarm at the horrible price

Israel will pay for that sin. The prophet speaks for God against sin, and this explains his anger. But that anger is directed toward his own people, and this explains the grief. The palpable pathos of woe oracles is due to the prophet's dual solidarities. Isaiah, for example, pronounced woe upon himself, not only because he himself was a person of unclean lips but also because he lived among a people of unclean lips. The prophet must speak for God, but in announcing oracles of judgment, the prophets knew that they were announcing the doom of their own people.

Woe oracles are also found in second-temple Jewish literature. The Qumran literature has notable woe oracles, including some against Jerusalem and its leaders.[19] First Enoch contains four series of woes (94:6–95:7; 96:4–8; 98:9–99:2; 100:7–9). Second Enoch 52 contains a series of alternating blessings and curses (cf. Luke 6:20–26). Later on, the Talmud will also contain exclamations of woe.[20]

Two important conclusions flow from this brief sketch of prophetic woe oracles. First, Jesus' pronouncements of woe upon the Jewish leaders were not innovative. His severe language must have sounded familiar to the Jewish leaders, given their ostensible acquaintance with the Tanakh. To the extent that these leaders were aware of second-temple sectarian literature, Jesus' woes would have sounded rather contemporary. Second, Jesus' pronouncement of woe oracles was not merely an exercise in spite against his enemies. Rather, as is made clear in 23:37, his lament comes from at least as much grief as anger.

The General Charge of Hypocrisy

Fourteen times in his gospel, Matthew speaks explicitly of hypocrites (6:2, 5, 16; 7:5; 15:7; 22:18; 23:13, 14, 15, 23, 25, 27, 29; 24:51). All but one (23:16) of the seven pronouncements of woe in Matthew 23 speak of the scribes and Pharisees as hypocrites. The words in the "hypocrite" group come not from the Hebrew Bible but from the Graeco-Roman world and are used to describe a variety of persons: those who gave an answer, interpreted an oracle, mimicked another person, or acted a part in a drama. At times the idea of pretending in order to deceive is present, but the word itself does not have a negative connotation. This word is used at times in the LXX to translate the Hebrew word *khanef,* which refers to a wicked or profane but not necessarily "hypocritical" person (e.g., Job 34:30; 36:13).[21] Philo, however, in his *Embassy to Gaius* (162), speaks of the Alexandrians' flattery of Gaius as deception and hypocrisy. In Matthew, hypocrites are more specifically those who live for fleeting human applause rather than for eternal divine approval (6:2, 5, 16). Hypocrites honor God outwardly but their hearts may be far from God (15:7–8). A hypocrite pretends sincere religious interest but questions Jesus with evil intent. Further, such a person says one thing but does another (23:3; cf. Rom. 2:21–24). Thus, in Matthew, hypocrisy involves religious fraud, a basic discrepancy or inconsistency between one's outwardly godly behavior and one's inner evil thoughts or motives.[22]

Do the prophets similarly condemn religious fraud? Isaiah 29:13 may be the most important text from the Prophets that condemns religious fraud. This passage, cited by Jesus in Matthew 15:7–9, concerns the religious leaders (Isa. 29:1, 10, 14, 20–21) of Jerusalem ("Ariel"; 29:1, 2, 7). The fraud being perpetrated here involves seemingly pious words and traditional rulings that in reality disguise hearts that are far from God, and plans that are thought to be hidden from God's sight (29:13). Israel's charismatic leaders, the prophets, are mute (29:10–12) and its judges are corrupt (29:20–21). But in spite of this, Israel's outward religious observances go on (29:1). Jesus applied this passage to certain Pharisees and scribes, who insisted on the ritual washing of hands before meals but dishonored their parents by the fraudulent claim that what might have been given to the parents had already been promised to God (Matt. 15:5). For Jesus, this *korban* practice (Mark 7:11), evidently sanctioned by the "tradition of the elders," violated and set aside God's law (Matt. 15:6).

Jesus' rebuke of hypocrisy is not only deeply rooted in the Tanakh, it is also similar to rebukes found in second-temple Jewish literature. The Psalms of Solomon 4r, for example, presents a withering critique of hypocritical religious and political leaders, including the wish that crows would peck out their eyes and that their corpses would not be buried (4:19–20). This critique may date from the first century B.C.E., when the Roman rule superseded the pro-Sadducee Hasmoneans.[23] The Assumption of Moses, an apocalyptic work dated variously from 165 B.C.E. to 135 C.E., predicts in chapter 7 the demise of hypocrites who behave unjustly and sensuously while at the same time being concerned for ritual purity. The

Community Rule (*Serek Hayakhad*) from Qumran divides humanity into the righteous—who will be eternally rewarded—and the
deceitful—who will be eternally punished—and includes "much
hypocrisy" (*rov khanef*) in a list of the vices of the deceitful (1QS
4:10). It is well known that later rabbinic literature was also sensitive to the problem of hypocrisy, even among the Pharisees.[24]

The Charge of Rejecting the Prophets

The charge that Israel has rejected its own prophets (23:29–31)
is perhaps the most serious accusation found in Matthew 23, since
it addresses the root cause of the other problems confronted there.
If Israel had listened to its prophets, Israel would not have pre-
vented people from entering the kingdom. If Israel had listened to
its prophets, casuistry in oaths and the elevation of trivial duties
over basic duties would not have become commonplace. If Israel
had listened to its prophets, matters of the heart, not the external
appearance of righteousness, would have remained primary. But
Israel had rejected its prophets throughout its history, and that rejection would reach its horrible culmination in the rejection of its
Messiah (23:32) and his messengers (23:34). This would bring the
guilt of innocent blood shed, from the first to the last book of the
Tanakh, upon Jerusalem (23:35–36).

This is not the first time Matthew points out that Israel has
rejected its prophets. The genealogy of Jesus stresses the exile to
Babylon, which was due, of course, to rejection of the prophets
(1:11–12, 17). The ministry of John the Baptist is presented in
terms of prophetic rebuke (3:7–12), and Israel's rejection of John
is explained as the rejection of an Elijah-like figure who is more
than a prophet (11:7–18; 17:12; 21:32). When Jesus' disciples are
persecuted, they are to be encouraged, because the prophets were
similarly persecuted (5:12). Rejection or reception of the ministry
of Jesus' disciples is described as the rejection or reception of a
prophet (10:41–42; 25:35–45). Jesus also repeatedly cites prophetic
literature, sometimes with an introduction that stresses Jesus' in-
credulity at the Jewish leaders' ignorance of the prophets' message
(9:13; 12:7; 13:14–15; 15:7–9; 21:13, 16, 33, 42). All of these elements combine, making it clear to the reader of Matthew that
Israel has rejected its prophets, and that by rejecting them, Israel
has failed to obey the law of Moses (5:17–48).

Jesus' charge that Israel has rejected its prophets clearly echoes many similar charges in the Tanakh itself. The Chronicler's sad commentary on the end of the southern kingdom stresses Israel's obstinacy in not merely ignoring God's message but in mocking God's messengers. The rejection of prophetic messages at last arrived at a place of "no remedy," and the exile to Babylon ensued (2 Chron. 36:15–16 NIV; cf. 24:17–22). Daniel's great prayer of confession is centered on the admission that "we have not listened to your servants the prophets" (Dan. 9:6, 10 NIV; cf. Jer. 25:4; 26:5; Neh. 9:26, 30). In terms of the "deuteronomistic" theology of the Tanakh, Israel's travails are Israel's own fault—Israel abandoned the Torah and rejected the prophets whom God sent to remind her of her obligations (Deut. 28:15ff.; 1 Kings 8:46ff.).[25] Notable examples of the rejection of the prophets include Ahab and Jezebel's rejection of Elijah and Micaiah (1 Kings 18–19, 22), Amaziah's rejection of Amos (Amos 7:10–17), Pashhur's persecution of Jeremiah (Jer. 20), Jehoiakim's murder of Uriah son of Shemaiah (Jer. 26:20–23), and Zedekiah's imprisonment of Jeremiah (Jer. 37–38). Even Jesus' "ironic imperative" telling the Jewish leaders to fill up the measure of their ancestors' guilt by killing him (23:32) has a prophetic ring to it (Isa. 8:9–10; Jer. 7:21; Amos 4:4–5; Neh. 3:14–15).[26] His allusion to the murders of Abel and Zechariah effectively sums up the entire history of the murder of God's prophets, found in the Tanakh, from Genesis (*Bereshit*) to 2 Chronicles (*Dibre Hayamim Bet*; 23:35; cf. Gen. 4:8ff.; 2 Chron. 24:21).[27]

Israel's rejection of the prophets is also mentioned in second-temple literature. The book of *Jubilees*, probably to be dated around 150 B.C.E., predicts the judgment that will come to Israel when they refuse to listen to the prophets (here called "witnesses") but instead kill them (1:12–14). The *Paraleipomena of Jeremiah*—which is probably a Jewish work with Christian interpolations or a Jewish-Christian work—mentions at the outset that the prophet Jeremiah must leave Jerusalem before God can allow the Babylonians to destroy it due to its sins. This is because Jeremiah's prayers buttress the city against its enemies (*Par Jer.* 1:1–1:1-8). This same work ends with a note about the desire of the people to kill Jeremiah as they had previously killed Isaiah (*Par Jer.* 9:19–31). The first century C.E. Jewish work the *Lives of the Prophets* recounts how twenty-three prophets died. Most are reported to have died peacefully, but seven are reported to have been martyred (chapters 1–3; 6–7; 15; 23). The composite Jewish-Christian book the *Martyrdom and Ascension of Isaiah* is obviously relevant here also. The book of Tobit describes Tobit's belief in the words of the prophets, and his conviction that the second temple would be destroyed and Israel scattered, and then finally that Israel would be restored, the temple rebuilt, and the nations converted (14:3–7).

Materials from Qumran also refer to Israel's rejection of the prophets. Commenting on Hosea 2:10, the document 4Q166 f1ii1–6 states that Israel forgot the God who gave them commandments through his servants the prophets and blindly revered false prophets as gods. The document 4Q266 f3ii18–19 states that Israel despised the words of the prophets (cf. CD, the "Damascus Document," 7:17–18); 4Q390 f2i5 predicts a coming time of evil when Israel will violate the statutes given to them by God's servants the prophets.

The mention of the martyrdom of Zechariah son of Berechiah in Matthew 23:35 causes some problems in identification, but clearly Matthew has in mind the murder of Zechariah the son of Jehoida in 2 Chronicles 24:21. This murder is recounted in the *Midrash Rabbah* on Lamentations (Proems 5, 23; cf. 1.16.51; 2.2.4; 2.20.23; 4.13.16) and in other rabbinic works.[28] Mathew's use of this story is not unlike that of the rabbinic materials in that the murder of Zechariah is a particularly egregious sin, one for which the victim implored God's retribution. For Matthew as well as for the rabbis, that retribution is put into the context of lament over the destruction of Jerusalem.

Conclusion

No one can doubt that the language of Matthew 23 is severe, and that it castigates certain Jewish religious leaders of Jesus' day in terms that make genteel modern folks extremely uncomfortable. And no one should deny that through the centuries many Christians have used this language as a justification of anti-Semitic attitudes and, worse yet, inquisitions, pogroms, and even the *Shoah*. But all this is due to a misunderstanding of Matthew 23 by the early Gentile church, a misunderstanding borne out of the arrogance against which Paul warned in Romans 11:18–21. It is ironic, then, that this (mis)understanding is held by modern Jews, as well as by modern Christians. Perhaps this lamentable history of a "Gentilized" misunderstanding can be alleviated somewhat by a "Judaized" understanding that stresses the Jewishness of Jesus' woe oracles and his concerns about hypocrisy and the rejection of the prophets. Jesus' denunciation of the Jewish leaders in Matthew 23 is in keeping with both the spirit of the prophets and the rhetoric of the times. This denunciation should not be minimized by denying that Jesus uttered it,[29] but neither should it be extrapolated to apply to the Jewish people as a whole, either then or now.

In the final analysis, the intellectual apologetic that has been argued above will certainly fall on deaf ears unless it is conveyed with a sensitive and loving spirit. In light of the sad history of Jewish-Christian relations, Gentile Christians have much to live down. Matthew 23 itself, especially 23:8–12, would be a good place for Christians to start a much needed character check. Matthew warns the disciples of Jesus that they too must be on guard against the sins charged to the Jewish leaders in Matthew 23 (7:1–5, 15–23; 19:30–20:16, 20–28; 22:1–14). Unless Christian Gentiles today are willing to love and respect Jewish people and grieve, as did Jesus (Matt. 23:37) and Paul (Rom. 9:1–3), for the sad state of Jewish-Christian relations, there is little reason to think that intellectual arguments will make any difference, or that the church's ultimate theological loose end will begin to be tied up.

Chapter 5

The Message of the Prophets and Jewish Evangelism

RICHARD E. AVERBECK

When I was first asked to write on the topic "The Message of the Prophets and Jewish Evangelism," I was in a quandary. Where does one start? I thought immediately about all the great prophetic oracles of Isaiah that are used in the New Testament in reference to Yeshua the Messiah. Isaiah 7:14, for example, references the promised child: "Therefore the Lord himself will give you a sign: The virgin will be with child and will give birth to a son, and will call him Immanuel."[1] Isaiah 9:6–7 prophesies,

> For to us a child is born, to us a son is given, and the government will be on his shoulders. And he will be called Wonderful Counselor, Mighty God, Everlasting Father, Prince of Peace. Of the increase of his government and peace there will be no end. He will reign on David's throne and over his kingdom, establishing and upholding it with justice and righteousness from that time on and forever. The zeal of the LORD Almighty will accomplish this.

Later, in Isaiah 53, is the well-known suffering servant passage that served in Acts 8 to bring the Ethiopian eunuch to belief in Jesus as his Savior:

> He was oppressed and afflicted, yet he did not open his mouth; he was led like a lamb to the slaughter, and as a sheep before her shearers is silent, so he did not open his mouth. By oppression and judgment he was taken away. And who can speak of his descendants? For he was cut off from the land of the living; for the transgression of my people he was stricken. (vv. 7–8)

Then, in Isaiah 61:1–2a, which Jesus read in connection with his own ministry in the synagogue at Nazareth (Luke 4:18–19), the prophet writes,

> The Spirit of the Sovereign Lord is on me, because the Lord has anointed me to preach good news to the poor. He has sent me to bind up the brokenhearted, to proclaim freedom for the captives and release from darkness for the prisoners, to proclaim the year of the Lord's favor.

Jesus left out the second half of verse 2, which refers to this day as "the day of vengeance of our God." That topic was not Jesus' concern on this particular occasion.

These are just a few of the main prophetic passages in Isaiah. This group, or any single one of them alone, could form the substance of this chapter. We have not even touched on the other prophetic books wherein multitudes of other relevant passages are found.

Then it occurred to me—at the very end of the prophetic section of the canon, it becomes readily apparent that the prophetic message is held open to the future, beyond the end of the Old Testament period. It looks forward to a new beginning. The last set of prophetic oracles uttered during the Old Testament period ends with Malachi 4:4–6 (3:22–24 in Hebrew):

> Remember the law of my servant Moses, the decrees
> and laws I gave him at Horeb for all Israel. See, I
> *will* send you the prophet Elijah before that great
> and dreadful day of the LORD comes. He *will* turn
> the hearts of the fathers to their children, and the
> hearts of the children to their fathers; or else I *will*
> come and strike the land with a curse.

Two of the greatest prophets of the Old Testament, Moses and
Elijah, are the focus here. The return of Elijah, in particular, "before that great and dreadful day of the LORD comes" proclaims
the promise of hope that the prophets hold out for Israel. It was a
promise unfulfilled in Malachi's day, left for the future.

I concluded that this passage, and the previously cited Isaiah
61 text about the anointing of the "Spirit of God" to "preach good
news," suggest the best point of departure for a discussion of "the
message of the Prophets and Jewish evangelism." This current
chapter, then, will (1) look at the close relationship between the
Holy Spirit and the institution of prophecy in the Old Testament,
(2) show how this relationship is relevant to new covenant ministry, and (3) conclude with the implications of this relevancy for
ministry today in the church and in the world—specifically evangelistic ministry.

From a biblical point of view, evangelism is, by definition, a
prophetic activity in its very essence. It stands in continuity with a
long line of prophetic activities that begin in the Torah and reach
through the Old Testament period into the New Testament ministries of John the Baptist, Jesus the Messiah, the apostles, the church
as a whole, and the individual Christian. Thus, our gospel message
is a prophetic message delivered by prophetic messengers.

Prophetic Spirit and Holy Spirit

The Old Testament traces a very close relationship between
the Holy Spirit and the institution of prophecy. That relationship
stretches from the Torah through the former and latter prophets,
and provides essential background for understanding the New
Testament work of the Holy Spirit.

The Torah

One of the most instructive Old Testament passages on the Holy Spirit is Numbers 11:17–29, where it first becomes evident that an especially close relationship exists between the institution of prophecy and the Holy Spirit.[2] The occasion is the Israelite complaint against Moses that they had nothing to eat in the wilderness except the *mannah* that the Lord provided. Moses, in turn, complained to the Lord that leading Israel was too heavy a burden.

The Lord's response included, among other things, a plan to get Moses some help from within the congregation—seventy elders who would help him bear the burden. These elders were to come to the tent outside the camp. The Lord said in verse 17, "I will come down and speak with you there, and I will take of *the Spirit* that is on you and put *the Spirit* on them. They will help you carry the burden of the people so that you will not have to carry it alone." As the story progresses in verse 25, "When the *Spirit* rested on them, they *prophesied*, but they did not do so again."

The close connection here between the coming of the Holy Spirit upon them and their distinctive prophetic behavior is clear, but *more* follows in the immediate verses. Two of the chosen seventy men had not gone outside the camp as they were supposed to, so the Holy Spirit simply came upon them in the camp. Joshua wanted to run and restrain them, but Moses stopped him and in verse 29 responded, "I wish that all the LORD's people were *prophets* and that the LORD would put *his Spirit* on them!"

The translation here is a bit troublesome. The verse would actually be better rendered, "O that the LORD would make the whole people *prophets* that the LORD would put *his Spirit* on them!" The implication is clear—to have the Holy Spirit come upon one in this way means that one becomes a prophet, and to become a prophet is to have the Holy Spirit come upon one in this way.

The Former Prophets

The same essential identity of this work of the Spirit with the prophetic calling appears in the former Prophets (Judges–2 Kings). It is seen, for example, in the anointing of Saul as king. After anointing Saul, Samuel tells him that on his way home Saul will meet a group of prophets who are "prophesying," and *"The Spirit of the LORD* will come upon you in power, and *you will prophesy* with them; and you will be changed into a different person" (1 Sam. 10:6).

Once again, *prophesying* was an easily identifiable manifestation of the Spirit, so when the people who knew Saul witnessed it, they responded, "What is this that has happened to the son of Kish? Is Saul also among the prophets?" (v. 11). Similarly, when Samuel anointed David in 1 Samuel 16, "from that day on the Spirit of the LORD came upon David in power" (v. 13). David is, of course, routinely referred to as a prophet.

The next verse says, "Now *the Spirit of the LORD* had departed from Saul, and *an evil spirit from the LORD* tormented him" (1 Sam. 16:14).[3] This "evil [Heb. רָעָה] spirit from the LORD" has long tormented interpreters of the Bible—almost as much as it tormented Saul.[4] One is tempted to see "evil spirit" as simply a troubled human spirit somehow imposed on him by the Lord because of Saul's disobedience. In 1 Kings 22:19–22, however, Micaiah reports his vision of the heavenly council in which the Lord was calling for someone to entice Ahab to go into battle so that he would meet his death. Micaiah recalls the following interchange in the heavenly council:

> Finally, *a* [lit. "the"] *spirit* came forward, stood before the LORD and said, "I will entice him." "By what means?" the LORD asked. "I will go out and be a lying spirit in the mouths of all his prophets," he said. "You will succeed in enticing him," said the LORD. "Go and do it."

It is important to recognize the difference between the expression "an evil spirit from the Lord" (1 Sam. 16:14a; cf. also "an evil spirit from God" in vv. 15–16, and "the spirit from God" in v. 23, which refers in this instance to the same "evil spirit"), and the common expression for the "the Spirit of the LORD/God" that is the focus of this chapter (e.g., 1 Sam. 16:13–14a; cf. 10:6, 10, etc.).

The "evil spirit" in 1 Samuel 16:14 is similar to that in 1 Kings 22. It cannot refer to the Holy Spirit, since the first part of the same verse says, "*the Spirit of the LORD* had departed from Saul." The term "an evil spirit," therefore, refers to some heavenly being (probably an angelic spirit) whom the Lord directed to carry out his judgments against Saul (cf. 1 Sam. 13:13–14; 15:24–35). I submit that this judgment came directly from God in the form of a "spirit" to cause "evil" in Saul's (human) "spirit."

"Evil" (Heb. רָעָה) in this case means "bad" in the sense of "troubled" or perhaps "distressed," not something morally bad. רַע is commonly used in this way, such as in Deuteronomy 7:15, where רָע refers to *horrible* diseases" (cf. 28:35). The spirit that God sent to torment Saul caused deep distress in his human spirit, so that he was driven to fits of extreme depression and rage. Later in this current chapter, I'll remark on the relationship between the Holy Spirit and a person's human "spirit."

Regardless of how one understands Saul's "evil spirit," the main point of the passage and our main concern here is the prophetic Spirit. In 1 Samuel 10, that spirit came upon Saul, and in 1 Samuel 16 was passed over to David, remaining with him from that day forward. David was thereby empowered by the prophetic Spirit to be the king of Israel.

The Latter Prophets

This prophetic power of the Spirit, which comes upon people, supplies the Old Testament background of Joel 2:28–32 (Joel 3 in the Hebrew Bible). Joel 2 provides, in turn, the key link between the Old Testament prophetic institution and the ministry of the New Testament church, beginning on the day of Pentecost. Joel 2:28–29 reads,

> [God says,] I will *pour out my Spirit on all people.* Your sons and daughters *will prophesy,* your old men will dream dreams, your young men will see visions. Even on my servants, both men and women, I will *pour out my Spirit* in those days.

As we've already observed, Malachi's predicted return of Elijah "before that great and dreadful day of the LORD comes" proclaims the promise of hope that the prophets hold out for Israel—a promise *un*fulfilled in Malachi's day.[5] At the advent of the kingdom of heaven, John the Baptist indeed came in "the *spirit and power of Elijah,* to turn the hearts of the fathers to their children and the disobedient to the wisdom of the righteous—to make ready a people prepared for the Lord" (Luke 1:17; cf. Matt. 11:7–15; 17:9–13; Mark 9:11–13; John 1:21). His ministry was to proclaim the coming of the one who would baptize "with the Holy Spirit and with fire" (Luke 3:16). Moreover, John's baptism inaugurated Jesus' ministry, and on that occasion *"the Holy Spirit* descended on him [Jesus] in bodily form like a dove" (Luke 3:22). After a time of satanic temptation in the wilderness, Jesus returned to Nazareth. There, he sat in the synagogue, reciting and proclaiming his mission as declared in the prophetic message from Isaiah 61 cited above, which begins *"The Spirit* of the Sovereign LORD is on me, because the LORD has *anointed* me [Heb. *māšaḥ* from which we get *Māšîʾah* "Messiah"] to preach good news to the poor" (Isa. 61:1; Luke 4:18–19).

Luke's narrative of the sequence of events that occurred at the beginning of Jesus' ministry also includes strong allusions to the Holy Spirit's activity. The allusions continue at the end of his gospel, where Jesus tells his followers, "I am going to send you what my Father has promised; but stay in the city until you have been clothed with *power from on high*" (Luke 24:49b). Then in Acts, at the very beginning of Luke's account of the early church, he immediately refers to these orders as being those that Jesus had given "through the *Holy Spirit*" (Acts 1:2). Jesus' instructions included the command to "wait for the gift my Father promised," that gift being a direct connection to the fact that "John baptized with *water*, but in a few days you will be baptized with the *Holy Spirit*" (Acts 1:4–5).

At this point we come to the well-known passage in Acts 1:8: "You will receive *power* when the *Holy Spirit* comes on you; and you will be *my witnesses* in Jerusalem, and in all Judea and Samaria, and to the ends of the earth." This Holy Spirit power was to remain all through the church age.

Clearly, then, the same Holy Spirit who empowered Moses, Saul, David, Elijah, and all the Old Testament prophets empowers us as well, we who have received salvation through Jesus the Messiah and are the present day prophets of the kingdom of God. We, too, have received the prophetic Spirit, and we are thereby empowered to proclaim the gospel.

The same Holy Spirit who indwells and transforms us into the image of our Messiah also empowers us for the prophetic ministry that is central to our evangelistic mission as the followers of Jesus the Messiah. The Holy Spirit empowered the ministry of John the

Baptist, he empowered the ministry of Jesus, and he is also the empowerment for our own prophetic ministry in the world. The birthday of the church, Pentecost, displayed this empowerment for all the world to see, at least all who were there in Jerusalem on that day. It was a display of the prophetic work of the Holy Spirit, and Peter explained it as such by citing Joel 2:28–32.

In the New Testament church, it is this very power of the prophetic Spirit that comes upon us when we are baptized by the Holy Spirit as believers in Jesus the Messiah. John the Baptist, in fact, proclaimed it: "I baptize you with water. But one more powerful than I will come, the thongs of whose sandals I am not worthy to untie. He will baptize you with the Holy Spirit and with fire" (Luke 3:16).

The Day of the Lord and the Day of Pentecost

The scope of this current chapter does not allow a full exposition of the book of Joel. It is clear on any reading of that book, however, that the prophetic oracle in Joel 2:28–32 looks forward to a new day. That future day would be inaugurated and characterized by an outpouring of the prophetic Spirit on people of all ages and walks of life. Furthermore, this day is closely linked with the prophetic anticipation of the coming day of the Lord, for in that day, the Lord says,

> I will show wonders in the heavens and on the earth, blood and fire and billows of smoke. The sun will be turned to darkness and the moon to blood *before the coming of the great and dreadful day of the* Lord. (Joel 2:30–31)

The day of the Lord is an important theme in Joel and elsewhere in the Prophets. In the particular passage above, the point is that day will be accompanied by the overwhelming outpouring of the Spirit referred to earlier in the passage. Thus, when this pouring out of the Spirit takes place, Joel's readers should look for the coming of this day of Lord in its wake.

There is no particular time given for this day in Joel. It could come any day, and it was imminent in the days of Joel. The outpouring of the Spirit in Acts, however, intensifies the imminence of Joel's day of Lord because the people at that time of Acts were witnessing the outpouring of the Spirit. We are, in fact, then, in the last days! That's the point Peter makes in Acts 2. So immediately following the quote of Joel 2, Peter begins preaching:

> Men of Israel, listen to this: Jesus of Nazareth was a man accredited by God to you by *miracles, wonders and signs*, which God did among you through him, as you yourselves know. This man was handed over to you by God's set purpose and foreknowledge; and you, with the help of wicked men, put him to death by nailing him to the cross. But God raised him from the dead, freeing him from the agony of death, because it was impossible for death to keep its hold on him. (Acts 2:22–24)

Peter continues, saying that this Jesus, having been raised from the dead and "exalted to the right hand of God, he has received from the Father the promised *Holy Spirit* and has *poured out* what you now see and hear" (Acts 2:33). By making reference to the *miracles, wonders, and signs* that God did among them to confirm Jesus as his ultimate prophet and his very Son, Peter seems to be implying that the "wonders in the heavens and on the earth" referred to in Joel 2:30–31 were inaugurated in Jesus' Messianic ministry. These things were attested to during his incarnation (John 20:30–31) and, perhaps, in a special way in the convulsions of nature that took place at the time of his death (Matt. 27:45, 51–54; Mark 15:33–39; Luke 23:44–49).

According to Acts 2:43, these signs and wonders continued through the apostles ("Many wonders and miraculous signs were done by the apostles"). At the same time, Peter ends his quote of Joel 2 with the first line of Joel 2:32: "And everyone who calls on the name of the LORD will be saved" (cf. Acts 2:21). Later, in response to the question, "What shall we do?" (v. 37), Peter responds, "Repent and be baptized, every one of you, in the name of Jesus Christ for the forgiveness of your sins. *And you will receive the gift of the Holy Spirit*" (v. 38). Everyone who would respond would receive the very same gift of the Holy Spirit that they had been witnessing on that day. In other words, they, too, would receive the prophetic Spirit.

According to verse 39, "The promise is for you and your children and for all who are far off—*for all whom the Lord our God will call.*" Notice how the sermon ends! Peter had begun with a quote of Joel 2 that ended with the *first* line of verse 32, "everyone who calls on the name of the Lᴏʀᴅ will be saved," and now he ends his sermon with a reference to the *last* of line of verse 32, where he assures his hearers that this promise is for those "whom the Lᴏʀᴅ calls." While other passages are cited in Acts 2, Joel provides the whole occasion and framework for the entire sermon.

My point here is this: *our* prophetic message in *our* day is to exhort people to call on the name of the Lord, and the Lord will add to the church all of those whom he calls.

The expression "call on the name of the Lord" has a long and fascinating biblical history, beginning in the last verse of Genesis 4. After the fall into sin in chapter 3 and the record of the degeneration of society in Genesis 4, the passage draws to a close with Adam and Eve having another son, Seth. Seth has a son Enosh, and the passage concludes, "At that time men began to *call on the name of the Lᴏʀᴅ*" (Gen. 4:26). The point is, the only proper response to the fall and its aftermath is to call on the name of the Lord. Abraham in Genesis 12 (see v. 8) did so in association with the building of the altar at Bethel, after he entered the Promised Land for the first time. Isaac did so at Beersheba (Gen. 26:25). Elijah made calling on the Lord the point of his confrontation with the prophets of Baal. His challenge to them, after they had built their competing altars, was, "*You call* on the name of your god, and *I will call* on the name of the Lᴏʀᴅ. The god who answers by fire—he is God" (1 Kings 18:24).

These are just a few examples of calling on the Lord in the Old Testament, not the end of the Bible's exhortations to do so. In Romans 10:12–13, for example, Paul says, "There is no difference between Jew and Gentile—the same Lord is Lord of all and richly blesses all who call on him, for, 'Everyone who calls on the name of the Lord will be saved.'"

This, then, is really our message. It is a prophetic message, and we are anointed and empowered by the Holy Spirit to function in this day and age as the prophets who are called to deliver it. This prophetic message is the essence of the evangelistic ministry of the church.

The Holy Spirit and New Covenant Ministry

This brings us to the relationship between the Old Testament work of the Spirit and the new covenant. There has been no small debate about this subject, so we need to set it in its largely biblical theological context.[6] Thus, we begin with the two major prophets of the exilic period, Jeremiah and Ezekiel, and the correlation between them in the New Testament.

Spirit, Heart, and Law in 2 Corinthians 3

Ezekiel 36 is largely a prophetic rebuke of Israel as a nation because they had profaned the holy name of the Lord "among the nations" (v. 22). The Lord was not about to leave it that way. God intended to act on behalf of his own name: "I will show the holiness of my great name, . . . Then the nations will know that I am the LORD, . . . when I show myself holy through you before their eyes" (v. 23). How is he going to do that? Verses 24–27 tell us:

> I will take you out of the nations; I will gather you from all the countries and bring you back into your own land. I will sprinkle clean water on you, and you will be clean; I will cleanse you from all your impurities and from all your idols. I will give you a *new heart* and *put a new spirit in you*; I will remove from you your *heart of stone* and give you a *heart of flesh*. And *I will put my Spirit in you* and move you to follow my decrees and be careful to keep my laws.

Ezekiel sees a restoration coming, and it will happen through a coming of the Spirit that will transform the people and the nation as a whole. According to the well-known new covenant passage in Jeremiah 31:31–33,

> "The time is coming," declares the LORD, "when I will make *a new covenant* with the house of Israel and with the house of Judah. . . . This is the covenant I will make with the house of Israel after that time," declares the LORD. "I will put *my law* in their minds and *write it on their hearts*. . . ."

The apostle Paul brings these two passages together in 2 Corinthians 3:3–6: "You show that you are a letter from Christ, the result of our ministry, *written not with ink but with the Spirit of the living God*" (v. 3a). Note the imagery in this passage, which combines the "Spirit" of Ezekiel 36 with the reference to writing in Jeremiah. Then Paul makes an obvious allusion (in v. 3b) to Jeremiah 31: "not on tablets of stone but *on tablets of human hearts*" making them "ministers of *a new covenant*" (v. 6a). Further, the Corinthians' (and our) ministry is one "not of the letter but *of the Spirit*; for the letter kills, but *the Spirit gives life*" (v. 6b). The "Spirit" of Ezekiel 36, then, provides the background to this Corinthian passage (Ezek. 37:7–9, 14 is perhaps an allusion to the life-giving power of the Spirit in the vision of dry bones).

In effect, the apostle Paul binds the work of the Spirit (Ezekiel) with the writing of the law on the heart (Jeremiah). We should not miss, however, that Ezekiel himself binds the Spirit and the law together in his own way: "I will put *my Spirit* in you and move you *to follow my decrees and be careful to keep my laws*" (Ezek. 36:27). This is actually another way of saying what Jeremiah 31 states in terms of writing the law upon the heart. The law and the Spirit go together. One cannot have the Spirit without bringing God's revealed law to bear upon one's life. Making God's law evident in one's life is, in fact, the essential nature of the sanctifying work of the Holy Spirit. It is interesting, too, that Ezekiel refers to putting God's Spirit "in you." Such is often taken to be a New Testament distinctive in the work of the Holy Spirit, that is, the dwelling of the Spirit in the believer.

The Holy Spirit and Israel

As remarked above, there has been a great deal of confusion about the relationship between the work of the Holy Spirit in the Old Testament and his work in the New Testament.[7] Scholars have debated whether the Holy Spirit "indwelt" Abraham, Moses, David, and Isaiah, much less the common believer who had Abrahamic faith. Some have even doubted that the Holy Spirit regenerated Old Testament believers in the first place. Several passages in the New Testament have given rise to these questions.

Jesus said, for example, "Whoever believes in me, as the Scripture has said, streams of living water will flow from within him" (John 7:38). The apostle John explained in the succeeding verse:

> By this he meant *the Spirit*, whom those who be-
> lieved in him were later to receive. *Up to that time*
> *the Spirit had not been given*, since Jesus had not yet
> been glorified. (v. 39)

Later, in John 14:16–17 Jesus promises,

> I will ask the Father, and he will give you another
> Counselor to be with you forever—*the Spirit of truth*.
> The world cannot accept him, because it neither
> sees him nor knows him. But you know him, *for he*
> *lives with you and will be in you*.[8]

Do these passages suggest that the apostles did *not* have the
Spirit, at least *not* in the same way they would have him in the
future, even though they certainly had Old Testament Abrahamic
faith?

The best answer from a biblical point of view arises naturally
out of our discussion earlier in this chapter about the prophetic
work of the Holy Spirit. The major difference between the work
of the Holy Spirit in the Old Testament as opposed to that in the
New Testament church is that not all Old Testament believers
were called and empowered by the Holy Spirit to serve as prophets, but all New Testament believers are called and empowered
by the Holy Spirit for prophetic ministry, more specifically, evangelistic prophetic ministry. In the Old Testament, many people
had Abrahamic faith but without the prophetic Spirit's coming
upon them, although some had Abrahamic faith and were also
called as prophets and empowered by the Holy Spirit. Elijah, for
example, was so anointed and empowered, but many if not most
of the "seven thousand in Israel" who had "not bowed down to
Baal" (1 Kings 19:18) were not so called and empowered. Elijah
was to take one of these who was loyal to God, Elisha, and pass
this special calling and empowerment on to him (1 Kings 19:16,
19–21; cf. 2 Kings 2).

I would argue that the Holy Spirit regenerated all believers even
in the Old Testament, and that he also carried on his sanctifying
work in their lives. Recall that Ezekiel was looking forward to a day
when the Israelites as a whole would have the sanctifying work of

the Spirit "in" them: "I will put my Spirit *in* you and move you to follow my decrees and be careful to keep my laws" (Ezek. 36:27a). The Spirit's being "in" someone was not, therefore, a foreign idea to the Old Testament prophets. God surely intended that the Holy Spirit accomplish his work in the life of his people in those days. The problem was, some had lived in rebellion to him and had, therefore, defiled his name among the people of the world. They had not shone forth the glory of the Lord as he had intended (cf. the glory of God in the people of God through the Spirit of God in 2 Cor. 3:17–18).

Jeremiah, too, looked forward to a day when the people would live the way God had always intended his people to live:

> "No longer will a man teach his neighbor, or a man
> his brother, saying, 'Know the Lord,' because they will
> all know me, from the least of them to the greatest,"
> declares the Lord. "For I will forgive their wickedness
> and will remember their sins no more." (Jer. 31:34)

The prophet Jeremiah was not implying that Israel as a whole did not know the Lord. The problem was, too many among the chosen covenant people of Israel did not know the Lord.

Yet, there would come a new covenant day in which all the people who were in this covenant would, by definition, truly "know the Lord." Either the law would be written on their hearts (Jer. 31:33), or they would not be part of this covenant community in the first place. They would be sanctified, to put it in Ezekiel's terms, by the Spirit's presence "in" them. Either the Spirit would move "in" their hearts to follow God's decrees and live according to his laws (Ezek. 36:27), or they would not be part of the community of faith in the first place. In that new covenant day such factors would define and delimit the community of faith.

There were only a select few in ancient Israel, however, who had the prophetic call and the empowerment of the Holy Spirit upon them to fulfill such a call. This is not the case in the New Testament church. All who are in this community of faith have both the commission (Matt. 28:18–20; Acts 1:8; 11:19–21, etc.) and the empowerment to carry it out (Acts 1:8; 2:38; 10:44–48, etc.).

The New Covenant Ministries of the Spirit

I'm not suggesting that everyone in the church has the special gift of "prophecy." On the contrary, we have definite references in the New Testament to the "apostles and *prophets*" as being especially gifted people who formed the "foundation" of the church (Eph. 2:20a), Jesus Christ himself being the "cornerstone" (v. 20b; cf. also Eph. 3:5; 4:11a; 1 Cor. 12:28a, 29a; Luke 2:25–32). Moreover, we know about "some prophets" in particular (Acts 11:27; note esp. Agabus, Acts 11:28 and 21:10–11; and Judas and Silas, Acts 15:32; and see esp. Acts 13:1–3) and even "prophetesses" (Acts 21:8–9; cf. Luke 2:36–38). Prophecy was a specific gift by which they functioned, and they sometimes spoke a word or oracle that had been directly vocalized to them in some way by the Lord, just as the Old Testament prophets were called to do (see, for example, Deut. 18:20).

This function of prophecy, is *not*, however, what I mean by the prophetic ministry of evangelism, to which all Christians are called and for which they are empowered by the Holy Spirit. What I refer to as our common prophetic evangelistic ministry is based on the principle of 1 Corinthians 12:13: "We were all baptized by *one Spirit* into one body—whether Jews or Greeks, slave or free—and we were all given the *one Spirit* to drink." This "one Spirit" is the prophetic Spirit that Jesus referred to in Acts 1. It was poured out on the day of Pentecost (Acts 2:33) and promised to all who would turn to Jesus (Acts 2:38; 10:44–48; 11:15–18; 15:7–9). This Spirit of God grants all varieties of gifts to the body (1 Cor. 12:1–12), all of which are given for the good of the body.

There is, of course, no small amount of debate in the church about the gifts of the Holy Spirit, especially the sign gifts. This current chapter does not engage in this debate. Instead, our concern here is with what all those in Messiah should hold in common, no matter what may be their views of the sign gifts. We all need to know and bear in our lives the full impact of the church's being by nature a "prophetic" institution, and that the Christian is by nature committed to prophetic ministry as a servant of Messiah in this world. The very origin of the church is based in the prophetic outpouring of the Spirit on all people who trust in Messiah, irrespective of their ages, social or economic status, intellectual capacities, or personal abilities. So whatever gift(s) from the Holy Spirit an individual may have (1 Cor. 12:14–30), we are all called to live out the love of God in this world by the power of the very same Holy Spirit (1 Cor. 12:31–13:13; see also, e.g., Rom. 5:5; Gal. 5:13–16; 1 Thess. 4:9–12; and Eph. 5:1–2). This includes a call to holiness of life (1 Thess. 4:7–8; Eph. 5:3–14) as well as a commitment to testify to the gospel of Jesus the Messiah (1 Thess. 1:5–8; Eph. 6:10–18), and an openness to the filling of the Holy Spirit (Eph. 5:18–20). The fruit of walking by the Spirit are such that "against such things there is no law" (Gal. 5:23).

The gifts and fullness of the Holy Spirit brings us back again to the Old Testament, for the gifts of the Spirit and being full of the Spirit have their background in the Old Testament. Bezalel, for example, was "filled . . . with the Spirit of God, with skill, ability and knowledge in all kinds of crafts" for the building of the tabernacle (Exod. 31:2–3; cf. 28:3; 35:31). God also gave "skill" to other craftsmen who worked on the tabernacle (Exod. 31:6). Similar to his doing so in the New Testament, the Holy Spirit in the Old Testament gifted people for specific ministries, only one of which was the special prophetic ministry. Moreover, like Stephen, who, through the laying on of hands by the apostles, was commissioned for special service in the early church because he was full of the Spirit (Acts 6:3–6), Joshua was commissioned by the laying on of Moses' hands for leadership in Israel because he was "a man in whom is the Spirit" (Num. 27:18–19, NIV has "spirit" but NASB has "Spirit"; cf. Deut. 34:9).

Prophetic Ministry Today

We have discussed above the prophetic nature of the church and the Christian message ("call on the name of the LORD"), as well as the relationship of the Spirit in the Old Testament to the new covenant ministry of the Holy Spirit. How does all this affect how we live today? A certain way of life comes with having a genuine prophetic ministry in this world.

The Prophetic Life of the Christian

The last of the Beatitudes in the Sermon on the Mount recalls the life of a prophet. In Matthew 5:11–12 Jesus says, "Blessed are you when people insult you, persecute you and falsely say all kinds of evil against you because of me. Rejoice and be glad, because great is your reward in heaven, *for in the same way they persecuted the prophets who were before you.*" In other words, a person who lives the Sermon on the Mount lives as a prophet today. The very nature of the prophetic life is that we do not fit into the world's scheme of things. If we do fit in, something is, in fact, terribly wrong.

Being different from the world in this way is part of the attraction of the gospel itself. At the end of Matthew 5, the first chapter of the Sermon on the Mount, Jesus reminds us that kingdom living makes us vulnerable. We are called to love not only our friends but also our enemies. To love one's neighbor does *not* mean that we need to love only the loveable ones:

> If you love those who love you, what reward will you get? Are not even the tax collectors doing that? And if you greet only your brothers, what are you doing more than others? Do not even pagans do that? Be perfect, therefore, as your heavenly Father is perfect. (Matt. 5:46–48)

The "perfect" that Jesus refers to here is a perfect love, which is a love that goes beyond loving the ones who love us back. Anyone can give love in return for love. But it takes the work of the prophetic Holy Spirit for us to live a prophetic life in the world, speaking the truth, but doing it based on a deep sincere love that cannot be thwarted by how people treat us.

The Prophetic Gospel of the Christian

So the church is by definition a prophetic institution, and is called to carry on a prophetic ministry in the world. If we do that well, however, we will meet with resistance. This hostility comes with the territory. Yeshua, our Messiah, encountered it (even to the point of death), and so will we, to one degree or another. At times, though, someone will come to us with a sincere desire to know the truth. Then we have a chance to do what our Messiah did when, for example, Nicodemus came to him. And here, once again, is a reference to the Spirit. Jesus told this Pharisee, "You must be born again." In response to further inquiry, Jesus added, "I tell you the truth, no one can enter the kingdom of God unless he is *born of water and the Spirit*" (John 3:5).

There has been some debate about what Jesus means here by "water" and "Spirit." It seems most likely that "water" is an allusion to water baptism, specifically the baptism of John the Baptist. Recall that many of the leaders of the Jews had gone to John to be baptized, and he had warned them that they needed to truly repent and bring forth appropriate fruits of repentance (Matt. 3). Personal religious piety and reputation are not sufficient for a spiritual rebirth. It takes an act of God—an act of the Spirit of God in particular—and for that to happen requires true repentance. Earlier in John's gospel we read that John the Baptist said, "The one who sent me to baptize with water told me, 'The man on whom you see the Spirit come down and remain is he who will *baptize with the Holy Spirit*'" (John 1:33). If John's baptism is what Jesus meant when he referred to being "born of water," then being "born of the Spirit" is an allusion to the "baptism of the Holy Spirit" by Jesus himself.[9]

In verse 8 of this passage, Jesus continues, talking about the mystery and power of the Holy Spirit: "The *wind* [*pneuma*] blows wherever it pleases. You hear its sound, but you cannot tell where it comes from or where it is going. So it is with everyone *born of the Spirit* [*pneuma*]." Jesus is here using a play on words. The words for "spirit" and even "[Holy] Spirit" in both the Old Testament (Hebrew *ruah*) and the New Testament (Greek *pneuma*) are the same words that are used for "wind" or "breath," and is the origin of the English "*pneuma*nia." The Holy Spirit (*pneuma*), then, is like the wind (*pneuma*) that blows. One cannot control it and cannot make it blow in a particular direction.

The Prophetic "Spirit" of the Christian

The Hebrew word *ruah* is used for the "wind" that blows the chaff away when one winnows grain (Ps. 1:4), thus leaving the essence of the grain. In Ezekiel 36 there is also a close connection between this kind of wind imagery and the Spirit of God. In the New Testament, too, *pneuma,* at 2 Thessalonians 2:8, is used for the "breath" that comes from the Lord's mouth to slay the Evil One. In the Old Testament *ruah* is used of a "human spirit" in all people. Genesis 45:27, for example, speaks of the reviving of Jacob's "spirit" when he heard that Joseph was still alive. In the New Testament, James puts it this way: "As the body without the spirit is dead, so faith without deeds is dead" (2:26). The human spirit is, then, the

part of us that makes our body alive rather than dead, and death
of the body is, in fact, associated with loss of the spirit. Jesus said
on the cross, "Father, into your hands I commit my *spirit*" (Greek
pneuma) and the narrator adds "When he had said this, *he breathed
his last*" (Greek *exepneusen*, note the root *pneuma* in this verb also;
Luke 23:46). *Ruah* and *pneuma* are used in a similar way in many
other passages.

All this is to highlight the close connection between the work
of the Holy Spirit of God and our human spirit, and how they
relate to the effectiveness of the gospel message. In 1 Corinthians
2, Paul argues that he is not concerned with the wisdom of this
world in his gospel testimony to the Corinthians, but is "resolved
to know nothing . . . except Jesus Christ and him crucified" (1 Cor.
2:2). His message was delivered "not with wise and persuasive
words, but with a demonstration of *the Spirit's power*" (v. 4). His
message was about "God's secret wisdom, a wisdom that has been
hidden . . . but God has revealed it to us *by his Spirit*" (vv. 7a, 10a).
Then he emphasizes the relationship between the Holy Spirit of
God and the human spirit:

> The *Spirit* searches all things, even the deep things
> of God. For who among men knows the thoughts
> of a man except the *man's spirit* within him? In the
> same way no one knows the thoughts of God ex-
> cept the *Spirit of God*. We have not received *the spirit*
> of the world but *the Spirit* who is from God, that
> we may understand *what God has freely given us*. (vv.
> 10b–12)

Power in the preaching of the gospel comes from the work of
the Holy Spirit of God in the human spirit of a person, convincing him or her of the things "God has freely given us."[10] And this
gospel is always "good news" for everyone—from the one who has
just trusted the Lord to the most seasoned veteran of the prophetic
ministry. This is so because, whether we have just received this
wisdom of God or have lived in it for many years, there are always
ways that the impact of the gospel has not been fully felt in us.
There are always aspects of our lives that need further application
of the things that God has freely given to us.

Summary and Conclusion

We have seen that there is a strong link between the prophetic message and evangelism. First, in the Hebrew Bible the institution of prophecy is intimately tied to the dynamic power of the Holy Spirit, and this Spirit of God is the prophetic Spirit.

Second, this prophetic work of the Spirit becomes the direct link between the Old Testament prophets and the coming of the Messiah—the ultimate prophet of God—in the New Testament. John the Baptist, who himself was a prophet—and more than a prophet according to Jesus (Matt. 11:9–10)—makes the connection clear when he proclaims the Messiah as the one who will baptize with the Holy Spirit.

Third, this prophetic work of the Spirit of God is also the most immediate and direct link from the Old Testament prophets to the New Testament church. This link is made evident from the quote of Joel 2 in Acts 2 at the birth of the church on the day of Pentecost. The link is even more evident in the action of God's Spirit on that day.

Fourth, the correlation continues in combining the new covenant of Jeremiah 31 with God's word through Ezekiel 36 about the Spirit of God *in all his people*. This Spirit's presence in all God's people is the nature of new covenant ministry!

Finally, our prophetic message is that God has made life freely available, and that life is found in his Messiah. That life is worked into our lives through the Holy Spirit, into whom we call people to be baptized. We have been given the Spirit of God to work in our human spirit so we can have not only the peace of God, but also the purpose of God in our lives. We have received the prophetic Holy Spirit so that we might live and serve as prophets in the midst of this perverse and corrupt generation. Every one of us, therefore, is called to a prophetic life.

In a sense, then, one way to understand and explain evangelism is to characterize it as a continuation of the Old Testament prophetic anointing. To receive Jesus as Messiah and Savior is to receive the Holy Spirit as well. And to receive the Holy Spirit is to become a spokesperson in the world—*to the Jew first*, and also to the Greek!

PART 2

THEOLOGY

By definition, theology is the "science of God," and as such, it has often been called the "Queen of the Sciences." But such a definition misleads, giving rise to the possibility of a disastrous misunderstanding. God is not a subject to be studied, as though through a microscope. For one thing, we have no such instrument. For another, God is impossible to know apart from the divine self-disclosure that must originate from beyond our own horizon. The veil of mystery must be parted from God's side, not ours, through the Word and the Spirit.

The task of the theologian, then, is to plumb the depths of how this divine self-disclosure addresses both the world in general and the body of Messiah in particular. The articles in this section engage the issues regarding Israel's future and Jewish evangelism from a variety of theological perspectives.

Chapter 6: "The Future of Israel as a Theological Question," by Craig A. Blaising

Dr. Blaising challenges the church to correct the widespread, supersessionist assumption that Israel has been deprived of a national future. He offers an alternative position, citing scholarship that affirms the connection of Jesus' teaching with the restoration of Israel. He demonstrates how supersessionism dangerously undermines a holistic Christology by de-emphasizing the Jewishness of Jesus.

Chapter 7: "The Holocaust and the Sacred Romance: A Return to the Divine Reality (Implications for Jewish Evangelism)," by Barry R. Leventhal

Dr. Leventhal explores the painful question of the Holocaust, reminding us that even this extremity of evil must be viewed through the prism of a scripturally based theology that does not seek easy answers. He also examines the church's stance toward Jewish evangelism in a post-Holocaust world and asks how affliction may be a means through which a loving God pursues us.

Chapter 8: "The Chosen People and Jewish Evangelism," by J. Lanier Burns

Dr. Burns considers the question of Jewish identity through the prism of the theological reflections of Abraham Joshua Heschel.

He urges those who would bring the gospel to the Jewish people to become knowledgeable about the broad spectrum of Jewish thinking, and become better equipped to address those whom we seek to reach.

Chapter 9: "To the Jew First: A Reformed Perspective," by Richard L. Pratt Jr.

Dr. Pratt takes a position on the gospel and the Jewish people that is rooted in Reformed theology. He articulates an alternative to both dispensationalism and replacement theology. Noting a widespread perception that Reformed theology does not properly address eschatology, Dr. Pratt stresses the relationship between Jewish evangelism and an eschatological vision of Israel's future.

Chapter 10: "To the Jew First in the New Millennium: A Dispensational Perspective," by Arnold G. Fruchtenbaum

Dr. Fruchtenbaum carefully exegetes Romans 1:16 and also examines the views of a variety of scholars, each holding differing interpretations. He then builds a case for this verse to be understood as an ongoing principle within a framework of dispensational understanding.

Chapter 6

The Future of Israel as a Theological Question

CRAIG A. BLAISING

The consistent message of Christianity for the past two thousand years is that salvation has been provided in Jesus the Messiah for Jews and Gentiles. The good news for Jews is also the good news for Gentiles—that forgiveness of sins and eternal life is a gift of God to the one who believes in Jesus. He is the foundation stone, foreseen by Isaiah—"Behold, I lay a stone in Zion for a foundation, a precious cornerstone, and the one who believes will not be ashamed" (Isa. 28:16). Both Jews and Gentiles received the message from the earliest days of Christianity, that everyone who believes in Jesus receives forgiveness of sins and the gift of the indwelling Holy Spirit, and thereby, immortal, everlasting life.

The message of the Christian church has been affirming with respect to the eternal future of individual Jews who believe in Messiah, just as it has with respect to individual Gentiles who believe in Messiah. Traditionally, however, the church has not affirmed the future of Israel—the ethnic, political, national Jewish

This chapter was also published as a paper in the *Journal of the Evangelical Theological Society* (September 2001): 435–50, with a slightly different introduction.

reality, which is the subject of practically the entire Bible, the special object of God's favor and grace, and the recipient of God's covenanted promises of blessing. The church has been faced, though, with seeing on the one hand a smattering of Jewish believers in Messiah (amidst a larger Gentile Christian reality) and on the other, a larger cohesive Jewish society, which did not believe. As a result, many Christians came to the conclusion not only that Israel was presently under divine judgment, but that God had completely rejected Israel to the point that no future for Israel remained except to wander the earth as a sign of divine displeasure until the final judgment at the end of time. As for God's covenanted promises regarding Israel's future, many Christian theologians adopted the view that those promises were transferred by God to the institution of the church. Thus, the church was seen to be the new Israel. Old Israel, Israel in the proper sense of the term, had been disinherited, dispossessed, and deprived of any place in the future plan of God.

Three things can be said about this traditional Christian view, that is, a future for individual believing Jews in Messiah, but no future for ethnic, national Israel in the plan of God. First, it has always been strange to Jews. Two, it is increasingly being rejected by Christians as not accurately representing the message of Jesus, his apostles, or Scripture generally. Three, given that the divine rejection of Israel has been deeply structured into Christian thought, if it is indeed true that God still has a future for Israel, then it will be necessary to examine the implications of that future for Christian theology.

In this chapter, then, readers will look first at how deeply the rejection of a future for Israel has affected Christian thought. This chapter then presents the biblical teaching that has convinced many that Israel indeed has a future in the plan of God. Finally, this chapter draws implications of that teaching for Christian theology.

Supersessionism

First, the rejection of Israel is an idea deeply ingrained in Christian thought. The church's traditional answer to the question of Israel's future is known as supersessionism: Israel has been replaced or superseded by the Gentile church. Supersessionism first arose after the suppression of the Bar Kochba revolt in A.D. 135, expressed in the writings of second-century Christians such as Justin

Martyr and Melito of Sardis, and also in the Letter of Barnabas.[1] It quickly spread to become the prevailing viewpoint of the Christian church.

R. K. Soulen, in his work *The God of Israel and Christian Theology*, suggests that we understand supersessionism in three types.[2] First is punitive supersessionism, which says that God has rejected the Jews because of their rejection of Messiah. The catastrophes of A.D. 70 and A.D. 135 were the political expressions of a fundamental divine abandonment of Israel in punishment for her rejection of Messiah. As a result, God has turned his back on the Jews and has embraced the Gentile church in their place.

More potent and far-reaching than punitive supersessionism, however, is economic supersessionism, which argues that the entire economy, or dispensation, of Israel, from Sinai to Messiah, was designed by God as a transitory symbol or type of an eternal, spiritual religion revealed by Messiah and embodied in Christianity. The nationalist, ethnic, physical defining features of Judaism are all, like the entire story of Old Testament Israel, a carnal symbol divinely intended to pass away when God brought the eternal spiritual antitype, the church, into being.

Finally, Soulen notes, we pass on to the most deeply embedded form of supersessionism—structural supersessionism—in which Scripture is habitually read with the distinctly Jewish or Israelitish elements of Scripture a mere background to the biblical story that moves primarily from universal creation to universal consummation by way of universal sin and universal redemption. Israel *per se* is not really even in the *main* story of the Bible.[3]

Because supersessionism is traditionally ingrained deeply into Christian thought, the question of a future for Israel is traditionally met with automatic rejection if not incomprehension. Today, though, supersessionism lives in Christian theology purely on the momentum of its own tradition as developments in the twentieth century have undercut its supposed historical and biblical bases.

Supersessionists believed that the catastrophes of A.D 70 and 135 signaled God's intention to make a complete end of Israel as a political, national entity. (The dramatic establishment of the state of Israel in 1948 under God's providence has belied, of course, that notion.) Supersessionists developed ways of reading the Bible that not only eliminated Israel from the main story, but also turned it into a symbol of the Gentile church and the spiritual realities that characterized the church's supposed future. They believed that the New Testament clearly set forth the spiritual religion of Christianity, to which the Old Testament covenants, promises, and narrative related as a symbol.

But revisions to this supersessionist way of reading Scripture began to appear as early as the seventeenth century as newly emerging millennial views began to argue for a future for ethnic, national Israel in the coming kingdom of Messiah.[4] In the late nineteenth century and through the twentieth century, belief in a future for Israel based on a literal rather than symbolic fulfillment of Old Testament prophecy became more widespread through the impact of premillennialism.[5] The awful genocide of the Holocaust impelled biblical scholars to reassess the anti-Jewish bias by which Scripture had been read. The result was a major shift of opinion on the New Testament expectation of a future for Israel. Key to this shift has been the development of a consensus regarding Paul's teaching in Romans 9–11 that there is, indeed, a future in the plan of God for Israel—not a redefined Israel, but ethnic-national Israel.[6]

Romans 9–11

It is worth emphasizing here the key features of Paul's argument. C. E. B. Cranfield expressed twenty-one years ago what is now broadly affirmed in New Testament studies: "These three chapters [Rom. 9–11] emphatically forbid us to speak of the church as having once and for all taken the place of the Jewish people."[7] The key hermeneutical points are the following: First, Paul states at the outset in Romans 9 that his concern is for his "brethren," his "kinsmen according to the flesh," "Israelites" (9:3–5 NASB). Second, Israel has failed to obtain the righteousness that is by faith (9:30–32; 10:2–21). They are enemies of the gospel (11:28), but Paul nevertheless prays for them that they might be saved (10:1). And third, he claims that God's Word concerning Israel will be fulfilled (9:6, 27–29; 11:1–5, 26–29), but in a twofold way—a fulfillment during the church age and an eschatological fulfillment. In the present time, God is fulfilling the Word that promised the salvation of a remnant as opposed to the whole of Israel (9:27–29; 11:1–7, 25).

In regard to this third hermeneutical point, Paul notes that, in his day, there is a remnant according to God's gracious election,

which includes "Israelites" such as himself (11:1–2, 5). The hardening of the majority of Israel in the present time is the way God has
chosen to extend the riches of salvation to the Gentiles (11:25).
This is a mystery in that whereas one might have expected Israel to
be blessed in full prior to blessing being extended to Gentiles, in actual fact, God will bring in the fullness of the Gentiles while Israel
is for the most part hardened. Thus, the first part of the fulfillment
of God's Word about Israel concerns the present time, the fulfillment of the Word that only a remnant would be saved (9:4, 6–12,
27–29; 11:5). But the second part of the fulfillment of God's Word
concerning Israel is what those who knew the Scriptures rightly
expected—the glorious blessing upon Israel nationally. Israel has
stumbled (9:32b–33; 11:9–11), and in that state of stumbling, God
is fulfilling his Word about saving a remnant. But, Paul says, they
have not stumbled so as to fall (11:11). If their failure has meant
riches for the Gentiles, how much more will the *fullness* of Israel
bring riches of blessing upon the world (11:12)?

The above fullness is contrasted to the part, the remnant, which
is being saved in the present time (11:7–26). Whereas Israel's rejection in the present time means the reconciliation of the Gentiles to
God, their future acceptance will mean life from the dead (11:15).
This is the language of reversal. Israel, which is now "an enemy
of God as regards the Gospel" (11:28); Israel, of which now only
a remnant is being saved (9:27–29; 11:5); Israel, for whom Paul is
praying and for whom he wishes himself accursed that they might
be saved (9:1–3; 10:1); Israel, which has missed the righteousness
of God by stumbling over the stumbling stone (9:32b–33; 11:9)—
Israel is nevertheless beloved for the sake of the forefathers (11:28).
The lump is holy because of the first bit of dough; the branches are
holy because of the root (11:16), and even if God has broken them
off, he is able to, and will, in fact, graft them in again (11:23–24).
According to the Word of the Lord, the redeemer will come from
Zion and remove ungodliness from Jacob. He will fulfill his covenant with them and all Israel will be saved (11:26–27).[8]

Among many interpreters of Paul, this is now the widespread
understanding of his teaching: a twofold bearing of the Word of
God on the status of Israel—a present time of hardening, in which
only a remnant from Israel is saved, and then an eschatological
salvation of Israel as a whole, which will mean even greater riches

for the world. This understanding accords well with the developing consensus concerning the focus of Jesus' ministry on Israel.

Jesus and the Restoration of Israel

Many biblical scholars working in historical, Jesus research share the view that the teaching and mission of Jesus can only be understood in terms of Jesus' vision for the restoration of Israel.[9] Jesus proclaimed the nearness of the kingdom of God to Israel—a kingdom that was as much political as it was spiritual; a kingdom that, in accord with the expectation of the Hebrew prophets, saw God's favor coming upon Israel nationally as much as upon Jews personally. The universal extent of the kingdom to Gentile nations, rather than contradicting the particularist focus on Israel, was its expected complement in the traditional way in which the prophets predicted a Messianic empire. The striking feature of this new consensus on Jesus is not only the nationalist particularity of Jesus' focus on Israel, but the consistency of that focus from the beginning of his ministry to the cross and resurrection. As Jim Scott has put it, "Jesus lived and died for the vision of the restoration of Israel."[10]

Scott McKnight, in his book *A New Vision for Israel: The Teaching of Jesus in National Context*, notes that Jesus proclaimed this vision at a crucial moment in Israel's history. Even as the eschatological kingdom was breaking forth in the ministry of Jesus, a severe judgment from God was imminent over the nation.[11] The rejection of Jesus and his message by the leaders of Israel made that judgment certain. Jesus himself warned Israel of the catastrophe that lay ahead. But he also set forth clearly and most certainly that God would bring the promised kingdom to a future fulfillment.[12] His apostles would rule the twelve tribes of Israel; they would inherit lands, cities, and houses in the age to come. Jesus assured his Jewish followers that the restoration of the kingdom to Israel was, indeed, certain, its time fixed by the Father in heaven, but not to be revealed in advance.[13]

In the meantime, the remnant of Israel, whose faith was in Jesus, would take the good news of the kingdom to the Gentiles. And in their fellowship, the inaugurated kingdom would manifest a presence until that time when, as Peter expressed it, God would bring in the *apokatastasis*, "the restoration of all that God spoke by the mouth of his holy prophets from of old" (Acts 3:19–21; cf. 1:3, 6–8).

As biblical scholarship makes ever more clear that Jesus and Paul taught a future for national Israel in the eschatological plan of God, the legitimacy of a supersessionist reading of Scripture grows ever more dim to the point of vanishing altogether. A new unified way of reading the Bible becomes possible, taking the Old Testament covenant promises to Israel in a literal rather than symbolic manner. And with the current reconstitution of Israel as a political reality after more than eighteen hundred years, the providential-historical argument for the end of Israel nationally has been thrown into question as well.

Are there theological reasons for believing that Israel has a future? Yes, because God is faithful to his Word. Yes, because, "For I, the Lord, do not change; therefore you, O sons of Jacob, are not consumed" (Mal. 3:6). Yes, because, "The gifts and calling of God are irrevocable" (Rom. 11:29).

Two Covenant Theology

In this current study, we need to note that another "yes" is being promoted in some corners of Christian theology. In the last few decades of the twentieth century, since the Holocaust, a number of Catholic and mainline Protestant theologians have proposed an alternative to supersessionism that is known generally as two covenant theology.[14] The key feature is the belief that Jews and Christians are related to God separately by distinct covenants: Christianity offers a covenant relationship to God for Gentiles through Jesus; Judaism offers a covenant relationship to God for Jews through Torah. These covenants are distinct yet divinely sanctioned ways for their constituents to relate to God. Thus, it would be categorically wrong to deny the legitimacy of a favorable relationship to God for Jews or Christians on the basis of one covenant or the other. So, even though most Jews do not believe in Messiah, according to two covenant theology, Christians should not deny that the Jews have a favorable relationship to God. Rather, they should affirm that Jews are in a favorable relationship to God precisely on the basis of Torah. Quite consistent with this, those who take this dual covenant view of Judaism and Christianity have repudiated Christian evangelism and mission to Jews not only as an affront but as a theological violation of God's covenant with Israel.

From an evangelical standpoint, there are many problems with the dual covenant theory. A number of these problems have been addressed in various publications, and I can only mention some within the scope of this paper.[15] Let us focus first on the claim concerning the covenant relationships of Israel and of the church to God. Does it make sense to say within the frameworks of the Tanakh and the New Testament that we could have two different God-approved religions, each with their own covenant relationships to God, existing side by side, separate but equal? Both Israel in the Tanakh and the church in the New Testament see themselves related to God through the covenant with Abraham. And consequently, both see their covenant relationship with God as entailing all peoples, as that covenant promised to bless Abraham and his seed, and in him or in his seed bless all peoples. The eschatological vision of Israel in the Tanakh is the mediation to the Gentiles of that blessing, the blessing with which she is herself blessed—for example, the shalom of Israel being extended to the Gentiles in Isaiah 2; Micah 4, and the Isaiah oracles concerning Yahweh the Savior of all nations (Isa. 42:1–6, 10–12; 45:22–25; 49:6–7, 22–26; 60:1–3). The latter is prefaced with the command to proclaim the good news of the Lord's favor to Zion and to all the nations (Isa. 40:9–11; 45:22–25). This vision is universal; it leaves no room for a people related to God by some other covenantal means. The church in the New Testament sees itself proclaiming new covenant blessings that flow from the covenant made with Abraham (Gal. 3:6–14). The New Testament sees both Jew and Gentile in Messiah, united in this new covenant blessing (Gal. 3:26–29).

The New Testament does, however, see Jewish and Gentile believers in different relationships to the law of Moses. We think of Acts 15, where the Jerusalem Council rejected the argument that Gentile believers had to be circumcised and had to observe the law of Moses. Jewish believers, however, continued to do so. James says, in Acts 21, that the Jewish believers in Messiah were zealous for the Torah (Acts 21:20). Paul himself practiced the law (Acts 12:21–26; 23:6; 24:13–21; 25:19; 28:17) but rejected the Pharisaic restrictions on table fellowship with Gentiles (Gal. 2:11–21; 1 Cor. 9:19–23), just as Jesus rejected those same restrictions used to discriminate among Jews (Matt. 9:10–13 et al.). But even though the New Testament does see Jewish and Gentile believers with different relationships to the law of Moses, it does not see this as a distinction between Judaism and the church. Rather, the church contains within its unity of new covenant blessing both Mosaic and Gentilic orders. The point is this: in regard to the vision in the Tanakh of Israel's covenant relationship to God and God's plan to bless Gentiles, or to the New Testament view of Jews and Gentiles in the church, neither presents a view of dual, unrelated covenants, one for Jews as Jews and the other for Gentiles as Gentiles. Further, both require evangelistic proclamation of covenant blessing to all peoples. Consequently, dual covenant theology is fundamentally incompatible with the biblical foundations of Israel's and the church's identities and missions.

A second problem of dual covenant theology in relation to evangelicalism is its primary orientation, which is not coming from the Bible but from modern pluralism. It proposes that Christianity and Judaism see each other as legitimately distinct religions. Doing so, however, creates further incoherence at the biblical level. Why? Because both Israel in the Tanakh and the church of the New Testament were profoundly exclusive—not of other peoples, but of other religions. No other religions are seen as sanctioned by God. To suggest, then, that Christianity and Judaism see each other as validly separate religions insults both Christianity and Judaism at their fundamental, that is biblical, levels.

But the biggest problem with two covenant theology as it concerns evangelicalism is its claim that Israel is related to God by covenant apart from Jesus the Messiah. Rosemary Reuther, in her book *Faith and Fratricide,* argues that Christology is the problem in Jewish-Christian relations, and consequently, Christology must be revised.[16] Many of those who endorse two covenant theology affirm that Jesus was not the Messiah of the Jews simply because he did not bring in the Messianic age. He may become that Messiah in the future, but he is not at present. Consequently, Jews cannot be said to be saved through faith in Jesus. Rather, they have their own covenant relationship with God apart from Jesus. That relationship is more or less like the covenantal nomism that E. P. Sanders says characterized the Jewish relationship to God in the first century and quite apart from the religion of Jesus advocated by the apostle Paul.[17]

The obvious problem with this for evangelical theology is its being entirely contrary to the teaching of the New Testament. The

Gospels uniformly present Jesus as the Messiah of Israel, from the angelic announcement to Mary and Joseph to the sign that was nailed to his cross (Matt. 27:37; Mark 15:26; Luke 23:38). After his ascension, the apostles proclaimed in Jerusalem that Israel should know that God had made Jesus Lord and Messiah (Acts 2:36), and that there is no other name under heaven given among men by which we must be saved (Acts 4:10, 12). As Peter declared to the Council of Israel, "He is the one whom God exalted to His right hand as a Prince and a Savior to grant repentance to Israel, and forgiveness of sins" (Acts 5:31). Further, the proclamation of Jesus as the Messiah of Israel is presented in the New Testament in terms of the fulfillment of Israel's covenants (Abrahamic, Mosaic, Davidic, and new covenants) in the twofold manner that we commonly recognize as the present and future fulfillment of the Messianic kingdom. The Israel of the future is the Israel of the kingdom of the Son of God, the Messiah, the Prince. To claim that Israel can be related to God by covenant apart from Jesus the Messiah is nothing less than a repudiation of New Testament Christianity.[18]

Theological Hermeneutics

Up to this point, I have addressed this chapter to the question of whether there are theological reasons for asserting a future for Israel. The answer is, contrary to supersessionism, yes. But it is not the yes of dual covenant theology. The yes to Israel's future is the yes spoken by the Scripture—both Tanakh and Christian Bible, both Old and New Testament alike. But that yes cannot be heard as the answer to an isolated question. The problem that we face here is the structural nature of supersessionism, the deep-set tradition of excluding ethnic, national Israel from the theological reading of Scripture. To put Israel back into the picture involves not a slight change of interpretation on a few passages, but involves an overall adjustment of the way Scripture is to be read.

We need to observe here that a heightened hermeneutical awareness *per se* does not automatically solve the theological problem of supersessionism. One must not underestimate the power of long-standing tradition in shaping the hermeneutical preunderstanding by which individual texts as well as whole portions of biblical literature are read—preunderstandings that are reinforced by the expositional commentary traditions in evangelical preaching and by traditional forms of theological catechesis in evangelical teaching.

Evangelicals affirm the consistent application of a grammatical-historical-literary hermeneutic. And evangelicals have produced excellent works on hermeneutics, from, for example, Osborn to Van Hoozer.[19] Also, evangelicals participate in the work of developing a canonical theology as can be seen, for example, in works from Dumbrell to Sailhamer.[20]

Although evangelicals are rich in hermeneutical theory, they are poor in its theological implementation. The tendency in evangelicalism is to rest confessionally on the theological work of predecessors rather than draw out of Scripture the faith afresh and ever richer by the hermeneutical methodologies that we spend so much time developing. In short, to take the future of Israel seriously as a theological question encumbers evangelical theology foundationally in the work of drawing out a canonical theology that is faithful to the theological work of predecessors. And as evangelicals do that, draw that theology out of the canon with Israel left in the story, what might be expected theologically?

Implications of a Nonsupersessionist Evangelical Theology

Here we can only sketch some of the possible implications of a nonsupersessionist evangelical theology. Those implications might be seen in the doctrine of God, in anthropology, Christology, ecclesiology, and eschatology.

Doctrine of God

With respect to an understanding of God, we in this current study would have to put foremost in our thinking that God is the God of Israel. He is the God of Israel, and also of the Gentiles. God created us all alike, but among this human creation, God chose Abraham and his descendants to bless, and to bless Gentiles in him. Our relationship to God is, therefore, not that of an undifferentiated mass, or even simply through the distinction of election to salvation, but by another election that adds complexity to the picture—the election of Israel among the peoples of the world.

When we talk about the attributes of God, first priority should be put not on apophatic or cataphatic methods, but on how he described himself to Moses on Sinai: "The Lord, the Lord God, compassionate and gracious, slow to anger, and abounding in loving-kindness and truth; who keeps loving-kindness for thousands, who forgives iniquity, transgression and sin; yet will by no means leave the guilty unpunished, visiting the iniquity of fathers on the children and on the grandchildren to the third and fourth generations" (Exod. 34:6–7). Note the emphasis on *loving-kindness and truth*. This is good news for a people to whom he has given promises of everlasting blessing. As a God who abounds in loving-kindness and truth, he can be relied upon to keep his Word. It is this God who became incarnate in the house of David two thousand years ago, revealing ever more fully his *grace and truth*. And it is he who has been receiving Gentiles to a table of fellowship with the remnant of Israel.

When we read the Bible, taking Israel and God's relationship to her seriously, we find in the matter of divine providence both a general providence—in which God works all things according to the council of his will—and a special providence overlaid upon the general in which he orders the ways of Israel in a special rather than general manner. We also find a personal engagement and re-lational reciprocity between God and Israel, one that goes beyond either this general or special providence and that cannot be simply dismissed as anthropomorphism. This relationship finds its cul-minating expression in the revelation of this very God of Israel *in* and *to* Jesus the Messiah, that revelation's being of an even greater complexity—the revelation of the triune God.

Anthropology

In the area of anthropology, having Israel truly in the divine plan confronts the myth of an undifferentiated humanity. Truly, we are all descended from Adam, but God thinks of us in the differ-entiated manner of the Abrahamic covenant. In Christianity, what happened to believers was not the universalizing of the particular. Rather, believers are experiencing the fulfillment of the plan to bless the various kinds of peoples through the particular mediation of Abraham's seed. Perhaps this means that more attention needs to be placed on ethnic and racial distinction as a variety intended by God for the enriching of the whole human race. Paul says that when the redeemer comes, he will remove ungodliness from Jacob, and that all Israel will be saved, and that this will mean riches for the world. Note: the riches for the world are not simply a direct gift from God to individuals, but a mediated result from the fullness of Israel. More serious attention may now need to be placed on the role of Israel as a people in the way God sovereignly blesses human life—not only the extension of salvation to Gentiles during Israel's hardening, but the regulation of the whole of Gentile life on the earth. Somehow, Israel and the Jewish people are taken up into God's ways of blessing human life on this side of the parousia—a point that might be seen in Thomas Cahill's recent work, *The Gifts of the Jews*.[21]

Christology

One of the most obvious effects of supersessionism in traditional Christology is the effacement of the Jewishness of Jesus from Christian confession. It is remarkable that the great creeds and confessions of the faith are silent on this point, being satisfied simply with the affirmation of Christ's humanity. In Scripture, however, not only the Jewishness of Jesus but also his Davidic lineage are central features of the gospel. Paul, in Romans 1, for example, summarizes the gospel in this way:

> The gospel of God, which He promised beforehand through His prophets in the holy Scriptures, concerning His Son, who was born of a descendant of David according to the flesh, who was declared the Son of God with power by the resurrection from the dead, according to the Spirit of holiness, Jesus Christ our Lord. (vv. 1–4 NASB)

This is the gospel that Paul says in Romans 1:16 is to the Jew first and also to the Greek. In 2 Timothy 2:8, Paul writes, "Remember Jesus Christ, risen from the dead, descendant of David, according to my gospel" (NASB). Matthew and Luke also emphasize, of course, the Davidic lineage of Jesus from the beginning of their gospel accounts. In Luke 1:32–33, Gabriel tells Mary that her son "will be great, and will be called the Son of the Most High; and the Lord God will give Him the throne of His father David; and He will reign over the house of Jacob forever, and His kingdom will have no end" (NASB).

The Davidic lineage is crucial, then, for understanding the New

Testament reference to Jesus as the Son of God, recalling the promise to David in 2 Samuel 7:14 concerning his descendant whom the Lord would raise up and whose kingdom the Lord would establish: "I will be a father to him and he will be a son to Me" (NASB). In other words, *Son of God* is, first of all, a covenantal term designating the fulfillment of the promise to David. The remarkable message of the New Testament is that in and through this Sonship a greater Sonship is revealed. Whereas Psalm 72 says that in him all the nations will be blessed—applying the Abrahamic promise to the Davidic King, indicating that it would be through the fulfillment of the Davidic covenant that the Abrahamic promise of mediated blessing would itself be fulfilled—Colossians 1 says that in him all things were created. The "in him" is the formula of mediated promise. But here it indicates a "him" who is greater than any descendant of David.

The point is, the incarnation is not just the union of God and humanity; it is the incarnation of the Son of God in the house of David as the Son of covenant promise. From a human standpoint, Jesus is not just a man, or generic man; he is that Man—that descendant of David who has a great inheritance and a future set forth in the eschatological fulfillment of God's plan for Israel. But in God the Son incarnate, those promises are ever more sure and certain, and they also receive a cosmic addition to the inheritance that is beyond—but not instead of—the initial scope of the promise. Paul goes on to say in Colossians 1:16 that all things were not only created "in him" but "for him"—the Son of God, God the Son incarnate as the covenant Son, the Son of David—as a gift from God the Father. If God the Father has given all things to his covenant Son, the Son of David, precisely because he is none other than God the Son, how could Israel's future be any more secure?

When we as believers think of Jesus Christ, then, clearly we must think of him as the Messiah of Israel. Israel's promises are guaranteed now not only by the Word and the Oath, as Hebrews 6 says, but by the union of Davidic Sonship and Divine Sonship, the inclusion of the covenanted Davidic inheritance in the inter-Trinitarian gift of all creation from the Father to the Son. This is why Jesus is the only way to partaking of the glorious inheritance of the kingdom for either Israel or the Gentiles, for one can only be blessed by God "in him."

Post-Holocaust theology is correct in calling Christianity to recognize the Jewishness of Jesus, but they have completely missed the New Testament message of which Jew he is. What about the charge that Jesus could not be the Messiah since he did not bring in the kingdom? Once again, post-Holocaust theology is unable to answer this question and stumbles over it because of its poor biblical foundation. The New Testament proclaims the inauguration of the kingdom in the preascension and ascension ministries of Jesus with the fullness of the kingdom yet to come. Those who believe in Jesus participate in the inaugural blessings of the kingdom.

Israel today, however—Israel who is mostly in unbelief—needs to see Jesus as the One who prophesied the destruction of the temple and the visitation of judgment on Jerusalem and the people. The temple has been in ruins since A.D. 70, and for over eighteen hundred years Israel was without any political presence in the land. The stark fact of the fulfillment of that prophecy, which was recorded in the New Testament, needs to be given serious attention. This same New Testament witnesses to the revelation of kingdom power and shalom in the ministry of Jesus, and sets forth Jesus as teaching that the kingdom will indeed come for Israel, although the time is not revealed. It is, as Jesus said, known only to the Father (Mark 13:32; Acts 1:7). But it will come, and as a sign, Jesus gave his own death and resurrection, his own enactment of the sign of Jonah (Matt. 12:38–50; Luke 11:29–32). Israel needs to consider this sign in light of the prophecy of Hosea 6:1–3:

> Come, let us return to the LORD, For He has torn us, but He will heal us; He has wounded us, but He will bandage us; He will revive us after two days; He will raise us up on the third day, that we may live before Him. "So let us know, let us press on to know the LORD. His going forth is as certain as the dawn; And He will come to us like the rain, like the spring rain watering the earth." (NASB)

The resurrection of the Son of David from the dead on the third day is the guarantee to Israel that after a season of being wounded and torn, the Lord will indeed raise them up to fully realize the kingdom promises. And when he does this for Israel, what will it mean for Gentiles? As Paul says, in Romans 11, it means "life from the dead" (cf. Ezek. 37:1–28).

Ecclesiology

When believing Gentiles realize that Israel does, indeed, have a future in the plan of God, it becomes obvious that we must lay aside the ecclesiology of supersessionism. While we recognize that the New Testament makes comparisons between Old Testament Israel and the New Testament church, and articulates the church's relationship to God covenantally through the covenants of Israel, we need to avoid the supersessionist reductionism, which simply identifies the church as the replacement of Israel. Such a view not only falls to the unwarranted arrogance of which Paul warned Gentile Christians (Rom. 11:17–18), but it has two other serious effects: (1) it impoverishes the church's understanding of the plan of God as revealed in Scripture; (2) it distorts the church's true identity. The church is not an essentially Gentile construct, even though since the second century, the majority of Christians have been Gentiles. The church's thinking of itself as Gentile and seeing itself as the replacement of Israel has, in fact, been the source of many a political misconstrual of its nature and mission. It is most important for an ecclesiology that keeps in view God's future for Israel to recover the meaning of the church as a fellowship anticipating the coming establishment of the kingdom in all its fullness for Israel and Gentiles.

As a consequence, this current fellowship is a table fellowship of Jewish and Gentile believers. It is a table fellowship of one kind of Gentile believers with other kinds of Gentile believers, and of all kinds of Gentile believers with Jewish believers—all of whom have received the inaugural blessings of the Messianic kingdom and who await that fullness. The vision of Jesus and the apostles was that in the church, Jewish believers and Gentile believers would sit down together in peace without Jews requiring Gentiles to become Jews. But in order to truly understand the vision today, we have to add, without Gentiles requiring Jews to become Gentiles.

Michael Wyshogrod, not a believer in Yeshua, has suggested that the key test of the church's overcoming of supersessionism will be its attitude toward Jewish believers.[22] This is most likely correct. But there is more at stake here than the problem of prejudice, the overcoming of cultural differences, or even the problem of anti-Semitism. The big question is, *What is authentic Judaism?* If we recognize that there is an Israel distinct from Gentiles in the plan of God, then what does it mean to be that kind of a Jew—a Jew of the kingdom—in relation to Gentiles of the kingdom and in comparison to the varieties of Judaism seen today?

It must be kept in mind that Jesus and the early disciples promoted an alternative vision of being Jewish to the various options of first-century Judaism. Jesus was not promoting Gentilism as opposed to Judaism, but a different kind of Judaism—one that belonged to the kingdom of God.[23] We know that he was engaged in disputes with Pharisees, Sadducees, and others over Torah and proper customs for observing Torah. The book of Acts clearly indicates that Jewish believers, including the apostles, practiced Torah, and it recognizes some tension over how their practice differed from that taught by the Pharisees. As a consequence of the destructions of A.D. 70 and 135, many of the Palestinian Jewish sects disappeared, and with them the sense that there are different ways of being Jewish.[24] Rabbinic Judaism arose out of the surviving Pharisaic sect and asserted itself as the only authentic way of being Jewish. And although the Jewishness of Jewish believers was not encouraged by the church and even suppressed for many years, Jesus' vision for authentic Jewishness—his way of observing Torah consistent with the shalom and fellowship of peoples in the kingdom of God—still remains. It stands as an alternative to the varieties of Judaism today as it was to the varieties of Judaism in the first century.

The key point about ecclesiology is that the postsupersessionist church needs to encourage, assist, and defend Jewish believers in their attempt to realize that vision, which Jesus, the Son of David, set forth for authentic Jewishness in anticipation of the coming kingdom of God. And the church needs to do this while at the same time promoting the table fellowship of Jewish and Gentile believers in Messiah.

Someone might object to a preservation of a certain kind of Jewishness, noting Paul's statements that there is no distinction between Jew and Greek (Rom. 3:22), that there is neither Jew nor Greek (Gal. 3:28), and that Jesus broke down the dividing wall, abolishing the enmity so as to make the two into a new man (Eph. 2:14–18). But Paul is speaking of sin, atonement, and the promised blessing of the Holy Spirit. In Messiah, the blessings of the resurrection and the gift of the Holy Spirit are given without distinction, just as they are to males and females without distinction. But soteriological equality does not lead to androgyny. Nor is it true that because all believers are saved with the same salvation that, as a consequence, our personalities have now become indistinguishable. Thus, both Jew and Gentile believers should see no contradiction between Paul's teachings on grace without distinction on the one hand, and on the other his expectation of an eschaton in which Israel is distinctively present. And if we in the church can grasp how those two fit together, then we also have the basis for grasping how Jews *as Jews* and Gentiles *as Gentiles* can truly fellowship together in blessings of salvation and sanctification by the Holy Spirit, blessings that they share without distinction.

Eschatology

To put Israel in the eschaton on the basis of a historical-grammatical-literary reading of Scripture is to put the *context* of future Israel there as well. And what that means is a new creation rather than a spiritual-vision eschatology.[25] In the history of the church, supersessionism and spiritual-vision eschatology fit hand in hand. What do I mean by spiritual-vision eschatology? I mean traditional eschatology, which sees eternal life as a timeless, changeless, spiritual existence consisting primarily in the human soul's full knowledge of God. This knowledge is understood to be like a direct view, vision, or beholding of God. This is the sum total of what eternal life is, and it defines what is meant by heaven. The resurrected body is expected to be a spiritual body in the sense that the body is composed of spiritual substance or has been transformed into spirit. The emphasis is on the individual's unchanging visionary-like epistemic experience of God. This spiritual-vision eschatology traditionally has seen earthly life as a symbol of spiritual realities.

Supersessionism fits well with this view in denying a future for Israel since a future for Israel literally has no place in a spiritual-vision eschatology. A future for Israel would demand a national and political reality in the eschaton with all its context of land and fruitfulness. This is all thought to be carnal by spiritual-vision ideology. It is simply not possible. As a result, Israel can only be a *symbol* of a spiritual people headed for a spiritual destiny.

To take the future of Israel seriously would demand that this spiritual-vision eschatology be modified at best or, at the most, replaced entirely with a different eschatological concept. This alternative—which spiritual-vision eschatology has thought was the only alternative—is not, however, carnal in every sense of the word carnal, in the manner say, of Muslim eschatology. Rather, the alternative is that which most biblical theologians see expressed in Scripture, that is, new-creation eschatology. New-creation eschatology emphasizes the liberation of the cosmos from sin, the bodily resurrection and glorification of the righteous, and the liberation of the cosmos to share in the liberty of the children of God. This eschaton is not to be seen as simply a continuation of the past, but does emphasize its continuity with the past as seen in the resurrection of the body. New creation does not see the eschaton as a timeless, changeless, or essentially visionary-like epistemic state. It is not eternal in the classic timeless sense but everlasting. New creation has a place for the earth, the cosmos, for the fullness of created life, but especially for resurrected human life living under the lordship of the resurrected Jesus the Messiah in fellowship with the triune God. It would see human life in created wholeness—not as undifferentiated individuals, but as differentiated individuals. But neither would new creation see them as *just* differentiated individuals, but rather differentiated in ethnic and communal dimensions as well, since these form essential elements of our identities. And what will we find here except Israel and the Gentiles who are together blessed by God, living under the lordship of Jesus the Messiah to the glory of God.

Some evangelicals have tried to adopt elements of new-creation eschatology within a spiritual-vision eschatology by positing a future for Israel that will be completely fulfilled in the millennium before the final judgment and the commencement of eternity—an eternity that they see in spiritual-vision terms. A limited duration kingdom alone, however, does not seem to do full justice to the biblical vision for Israel and the Gentiles. But that form of premillennialism has been a necessary step for some on the way to a full new-creation eschatology. Does the adoption of new-creation eschatology mean the end of premillennialism? *Me genoito!* Rather, the same hermeneutics by which Gentile believers come to embrace new-creation eschatology without doubt leads to the inescapable conclusion that the vision Jesus gave to John recorded in Revelation 20 was precisely that of a millennial kingdom between the parousia and the final judgment. Today, while many premillennialists are coming to adopt a more consistent new-creationist eschatology, many amillennialists who have come to a new-creationist eschatology are reexamining the traditional objections to a premillennialist reading of Revelation 20, objections of which many were forged within a precommitted framework of supersessionist, spiritual-vision eschatology.

In conclusion, does Israel have a future in the plan of God? Yes—a *yes* that needs to be worked through our theological thinking, removing the *no* that was deeply embedded in traditional theology by supersessionism. What are the theological implications of a future for Israel? This current study has only touched upon some of the implications—implications for an understanding of God, of humankind, of Messiah, of the church, and of the nature of the eschaton. Much more could be said. But I will close with Paul: "Oh, the depth of the riches both of the wisdom and knowledge of God!" (Rom. 11:33 NASB). Perhaps we as Gentile believers will find that just as the future fullness of Israel is the occasion for riches to the world, so even now our theological knowledge stands to be enriched when we consider that *all* of the promises of God concerning Israel are *yes* and *Amen* in Messiah Jesus!

Chapter 7

The Holocaust and the Sacred Romance

A Return to the Divine Reality
(Implications for Jewish Evangelism)

BARRY R. LEVENTHAL

> I believe in the sun when it is not shining.
> I believe in love even when feeling it not.
> I believe in God even when He is silent.[1]

Like a child's tiny nightlight, these anonymous words, scribbled on the wall of a cellar in Cologne, Germany, during the Second World War, shine forth like a beacon through the darkness of the Holocaust—not just during the war, but also down to our own day. They are words that penetrate to the very heart of the Holocaust, words that force each of us to come to grips with the Nazi genocide of six million Jews—men, women, and children. What can we say to God's so-called silence? How can we as Messianic Jews help others, especially our Jewish family members and our Jewish friends, see through the dark night of the Holocaust and still be willing to hear the words of the good news of the gospel? Indeed, does the gospel itself still have any saving relevance in our post-Holocaust world?

All of these questions have major implications for Jewish evangelism. In addressing these implications, I first by way of introduction need to define the Holocaust. Next I will present a brief explanation of Judaism's relationship to the Holocaust, as well as Christianity's. I then lay down two preliminary cautions in approaching the Holocaust, and discuss three barriers that are often encountered against the good news of the gospel.

Defining the Holocaust

Before delving into the difficult subject of the Holocaust, we need to define it. The most authoritative definition is found in the *Encyclopaedia Judaica* in a lengthy article by Jacob Robinson:

> The "Holocaust" (also known as the Catastrophe [the *Shoʾah*], [the *Churban*]) is the most tragic period of Jewish Diaspora history and indeed of modern mankind as a whole. It started in Germany on January 30, 1933, with the accession of the Nazis to power, and ended on May 8, 1945, with the unconditional surrender of Nazi Germany. The twelve years of the Nazi anti-Jewish *Aktion* (1933–1944) constitute an uninterrupted progression toward an ever-increasing radicalization of objectives and barbarization of methods in constantly expanded territories under direct Nazi control or under decisive Nazi influence, to the accompaniment of vicious, sometimes obscene, anti-Jewish propaganda. The consequences of the Holocaust are of decisive significance for the Jewish present and future: those consequences are still evident now and will be experienced for generations to come.
>
> The nature of the Holocaust is unique. Millions of Jews—some for periods of twelve years—lived under the all-pervading Nazi power, enduring its threats and its *Aktionen*. The Jews lived in agony. Tortured by anxiety, insecure in the present, unable to anticipate the future, torn between hope and despair, they

were helpless in the face of a tremendous machine always ready to crush them. The psychological effects on those who had to live through this period of total persecution are beyond even superficial description. [The task of the Holocaust historian is to] attempt to trace at least the external events—the extraordinary human suffering of a specially selected "race," pursued over the length and breadth of a continent and beyond, condemned to mass murder. Integrated or segregated, educated or ignorant, rich or poor, young or old, every Jew was condemned. East European Jewry, however, was especially singled out, in the belief that by destroying this reservoir of Jewish population and culture, the Nazis would have the ultimate "solution" to the "Jewish question."[2]

It must also be remembered that when Robinson refers to the systematic slaughter of six million Jews, one and half million were Jewish children. Added to this number is another six million non-Jews also killed during the Second World War. It is virtually impossible to wrap one's mind around six million of anything, let alone six million Jews. In terms of annihilating six million Jews, what does this figure mean? It means that during the twelve-year period (1933–1945), almost 1,400 Jews, on average, were slaughtered each and every day in the Holocaust kingdom! Is it any wonder that the Jewish people have such an agonizing time in dealing with the reality of the Nazi genocide.[3]

Judaism and the Holocaust

The Holocaust has permanently scarred the face of contemporary Judaism.[4] This excruciating wound will probably never heal. It will last as long as Judaism itself. The Holocaust has forced every Jewish person to reevaluate Judaism's very identity.[5] Every facet of Jewish life feels the pain of this scar, from the simple outlook of childhood to the complex perspective of old age.

The Simplicity of Childhood

This simplicity is reflected in the innocent faith of Anne Frank in the classic book *The Diary of a Young Girl*: "Who has inflicted this upon us? Who has made us Jews different from all other people? Who has allowed us to suffer so terribly up till now? It is God that has made us as we are, but it will be God, too, who will raise us up again."[6] This kind of simplicity is also mirrored in the intriguing reflection of a Hasidic rabbi trapped inside the Holocaust kingdom: "For the faithful, there are no questions; for the non-believer, there are no answers."[7]

The Complexity of Old Age

But the wizened, complex perspective of old age is also reflected in the words of Eli Wiesel, himself a Holocaust survivor and story-teller. He says the Holocaust "could not have been without God, nor could it have been with God. It cannot be conceived on any level."[8] Even Jewish-Christian scholars like the late Jakob Jocz recognize the traumatizing effect of the Holocaust on modern Judaism: "Auschwitz casts a black pall upon the civilized world. Not only is man's humanity put under a question mark, but God himself stands accused. Jews are asking insistently, 'Where was God when our brothers and sisters were dragged to the gas ovens?'"[9] Striking the same dark note, but also contrasting Christian theologians with Jewish theologians, Seymour Cain makes the following astute comments: "Auschwitz, or 'The Holocaust,' looms as the stumbling block of Jewish theology. Whatever may be the case with Christian theologians, for whom it seems to play no significant generative or transformative role, the Jewish religious thinker is forced to confront fullface that horror, the uttermost of evil in Jewish history."[10]

Christianity and the Holocaust

Sad to say, Seymour Cain's words seem to reflect a distressing truth. For Christian theologians, the Holocaust seems to have moved them to either of two extremes.

Extreme #1: Rejection of Jewish Missions

On one hand, some Christian theologians maintain that Yeshua's worldwide missionary mandate, the Great Commission (Matt. 28:16–20), is no longer a viable option in our post-Holocaust world. Jewish evangelism in particular is, in fact, not only deemed obsolete and irrelevant, but even abhorrent and repugnant. They argue that Christians have no right to preach a gospel of love to the Jewish people, the very people who suffered the atrocities of the Holocaust in so-called Christian lands. It is not unusual to find whole Christian denominations that have abandoned all forms of Jewish missions.

Many use a so-called *dual covenant theory* to support such a wholesale desertion of Jewish missions. A dual covenant theory holds that the Jewish people do not need the good news of the gospel because they have their own covenant with God. While the Gentiles have their own new covenant with God, the Mosaic covenant is supposedly sufficient for a Jewish person's right standing with God. In other words, Jesus may be the Messiah for the Gentiles, but certainly not for the Jews. This is, of course, in direct contradiction to the teachings of Moses himself, as well as Jesus the Messiah and his apostles.[11]

Extreme #2: Indifference Toward Jewish Missions

On the other hand, even some evangelical churches have grown indifferent toward Jewish missions. They have forsaken, therefore, any kind of robust Jewish missions. In its place a general apathy has set in. The post-Holocaust realization has sent the evangelical world into a flight from missions in general and Jewish missions in particular. There seems to be a lack of biblical commitment concerning God's everlasting promises for the Jewish people (cf. Rom. 11:1–36; etc.). Not only has Paul's fundamental missionary mandate, "to the Jew first" (Rom. 1:16–17), been abandoned by many evangelicals, even taking the gospel to the Jew *at all* has been jettisoned by some.[12]

A part of the evangelical indifference toward Jewish missions can be attributed to the evangelical church's embrace of an Augustinian *replacement theology*. Replacement theology teaches that, since the Jews have rejected their own Messiah, God has now "replaced" them with the church. As a result, all of the Old Testament promises to ethnic Israel are now being, and will continue to be, spiritually or allegorically fulfilled in the church, the so-called "New Israel."[13]

Two Cautions

Before getting to the heart of this study of Jewish evangelism, we need to address by way of further introduction yet another matter. As Messianic Jews seek to share the good new of Israel's Messiah with our Jewish people, we need to be cautious in two areas, especially in light of the Holocaust.

Caution #1: Avoid Transgressing the Boundaries of Biblical Revelation

First, when we deal with suffering and evil, particularly the evil of the Holocaust, we must not transgress the boundaries of biblical revelation. In other words, leaving all of our arrogance behind, we must leave room for biblical mystery. Doing so requires a humble reverence before God, knowing that in God's mysterious ways, he sometimes conceals himself.

In its grappling with evil and suffering, the book of Job certainly declares this truth. Job 11:7–8 (NASB)[14] asks these rhetorical questions: "Can you discover the depths of God? Can you discover the limits of the Almighty? They are high as the heavens, what can you do? Deeper than Sheol, what can you know?" Job 36:26 says, "Behold, God is exalted, and we do not know Him; the number of His years is unsearchable."

Likewise, the book of Proverbs maintains the same truth. Proverbs 16:4 says, "The LORD has made everything for its own purpose, even the wicked for the day of evil." Proverbs 19:21 says, "Many plans are in a man's heart, but the counsel of the LORD will stand." Proverbs 21:1–2 also says, "The king's heart is like channels of water in the hand of the LORD; He turns it wherever He wishes. Every man's way is right in his own eyes, but the LORD weighs the hearts." Likewise, Proverbs 21:30–31 says, "There is no wisdom and no understanding and no counsel against the LORD. The horse is prepared for the day of battle, but victory belongs to the LORD." And Proverbs 25:2 says, "It is the glory of God to conceal a matter, but the glory of kings is to search out a matter."

Even the book of Ecclesiastes supports this same truth. Ecclesiastes 3:10–11 says, "I have seen the task which God has given the sons of men with which to occupy themselves. He has made everything appropriate in its time. He has also set eternity in their heart, yet so that man will not find out the work which God has done from the beginning even to the end." Likewise, Ecclesiastes 8:16–17 says, "When I gave my heart to know wisdom and to see the task which has been done on the earth (even though one should never sleep day or night), and I saw every work of God, I concluded that man cannot discover the work which has been done under the sun. Even though man should seek laboriously, he will not discover; and though the wise man should say, 'I know,' he cannot discover."

The prophet Isaiah concluded the same thing. Isaiah 55:8–9 says, "'For My thoughts are not your thoughts, nor are your ways My ways,' declares the LORD. 'For as the heavens are higher than the earth, so are My ways higher than your ways and My thoughts than your thoughts.'"

The New Testament also proclaims that, at times, God hides himself. In Matthew 11:25–26, the Lord Yeshua made this clear in his own ministry: "At that time Jesus said, 'I praise You, Father, Lord of heaven and earth, that You have hidden these things from the wise and intelligent and have revealed them to infants. Yes, Father, for this way was well-pleasing in Your sight.'"

And finally, the apostle Paul, in concluding his marvelous argument on God's sovereign plans for Israel, moves into his closing doxology with these words (Rom. 11:33–36): "Oh, the depth of the riches both of the wisdom and knowledge of God! How unsearchable are His judgments and unfathomable His ways! For who has known the mind of the LORD, or who became His counselor? Or who has first given to Him that it might be paid back to Him again? For from Him and through Him and to Him are all things. To Him be the glory forever. Amen."

One particular saying of the rabbis is pertinent here, especially in light of the Holocaust. The Talmud says, "It is not in our power fully to explain either the prosperity of the wicked or the suffering of the righteous" (*Pirke Avoth* 4:15).

So then, the first caution: we must not transgress the boundaries of biblical revelation. Leave room for mystery. At times God conceals himself.

Caution #2: Do Not Avoid the Pronouncements of Biblical Revelation

Second, on the other hand, when we deal with the suffering and evil of the Holocaust, we must not avoid the pronouncements of biblical revelation. We must be willing to wrestle with God over the painful crisis of the Holocaust. In other words, we must draw near to God with all of our complaints within a covenant context.

Yes, we need a humble reverence, but we also need a holy boldness. Yes, at times God conceals himself, but he also *reveals* himself.

Moses, in Deuteronomy 29:29, says, "The secret things belong to the LORD our God, but the things revealed belong to us and to our sons forever, that we may observe all the words of this law." When God reveals himself, he is granting us an open invitation to come into his presence and deal with the matters at hand, especially matters of sin, judgment, and suffering.

The wisdom literature further affirms Moses' statement. Even though mysteries abound, God has spoken in his Word. Proverbs 30:2–6 says, "Surely I am more stupid than any man, and I do not have the understanding of a man. Neither have I learned wisdom, nor do I have the knowledge of the Holy One. Who has ascended into heaven and descended? Who has gathered the wind in His fists? Who has wrapped the waters in His garment? Who has established all the ends of the earth? What is His name or His son's name? Surely you know! Every word of God is tested; He is a shield to those who take refuge in Him. Do not add to His words or He will reprove you, and you will be proved a liar."

The prophet Isaiah, in the opening chapter of his book, invites rebellious Israel to the revealed Word of God (Isa. 1:18): "'Come now, let us reason together,' says the LORD. 'Though your sins are as scarlet, they will be as white as snow; though they are red like crimson, they will be like wool.'" And as noted above in Isaiah 55:8–9, the thoughts and ways of God are insurmountably beyond us. The prophet continues, however, in the same passage (Isa. 55:10–11), "For as the rain and the snow come down from heaven, and do not return there without watering the earth and making it bear and sprout, and furnishing seed to the sower and bread to the eater; so will My word be which goes forth from My mouth; it will not return to Me empty, without accomplishing what I desire, and without succeeding in the matter for which I sent it."

The prophet Jeremiah, likewise, affirms that God is a revealing God (Jer. 29:11–13): "'For I know the plans that I have for you,' declares the LORD, 'plans for welfare and not for calamity to give you a future and a hope. Then you shall call upon Me and come and pray to Me, and I will listen to you. You will seek Me and find Me when you search for Me with all your heart.'"

The New Testament once again reaffirms this message. The Lord

Yeshua made the following promises to his disciples (Matt. 7:7–11), "Ask, and it will be given to you; seek, and you will find; knock, and it will be opened to you. For everyone who asks receives, and he who seeks finds, and to him who knocks it will be opened. Or what man is there among you who, when his son asks for a loaf, will give him a stone? Or if he asks for a fish, he will not give him a snake, will he? If you then, being evil, know how to give good gifts to your children, how much more will your Father who is in heaven give what is good to those who ask Him!"

So we must remember, that while God may conceal himself at times, he also does reveal himself. And as God did to our forefather Jacob, he invites us into his personal presence to grapple over issues like the Holocaust.

Holocaust survivor and philosopher Emil Fackenheim echoed this biblical pattern when he insisted, "Is not . . . the Jew of the generation of Auschwitz required to do what, since Abraham, Jeremiah, and Job, Jews have always done in times of darkness—contend with the silent God, and bear witness to Him by this contention."[15]

Eli Wiesel, in a television interview, likewise affirmed this same biblical posture: "For a Jew to believe in God is good. For a Jew to protest against God is still good. But simply to ignore God, that is not good. Anger, yes. Protest, yes. Affirmation, yes. But indifference to God, no. You can be a Jew with God; you can be a Jew against God; but not without God."[16] Elsewhere, Wiesel also rightly stated that the Jew must remember, this protest against God must remain within a covenant context: "I believe that God *is* part of our experience. The Jew, in my view, may rise against God, provided he remains with God."[17]

So we always need to keep these two cautions in front of us, especially when we think about our own struggles with the Holocaust, as well as when we think about how to communicate the good news of the gospel of Yeshua the Messiah to our Jewish friends, neighbors, colleagues, and family members.

Three Barriers

When we share the good news of the gospel with anyone, we should not be surprised to encounter barriers to the gospel. The forces of evil are totally committed to erecting barriers against the kingdom of light. Therefore, anytime we encounter another person without a knowledge of the gospel, especially a Jewish person in our post-Holocaust setting, we must be aware of three potential barriers—actually two potential barriers and one actual barrier.[18]

Barrier #1: The Emotional Barrier

The first potential barrier is *the emotional barrier*. People have been burned in the name of Christianity, by painful things done in the name of Jesus. For many of us who are Jews, the first time we heard the name "Jesus" may have been in an anti-Semitic context. These kinds of hurtful contexts raise emotional barriers against the gospel. This barrier is even more severe in our post-Holocaust context. It is not uncommon to hear Holocaust survivors say that, when the Nazis came into their neighborhoods to load the Jewish community into trucks headed for the concentration camps, their so-called Christian neighbors simply drew their curtains closed rather than see and therefore have to do something for them. Is it any wonder that these Jewish folks have a major emotional barrier against the gospel? They may have never really known a faithful Christian, only hypocrisy. Instead of being "provoked to jealousy" toward the good news of the gospel through the life and love of a Christian, they have been provoked to fear, anger, and hatred toward Jesus and his love for them.[19]

How do we overcome this emotional barrier? The answer is through loving and genuine relationships—personal, ongoing, intimate relationships, so that the Sacred Romance we have experienced will spill over upon them. It takes time and its takes effort.[20]

Barrier #2: The Intellectual Barrier

The second potential barrier is *the intellectual barrier*. People have valid questions about the Christian faith and worldview. These questions may have arisen in a classroom lecture that criticized or attacked the Christian faith. They may have arisen from the reading of a book written by a skeptic. Or, in our case, these kinds of questions may have arisen from an event like the Holocaust: Where was God in the Holocaust? How could a good and loving God allow such evil and suffering? These are valid questions that erect this intellectual barrier against the gospel.

How do we overcome this intellectual barrier? These kinds of questions give us a wonderful opportunity. Providing some basic answers to the often painful riddles and contradictions of life in a loving and honest way is, of course, the role of basic Christian apologetics. The term *apologetics* has been defined as "the discipline that deals with a rational defense of [the] Christian faith. It comes from the Greek word *apologia*, which means to give a reason or defense" (cf. 1 Peter 3:15; Phil. 1:7, 16; Jude 3; etc.).[21] Therefore, basic apologetics is one of God's tools for providing the pre-evangelism answers to the intellectual barrier.[22]

Barrier #3: The Volitional or Moral Barrier

The third barrier is *the volitional* or *moral barrier*. Whether or not someone has an emotional barrier or an intellectual barrier to the gospel, everybody has the third barrier, and that is the volitional barrier: rebellion in the human heart against God—human depravity. Even if we could love a person perfectly to remove the emotional barrier, even if we could give all the answers and all the truth to remove the intellectual barrier, it doesn't mean that person will become believers. The Lord Yeshua was love incarnate and truth incarnate, yet he was rejected by many because the human heart is rebellious against God.

How do we overcome this volitional or moral barrier? On our own we cannot. Only the Holy Spirit can. That's why Yeshua said in John 16:7–8, "But I tell you the truth, it is to your advantage that I go away; for if I do not go away, the Helper [the Holy Spirit; cf. 14:16–17] will not come to you; but if I go, I will send Him to you. And He, when He comes, will convict the world concerning sin and righteousness and judgment." Therefore, we must commit ourselves to praying that the Holy Spirit will do his convicting work in the human heart.

So as God gives us opportunities to share the good news of Yeshua with our Jewish friends and family members, we must love them with the authentic love of God, give them answers to their probing questions, and then pray that the Holy Spirit will move in their hearts.

The Sacred Romance

In light of the above two extremes that are common in the post-Holocaust world, as well as the three barriers to the gospel, how should we who are committed to Jewish missions, respond?

What should be our approach to our Jewish friends and associates? In a recent book titled *The Sacred Romance*, authors John Eldredge and Brent Curtis remind us that God is totally committed to pursuing and wooing humanity to himself.[23] The universe is engulfed in a cosmic love affair. Eldredge and Curtis also remind us, however, "There are only two things that pierce the human heart, . . . one is beauty. The other is affliction. And while we wish there were only beauty in the world, each of has known enough pain to raise serious doubts about the universe we live in. From very early life we know another message, warning us that the Romance has an enemy."[24] The Scriptures affirm, though, that there is a redemptive side to affliction:

> This is my comfort in my affliction, that Your word has revived me. (Ps. 119:50)

> Before I was afflicted I went astray, but now I keep Your word. (Ps. 119:67)

> It is good for me that I was afflicted, that I may learn Your statutes. (Ps. 119:71)

> If Your law had not been my delight, then I would have perished in my affliction. (Ps. 119:92)

> I am exceedingly afflicted; revive me, O Lord, according to Your word. (Ps. 119:107)

> Look upon my affliction and rescue me, for I do not forget Your law. (Ps. 119:153)

But a major dilemma with affliction is that it can turn us either toward God or away from him. It may cause us to seek God's face or to shake our fist in his face. For many Jewish people, the affliction and agony of the Holocaust have turned them away not only from the good news of the messiahship of Yeshua, but from any kind of belief in God.[25]

In drawing us to himself, God pierced many of our hearts with the beauty of life. But for others of us, it may have taken affliction, the arrows that God permitted to penetrate our hearts.

As we will see later, this is what happened during the Holocaust. Thousands and thousands of Jewish people came into a living faith with Yeshua the Messiah. We don't know how many, but reliable documented testimony indicates that thousands of Jews came to saving faith during the Holocaust, most of whom did not survive.[26] In God's Sacred Romance pursuit of us, he may allow arrows of affliction to fly against us. Because God's own people are so prone to idolatry and the mad pursuit of other things, God must often come against them. God is, indeed, a jealous God.[27] "Jealousy" is a Sacred Romance term. Like a faithful husband, the covenant Lord pursues his adulterous wife, Israel.[28]

The Return to the Divine Reality

We now come to the heart of what matters in evangelizing Jews in a post-Holocaust world. When the Hebrew Bible speaks of Israel's "return" to God, one of the major words it uses is *shuv*. This term is used a total of 1,054 times in the Hebrew Bible. For 890 uses of the term, the basic idea is "to turn back, to return." But in the remaining 164 times, the term is used in a covenant context between God and Israel; in this sense the idea is "to repent," a turning from evil and a return to God, a turning from unbelief and a returning to belief. In the examples below, I've used italics for emphasis:

> When you [Israel] are in distress and all these [judgments] have come upon you, in the latter days you *will return* to the LORD your God and listen to His voice. (Deut. 4:30)

> . . . and [if] My people [Israel] who are called by My name humble themselves and pray and seek My face and *turn* from their wicked ways, then I will hear from heaven, will forgive their sin and will heal their land. (2 Chron. 7:14)

> A remnant *will return*, the remnant of Jacob, to the mighty God. For though your people, O Israel, may be like the sand of the sea, only a remnant within them *will return*; a destruction is determined, overflowing with righteousness. (Isa. 10:21–22)

"If you *will return*, O Israel," declares the Lord, "then you *should return* to Me. And if you will put away your detested things from My presence, and will not waver, and you will swear, 'As the Lord lives,' in truth, in justice and in righteousness; then the nations will bless themselves in Him, and in Him they will glory." (Jer. 4:1–2)

Come, let us *return* to the Lord. For He has torn us, but He will heal us; He has wounded us, but He will bandage us. (Hos. 6:1)

Return, O Israel, to the Lord your God, for you have stumbled because of your iniquity. Take words with you and *return* to the Lord. Say to Him, "Take away all iniquity and receive us graciously, that we may present the fruit of our lips." (Hos. 14:1–2)

"Yet even now," declares the Lord, "*return* to Me with all your heart, and with fasting, weeping and mourning; and rend your heart and not your garments." Now *return* to the Lord your God, for He is gracious and compassionate, slow to anger, abounding in lovingkindness and relenting of evil. (Joel 2:12–13)

Therefore say to them, "Thus says the Lord of hosts, '*Return* to Me,' declares the Lord of hosts, 'that I *may return* to you,' says the Lord of hosts." (Zech. 1:3)

From the days of your fathers you have turned aside from My statutes and have not kept them. "*Return* to Me, and I *will return* to you," says the Lord of hosts. But you say, "How shall we return?" (Mal. 3:7)

One thing is certain, then: the heart of God is seeking the heart of Israel. The Sacred Romance will settle for nothing less than the total *return* of our Jewish people to God and to the divine realities. Since all of us believing Jews are faithful disciples of the Lord Yeshua,

how can we go about proclaiming God's Sacred Romance for our
Jewish people, especially in light of the Holocaust? As the covenant
Lord continues his pursuit of his people Israel, how can we help
them return to and recover their God-ordained divine realities?

What, though, do I mean by *divine realities*? There are at least
three basic divine realities, and without a return of the Jewish people
to these three divine realities, we will not be able to present to them
the messiahship of Yeshua and his atoning death.[29] These three divine realities function, then, as a kind of pre-evangelism and are,
therefore, foundational to any presentation of the gospel itself.[30]

The First Return to Reality: The Biblical Revelation of the Reality of Sin and Depravity

Perhaps the most theologically shattering return to reality for
contemporary Judaism was the Holocaust's dramatic demonstration of the fundamentally flawed state of the human condition.
The pre-Holocaust illusion, reflecting an Enlightenment thinking
that man is basically good, went up with the smoke of the Nazi
gas chambers. This flawed and certainly unbiblical reasoning that
God is the Father of us all and that we are all brothers and sisters
seemed utterly devoid of any meaning in the post-Holocaust reality. This Enlightenment reasoning of eighteenth-century Europe
spilled over into the Jewish Enlightenment, called the *Haskalah*,
the Hebrew term for the Enlightenment/Emancipation movement
and ideology that began within Jewish society in the 1770s and
continued until the early 1880s.[31]

This pre-Holocaust Jewish Enlightenment thinking emphasized the innate goodness and rationality of man. Rabbinic Judaism
has traditionally maintained that a human being is born into this
world with a morally neutral, blank slate inscribed upon by his or
her own moral choices, and each person chooses whether to follow
his or her evil or good impulse. The concepts of original sin and
total depravity are flatly rejected. Instead, according to the rabbis,
two conflicting impulses are present and at work in human nature:
the *yetzer ha-tov*, the good inclination, urges a human being to do
right; the *yetzer ha-ra*, the evil inclination, entices him or her to
do evil. In other words, man's "natural instinct" (*yetzer*) is basically neutral, capable of both good and bad deeds, dependent upon
man's free will in making moral choices.[32]

This is, of course, a direct contradiction to biblical revelation. The Old and New Testaments alike affirm that one is born with a sin nature, inherited from one's parents at conception. Therefore, all of us are prone to sin from the very core of our being. Biblical theologians call this "total depravity."[33] Theologian Norman L. Geisler defines "total depravity" in the following words:

> Since the whole person is made in God's image, and since sin affects the whole person, the first thing to be said is that the effect of sin on God's image in fallen human beings is pervasive, extending to every dimension of his being—body and soul, mind and will. Hence, it is in this sense that sinful humanity is appropriately described . . . as "totally depraved." This *does not* mean that fallen humans are as sinful as they could be, but it *does* mean that apart from Christ we are not as good as we should be (in accordance with God's perfect nature and the perfection with which He created us). Sin *does* penetrate and permeate our whole being. Humans *are* born wholly, not partially, depraved; that is, every aspect of our being is affected by sin. No element of human nature is unaffected by inherited evil, even though no aspect is completely destroyed by it.[34]

The Jewish Return to the Reality of Sin and Depravity

The Holocaust has forced Jewish theologians and philosophers to do some radical rethinking concerning the very nature of the human condition. Much of this post-Holocaust Jewish discussion reflects a return toward the biblical reality of sin and its pervasive impact on *all* human beings. Take, for example, the following penetrating statements. Jewish author Max Picard, in his book on the Holocaust, dared to title his book, *Hitler in Our Selves*.[35] Israel W. Charney makes the same point: "We ourselves must come to terms with the horrible violence that has been to us a mirror of the violence that lurks within us too."[36]

Daniel Polish, reflecting on the Holocaust, is forced to make the following comments:

As a result of the *shoah* [the Holocaust], some ideas of recent generations have been repudiated altogether. Jewish thought since the emancipation [the *Haskalah*, the Jewish Enlightenment] reflected the optimism of the general intellectual climate. A mood prevailed which affirmed human nobility. Reason was celebrated, and with it a sense that human moderation and understanding would carry the day for the cause of virtue. Mankind, it was felt, had virtually approached the limits of its perfectibility. Pockets of corruption may have persisted, it was believed, but they would be quickly overcome by the forces of right. Humanity shines less radiant now than to those teachers of hope, many of whom themselves, perished in the cataclysm. Our eyes have been seared by the flames of hell. Whether they see more clearly for that, or suffer a painful stigmatism, we cannot say. But to us, humanity appears less noble and less the proper object of veneration. We see the human spirit as capable of base depravity as of elevation. We see human actions as readily responsive to the impulses for evil as to the good.[37]

Eugene B. Borowitz maintains that "it is no longer possible to make the goodness of man the cornerstone of Jewish faith."[38] Abba Eban echoes this realization as well: "Until the Nazi Holocaust there was the innocent assumption that no man, however depraved, can stand unmoved before the innocence and fragility of childhood. The human race can no longer allow itself even this consolation."[39]

Frederick Sontag also maintains that "we must abandon any idea of 'progress,' or notion of the gradual uplift of humanity in modern times, that moves along a scale of increased sophistication. We now realize that horror comes from the intellectually advanced as well as from the primitive. Destruction knows no time or place. It is as much home in universities as in primitive villages."[40]

Morris Shapiro makes the following statement concerning our post-Holocaust reality: "The Holocaust has taught us this simple lesson, that every member of *homo sapiens*, if not humanized, is a potential Eichmann."[41] In like manner, Dennis Prager and Joseph Telushkin make the following assertion: "The Holocaust may make faith in God difficult; but it makes faith in man impossible. Along with the six million Jews, and tens of millions of other murdered by the Nazis and Communists, we must bury the doctrine which enabled Communism and Nazism to rise: the belief that man is the highest being. After Auschwitz . . . , we have two choices: belief in man under God or belief in nothing."[42]

Michael Berenbaum strikes the same dismal chord:

> Why is the Holocaust an unrelenting event? The Holocaust, by its scope, nature, and magnitude, transforms our understanding of human culture and human existence. An unspoken premise of advocates of culture and education is that the refinements of culture and learning somehow make us into better people and intensify our moral worth. Yet the Holocaust was perpetrated not by the least cultured and least sophisticated of nations, but by the most cultured and most advanced of societies. Furthermore, the elements within that society that proved capable of perpetrating the evils were not the least cultured, but came from all spectrums of society, including philosophers and scientists, musicians and engineers, lawyers and ministers, artists and intellectuals. No segment of German society proved immune. . . . We see that people could love good music and kill young children. They could be admirable husbands and concerned fathers, yet spend their days in constant contact with death and destruction. Human society can be organized and given meaning in such a way that the enterprise with death becomes triumphant. This is possible in the twentieth century with technology facilitating the process.[43]

The most respected historian and storyteller of the Holocaust, Eli Wiesel, makes this same point in his writings. Wiesel, at a symposium in 1967, for example, made the following statement:

If the Holocaust proved anything, it is that it is possible for a person both to love poems and kill children; many Germans cried when listening to Mozart, when playing Haydn, when quoting Goethe and Schiller—but remained quite unemotional and casual when torturing and shooting children. Their act had no effect on their spirit; the idea had no bearing on the source of inspiration. Heidegger served as Chancellor of the Freiburg University under the Nazis. Karl Orf, the composer, was Goebbels' favorite musician. As for Van Karajan, he did not lose his talent when conducting in Berlin and elsewhere, wearing a Nazi uniform. Something then must be wrong, not only with their concept of evil but with man as well.[44]

Elsewhere, Wiesel also reasserts that since the Holocaust we must come to grips with the idea that something is inherently wrong with the human condition:

How is it possible that the same civilization that produces Goethe, Bach, Voltaire, and Rousseau could also have produced such dehumanization of man. Something must be wrong with man himself and with man's vision of himself, and something must be wrong with culture if Germans could quote Schiller and Fichte at the same time they were killing Jews. Something must be wrong with books and language if people who write so impressively and who play music so artistically could become allies of non-human death. And something must be wrong with us if during those years of the Third Reich all movements of the spirit failed. Communism failed. Rationalism failed. And religion failed. Evil's conquest was easy, too easy.[45]

Bernard J. Bamberger maintains that we should not have been surprised at the deliberate evil of the Holocaust:

There are no words, no concepts adequate to the facts of the Holocaust. It was not a spontaneous outbreak of popular blood lust, but a coldly conceived program of extermination, carried out with highly organized efficiency. To facilitate the physical destruction of the victims, their moral degradation and corruption were also deliberately planned. The ghastly deeds of the Nazis are beyond description and beyond comprehension. And these crimes were compounded by the failure of the "democratic" nations to do anything to stop the slaughter long after they well knew what was happening in the death camps. But it is not clear why so many theologians should regard Auschwitz as a boundary mark in the history of religious thought. What Auschwitz teaches, if it teaches anything, is that we have underestimated man's capacity for evil. We have too often assumed that men are guided by self-interest, and that their evil deeds are the result of a misguided urge to protect or aggrandize themselves. We have not recognized that men may be attracted to evil because it is evil, may even embrace it in a mad ecstasy. But our failure to take this fact into account does not mean that it never had been known. An attentive reading of the Bible makes plain the truth that moral evil is sometimes more than mere deficiency; it can be a dynamic, demonic force in human life.[46]

C. S. Lewis certainly got it right when he said, "When natural things look most divine, the demoniac is just round the corner."[47]

The Biblical Return to the Reality of Sin and Depravity

Bamberger has pointed us in the right direction—an attentive reading of the Bible. For the biblical revelation has clearly and concisely articulated the reality of sin and depravity. Long before the Holocaust, the New Testament articulated the depraved nature of the human heart.[48] This is clearly seen in the following table.

New Testament Images of the Human Condition
("Total Depravity")

The Human Condition	In the Teachings of Jesus	In the Teachings of the Apostles
1. "Sinners"	Matt. 9:10–13 // Mark 2:15–17 // Luke 5:30–32; Matt. 11:19 // Luke 7:34; Matt. 26:45 // Mark 14:41; Luke 6:32–34; 13:1–5; 15:1–2, 7, 10; 18:13	Rom. 3:7; 5:8, 19; Gal. 2:15–17; 1 Tim. 1:9, 15; Heb. 7:26; 12:3; James 4:8; 1 Peter 4:18; Jude 15
2. "Dead"	John 6:50; 8:21–24; Luke 15:24, 32	Rom. 1:32; 6:21–23; Eph. 2:1, 5
3. "Lost"	Matt. 18:11; Luke 15:24, 32; 19:10	
4. "Debtors"	Matt. 6:12; 18:27, 32; Luke 7:41–50	Col. 2:14
5. "Blind"	John 9:39–41 (cf. 8:12; 12:36)	2 Cor. 4:3–6 (cf. 3:14–16)
6. "Sick"	Matt. 9:12 // Mark 2:17 // Luke 5:31	1 Peter 2:24 (cf. Isa. 53:5)
7. "Enslaved"	John 8:30–36	Rom. 6:17–22; Titus 3:3
8. "Thirsty"	Matt. 5:6; John 4:7–14; 6:35	
9. "Hungry"	Matt. 5:6; John 6:35	
10. "Defiled"	Matt. 15:10–11, 15–20 // Mark 7:14–23	Jude 23
11. "Unclean"	Matt. 23:27	1 Cor. 7:14; 2 Cor. 6:17
12. "Ignorant"	Luke 23:34	
13. "Evil from the heart"	Matt. 15:18–20 // Mark 7:20–23	
14. "Hypocrites"	Matt. 6:2, 5, 16; 7:5; 15:7; 22:18; 23:13, 14, 15, 23, 25, 27, 29; 24:51; Mark 7:6; 12:15; Luke 6:42; 12:1, 56; 13:15; Matt. 23:28	1 Tim. 4:2

15. "Full of hypocrisy"	Matt. 23:16–24	
16. "Blind guides"	Matt. 23:27–28ff.	
17. "Whitewashed tombs"	Matt. 23:28	
18. "Full of . . . lawlessness"	Matt. 23:28	
19. "Lawless"		1 Tim. 1:9
20. "Sons of disobedience"		Eph. 2:2
21. "Disobedient"		2 Thess. 1:8–9; Titus 3:3
22. "Children of wrath"		Eph. 2:3
23. "Fallen short"		Rom. 3:23
24. "Without strength"		Rom. 5:6
25. "Enemies"		Rom. 5:10
26. "Rebels"		1 Tim. 1:9; Titus 1:10; Jude 11
27. "Ungodly"		1 Tim. 1:9; 1 Peter 4:18
28. "Unholy"		1 Tim. 1:9
29. "Profane"		1 Tim. 1:9; Heb.12:16
30. "Immoral"		1 Tim. 1:10
31. "Blasphemers"		1 Tim. 1:13
32. "Arrogant"		1 Tim. 1:13
33. "Ignorant"		Acts 3:17; Eph. 4:17–18; 2 Thess. 1:8–9; 1 Tim. 1:13
34. "Deceived"		1 Tim. 4:1; 2 Tim. 3:13; Titus 3:3
35. "Seared consciences"		1 Tim. 4:2
36. "Foolish"		Rom. 1:21–23; Titus 3:3
37. "Imposters"		2 Tim. 3:13
38. "Evil"		Heb. 10:22; 2 Tim. 3:13
39. "Hardened in heart"		Eph. 4:18–19
40. "Stiff-necked and uncircumcised in heart and ears, always resisting the Holy Spirit"		Acts 7:51
41. "Adversaries"		Heb. 10:27
42. "Antichrists"		1 John 2:18–19
43. "Dreamers"		Jude 8
44. "Brute beasts"		Jude 10 (KJV)
45. "Excluded from the life of God"		Eph. 2:12; 4:18 (KJV)

It should not be surprising that these New Testament descriptions of the human heart have spilled over into secular human history as well, even into our own sophisticated world of today. Christian theologian D. A. Carson gives us a grim reminder of the fallout from man's propensity for evil, especially in the twentieth century, the bloodiest century in human history:

> There is now a vast literature on the Holocaust, in which 6 million Jews were systematically exterminated. Much of this literature treats the Holocaust as an aberration, a singularity that we must never permit to happen again, a horrific brutality that destroys meaning. We are told that we must not compare it with other orgies of violence lest we trivialize it. Yet the sad truth is far worse: in this century alone it is only one of a string of similar holocausts. Probably 10 million will die in central Africa from AIDS. Twenty to 50 million Chinese died under Chairman Mao. The same percentage of Cambodians died under Pol Pot as Jews under Hitler. We do not know how many Soviet citizens died under Stalin. The suffering inflicted by Idi Amin is incalculable.[49]

The secular world continues to be wantonly indifferent to such atrocities. Thus, the words of *National Geographic* reporter Lewis M. Simons are even more staggering:

> More than 50 million people were systematically murdered in the past 100 years—the century of mass murder: From 1915 to 1923 Ottoman Turks slaughtered up to 1.5 million Armenians. In mid-century the Nazis liquidated six million Jews, three million Soviet POWs, two million Poles, and 400,000 other "undesirables." Mao Zedong killed 30 million Chinese, and the Soviet government murdered 20 million of its own people. In the 1970s the communist Khmer Rouge killed 1.7 million of their fellow Cambodians. In the 1980s and early '90s Saddam

Hussein's Baath Party killed 100,000 Kurds. Rwanda's Hutu-led military wiped out 800,000 members of the Tutsi minority in the 1990s. Now there is genocide in Sudan's Darfur region. In sheer numbers, these and other killings make the twentieth century the bloodiest period in human history.[50]

Many people find it difficult to swallow this reality of innate sin and depravity, especially those committed to a so-called liberal mind-set. They would rather blame the world's problems on God. Alister McGrath elaborated on this when he said,

> Many people seem unable to cope with this harsh reality [i.e., the loss of the Western liberal dream]. Instead of acknowledging that there seems to be something wrong with human nature causing people to inflict suffering on others, they have taken the easy way out, blaming God for all the ills of the world. Many Jews became atheists as a result of the events that took place in the Second World War, especially in the extermination camps. But it wasn't God who engineered the Holocaust; it was human beings. It wasn't God who developed the atom bomb or who dropped it on Hiroshima. It wasn't God who directed the liquidation squads during Stalin's purges. It was sinful and fallen human beings. This dreadful truth shatters the shallow and facile optimism of liberalism, which insists in the most doctrinaire manner upon the basic goodness of humanity, and ignores humanity's darker side.[51]

Dietrich Bonhoeffer was a German Christian leader who lived through the Holocaust and was murdered by the Nazis just before the end of World War II. He thus witnessed the face of evil first-hand, and courageously bore witness to its deceptive and destructive nature:

> The message of God's becoming human attacks the heart of an era when contempt for humanity or

idolization of humanity is the height of all wisdom, among bad people as well as good. The weaknesses of human nature appear more clearly in a storm than in the quiet flow of calmer times. Among the overwhelming majority of people, anxiety, greed, lack of independence, and brutality show themselves to be the mainstream of behavior in the face of unsuspected chance and threats. At such a time the tyrannical despiser of humanity [i.e., Adolf Hitler] easily makes use to the meanness of the human heart by nourishing it and giving it other names. Anxiety is called responsibility; greed is called industriousness; lack of independence becomes solidarity; brutality becomes masterfulness. By this ingratiating treatment of human weaknesses, what is base and mean is generated and increased ever anew. The basest contempt for humanity carries on its sinister business under the most holy assertions of love for humanity. The meaner the baseness becomes, the more willing and pliant a tool it is in the hand of the tyrant. The small number of upright people will be smeared with mud. Their courage is called revolt, their discipline Pharisaism, their independence arbitrariness, and their masterfulness arrogance.[52]

Is it any wonder that, in light of all of this, God is forcing our Jewish people to face this first divine reality—the biblical revelation of sin and depravity. This first biblical reality naturally forces, of course, Judaism to face a second painful reality.

The Second Return to Reality: The Biblical Revelation of the Realities of Life and Death, of Time and Eternity

The Holocaust also forces us to come to grips with the realities of life and death, and of time and eternity. Contemporary Judaism cannot escape the turmoil of a world that has seemingly lost every human basis for meaning, purpose, and value. If there is *any* basis at all for meaning, purpose, and value in a post-Holocaust world, it cannot be laid upon faith in humanity.

It must be laid upon faith in the divine, that is, from God's bibli-cal revelation. Only when our Jewish people reconnect with the divine reality of life and death, and of time and eternity, as re-vealed in the Word of God, will they be able to hear the good news of the gospel. So once again, it is God's Sacred Romance that is forcing our people to reassess this biblical revelation. In doing so, we can come to understand that God is attempting to prepare us all, as the Puritan doctrine of old put it, "to die a good death."

How, though, does the Bible describe life and death, time and eternity? The Word of God through metaphor and simile presents temporal life in such terms as the wind, the grass, a leaf, a flower, a vapor, a cloud, a shadow, a dream, a handbreadth. In other words, this present passing life is portrayed as brief, fleeting, vain, futile, empty, fragile, painful, unpredictable. Below is a summary of the Bible's teaching on the nature of earthly life. A return to these teachings is a return to this second biblical reality.

1. The brevity of life: Genesis 47:9; Job 10:9; 10:20–21; 13:12, 25, 28; Psalms 89:47–48; 90:10; 146:4; Isaiah 2:22.
2. Life as empty, vain, and futile: Job 7:1–3ff. (Heb. *shav*: "emptiness, vanity"; 53x in Old Testament); 15:31; Psalm 89:47–48; Ecclesiastes 1:2, 8, 14; 2:11, 15, 19, 21, 23, 26; 3:19; 4:4, 7, 8, 16; 5:10; 6:2; 12:8 (Heb. *hebel*: "vapor, breath, vanity"; 80x in Old Testament; 22x in Ecclesiastes); Isaiah 49:4.
3. Life as a shadow: 1 Chronicles 29:15; Job 8:9; 14:1–2; Psalms 102:11; 144:3–4; Ecclesiastes 6:12.
4. Life as a weaver's shuttle: Job 7:6–10.
5. Life as a courier: Job 9:25–26.
6. Life as a handbreadth (the width of the human hand): Psalm 39:4–5.
7. Life as straw/chaff: Job 21:17–18; Psalm 78:39.
8. Life as the grass: Psalms 90:5–6; 102:11; 103:14–16; Isaiah 40:6–8, 24; 51:12; James 1:10–12; 1 Peter 1:24.
9. Life as a leaf: Isaiah 64:6.
10. Life as a flower: Job 14:2; 15:31–33; Psalm 103:14–16.
11. Life as a vapor: James 4:14.
12. Life as a breath: Job 7:7; Psalms 39:4–5; 144:3–4.

The Bible also describes the reality of death, and that for *all* death is

1. inevitable: Job 7:8–10, 21; 21:23–26; Ecclesiastes 3:2, 19–21; Romans 5:12, 14; 1 Peter 1:24.
2. at an unknown time: Genesis 27:2; Psalm 39:4, 13.
3. near: Joshua 23:14; 1 Samuel 20:3.
4. a separation (of the soul/spirit from the body): Ecclesiastes 12:7.
5. a loss of all earthly goods: Job 1:21; Psalm 49:1–20; Luke 12:13–21ff.; 1 Timothy 6:7.

Death for *the unbeliever* is

1. a judgment: Genesis 2:17; 3:19; Romans 5:12–21; 2 Thessalonians 2:5–9; Hebrews 9:27.
2. painful: Job 15:17–20; 1 Corinthians 15:55–56.
3. fearful: Hebrews 2:14–15; cf. Matthew 10:28; Luke 12:4–5.
4. a terror: Job 15:21–22.
5. a distress and an anguish: Job 15:22–24; Luke 16:19–31.
6. a loss of all earthly goods: Job 15:25–35; Luke 16:19–31.
7. a ruination: Job 15:28; Psalm 49:1–20.
8. to perish: John 3:16; 1 Corinthians 1:18; 2 Corinthians 2:15–16; 4:3; 2 Thessalonians 2:10.
9. eternal destruction: Matthew 7:13; 2 Thessalonians 1:9; cf. 1 Thessalonians 5:3.
10. retribution: 2 Thessalonians 1:8.
11. dying in one's sins: John 8:21, 24.
12. an eternal separation from God (spiritual death): Luke 16:19–31; Romans 6:23; 2 Thessalonians 1:9; cf. Daniel 12:1–3; Matthew 25:46; John 5:24–29; 1 Corinthians 15:20–28; Revelation 6:8; 20:6, 14.
13. hell/hades: Revelation 6:8; 20:14.
14. the lake of fire: Revelation 19:20; 20:10, 14, 15; cf. Matthew 25:41, 46.
15. torment: Luke 16:23.

Death for *the believer* is

1. rest: Job 3:13, 17–19; Isaiah 57:2; 2 Thessalonians 1:7; Hebrews 4:9–11; Revelation 6:11; 14:13.
2. peace: Psalm 37:37; Isaiah 57:1–2.
3. paradise: Luke 23:39–43; cf. 16:22; 2 Corinthians 12:4.

4. gain: Philippians 1:21 (Gr. *kerdos*: "profit, winnings"; cf. 3:7).
5. better: Philippians 1:23.
6. fullness of joy: Psalm 16:11; cf. Matthew 25:21, 23.
7. pleasures forever: Psalm 16:11.
8. to dwell securely: Psalm 16:9.
9. to be at home: 2 Corinthians 5:8.
10. a refuge: Proverbs 14:32 (NIV).
11. to be with the Lord: 2 Corinthians 5:8; Philippians 1:23; cf. Ecclesiastes 12:7; Romans 14:7–8; 1 Corinthians 3:21–23; 1 Thessalonians 4:17.
12. to depart/be released (Gr., "setting sail, striking camp"): Philippians 1:23; 2 Timothy 4:6.
13. to be asleep (the physical body until the resurrection): Acts 7:60; 1 Thessalonians 4:13–18; 5:9–10.
14. the final victory: 1 Corinthians 15:55–57.
15. to be glorified: 2 Thessalonians 1:10; cf. Romans 8:16–17; Philippians 3:20–21.
16. heaven: John 14:1–3; Acts 7:54–60; etc.
17. rewards for faithfulness, stewardship, and suffering for Messiah's sake: Matthew 19:23–29; Mark 10:28–30; Luke 19:11–27; Romans 8:16–17; 1 Corinthians 3:10–15; 4:1–5; 9:24–27; 2 Corinthians 5:9–10; Galatians 6:7–10; Ephesians 6:7–8; Philippians 4:1; Colossians 3:22–25; 1 Thessalonians 2:19–20; 1 Timothy 6:12–19; 2 Timothy 2:11–13; Hebrews 10:32–36; James 2:5; 2 Peter 1:2–11; 1 John 2:28–3:3; 2 John 8; Revelation 2:10, 25–28; 3:10–11, 21; 5:9–10; 20:4, 6; 21:5–8; 22:12; *crowns*: 1 Corinthians 9:25; 1 Thessalonians 2:19; 2 Timothy 4:7–8; James 1:12; 1 Peter 5:1–4; cf. Revelation 4:10.
18. precious in the sight of the Lord: Psalm 116:15.
19. eternal life: John 11:25–26; cf. 3:16; 5:24; 10:27–30; 17:3; Romans 8:28–39.
20. "Blessed [for those] who die in the Lord": Revelation 14:13; cf. 1 Corinthians 2:6–16.

In summary, then, according to divine revelation, there are only two ways to die. The Lord Yeshua, in speaking to the most religious people of his day, said of those who rejected a saving relationship with him, "You . . . will die in your sins" (John 8:21, 24). That is one way to die. There is only one other way to die: "Blessed are the dead who die in the Lord" (Rev. 14:13). God is using the Holocaust to cause our Jewish people to face the answer to this question of eternal reality: "Will you die in your sins or will you die in the Lord?" This second biblical reality should force our Jewish people to face a third and future agonizing reality.

The Third Return to Reality: The Biblical Revelation of "the Time of Jacob's Trouble" and "the Day of the Lord"

The third and final reality is eschatological. It is the biblical revelation of a future "time of Jacob's trouble," elsewhere in the Bible called "the day of the Lord" or "the great tribulation." Although most Jewish scholars feel that a repeat of the Nazi Holocaust is highly unlikely, the truth is that the Nazi genocide of six million Jews was a harbinger of Israel's future and final Holocaust, which will be much more devastating than Hitler's Holocaust. According to Holy Scripture, the future of our Jewish people is more ominous than one can imagine. From a human standpoint, it will, in fact, be the worst deluge of evil on the earth since the beginning of man's existence. Unless our Jewish people return to this biblical reality, they will not sense the precarious nature of their existence and will therefore continue to evade God's good news of the gospel.

How does the Word of God describe the devastation of this future and final Jewish Holocaust?[53] First, the Bible describes "the time of Jacob's trouble" as unprecedented in its severity and unparalleled in human history.

> Alas! for that day is great, there is none like it; and it is the time of Jacob's distress. (Jer. 30:7)

> Now at that time Michael, the great prince who stands guard over the sons of your people [Israel], will arise. And there will be a time of distress such as never occurred since there was a nation until that time. (Dan. 12:1)

> Blow a trumpet in Zion, and sound an alarm on My holy mountain! Let all the inhabitants of the land tremble, for the day of the LORD is coming; surely it

is near, a day of darkness and gloom, a day of clouds and thick darkness. As the dawn is spread over the mountains, so there is a great and mighty people; there has never been anything like it, nor will there be again after it to the years of many generations. . . . The LORD utters His voice before His army; surely His camp is very great, for strong is he who carries His word. The day of the LORD is indeed great and very awesome, and who can endure it? (Joel 2:1–2, 11)

"It will come about in all the land," declares the LORD, "that two parts in it will be cut off and perish." (Zech. 13:8)

For then there will be a great tribulation, such as has not occurred since the beginning of the world until now, nor ever will. Unless those days had been cut short, no life would have been saved. (Matt. 24:21–22)

But, second, along with such destruction, the Bible describes "the time of Jacob's trouble" as a time of salvation for Israel's believing remnant (emphases added in Scripture below).[54]

Alas! for that day is great, there is none like it; and it is the time of Jacob's distress, *but he will be saved from it.* (Jer. 30:7)

Now at that time Michael, the great prince who stands guard over the sons of your people [Israel], will arise. And there will be a time of distress such as never occurred since there was a nation until that time; *and at that time your people, everyone who is found written in the book, will be rescued.* (Dan. 12:1)

"It will come about in all the land," declares the LORD, "that two parts in it will be cut off and perish; *but the third will be left in it. And I will bring the third part through the fire, refine them as silver is refined, and test them as gold is tested. They will call on My name, and I will answer them; I will say, 'They are My people,' and they will say, 'The LORD is my God.'"* (Zech. 13:8–9)

In that day the LORD will defend the inhabitants of Jerusalem, and the one who is feeble among them in that day will be like David, and the house of David will be like God, like the angel of the LORD before them. And in that day I will set about to destroy all the nations that come against Jerusalem. I will pour out on the house of David and on the inhabitants of Jerusalem, the Spirit of grace and of supplication, so that they will look on Me whom they have pierced; and they will mourn for Him, as one mourns for an only son, and they will weep bitterly over Him like the bitter weeping over a firstborn. (Zech. 12:8–10)

For then there will be a great tribulation, such as has not occurred since the beginning of the world until now, nor ever will. Unless those days had been cut short, no life would have been saved; *but for the sake of the elect those days will be cut short.* (Matt. 24:21–22)

In summary, the Bible declares that Israel is facing both a precarious as well as a glorious future. "The time of Jacob's trouble" will descend like a fury on Israel, but a believing remnant will be saved out of it. Whereas Hitler slaughtered one-third of the world's Jewish population, the final "day of the LORD" will see two-thirds destroyed. And yet, one-third will survive.

Conclusion

Jewish history and prophecy alike demonstrate that God is playing out the great drama of his Sacred Romance on the stage of Jewish suffering. This is most graphically seen in the past Nazi Holocaust as well as in Israel's future and final Holocaust. For Israel and the Jewish people, the way of the Sacred Romance is both se-lect and secure: "You only have I chosen among all the families of the earth; therefore I will punish you for all your iniquities" (Amos 3:2).

C. S. Lewis, more than most, dramatically portrayed the place of pain and suffering in the Sacred Romance:

> The human spirit will not even begin to try to surrender itself as long as all seems to be very well with it. Now error and sin both have this property, that the deeper they are the less their victim suspects their existence; they are masked evil. Pain is unmasked, unmistakable evil; every man knows that something is wrong when he is being hurt. . . . But pain insists upon being attended to. God whispers to us in our pleasures, speaks to us in our conscience, but shouts to us in our pains: it is His megaphone to rouse a deaf world. . . . No doubt pain as God's megaphone is a terrible instrument; it may lead to final and unrepented rebellion. But it gives the only opportunity the bad man can have for amendment. It removes the veil; it plants the flag of truth within the fortress of a rebel soul. . . . The creature's illusion of self-sufficiency must, for the creature's sake, be shattered; and by trouble or fear of trouble on earth, by crude fear of the eternal flames, God shatters it "unmindful of His glory's diminution."[55]

God's megaphone of pain and suffering, demonstrated in Israel's past and future holocausts, have drawn—and will continue to draw—our Jewish people back into the divine reality. And when Israel's final, believing remnant is roused out of its deafness and comes to a saving relationship with the Lord Yeshua, then Isaiah's prophetic confession will have come to pass:

> I shall make mention of the lovingkindnesses of the LORD, the praises of the LORD, according to all that the LORD has granted us, and the great goodness toward the house of Israel, which He has granted them according to His compassion and according to the abundance of His many lovingkindnesses. For

He said, "Surely, they are My people, sons who will
not deal falsely." So He became their Savior. In all
their affliction He was afflicted, and the angel of His
presence saved them; in His love and in His mercy
He redeemed them, and He lifted them and carried
them all the days of old. (Isa. 63:7–9)

In the meantime, our passion and prayer for our Jewish friends
and family members will echo the prayer of the apostle Paul:

Brethren, my heart's desire and my prayer to God for
[our Jewish people] is for their salvation. (Rom. 10:1)

Chapter 8

The Chosen People and Jewish Evangelism

J. LANIER BURNS

I am not ashamed of the gospel, because it is the power of God for the salvation of everyone who believes: first for the Jew, then for the Gentile. . . . What advantage, then, is there in being a Jew, or what value is there in circumcision? Much in every way! First of all, they have been entrusted with the very words of God. . . . For I could wish that I myself were cursed and cut off from Messiah for the sake of my brothers, those of my own race, the people of Israel. Theirs is the adoption as sons; theirs the divine glory, the covenants, the receiving of the law, the temple worship and the promises. Theirs are the patriarchs, and from them is traced the human ancestry of Messiah, who is God over all, forever praised! Amen. (Rom. 1:16; 3:1–2; 9:3–5 NIV)

These verses from perhaps the most famous Messianic Jew who ever lived, the apostle Paul, set the tone for this chapter on the chosen people and Jewish evangelism. This chapter is, then, a call to evangelism in general and Jewish evangelism in particular. Special challenges in Jewish evangelism will herein be understood in light of the writings of Abraham Joshua Heschel, a leading spokesman for his people in the mid-twentieth century.

In Romans, Paul emphasizes "to the Jew first" in accordance with a biblical priority that had endured from Abraham's commission to bless the world through the chosen fathers Isaac and Jacob (9:6–14). Jewish election traced the "human ancestry of Messiah" (9:5) and formed the initial core of the church in Acts. In addressing the problem of Jewish unbelief in Romans 10, Paul responded, "Did God reject his people? By no means!" (11:1 NIV), and proceeded to show by means of the olive tree analogy that evangelizing Gentiles as "wild" (v.17) branches would lead to the salvation of "all Israel" (v. 26). This prelude to the fulfillment of God's promises points to John's Revelation, where the highway to the new heavens and earth is paved with Old Testament asphalt. Should we, then, evangelize Jews and, in volumes such as this current one, encourage others to do so? The answer is that this priority is a divine imperative.

Initially, I will assume, with Paul, that the most basic problem of Jewish evangelism is that all believers do not evangelize as they should. Citing Joel and Isaiah, Paul asked, "How can they believe in the one of whom they have not heard?" (Rom. 10:14). Such neglect is not, however, universally the case. Because many Jews have been assimilated with cultures through means like intermarriage to the point that their Jewish identity has been reduced to a mere thread, many new believers may not be aware of their Jewishness. I have known many people who combined their newly discovered roots and their faith in a refreshing desire to see their fellow Jews come to a saving knowledge of their mutual Messiah.

As will be seen, this assimilation is symptomatic of the breadth, as well as the problematic nature, of intentional Jewish evangelism. In this chapter, I deal with the breadth of the subject by focusing on a representative scholar whom I have studied for a number of years, Abraham Joshua Heschel (1907–72). His work has given me helpful insight into his Old Testament as well as his people. The distinctive problems of Jewish evangelism will be placed under the headings of four needs: their diverse commitments, their mutual identity, their sensitivities about doctrine, and our need for recognition of this priority in our programs and curricula. I trust that an understanding of these needs, combined with Heschel's insights, will be helpful for the reader.

Heschel was born in 1907 into a distinguished line of the Hasidim, ordained a rabbi in his teens, and received his doctorate for his work on the prophets at the University of Berlin (1933).[1] The work was very influential in biblical studies, and his own life and thought. In an autobiographical interview a few days before his death, he stated, "May I make a personal statement here? I have written a book on the prophets, a rather large book. . . . And, really, this book changed my life. . . . I have learned from the prophets that I have to be involved in the affairs of men, in the affairs of suffering man."[2] Heschel was a leading educator in Europe until 1940, before narrowly escaping the Holocaust. From 1940–45 he served as Professor of Philosophy and Rabbinics at Hebrew Union College. He then became Professor of Jewish Ethics and Mysticism at the Jewish Theological Seminary of America, a post he held until his death twenty-seven years later. He was eulogized as "scoring singular success in word and deed in relating yesterday's wisdom to today's perplexities . . . a noble soul, a profound intellect, and a wise guide."[3] A prolific writer in philosophy, biblical studies, and Jewish tradition, Heschel wrote definitive works in three languages: English, Hebrew, and Yiddish. In this chapter I focus on one of his works, *Israel: An Echo of Eternity*, that illustrates many aspects of his passions and our current subject.[4]

In all of his writings Heschel's central premise is divine revelation. Through revelation, God reaches people and communicates his plan for history's fulfillment. In the mid-1960s, when "God-is-dead" theologians were developing their funereal icon, Heschel denounced the movement as a fad. Humanity and its conscience may be dead, he asserted, but God is very much alive. He wrote, "Some of us are like patients in the state of final agony—who scream in delirium: the doctor is dead, the doctor is dead."[5]

His thinking about revelation is developed in concentric layers. The foundational core is God's initiation of history with his covenantal pledge/promise of Israel's destiny. The second level is Israel as God's questing people, who bridge God's promise and humanity's hope. The third level transitions to spatial aspects of land and city, both of which are personified as maintaining dialogue with God and his people. Revelation, people, and land are indivisibly linked. The visible bond that unifies and focuses all aspects of "the chosen people" is Jerusalem. Therefore, Heschel was an eloquent spokesmen for his people, underscoring their chosenness and responding to challenges that might undermine their identity.

Our Need to Understand Jewish Diversity

The first of four needs in intentional Jewish evangelism is our need to understand their diversity. According to the American Jewish Yearbook, American Jews are divided into four groups: Orthodox (6 percent), Reform (40 percent), Conservative (35 percent), and a large number of so-called secular Jews, who are more concerned with cultural assimilation than religious distinctives. Significant differences distinguish appropriate evangelism of these groups.

Orthodox Judaism is the most committed, religious core. Practically speaking, they are usually reached only by Messianic Jews who have retained their distinctiveness. This is the oldest and most traditional group, and it reveres the Torah as Yahweh's Word. In Orthodox thinking, humanity is morally neutral, and sins can be atoned for by a more devout observance of the body of Jewish law (the Halakhah). Accordingly, the Jews are God's chosen people who need to maintain relationship with God, while non-Jews are obliged to become proselytes. Messiah is a human, who will deliver Jews from non-Jewish kingdoms, and who will establish righteousness by judgments. Orthodox Jews believe that there will be a physical resurrection, and righteous people will live forever in the world to come.

At the opposite extreme are the Reformed and secular Jews. Reform Judaism emerged in eighteenth-century Europe with emancipation from ghetto life and a concomitant desire to assimilate with European cultures. The Bible, they believe, is insightful about Jewish history and culture, but truth is relative, and a minimalist "God concept" is adequate. Hence, the law evolves, and must be adapted to civilizing ideals. Sins are social ills, and humanity is basically good, so education can help us evolve into a better people and society and, perhaps, help us create a utopia of peace. The spectrum of commitment in these groups ranges from religiously aware to secularly uncaring citizens. They believe that there is no afterlife, and some of these people opt for New Age notions of an ongoing life force.

Conservative Judaism occupies the middle ground, a nineteenth-century reaction to the assimilationist tendencies of the Reform and secular majority. The Bible is the Word of God, and man is in a continuing revelatory process. Conservatives gravitate toward the Reformed view of God, man, and social evil, but it insists on the necessity of maintaining Jewish identity.

We should, of course, share our faith with all of the people that we know, Jewish people being no exception. The point, however, is that we need to know our audience, since Jewish people are diverse in the depth of their knowledge of the Bible and in their commitment to the Old Testament doctrines and ideals. On the other hand, my observation has been that most Jews care deeply about their heritage and identity. I would note that the following principle applies to all evangelism: the depth of religious or ethnic commitment of a person is inversely proportional to that person's willingness to consider a new, and sometimes costly, direction in his or her life.

Heschel was interesting with his European background and adopted American context for ministry. He expressed in vivid terms an eclectic approach that is Orthodox in doctrine, Conservative in identity, and Reformed in application and expression. One of his stated goals in ministry was to preserve Jewish identity in a post-Holocaust world that desperately needed the ideal of shalom. The Old Testament, for him, is the Word of God that is to be interpreted literally to avoid allegorizing Israel's promises.[6] He emphatically affirms,

> Far from being a new relic of ancient literature, a book on the shelf gathering dust, the Bible in our lives is living power, radiating anticipations, throwing illuminations. . . . It is a book alive, a book that goes on and extends into the present—always being written, always disclosing and unfolding. We are in labor with biblical visions.[7]

Heschel asserts that God is Yahweh, the covenant God of Israel, whom he has characterized primarily as abiding presence in commitment to his pledge of the land to the Israelites. Heschel's "pathos" toward Israel was expressed in a more personal way than most Jewish thinkers; indeed, he has been immanently and intimately concerned for his people, and through them concerned for creation. Heschel repeatedly opposed the self-centered, man-like gods of paganism as well as the impersonal, philosophical notions of an Unmoved Mover against the other-centered, passionate God of the prophets. The bridge between Israel and all people he believed is that human life is structured by "polarities," or paradoxical tensions between seemingly irreconcilable truths such as the ability of finite people to know an infinite God, and the agency of a particular nation to bring universal redemption to creation. The creation of humanity in the image of God in this light was expressed by Heschel in the following terms: "The ultimate meaning of the State of Israel must be seen in terms of the vision of the prophets: the redemption of all men."[8] Or, beyond the Jews, the Bible is "the story of God's quest for righteous people," all of whom possess God-consciousness as a significant part of their quest for meaning on earth.[9] Again, the promise of the land extends through Abraham to an eschatological peace for the earth: "At the end of days, in a climax of days, there will be a new dawn of history. Redemption will come, cleansing the world from war and hatred. This is God's pledge and Israel's hope . . . the grand design."[10] In short, "eternity," for Heschel, is the echo of God's Word through Israel. Israel's divinely bestowed responsibility is to make the world aware of our responsibility for a Torah-type of holiness.

Heschel's view of God's pledge of the land gave him a Conservative concern for Jewish identity. Rather than fearing that an assimilationist approach might ultimately compromise Jewish identity, he felt instead that exile from the land and anti-Semitic persecutions had caused Jews to lose heart for embracing their distinctive contribution to the world. On the other hand, he expressed Jewish holiness in a Reformed-like, sacrificial involvement in issues of social justice and peace to the extent that all of life was sacred. He was a postmillennial Jew, meaning that he believed Israelite involvement in the historical evolution of the world would usher in a new world order of peace. His specific illustration of this evolution was the Jewish reclamation of desertlike land as an example for all underdeveloped nations. He was well known for his involvement in secular activities, political and social, that he felt would advance the sacredness of peace and justice in the world. A thorough knowledge of Heschel gives a student an awareness of Jewish diversity, ecumenically expressed by his eclectic concerns.

Our Need to Understand Jewish Identity

The second of four needs in intentional Jewish evangelism is that of understanding the liturgical nature of Jewish life. In light of Judaism's emphasis on religious life, it is understandable if many Jews view evangelical Gentiles as puritanical in lifestyle, having arbitrary rules for proper behavior, being overly conservative in political allegiance, and shallow in worship. As regards worship, in comparison to the commonly observed Christian holy days, for instance, the Jewish calendar has a number of annual holy days: Purim in February or March, Passover in March or April, Shavuot in May or June, especially sacred Yom Kippur (Atonement) with New Year and Tabernacles in September or October, and Hanukkah in November or December. All this in addition to the weekly Sabbath, of which most people are aware whether for religious reasons or mere connection with Jewish heritage. Finally, Jews are more conscious than most people of rites of passage in life. Circumcision of sons occurs on the eighth day after birth. Bar (or Bat) Mitzvah celebrates the coming of age at thirteen. Weddings are a high celebration of Jewish identity and tradition. Under the chuppah (or canopy), a glass is broken to symbolize the destruction of Jerusalem.

These occasions are important to Jews, connecting them with their identity and heritage. On these occasions we could honor Jewish people with their greeting cards. These occasions remind us that Jews are proud of their identity and that gospel conversations will probably not be heard apart from a personal relationship.

Is this not true, though, of us all? When someone inquires about our most basic beliefs, commitments, and destiny, are we not more receptive to spiritual reflection during special moments and in personal relationships than, for example, during the Miami vs. Florida football game? Evangelizing people, Jews being no exception, involves the most fundamental needs of human spiritual life—like a person's need of forgiveness. The Jewish mind usually reflects on forgiveness during Yom Kippur, the Day of Atonement. So that would be a special time when we can visit together with our Jewish friends and talk about our need as humans for forgiveness from sin and the provision of our Jewish Messiah for that need.

Heschel extends these Jewish distinctives into the all-important issue of Israel and the Holy Land. "Even before there was a people," he wrote, "there was a promise. The promise of a land. . . . Pagans have idols, Israel has a promise. We have no image, all we have is hope."[11] And further, the Bible is "above all a reality of living in the present tense" to the extent that "to abandon the land would be to repudiate the Bible."[12] And further still, "intimate attachment to the land, waiting for the renewal of Jewish life in the land of Israel, is part of our integrity, an existential fact. Unique . . . it lives in our hopes, it abides in our hearts."[13] Therefore, the reader is not surprised when Heschel relates the liturgical year to sorrow for the destruction of the land and celebration for its renewal. Jerusalem is, he noted, "the recurring theme of our liturgy."[14] God's pledge makes the land "inspired" and "mysteriously forceful," which has formed an "unending dialogue" between Jews and the Holy Land. Jerusalem as the symbol of Jewish consciousness is so central that Heschel speaks kindly about both Christianity and Islam, both of whom have had a share in the reclamation of the Holy Land. On the other hand, he vents toward the self-defeating hatred held, and political perversions espoused, by the Arabs.[15] I summarize this important point of empathy for Jewish people with an extended quote from Heschel:

> Jerusalem is a *witness*, an echo of eternity. . . . In Jerusalem there are houses, sewage, buses, lampposts. Yet she is more than a city among cities; she is a city full of vision, a city with extraordinary dimension. . . . Her power is in her promise. Her very being is an earnest, a promise and a pledge. . . .
>
> Between the middle of May and the middle of June, 1967, the Jewish people had a "rendezvous with history [Israel's stunning Six-Day War victory over the Arabs]," . . . I had not known how Jewish I was. . . . One of the insights learned from the great crisis of May, 1967, is the deep personal involvement of every Jew in the existence of Israel.[16]

From Heschel's words, we must realize that many events in today's world touch the notion of "home" in the Jewish heart.

Gentiles have had trials in this fallen world, but we had best understand the ramifications of long-term anti-Semitism in certain Christian traditions, and twentieth-century persecutions in particular, if we are to gain a sympathetic hearing with our Jewish friends.

Our Need to Understand Jewish Opposition to Conversion

The third of four needs in intentional Jewish evangelism is to understand Jewish attitudes toward key doctrines and conversion in general. We might refer to these as distinctive sensitivities that stand in the way of Jewish acceptance of the gospel. Judaism is a religion of deed (of works) in which the grace of God was manifested in their chosenness to be his agents of redemption in the world. Jews—at least those who care about acceptance with God—see themselves as the chosen people, so why talk about salvation? Salvation from what? Our doctrine of salvation is accompanied by an extensive theological reflection about possibilities in our afterlives. Jews traditionally have been far more concerned with right living and peacefulness now. As a result, our attempts at evangelism can be no more meaningful than two "ships passing in the night." Rather than focusing on the common Christian understandings of salvation, we would do better to go to the Old Testament and show that Israel and its leaders needed the full redemption that Messiah has brought as the Lamb of God.

Heschel brings these tensions with the gospel into clear focus. History, he holds, is a "reciprocal relationship" between God and Israel, his covenant establishing both his will and his need of people to fulfill it. There are, Heschel asserted, mutual needs and deeds of God and humanity that operate together in the grand design for Sabbath on earth through Israel. For the accomplishment of this grand design, Heschel said, "God needs the help of man. . . . His will does not dominate the affairs of men."[17] He strongly opposed the individualistic approach of evangelical Christianity: "The ultimate concern of the Jew is not personal salvation but universal redemption." Thus, in Heschel's estimation, Paul's doctrine of justification by faith is wrong. In Heschel's words, "Judaism stands or falls with the idea of the absolute relevance of deeds. Even to God we ascribe the deed. *Imitatio dei* is in deeds as the source of holiness."[18] Accordingly, Heschel uses Christian language for salvation with reference to the land: "The Jews go to Israel not only for physical security for themselves and their children," he wrote, "they go to Israel for renewal, for the experience of resurrection."[19] He acknowledges the Christian tradition that Jews would be barred from the land as punishment for the crucifixion of the Messiah, but he traces the curse to Chrysostom in the fourth century. The apostles, however, Heschel noted, did not recognize a post-crucifixion curse, and agreed with the rabbis in their expectation about the Jewish kingdom of Messiah, as is expressed in Acts 1:6–7. Heschel's polarities of thought allowed for a vague acceptance of a Messiah. Although he favored a redemption through national process, he allowed, "It was in this land that a man of Israel, the son of an Israelite carpenter, proclaimed the gospel of love to the pagan world and cleared the way for the days of the Messiah."[20] One wonders if this Messiah, even with Heschel's capital "M," is anything more than a particularly adept Israelite politician in a utopian world of peace?

We can address the Heschels of the world with the gospel, remembering that, if we lived in a graceless world, the gospel would be just as offensive for us as it has been for any Jew. We can show how the Hebrew Bible pointed to a Messiah, who did not renounce his Jewishness as he solved the sin problem of the world. This Messiah was committed to the fulfillment of the Law (Matt. 5:17–18), to the deepest meanings of the Seder (Matt. 26; Luke 22), and to the fulfilling promises that God had made to Israel. The New Testament, from beginning to end, is, in fact, intricately interwoven with Old Testament citations and allusions. The church was founded on Abrahamic faith in the completion of Calvary's atonement and resurrection. Further, only after extraordinary signs and wonders and painful confrontations were Gentiles accepted into the family of God's church. Hardly a day has gone by that I do not remember with thankfulness my adopted Semitic heritage and glorious future that Israel's Messiah, the Father's Lamb and Judah's Lion, will accomplish on my behalf. In other words, I am the recipient of blessings that Israel has brought to the world. It has seemed unnatural to me that Jews reject these Israelite gifts, while Gentiles like me accept them with thankfulness. This in part is, of course, what Paul argues in Romans 11.

Nevertheless, Heschel strongly resisted the completion of the Hebrew faith by Jews joining the Christian church. Christian "missions" to the Jews are wrong, he emphatically argued, because they will ask Jews to cease to be Jewish. He shared the very common objection among his people that to accept Christianity is to turn one's back on Jewish people, history, and lifestyle. Recall that there have always been serious social consequences for such "betrayal." In John 9:22, the blind man's parents referred the questioning Pharisees to their son "because they were afraid of the Jews, for already the Jews had decided that anyone who acknowledged that Jesus was the Messiah would be put out of the synagogue." In John 12:42–43, "Many even among the leaders believed in him. But because of the Pharisees they would not confess their faith for fear they would be put out of the synagogue; for they loved praise from men more than praise from God" (NIV). Finally, we note Heschel's words,

> The mission to the Jews is a call to betray . . . the sacred history of their people. Very few Christians seem to comprehend what is morally and spiritually involved in supporting such activities. We are Jews as we are men. The alternative to our existence as Jews is spiritual suicide, extinction. It is not a change into something else. Judaism has allies but no substitutes.[21]

The Ecumenical Council's renunciation of such endeavors was, in fact, the result of Heschel's dialogues with Popes John XXIII and Paul VI.

The need to understand Jewish attitudes reminds us that Jewish evangelism will not be an exercise in instant gratification. A history of anti-Semitism, pogroms, and theological neglect of the divine imperative to evangelize with "the Jew first" has placed a number of pitfalls in our way. I do not think that the evangelism of most Jews, however, is substantially different from the evangelism of most people. We are all sinners in need of the Savior. We can only be saved through the Holy Spirit "by grace through faith" alone. We resist God's grace because we fear that he might make a difference in a lifestyle that we have built for ourselves, sometimes full of residual sins and baleful influences. But a godly life with biblical fidelity is far better than the deceitful pleasures that excuse our resistance to God's will, which far surpasses our self-centered desires. Is fear of change, then, not the evangelistic hurdle that we all must jump in addressing our relationship with the Savior? The question is, will we love God and neighbor to the point that we will in turn embrace people with the gospel, even if such relationships inconveniently interfere with our mirages of the "good life"?

Our Need to Prioritize Evangelism in Programs

We come now to the fourth of four needs in intentional Jewish evangelism. It is the need to place evangelizing as a priority in our church programs and seminary curricula. Every educator and church leader knows that various activities have mandated priorities in the lives of their students and congregations. The members of a community will grow to accept an activity with adequate training and exposure, and then they mutually support one another in its accomplishment. In the present case, I'm speaking of an ongoing class in evangelism that incorporates becoming familiar with the belief systems of different people, as well as ways to develop friendships and speak inoffensively to nonbelievers.

During the 1990s the Jewish Outreach Institute reported that interfaith marriage for Jews was about 50 percent, with rates varying from 60 percent in California to about 25 percent in New York. As a result, about 800,000 children come from interfaith marriages out of a total Jewish population of approximately 5.5 million in America.[22] These statistics mean that the majority of Jews are religiously uncommitted to the point of marrying outside of their religion and do not have articulated objections to the gospel as did Heschel, who spoke for large number of Jews midcentury.

Thus, the fields are white, so we pray that the laborers will not be few. Sporadic evangelizing activities of scattered church members never achieve the strength that comes from mutual support that carries the laborer through difficult situations. As a result, unsponsored ideas fall by the wayside. I have long felt that many churches have neglected intentional evangelism, opting to let the professionals do the awkward or threatening things for which they are paid. Jewish evangelism and any ethnic outreach will be tougher than dutifully listening to an entertaining message. But evangelism that will involve Jews can be one of the most refreshing and rewarding activities for a believer. When a believer sees new birth and then disciples God's children to a maturity at which they, too, can reproduce, that believer experiences a fulfillment that is grounded in God's Word. This sense of fulfillment brings in turn a sense of worth in that we can all be vitally involved in the divine imperatives that God has given us.

Conclusion

I've suggested that an adequate evangelistic outreach will include a number of people who have mixed Jewish ancestry. Fostering evangelistic efforts by most Christians is probably our biggest challenge. Within that broad effort, we have four needs in intentional Jewish evangelism. We need first to understand the diversity among Jews so that we can speak more intelligently to our audiences. We also need to understand Jewish liturgical traditions so that we can relate our message to the significant times of their calendar. Third, we need to understand Jewish sensitivity to language that addresses their concerns about meaning in this life, language that does not threaten their Jewish identity. We must remind ourselves that Jewish identity was the primary concern expressed in *Jewish News*.[23] Finally, we need to prioritize Jewish evangelism in our programs and curricula. Otherwise, we will not be training people in the importance of this divine imperative. I would suggest that all of these topics are broad and easier to talk about than to practice. If we could devote some of our reading to excellent Jewish writing by thinkers like Heschel, we can better acquaint ourselves with the thoughts and lifestyles of the people whom we are trying to reach with the gospel.

Chapter 9

To the Jew First

A Reformed Perspective

RICHARD L. PRATT JR.

Christians of all denominations should draw encouragement at the widespread, interdenominational interest in the important topic of witnessing to Jews who have not acknowledged Jesus as Messiah. It is only fitting, then, that my branch of the church, the Reformed tradition, should take part in this discussion. The Calvinistic tradition has without doubt many things to learn in this area, and perhaps a few things to contribute to an interdenominational discussion.[1]

This current study thus looks at four major, long-standing Calvinistic doctrines upon which the Reformed tradition has been relatively unified, and that have implications for gospel ministry to unbelieving Jews. In doing so, and to insure that the perspectives here reflect some breadth of agreement, I will draw upon confessional resources, especially the *Westminster Confession of Faith*,[2] rather than direct exegetical work with the Bible. I will also direct attention to some of the practical implications that each of these doctrines has for gospel ministry to Jews who do not follow Jesus as their Messiah.

The four theological emphases within the Reformed tradition to which we now turn our attention are as follows: (1) the doctrine of the covenant of grace; (2) Calvinistic perspectives on the people of God; (3) the relationship of law and gospel; (4) the Reformed doctrine of eschatology, which will draw attention to several important issues.[3]

The Covenant of Grace

The term *covenant* is so closely associated with Reformed theology that the words *covenant* and *reformed* are often used interchangeably. In many circles, "Reformed theology" is "covenant theology"; "covenant theology" is "Reformed theology." This close association reflects a central feature of Reformed systematics as being the doctrine of covenant.

We should note that Reformed covenant theology has undergone significant historical developments. Covenant did not dominate early Calvinistic thinking, but rose to prominence through the Reformed scholastics of the seventeenth century. Since then, however, covenant has played a formative role in nearly every corner of the tradition.[4] In contemporary Calvinism, significant adjustments have been made in the light of recent analyses of ancient Near Eastern texts, but covenant remains a central organizing feature of Reformed theology.[5]

One of Reformed covenant theology's most important features is the idea of the covenant of grace outlined in the *Westminster Confession*.[6] To understand this doctrine, we must remember that the highly scholastic Westminster Assembly did not use the term *covenant* in precisely the same way that the Bible does. Rather, the term was used as a theological construct to designate the manner in which God reveals himself to humanity.

Within this framework, God reveals himself in two covenants. The Westminster Assembly called the first covenant the "covenant of works"[7] or "covenant of life."[8] This covenant describes the relationship between God and our first parents during their probation in Eden. The assembly identified the second covenant between God and humanity as the "covenant of grace." This covenant was made with Messiah and governed divine-human relations from Genesis 3:15 to the Messiah's second coming. At times, this traditional vocabulary leads to confusion because many evangelical groups associate the "covenant of works" with Moses, and the "covenant of grace" with the New Testament. By contrast, the Reformed tradition limits the "covenant of works" to the time before the fall, and assigns the entire history of redemption, including both the Old and New Testaments, to the "covenant of grace."

Despite the historical breadth of the covenant of grace, the

Reformed tradition has always acknowledged differences between the Old Testament and New Testament periods. Yet it has also insisted that both Testaments are substantially unified and differ only administratively; as the Westminster Assembly put it, the one covenant of grace "was differently administered in the time of the law, and in the time of the gospel,"[9] but "there are not . . . two covenants of grace, differing in substance, but one and the same, under various dispensations."[10]

To be sure, this theological perspective raises many questions. What precisely is the difference between the "substance" and "administration" of a covenant? Are not "substance" and "administration" reciprocally related? Reformed theologians continue to explore these interesting questions, but we must set them aside in order to focus our discussion in a different direction.

Perhaps the most important implication of the covenant of grace is that there has always been only one way of salvation. The way of salvation in the Old Testament era was essentially the same as it is for Christians today. As the *Westminster Confession* put it, Old Testament believers looked to "the promised Messiah, by whom they had full remission of sins, and eternal salvation."[11] The divine purposes behind the religious arrangements of the Old Testament were "for that time, sufficient and efficacious, through the operation of the Spirit, to instruct and build up the elect in faith in the promised Messiah."[12]

No doubt, many aspects of this affirmation need to be clarified. How did the concept of the eschatological Messiah develop in the Old Testament? How much did Old Testament believers understand about the Messiah? While Reformed theologians may answer these questions differently, all agree that Messiah was the implicit or explicit object of saving faith even in the Old Testament. His death and resurrection have always been the basis of salvation for all who believe.

The Calvinistic emphasis on one way of salvation in the one covenant of grace has at least two significant implications for gospel ministry to unbelieving Jews. First is the need to stress retrospective continuity. Evangelism of Jews from a Reformed perspective should stress the continuities between Old Testament and New Testament faith. Because Gentiles have dominated in the church for so long, Christianity has transformed remarkably from its biblical roots. To be sure, some of these changes have resulted from encroachments of paganism, while others have rightly come about as the church has sought, as Paul put it in 1 Corinthians 9:22, to "become all things to all people" (ESV). Nevertheless, the distinctively Gentile flavor of most denominations often makes Christianity appear to be an entirely Gentile religion. This appearance, in turn, erects enormous barriers between the church and Jews.

The manner in which Christians present the gospel can either ameliorate or exacerbate this unfortunate situation. Christian groups who have no doctrine like the covenant of grace that unifies the Testaments often run the risk of worsening the tension. Many feel free, if not compelled, to present Christianity in ways that focus on distinctively Gentile interests and needs. Reformed theology, however, can help resolve some of these tensions because it stresses the continuities between the Testaments. Because the Reformed tradition enthusiastically embraces the Old Testament's authority over the modern church, it can present Messiah in ways that emphasize the Old Testament concerns that many Jewish communities still treasure so highly.

The second implication speaks to the need for evangelism to stress prospective continuities between the Testaments. The unity of the covenant does draw New Testament believers not simply retrospectively toward Old Testament faith. It also presses those oriented toward Old Testament revelation to look prospectively toward Jesus and the New Testament. So many Christian groups have given our era the unfortunate distinction as the "Gentile age." Thus, a number of evangelicals have tended to minimize the call for Jews to place their faith in Jesus as the Messiah. At times, these evangelicals come close to treating Old Testament Israelite faith and Christianity as different but equally legitimate ways to reach the same goal of salvation.

According to traditional Calvinism, nothing could be further from the truth. The unity of the covenant of grace portrays Christian faith as the unwavering focus and goal of the Old Testament. The faith structures of the Old Testament always anticipated Jesus. As the Westminster Assembly put it, those structures were "all foresignifying Christ to come."[13] In this sense, God designed Old Testament faith to point to Jesus and the faith structures he and his apostles taught. To reject explicit commitment to Jesus of Nazareth, therefore, is to reject Old Testament faith itself. The Reformed concept of the unity of the covenant of grace makes evangelism of Jewish communities an absolute necessity, whether those communities are faithful or unfaithful to Old Testament religion.

The People of God

A second Calvinistic outlook having significant implications for our topic is the doctrine of the people of God. This doctrine addresses the relationship between Old Testament Jews and the New Testament church. Many evangelicals hold one of two common yet unfortunate positions on this issue: (1) separation theology; (2) replacement theology. As we will see, however, the Reformed tradition actually holds a third position.

The first position, separation theology, views Israel and the New Testament church as two relatively separate peoples of God. This viewpoint has become popular in recent decades through Scofieldian dispensationalism, and continues to varying degrees in many contemporary expressions of dispensationalism. In general, separation theology radically distinguishes the divine program for ethnic Israel from that of the New Testament church. Ethnic Israel often receives the designation of "the earthly people of God" because they are thought to be destined to receive the land of Canaan and to experience an earthly salvation in the millennium and beyond. The Gentiles of the New Testament church are frequently described as "the spiritual or heavenly people of God" because they are thought to be destined to receive the inheritance of an eternal heavenly existence. These Old Testament and New Testament promises continue alongside each other as largely independent programs.

The second position, replacement theology, holds that ethnic Israel has ceased to be special in the eyes of God. This outlook has dominated a number of denominations throughout the centuries. In this view, God has abrogated the special covenant status of ethnic Israel and replaced Israel with the Christian church. At times, this replacement is thought to be so categorical that Jews no longer have any special role whatsoever in the plan of God.

I'm sad to say that many Christians outside the Reformed tradition characterize the Calvinistic position as replacement theology. I suspect this misperception stems largely from the strong rhetoric many Reformed theologians employ against the separation theology of dispensationalism. The Reformed position differs, however, from both separation and replacement theologies. It is more accurate to describe the Reformed view on the people of God as "unity theology." In this outlook, the New Testament church is one with Israel of the Old Testament. The promises to Israel are not abrogated, but extended and fulfilled through the salvation of both Jews and Gentiles in the New Testament community.

Reformed theologians have displayed their unity theology in a number of ways. Calvin's interpretation, for instance, of Paul's statement in Romans 11:26 that "all Israel will be saved" points to this strong sense of unity. In Calvin's view, "all Israel" refers neither to believing Jews alone nor to believers within the New Testament church alone. Instead, "all Israel" denotes the combined number of believing Jews and Gentiles from both the Old and New Testaments periods. As Calvin himself put it,

> When the Gentiles shall come in, the Jews also shall
> return . . . and thus shall be completed the salvation
> of the whole Israel of God, which must be gathered
> from both, and yet in such a way that the Jews shall
> obtain the first place, being as it were the first born
> in God's family.[14]

Whether or not Calvin's interpretation of this verse is correct, it set the course for a continuing posture of the Reformed tradition. In line with Calvin's view, it is common for Reformed theologians to speak of Israel as the church and the church as Israel.[15] This interchangeability of terms points to the organic unity that Reformed theology understands to exist between Old Testament Israel and the New Testament church. From the Reformed perspective, believing Gentiles have always been adopted into the family of Abraham by faith in Abraham's great Son. Gentile believers are made a part of Israel, and thus they, alongside Jewish believers from both Testaments, inherit the promises given to Abraham. There is neither separation nor replacement. Instead, the two have become one.

Unity theology may be further explained by drawing attention to several beliefs that characterize the doctrine of the church in the Reformed tradition. First, the Reformed outlook on the unity of the invisible church makes absolutely no distinction between ethnic Israel and the church. The *Westminster Confession* defines the invisible church in this manner:

> The catholic or universal church, which is invisible, consists of the whole number of the elect, that have been, are, or shall be gathered into one, under Christ the Head thereof.[16]

The full number of the elect from all ages and nations comprise the one invisible church. In this respect, absolutely no distinction exists between the believing Jews of the Old Testament era and the believing Jews and Gentiles of the New Testament era. All the elect have equal status and utter unity in the invisible church.

Second, Reformed theology also stresses the unity between the visible communities of God's people in the Old and New Testaments. The Westminster Assembly defined the visible church as that community

> consist[ing] of all those throughout the world that profess the true religion; and of their children: and is the kingdom of the Lord Jesus Christ, the house and family of God, out of which there is no ordinary possibility of salvation.[17]

As regards the visible church, however, the *Westminster Confession* notes one important distinction in a parenthetical comment within 25.2. It remarks that during the New Testament period the visible church is "not confined to one nation, as before under the law [but] . . . consists of all those throughout the world that profess true religion." The visible New Testament church simply extends the visible Old Testament church to all the nations of the earth. Even on the level of visible communities, Old Testament Israel and the New Testament church are not two separate peoples, existing alongside or in opposition to each other.

Third, the unity of the visible communities is also evident in the ways Reformed theology has taught that the New Testament visible church includes both believers and unbelievers, just as Old

Testament Israel did. This outlook on the church differs from that of many groups who teach that the New Testament church consists only of true believers. In the Reformed tradition, Jeremiah's promise that everyone will know the Lord (Jer. 31:34) in the new covenant is not completed until the return of Messiah. For this reason, at the present time, membership in the visible church consists of believers and unbelievers, just as citizenship in Old Testament Israel consisted of believers and unbelievers.

Fourth, the unity of the visible Old and New Testament communities appears under Calvinistic belief in that the children of believers are part of the visible New Testament church.[18] As the Westminster Assembly put it, the visible church consists of those who "profess the true religion . . . and . . . their children."[19] All Reformed paedo-baptists and a number of Reformed Baptists believe that children within the New Testament church hold a status much like that of Israelite children in the Old Testament. They are the expected (although not guaranteed) heirs of the promises of grace. This biological dynamic rests on the conviction that the New Testament church is a continuation of Old Testament Israel.

Fifth, Reformed theology has emphasized the unity of Israel and the church by applying Old Testament remnant theology to the church. This connection appears in two ways. The first connection is the threat of divine judgment. Such judgment stands over the New Testament church just as it stood over Old Testament Israel. Calvinism does not distinguish Old Testament Israel as under judgment and the New Testament church as under grace. The Westminster Assembly plainly stated, "Some [churches] have so degenerated, as to become no churches of Christ, but synagogues of Satan."[20] As Old Testament Israel experienced divine judgment for flagrant apostasy, New Testament apostates will suffer divine wrath individually and corporately, temporally and eternally. The second connection is the promise of a righteous remnant. Just as the Old Testament promised a righteous remnant would continue even through Israel's darkest hours, so the Reformed tradition has affirmed that "nevertheless, there shall be always a church on earth, to worship God according to his will."[21] This application of Old Testament remnant theology points again to the Calvinistic belief in the unity of the people of God in both Testaments.

To be sure, Reformed unity theology raises questions that need to be explored further. Reformed theologians, for example, still have not reached much consensus on the status of physical descendants of believers after multiple generations have passed with little or no evidence of saving faith. In this regard, unbelieving Jews today may have a status among God's people similar to non-Christian Gentiles who have distant Christian ancestors. One thing is clear to all in the Reformed tradition: physical descent does not determine salvation. Yet Paul's remarkably paradoxical statement in Romans 11:28 strongly suggests that a special status extends through multiple generations. Speaking of unbelieving Jews, he says, "As far as the gospel is concerned, they are enemies on your [the Gentiles'] account; but as far as election is concerned, they are loved on account of the patriarchs, for God's gifts and his call are irrevocable." This passage asserts that a special status of some sort continues for Jews who are distant physical descendants of the Old Testament believers. Perhaps a similar status applies as well to Gentiles with Christian ancestry, but this issue remains to be explored more fully in the Reformed tradition. Despite a number of lingering uncertainties, Reformed theologians unquestionably affirm continuity between the visible people of God in both Testaments.

The Reformed perspective on the unity of God's people has at least two important implications for gospel ministry to Jewish communities. First, Gentiles must carry out evangelism of Jews with a strong sense of indebtedness. Throughout the history of Christianity, Gentile Christians have evangelized Jewish communities with apparently little awareness of the gratitude they owe to ethnic Israel. Even when anti-Semitism has not dominated Gentile Christian attitudes, outreach to the lost in ethnic Israel has not differed noticeably from outreach to lost pagans. Yet, if the Reformed perspective is right, then Gentile Christians owe a tremendous debt to ethnic Israel because Gentile Christians practice a faith that they inherited from Jews. In this regard, we should be mindful of Paul's words to the Gentiles in Rome: "Do not boast over those branches [unbelieving Jews]. If you do, consider this: You do not support the root, but the root supports you" (Rom. 11:18 NIV). Calvinistic unity theology stresses the gratitude that every Gentile believer owes to ethnic Israel. Although we must not diminish the teachings of the New Testament that may offend non-Christian Jews, the practices of Gentile Christian evangelists should demonstrate the utmost appreciation for the ethnic Israel to whom they owe so much.

The second implication of unity theology in gospel ministry to Jews is that the visible Christian church has no claim to moral superiority over ethnic Israel. Throughout its history, Gentile Christians have frequently disdained Jews as "covenant breakers," "God haters," and "Christ killers." Most of the time, this treatment of ethnic Israel has been coupled with the belief that the Christian church is of a higher moral character. According to the Reformed doctrine of the visible church, however, the New Testament church also contains much impurity. In Romans 11:18–21, the apostle Paul warned Gentile Christians of his day not to "act arrogantly" toward unbelieving Jews under divine judgment because apostasy and divine judgment were possibilities for the Gentile visible church as well. Judgment can come upon them as "unnatural branches" as it came upon the "natural branches" of Old Testament Israel. As history has demonstrated repeatedly, Paul's warning has become reality. It is a matter of record that the predominantly Gentile church has repeatedly turned from covenant fidelity and has suffered the judgment of God for these apostasies. For this reason, evangelism of Jews must be carried out with a high degree of humility. We must always be ready to admit the enormous failures of the Christian church.

Law and Gospel

The Reformed tradition has also espoused an outlook on law and gospel that should inform gospel ministry to Jews. In Reformed confessions and catechisms, the terms "law" and "gospel" commonly distinguish the Old Testament from the New Testament, but it is important to see that this distinction is by no means absolute.[22] In the Calvinistic perspective, the gospel of Messiah held an essential place in the law of Moses, and Mosaic law plays a central and positive role in the age of the gospel; law and gospel are not in opposition, but are two harmonious dimensions of life under the mercy of God in both Testaments.

In this respect, important differences arise between the Reformed and the Lutheran traditions. Put simply, the Lutheran Church in contrast with Reformed theology has exhibited a largely negative assessment of the law. It is well known that Luther's catechisms and sermons on the law primarily focused on the *usus pedigogicus*, the law as an instrument of sin leading to belief in Messiah. The *usus dvilus*, law as restraining sin, also received attention quite early. Luther himself, however, never formally established a place for *usus normativus*, the third use of the law as a moral guide for believers. Given Luther's personal religious history, his orientation is not surprising. It was not until the Melancthonian *Formula of Concord* (1577–1580) that the Lutheran tradition formally affirmed the *tertius usus legis* ("third use of the law")—the law as moral guide for followers of Messiah.[23] Still, the third use of the law has not held a strong position in Lutheran theology. In this regard, Luther's negative assessment of the law continues to characterize the Lutheran tradition.[24]

Calvinism, however, has taken a very different approach. Calvin's commentary on the seventh chapter of Romans argues that the law as moral guide was actually the primary use of the law. This position led Calvin to a much more positive assessment. Commenting on Romans 7:10, Calvin said,

> The commandment shows us a way of life in the righteousness of God, and . . . was given in order that we by keeping the law of the Lord might obtain eternal life, except our corruption stood in the way. . . . We must thus distinguish between the character of the law and our own wickedness. It hence follows, that it is incidental that the law inflicts on us a deadly wound, as when an incurable disease is more exasperated by a healing remedy. . . . This remains unaltered, that it is not in its own nature harmful to us, but it is so because our corruption provokes and draws upon us its curse.[25]

From Calvin's viewpoint, the law of Moses reflected the moral nature of God and was designed in the first place to show humanity the path to life. The law increased sin and led to death only because of humanity's fall into sin. For this reason, Calvin stressed the law as a gracious gift from God.[26] It is a blessing even for Christian believers, and guides them in the way of grateful living before God.[27] In a word, Calvin was much more positive than Luther in his assessment of the Mosaic law as a guide for Christians. This more positive outlook has characterized Reformed theology throughout the centuries.

The *Westminster Confession* devoted, in fact, an entire chapter to the subject, "Of the Law of God." First, the Westminster Assembly declared that the moral structures of God's law actually preceded Moses. The first and second paragraphs, chapter 19 of the *Confession* declare, "God gave to Adam a law"[28] and this same law was "delivered by God upon Mount Sinai, in Ten Commandments."[29] In this view, it was never morally acceptable to steal, break Sabbath, dishonor parents, and so forth. These laws were codified in the days of Moses, but had already "bound [Adam] and all his posterity."[30]

Beyond this, in the Calvinistic outlook, God, through the ministry of Moses, added two features to this preexisting moral law. First, in the language of Westminster, God ordained for Israel "as a church under age, ceremonial laws."[31] Second, he gave to Israel "as a body politic . . . sundry judicial laws."[32] It is true that establishing sharp divisions between moral, ceremonial, and judicial laws is without doubt problematic. Countless theologians within and without the Reformed tradition have challenged the value of these categories. Nevertheless, even operating with this threefold division, the Reformed tradition has affirmed the moral relevance of all aspects of Mosaic law. As the Westminster Assembly put it, the moral law is "binding in all times and circumstances what ever it says."[33] Even though the ceremonies of the Old Testament, such as sacrifice and temple worship, are not to be performed by New Testament believers, they are not irrelevant because they "[prefigured] Christ" and "[held] forth divers instruction of moral duties."[34] Moreover, even the judicial laws maintain relevance for the New Testament period as far as "the general equity thereof may require."[35]

It is not surprising, then, that Reformed theologians have emphasized that followers of Messiah benefit tremendously from attention to the law of God. The *Westminster Confession* devoted, in fact, the overwhelming majority of its attention to the law of God, affirming positive declarations of its usefulness and value for life in the New Testament period. Consider the following sample:

> Although true believers be not under the law, as
> a covenant of works, to be thereby justified, or

> condemned; yet it is of great use to them, as well as
> to others, in that, as a rule of life informing them of
> the will of God, and their duty, it directs and binds
> them to walk accordingly. . . . It is likewise of use to
> the regenerate, to restrain their corruptions.[36]

As this passage makes clear, from a Reformed perspective the law of God is "of great use" to believers and unbelievers alike even in our day.

If this confessional statement does not make the point clear, the positive outlook on Mosaic law in the Reformed tradition should be evident in various Calvinistic political experiments. The social structures of Calvin's Geneva, for example, the Puritans' England, and the Puritan colonies of America demonstrate how prone Reformed theologians are to view the Mosaic law as a positive resource for guiding moral and political life. Even in our own day, it is not uncommon to hear Calvinists, often known as "theonomists" or "reconstructionists," enthusiastically recommending that contemporary civil governments enforce Old Testament judicial laws as much as possible. To be sure, Reformed theologians disagree about the details of these views, but the propensity of the Reformed tradition to emphasize the third use of the law appears throughout its history.[37]

What are some implications of this focus of Reformed theology for gospel ministry to Jews? At least one important implication comes to mind. Evangelism guided by Reformed theology insists that the law of Moses remains God's law for his people today. Contrary to many Christian traditions, Reformed theology does not present Christianity as opposed to the guidance of Mosaic law. Christian traditions that tend toward antinomianism often require Jewish believers to abandon their traditions such as Sabbath-keeping, annual Feasts, and dietary observances. In effect, these Jews are told that they must live as Gentiles to demonstrate loyalty to their Jewish Messiah Jesus.

In a positive trend in recent years, a number of Messianic Jewish congregations have resisted this widespread antinomianism. These congregations endorse practices that some Gentile Christians are likely to consider contrary to the teaching of the New Testament. Yet the members of these congregations see themselves as remaining Jews when they receive Jesus as the Messiah. They see no need to abandon biblical or postbiblical traditions.

As might be expected, the existence of these Messianic Jewish communities has raised tensions in the broader Christian church. Their beliefs and practices are so different from those of typical Gentile churches that some Gentiles view these congregations as unusual. On occasion, some of these congregations react with an attitude of superiority over their Gentile brothers and sisters. It would appear, then, that we are not far from the ethnic tensions that severely divided the first-century church. This disharmony compels us to examine more closely how we should relate the law of Moses to life in Messiah.

The positive Reformed outlook on Old Testament law can greatly mollify these divisions. Reformed theology finds all Mosaic law valuable for Christian living, and promotes open attitudes toward Messianic Jews who wish to preserve their distinctively Jewish practices. Just as the book of Acts indicates that the apostles did not forsake their Jewish traditions as they followed Messiah,[38] so Reformed evangelism today should not discount many of the practices of contemporary Messianic Jewish congregations.

To be sure, disagreements will arise over how biblical and post-biblical Jewish traditions should be applied today. It is unlikely that full agreement will ever be reached on these matters. Yet the Reformed emphasis on the law as a moral guide for believers should at least help us clarify where the crucial issues lie. From the vantage point of Reformed theology, there is no problem for Messianic Jews to explore the applications of Old Testament laws to life today. This exploration, in fact, should be applauded and pursued by Gentiles as well.

The Reformed outlook on Old Testament law also clarifies the nature of Jews coming to faith in Jesus. On the one hand, to be a Messianic Jew does not mean lessening one's pursuit of obedience to the law of Moses. On the contrary, it implies a new empower-ment from the Holy Spirit to fulfill the requirements of the law under the lordship of Messiah. Even those postbiblical Jewish tra-ditions that aid in the process of sanctification are acceptable in principle. In a word, Reformed evangelists should be clear that Jews do not have to become Gentiles in order to follow Jesus.

On the other hand, Reformed theology encourages Messianic

Jews to remember that all traditional practices must be reinterpreted and modified in light of the revelation of Jesus the Messiah. It may be acceptable, for instance, to maintain a Kosher diet for reasons of health or tradition, but to do so that it separates oneself from Gentile Christians contradicts New Testament teaching on the unity of the church.[39] While the Reformed tradition does not ask Jews to forgo their Jewishness in order to follow Messiah, it does insist that their Jewishness be completely defined by Messiah. Moreover, while in principle Jews need not live like Gentiles, they must at times be willing to accommodate themselves to Gentiles for the sake of the gospel.[40]

Nevertheless, it is incumbent upon Jewish and Gentile believers alike to pursue obedience to God's law together. The question before Reformed churches is not *whether* the law of Moses applies to the Christian life, but *how*. To neglect the law of Moses is to neglect the moral perspectives of Jesus himself, who insisted that "anyone who breaks one of the least of these commandments and teaches others to do the same will be called least in the kingdom of heaven" (Matt. 5:19). Our task is to discern how to observe the Mosaic law in the New Testament era. Should these observances be the same for Gentiles and Jews? To what degree should cultural and personal variations be permitted?

In all events, it should be clear from a Reformed perspective that evangelism of Jews should never give the false impression that loyalty to Moses precludes love for Messiah. On the contrary, Christian evangelism should affirm that wholehearted devotion to Messiah expresses itself in wholehearted devotion to Mosaic law.

Eschatology

The Reformed perspective on eschatology also provides significant guidance for evangelizing Jews. It is an unfortunate perception that the terms "Reformed" and "eschatology" do not go together in the minds of many Christians. Most evangelicals have difficulty believing that Reformed theology has much to say about eschatology. There are at least two reasons for this misperception. First, unlike many contemporary evangelical groups, Reformed theologians seldom give themselves to sketching out particular end-time scenarios. We have remained largely skeptical of proposed dates and sequences of events. Second, Reformed ecclesiastical bodies have normally allowed a wide variety of views among their members and officers. Reformed confessions and catechisms do not endorse particular positions on questions that preoccupy many evangelical groups. They simply affirm basic beliefs such as the return of Messiah in glory, the resurrection of the dead, judgment, and the final new creation.

Despite this variety, it is fair to say that the Reformed tradition has largely been divided between amillennial and postmillennial eschatologies. On occasion, premillennial Reformed theologians have appeared, but this position has not been widespread. For this reason, this current study will concentrate attention on the eschatological hopes of Reformed theologians who endorsed amillennial or postmillennial positions.

The Reformed tradition has typically affirmed a very important eschatological role for ethnic Israel in at least two ways. First, Calvinists have strongly affirmed that the land promises to Israel will be fulfilled when redeemed Israel possesses the entire earth. Many evangelicals assume that only premillennial eschatology affirms the abiding validity of Israel's land promises. In this view, to deny the premillennial return of Messiah is to deny God's faithfulness to his earthly promises and to replace them with spiritual blessings. It should be pointed out, however, that neither Reformed amillennial nor postmillennial eschatologies suggest that the earthly promises to Israel's patriarchs have failed. On the contrary, Reformed eschatology sees the fulfillment of Israel's land promises on a grand scale. It is true that amillennialism and postmillennialism do not typically make much of the recent establishment of the state of Israel. Nor do they believe in a thousand-year reign to follow Messiah's appearance. Instead, the land of Canaan was a mere foretaste, a first step toward total world dominion by the people of God.[41] Reformed theology has looked to the eschatological new heavens and new earth as the fulfillment of Israel's hopes of a land. In the new creation, redeemed Jews and engrafted Gentiles will possess the entire new earth, the geographical center of which will be the land of Canaan and the New Jerusalem.

Second, Reformed theologians have dealt very seriously with the implications of Paul's paradoxical statement in Romans 11:28–29 regarding Israel: "As far as the gospel is concerned, they are enemies on your account; but as far as election is concerned, they are loved on account of the patriarchs, for God's gifts and his call are irrevocable" (NIV).[42] As a result, Reformed theology has been united in affirming a hope for the redemption of ethnic Israel.

This hope for redemption has taken two basic forms. In the first, some Reformed theologians have argued that Paul simply assured his readers that the Jews have not been cut off entirely from the grace of God. For this reason, the church will always have Jews among it numbers.[43] In the second form, other Reformed theologians have understood Romans 11 to teach that there will be a large-scale acceptance of Jesus by Jews before the second coming. For example, the answer to *Westminster Larger Catechism* question 191 states that in the second petition of the Lord's Prayer ("Thy kingdom come"), we should pray among other things that "the Jews [may be] called." This too is the opinion expressed in the marginal notes on Romans 11:26 in the Geneva Bible.[44] Other well-known theologians have taken this position as well. Charles Hodge, for example, wrote, "The second great event, which, according to the common faith of the church, is to precede the second advent of Christ, is the national conversion of the Jews."[45]

This future hope for the widespread restoration of ethnic Israel has followed two basic patterns in Reformed theology. In the first, postmillennialists often look upon this event as the final stage of the Messiah's victorious church. The gospel goes forth to all the world, and ethnic Israel joins in the worldwide redemption, which ushers in the return of Messiah. In the second pattern, amillennialists tend to understand ethnic Israel's eschatological restoration as a divine response to Gentile apostasy, not as a great climax of the gospel's victory over the world.[46]

Despite these differences, one common element appears in the Reformed tradition on the future restoration of ethnic Israel: any large-scale Jewish restoration must come through the preaching of the gospel. This position strongly opposes any eschatology that provides ethnic Israel with an alternative avenue of salvation. The Reformed vision of Israel's future absolutely dismisses the popular notion that unbelieving Jews will have the opportunity to believe in Messiah when they see him coming in glory. When Messiah appears in glory, it will be too late for unrepentant Gentiles and Jews alike. The Divine Warrior will strike out in judgment against the rebellious nations of the earth as well as apostates in Israel.

What are the implications of Reformed eschatology for gospel ministry to Jews? At least two come to the foreground. In the first, the Reformed outlook draws attention to the kind of hope we offer to Jews in the gospel of Messiah. The Christian faith points to the fulfillment of Israel's hopes for earthly victory and prosperity. From the time of the exile of Israel and Judah until now, the persecution and suffering of the righteous in Israel has created severe theological and physical crises. The laments have risen heavenward throughout the millennia. What has happened to the promises to the patriarchs? Has God forgotten his promise to give Israel victory over the nations that have persecuted her? When will God bring justice and victory for his people? These hopes are concrete, physical, and earthly, but they often seem foreign to the Christian gospel. From the Reformed perspective, however, these earthly hopes are nothing other than the inheritance all believers have been promised in Jesus.

The Christian gospel is the proclamation that these very real, corporeal, earthly hopes are fulfilled through the work of Messiah. The gospel announces that in Jesus is the inauguration of that kingdom. Already the stronghold of evil has been broken through the death and resurrection of Messiah. In the ongoing work of the Spirit today, we see different aspects of this eschatological vision fulfilled throughout the world. Moreover, every hope of the faithful remnant of Israel will come to complete fruition in the return of Messiah.

From the Reformed perspective, the Christian gospel, which we announce to Gentile and Jew alike, does not promise an individual salvation of eternal heavenly bliss. Instead, the Christian gospel announces that the earthly hopes of God's people Israel will become a never-ending historical reality on the new earth at Messiah's return. At that time, the enemies of God's people will be destroyed, the earth will be renewed, and God's people will inherit the earth. This focus of the Christian gospel is often lost from contemporary evangelism, but it must be reaffirmed in the strongest terms, especially in ministry to Jews.[47]

A second implication of Reformed eschatology in witnessing to Jews recalls that the Reformed tradition insists that like Gentiles, Jews can experience the future glory of the kingdom of God only by receiving the gospel of Messiah now. As a result, Christians have

an urgent responsibility to bring the gospel to Jewish communities. Our hearts should break over the condition of Jews who live
apart from their Messiah. Our love and high regard for the people
who received God's irrevocable call should stir our hearts to bring
them the good news of Messiah so that they might be rescued from
the coming judgment.

Moreover, whether or not we believe that there will be a large-
scale restoration of Jews to Messiah, focusing evangelistic attention on Jewish communities is our eschatological responsibility.
Evangelical organizations frequently focus on Jesus' words that "this
gospel of the kingdom will be preached in the whole world as a testimony to all nations, and then the end will come" (Matt. 24:14). As a
result, these organizations work diligently to spread the gospel to every identifiable Gentile people group. We should, of course, applaud
these efforts. But when this focus on Gentiles entirely displaces
evangelistic concern for ethnic Israel, it has gone too far. Insofar as
Christian eschatology leads us as believers to expect our age to include the restoration of Jews, we are responsible to reach not just the
Gentile world for Messiah, but to reach Israel as well.

Conclusion

I began this chapter suggesting that the Reformed tradition has
a lot to learn about, and some things to contribute to, shaping gospel ministry to Jews. This chapter is a call for Reformed churches
to reconsider their commitments to this task. The Reformed tradition has been so oriented toward the Gentile world that we in the
Reformed church have often failed to seek the lost in Israel. It is
time for us to follow through with the implications of Reformed
theology by reaffirming and applying our commitments to this
ministry opportunity. At the same time, it would appear that
Reformed theology also has perspectives that can contribute to re-
assessments within other traditions. The unity of the Testaments
in the covenant of grace, the one people of God, the harmony of
law and gospel, and the eschatological vision of Israel's future offer outlooks that may enhance the efforts of other branches of
the church as well. In all events, every Christian tradition should
search deeply within itself and interact with other theological perspectives to find every legitimate and effective way to bring the
gospel to those Jews who still have not found their Messiah.

Overture on Jewish Evangelism
20th General Assembly
Presbyterian Church in America

Whereas Messiah Jesus commanded that "repentance and forgiveness of sins be preached in His name to all nations *beginning at Jerusalem*" (Luke 24:47);

Whereas there has been an organized effort on the part of some who claim to profess the name of Christ to deny that Jewish people need to come to Him to be saved;

Whereas these people have spread a false hope and security that Jewish people can inherit eternal life apart from the faith in God's New Covenant promises foretold by the Jewish prophets (Jeremiah 31:31; Isaiah 53);

Therefore, the 20th General Assembly of the PCA re-affirms that we are "not ashamed of the gospel, because it is the power of God for the salvation of everyone who believes: *first for the Jew*, then for the Gentile" (Romans 1:16);

Re-affirms that "salvation is found in no one else, for there is no other name under heaven given to men by which we must be saved" (Acts 4:12) and "at the name of Jesus every knee should bow" (Philippians 2:10);

Re-affirms that anyone and everyone—Jewish or Gentile—who fails to receive Jesus, Messiah of Israel, as Savior and Lord, as taught in the New Covenant, will perish eternally; for Peter, appointed as Apostle to the Jewish people (Galatians 2:7), pleaded with the men of Israel, "save yourselves from this corrupt generation" (Acts 2:1–41);

Re-commits itself to prayer for all peoples—Jewish & Gentile, to turn to the God of Israel and His Holy Messiah Jesus in faith, as the Westminster Larger Catechism states, we are to pray that "the gospel [be] propagated throughout the world, *the Jews called*, the fullness of the Gentiles brought in" (Westminster Larger Catechism answer to Question 191);

Re-commits itself to the preaching of the gospel of Christ to all peoples—Jewish & Gentile, and condemns as the worst form of anti-Semitism withholding the gospel from the Jewish people; *Condemns* as erroneous the false teaching held by some that salvation for Jews today is possible *apart from the gospel of Christ* due to the Abrahamic Covenant, for this heresy necessarily involves denying the completed atonement for sin accomplished through our Messiah (Hebrews 9:15).

We therefore *re-affirm*, in accord with the Scriptures and the Westminster Confession of Faith and Catechisms, that it is our duty, as Messiah's people, to take the gospel to all the peoples of the earth, including the Jewish people. We call the Jewish people, through whom Jesus came, to join us in faith in their own Messiah, obedience to their own King, Jesus the "King of the Universe," and in the proclamation of His gospel to all peoples, for that same Jesus will one day return to judge the world (Acts 1:11).[48]

Chapter 10

To the Jew First in the New Millennium

A Dispensational Perspective

ARNOLD G. FRUCHTENBAUM

Romans 1:16 reads as follows in the *American Standard Version*:[1]

> For I am not ashamed of the gospel: for it is the power of God unto salvation to every one that believeth; to the Jew first, and also to the Greek.

The verse has two verbs. The first verb, *epaischunomai*, meaning "to be ashamed," controls the first clause. It is in the Greek present tense, emphasizing continuous action; Paul is continuously not ashamed of the gospel.

The second verb is *estin*, meaning "is," also in the Greek present tense, emphasizing continuous action. The exegetical question concerns whether the verb controls only the second clause or the second and third clauses. The second clause tells us that the gospel is *the power of God unto salvation*, and as the Greek present tense emphasizes, this is always true. Thus far, there is no debate among the commentaries. The real question is whether the verb "is" also controls the last clause: *to the Jew first, and also to the Greek.* If it does, then it would also teach that the gospel is continuously *to the Jew first, and also to the Greek.* If it does not, then Paul is making nothing more than a historical statement that the gospel came to the Jew first and has no ongoing relevance.

Important to this same discussion is Paul's use of the phrase two more times in Romans 2:9–10:

> . . . tribulation and anguish, upon every soul of man that worketh evil, of the Jew first, and also of the Greek; but glory and honor and peace to every man that worketh good, to the Jew first, and also to the Greek. (ASV)

The question also is, of course, *Do these two verses speak of an ongoing situation or a purely historical situation?* Are these two verses describing a principle that is always true? Or was it only true at one time, but no more? How one concludes the meaning of these two verses will, in turn, help to properly interpret Romans 1:16.

The final question of this current study is, *What is the exact meaning of the word,* first *(proton)?*

The Various Views

A survey of some exegetical commentaries, from both past and present, indicates more than one view among the commentators.

The view of Charles Hodge is,

> *To the Jew first, and also to the Greek.* To render *first,* here *especially,* would make the apostle teach that the gospel was peculiarly adapted to the Jews, or specially designed for them. But he frequently asserts that this is not the case, chap. iii. 9, 22, 29; x. 12. [*First,*] therefore, must have reference to time, "To the Jew in the first instance, and then to the Greek." Salvation, as our Saviour said to the woman of Samaria, is of the Jews. Of them the Messiah came, to them the gospel was first preached, and by them preached to the Gentiles. The apostle often, as in the present instance, says Jews and Greeks,

for Jews and Gentiles, because the Greeks were the Gentiles with whom, at that period, the Jews were most familiar.[2]

In his first quote, Charles Hodge rejects the view that the word *proton* is to be taken as "especially," which he defines that "the gospel was peculiarly adapted to the Jews, or specially designed for them," because he feels that would contradict other passages that teach against the gospel being particularly designed for the Jews. His conclusion, then, is that in this case *proton* should be taken as a "reference to time," and therefore concludes with a historical view of Romans 1:16. The Messiah came from the Jews, and the gospel was first preached to the Jews before it was preached to the Gentiles. It should be noted that he does not draw his conclusion exegetically from the text, nor the meaning of the word. It is based purely on his belief that other passages negate any ongoing validity of the principle to the Jew first. But he takes the exact opposite view on Romans 2:9–10:

> *Of the Jew first, and also of the Greek.* It becomes now apparent that the apostle, in laying down these general principles of justice, had the Jews specially in view. God, he says, will render to every man according to his works, to the good, eternal life; to the evil, tribulation and anguish. And lest the *every man* should fail to arrest attention, he adds expressly, that the Jew as well as the Greek is to be thus judged. The word [*first*] may express either order or preëminence. If the former, . . . The judgment shall begin with the Jews, and extend to the Gentiles. If the latter, the sense is, The Jew shall not only be punished as certainly as others, but more severely, because he has been more highly favoured. "The Jew first," is equivalent then to the Jew especially. The same remark applies to the following verse. If the Jew is faithful, he shall be specially rewarded. What is true of all men, is specially true of those to whom God has revealed himself in a peculiar manner.[3]

In this case he does take the meaning to be "specially." Therefore, the Jew will be either specially rewarded or specially judged. While John Calvin took this verse as historical in the sense that judgment begins with the Jews and extends to the Gentiles, Hodge himself takes it as an ongoing principle and not a purely historical situation. As to why this should differ from Romans 1:16, Hodge does not explain.

William Shedd also takes a historical view on Romans 1:16:

> . . . first in the order in which the gospel was to be preached; because "salvation is of the Jews," John iv. 22, and Jerusalem was the natural point of departure.[4]

But on Romans 2:9–10, Shedd states,

> . . . first in order, as in Acts iii. 26, and first in degree: pre-eminence in privileges, if abused, carries pre-eminence in condemnation.[5]

Shedd's view is the same as Hodge's: Romans 1:16 is taken to be purely historical, while Romans 2:9–10 is taken to be perpetual.

The view of John Murray on Romans 1:16 is expressed as follows:

> "To the Jew first, and also to the Greek." Since Paul was the apostle to the Gentiles and since the church at Rome was preponderantly Gentile (*cf.* vs. 13), it is the more significant that he should have intimated so expressly the priority of the Jew. But it was the divine economy that the gospel should have been preached first of all to the Jew (cf. Luke 24:49; Acts 1:4, 8; 13:46). It does not appear sufficient to regard this priority as that merely of time. In this text there is no suggestion to the effect that the priority is merely that of time. The implication appears to be rather that the power of God unto salvation through faith has primary relevance to the Jew, and the analogy of Scripture would indicate that this pe-

culiar relevance to the Jew arises from the fact that the Jew had been chosen by God to be the recipient of the promise of the gospel and that to him were committed the oracles of God. Salvation was of the Jews (John 4:22; *cf.* Acts 2:39; Rom. 3:1, 2; 9:4, 5). The lines of preparation for the full revelation of the gospel were laid in Israel and for that reason the gospel is pre-eminently the gospel for the Jew. How totally contrary to the current attitude of Jewry that Christianity is for the Gentile but not for the Jew.

This priority that belongs to the Jew does not make the gospel less relevant to the Gentile—"and also to the Greek." The Gentile as fully as the Jew is the recipient of salvation and so, in respect of the favour enjoyed, there is no discrimination.[6]

Although Murray shares the same postmillennial eschatology of Shedd and Hodge, he differs with both of them on the issue of Romans 1:16. He emphasizes that this verse does teach "the priority of the Jew." While it includes the historical concept that the gospel was "preached first of all to the Jew," he does not feel that history exhausts the meaning of the verse and denies that this priority "is merely that of time." Murray concludes that the meaning of the verse is that the gospel "has primary relevance to the Jew" because the Jews are the chosen people of God. And so "the gospel is pre-eminently the gospel for the Jew." What Murray does not clearly state is how this involves the practical realm of evangelism; and does it give priority to the Jew first in the realm of evangelism? He comes closer to that view than the previous authors quoted. But since he has denied that the gospel is preeminently for the Jew only in terms of time, in this case it is an ongoing priority and, therefore, in practice it opens the door to the fact that evangelism throughout this age is also to the Jew first. On Romans 2:9–10, Murray states,

> "Of the Jew first, and also of the Greek" (cf. 1:16). The priority of the Jew applies to condemnation and damnation as well as to salvation. As the gospel applies to him not only with a priority of time but of relevance, so the enhancement of his privilege and

responsibility magnifies correspondingly the weight of his retribution, a clear proof that the priority that belongs to the Jew by reason of the dispensation of grace will be taken into account and applied in the adjudications of the final judgment. . . . "To the Jew first, and also to the Greek." The repetition of this formula indicates that the priority of relevance which belongs to the gospel in reference to the Jew is carried through in the final administration of reward—the Jew will have priority in the bestowal of glory itself. The final judgment will take account of the priority of the Jew not only in the dispensing of retribution (vs. 9) but also in the dispensing of bliss.[7]

Murray is more consistent than either Hodge or Shedd and makes all three appearances of the phrase as ongoing reality that will continue with the final dispensing of judgment and reward.

J. P. McBeth's view of Romans 1:16 is purely historical.

Ιουδαίω τε πρῶτον . . . (to the Jew first and also to the Greek). "Greeks" includes all Gentiles, and "Jew and Greek" includes all mankind. και (and), a co-ordinate conjunction, denotes the equality of the Gentiles with the Jews in gospel privileges and grace.

The gospel was divinely appointed to be first preached to the Jews, and then to be given equally to the Gentiles. The Messiah was promised as the seed of Abraham and to be the Son of David, and to sit upon His father's throne. From the very nature of the promise of the Messiah, it was only natural that the gospel should be first preached to the Jews. Not that the Jews had any pre-eminence in privilege or grace; but of inevitable necessity, the Messianic message must first be proclaimed by and to those who first have the Messiah. And yet the emphasis is not upon the point of time, but rather upon the responsibility of leadership in the proclamation of the gospel. Paul is glad to refer the priority of responsibility to the Jews in the form of a compliment, in order that this might be a shield in warding off later attacks from the Jews upon certain doctrines in the Epistle.[8]

In McBeth's presentation, not only is Romans 1:16 merely expressing a historical view, it seems to be just an accident of history or, in his term, an "inevitable necessity," since the Messiah came from the Jews and would naturally proclaim it first to those for whom he came. McBeth's view on Romans 2:9–10 is,

> Ιουδαίου πρῶτον (to the Jews first). Wrath and indignation together with tribulation and anguish will punish every soul that works evil. Certainly the Gentile will have his rightful place in the judgment, but the Jew will precede the Gentile. In 1:16, Paul accorded the Jew first place in leadership and responsibility. Who shall be first in the judgment but he who defaulted in his responsibility? The person most responsible is most guilty when unfaithful to a trust. Ability brings added responsibility. The Jew is accountable for all that he could have been and is not. The Jew gladly accepted the honor, as Paul accorded first place to him in 1:16. It is self-evident that his being first in leadership and responsibility gives him first place also in the judgment by reason of his failure to discharge known duty.
>
> 2:10
>
> Paul startled every Jew by the horror of a worse judgment for them than even the Gentiles deserve. But this verse holds out hope to them and seeks to allure them into duty by stating that the first place in rewards is yet reserved for the Jew, if only he will be faithful in his place of responsibility. This verse indicates that first place in the reward of glory, honor, and peace will just as easily go to the Gentile, when he outstrips the Jew in the righteousness of God. The Jew has no monopoly on first honors in reward, and the Gentile is not underprivileged. This place is for either Jew or Gentile who can meet the requirements (Matt. 20:23).[9]

It is hard to escape the feeling that McBeth is trying to conclude the opposite of what Paul is saying. McBeth is content to see that the judgments of verse 9 will fall upon the Jew first. He is reluctant to say the same thing for the blessings of verse 10. Therefore, blessings "will just as easily go to the Gentile, . . ." and "[t]he Jew has no monopoly on first honors in reward, . . ." In other words, judgment upon the Jew first: Yes! Rewards: No!

In the case of F. F. Bruce, in his commentary[10] he limits his comments only to the first phrase, "I am not ashamed of the gospel of Christ." He totally skips commenting on the rest of verse 16. This is also true of his treatment of Romans 2:9–10. He comments on verse 8 and then skips over to verse 11, totally bypassing verses 9 through 10.[11] This is all rather surprising coming from a Greek scholar of his caliber.

Douglas Moo, in his recent commentary on Romans, has this to say about Romans 1:16:

> Yet it is typical also of Romans that Paul does not rest content with a reminder of the universalism of the gospel but immediately introduces a note of particularism: "to the Jew first and then to the Greek." What is the nature of the Jew's priority ("first") over the Gentile? Some scholars, indeed, have sought to remove any sense of priority from the phrase, but without success. Paul clearly accords some kind of priority to the Jew. Some suggest that no more is involved than the historical circumstance of the apostolic preaching, which, according to Acts, began with the Jews and moved to the Gentiles. But Paul must intend more than simple historical fact in light of the theological context here. If we ask what precedence Paul accords Israel elsewhere in Romans, we find that his emphasis is on the special applicability of the promise of God to that people whom he chose (3:2; 9–11). However much the church may seem to be dominated by Gentiles, Paul insists that the promises of God realized in the gospel are "first of all" for the Jew. To Israel the promises were first given, and to the Jews they still particularly

apply. Without in any way subtracting from the equal access that all people now have to the gospel, then, Paul insists that the gospel, "promised beforehand . . . in the holy Scriptures" (1:2), has a special relevance to the Jew.[12]

Moo is a historic premillennialist. He rejects any scholarly attempt to remove the concept of priority from the word "first." He also rejects the purely historical view—that it means no more than that the gospel first went to the Jews before going to the Gentiles. Rather he sees "to the Jew first" as an ongoing principle, but applies it only in the realm of the promises of God having "a special relevance to the Jew." These promises of God are primarily for the Jew. Thus, "[t]o Israel the promises were first given, and to the Jews they still particularly apply." While Moo sees this as an ongoing principle and reality, he does not make any specific application to the issue of evangelism. Moo's view on 2:9–10 is,

> . . . In using the phrase "every soul of a person," Paul apparently wants to emphasize again the utter impartiality of God's judgment. And, once again, this point is directed particularly to the Jew, as the last phrase of the verse—"for the Jew first and then for the Greek"—indicates. In an ironic twist, Paul uses the same phrase that maintained the priority of the Jew as the recipient of the good news of salvation (1:16) to assert the same priority in judgment. As the word of the promise has gone "first" to the Jew, so does punishment for failure to respond to that word go "first" to the Jew. In contrast to the Jews' tendency to regard their election as a guarantee that they would be "first" in salvation and "last" in judgment, Paul insists that their priority be applied equally to both. . . . And, more simply than in v. 7, Paul describes those who inherit these blessings as "everyone who does good." But he also continues the theme of v. 9 with his addition of the phrase "for the Jew first and then for the Greek."[13]

Here, Moo reasserts the principle of priority, applying it to both judgment and blessing.

Alva J. McClain, a dispensational writer, states the following:

> To add on to the first: "It is the power of God unto salvation to every one that believeth; to the Jew first, and also to the Greek." "The gospel is for everyone." The word *Greek* in the text was a term very often used by the Jews to mean all the Gentiles. The gospel has no racial boundaries. It even ignores degrees of goodness or badness. The ignorant and the wise, the high and the low—the gospel is for all. It is like the air we breathe, the rain that falls from heaven—it is for everybody.[14]

One would expect more comment from a dispensational writer concerning the phrase, "to the Jew first." McClain says nothing more about this verse except that the gospel is for all without "racial boundaries"; he does not comment at all on the key phrase. McClain's view on 2:9–10 is,

> When God reveals a certain truth in a certain age, there are two classes that emerge. One class is obedient to the truth, and the other is rebellious. For them that rebel there shall be "wrath and indignation" from God's side (v. 8); "tribulation and anguish" on man's side (v. 9). This will be true for "The Jew first, and also the Greek." That is an awful priority, isn't it? Did you ever think of it? What was the Jew morally? He said, "I am first." And he was first, too. But in a larger sense than he ever dreamed of! For if God would render to him first from the standpoint of righteousness, He would also render to him first from the standpoint of responsibility. Revelation of truth determines priority in the mind of God. On the positive side the principle of judgment follows the same order (v. 10).[15]

Here, McClain does comment on the phrase and sees it as emphasizing priority in both judgment and blessing.

C. K. Barrett expresses his view of Romans 1:16 as follows:

> The Gospel means salvation for *everyone* who has faith, but it was delivered to the *Jew first, and then the Gentile too.* . . . That the Jews were the first to hear the Gospel is to Paul more than a fact of history; it was due to God's election (see especially chs. ix–xi). It was inconceivable that God's Anointed should appear outside the context of Messianic prophecy, where alone there existed a vocabulary suitable for describing him.[16]

Barrett also takes a purely historical view, although he credits the historical view due to God's national election of Israel. Barrett's view on 2:9–10 is the opposite:

> Both for good and ill the Jew retains a certain priority (cf. i. 16)—not necessarily an enviable priority; but inevitably must be added—and the Gentile too.[17]

The Jew does retain a priority "[b]oth for good and ill" and, hence, these verses at least have an ongoing significance.

The view of Sanford C. Mills on Romans 1:16 is expressed as follows:

> We have examined the greater portion of Romans 1:16. Now look at the last phrase of the verse, ". . . to the Jew first, and also to the Greek." This epistle to the church at Rome was written to an established church. The so-called "church age" had been in existence for 25 years. Paul's proclamation in this letter that the Gospel was "to the Jew first, and also to the Greek," was, we believe, without qualification and is just as applicable today as it was in Paul's time. It will not do merely to state that Paul had preached the Gospel to the Jews and then rejected them since they rejected him at Corinth because he said to them, "from henceforth I will go to the

Gentiles" (Acts 18:6). It is true that he did say this to the Jews at Corinth, but let us follow Paul as he goes to the next city, and the next city: inevitably and invariably he goes to the Jews.[18]

Mills's view is that this principle is ongoing rather than purely historical and, in his case, he also applies it to evangelism and, subsequently, uses Paul's activities in the book of Acts as evidence as he went from city to city, "to the Jew first."

The View of Joseph Hoffman Cohn

Joseph Hoffman Cohn, for many years the general secretary of the American Board of Missions to the Jews (now Chosen People Ministries), wrote extensively on the mission's policy of "to the Jew first." It was his custom every year, in the January issue of *The Chosen People*, to write an article on Romans 1:16. All his articles from January 1918 until January 1948 were incorporated into a book titled *Beginning at Jerusalem*. Typical of his position is the view expressed in the January 1919 issue:

What *Is* God's Plan?
January, 1919

May we urge again God's plan for the Jews? If the Bible be true, and if words mean what they say, then it is inevitably true that every real Christian must give the Gospel "to the Jew first." Our Lord's own parting words were, "Beginning at Jerusalem." We resent any perverted interpretation of this phrase as meaning "begin in your home field." It does not mean that, it means just what it says—begin with the Jewish people. We resent further, the absurd avoidance of the issue by the assertion that "the Jews had it first." The mere fact that Jews were given the Gospel nineteen hundred years ago, will never excuse you for neglecting the Jew of today, of this very hour, of this very generation. It is outrageously unfair to judge the Jew of the present day because of what did or did not happen two thousand years ago.

The truth is, that God's plan for world evangelization has never been changed. That plan was, and is now, that we, as believers in the Lord Jesus Christ, shall make known His salvation to all the earth, "To the Jew First." This means that in every generation we are to preach the Gospel to the Jew first. It means, further, that in your church, in your Sunday school, and in your Missionary Society, you are faithfully to follow this divine plan, and you are to set aside unto Him the first part of your offering for missions, to be used in giving the Gospel literally "to the Jew first."[19]

In the January 1925 issue, he wrote,

The sainted Scotch preacher, Robert Murray Mc-Cheyne, became, early in his ministry, profoundly convinced of the importance of the "To the Jew first" doctrine, and this conviction influenced his life activities. We came across, recently, a sermon of his dealing with this very subject, and we can do our readers no greater service than to give at least some important extracts:

"Paul glories in the Gospel as the power of God unto salvation to the Jew first; from which I draw this Doctrine—that the Gospel should be preached first to the Jews.

"(1) Because judgment will begin with them—'Indignation and wrath to the Jew first,' Romans 2:6–10. It is an awful thought that the Jew will be the first to stand forward at the bar of God to be judged. When the great white throne is set, and He sits down upon it, from whose face the heavens and earth flee away, and great and small stand before God, is it not a striking thought that Israel—poor, blinded Israel—will be the first to stand in judgment before God?

"Is this not reason, then, why the Gospel should first be preached to the Jew? They are ready to perish. The cloud of indignation and wrath that is even now gathering above the lost will break first

upon the head of unhappy, unbelieving Israel. And
have you none of the bowels of Christ in you, that
you will not run first to them that are in so sad a
case?"[20]

Another example comes from the January 1940 article:
    With reference to your question as to the doctrine
    of "to the Jew first";—If we are to accept the inter-
    pretation which you give, that in the epistles, "to
    the Jew first," no longer holds, then how are we to
    explain such a passage as Romans 1:16? Or Romans
    2:9–10? This latter passage deals with future pun-
    ishment and has yet to be fulfilled.
        You quote Acts 13:46, "Lo, we turn to the
    Gentiles," but you apparently did not notice, in
    the chapter immediately following, Acts 14:1, that
    when they went into the next town, Iconium, they
    went again "to the Jew first." It is a matter of prin-
    ciple, for in Acts 13:46, Paul says, "it was *necessary*
    that the word should *first* have been spoken to you."
    This gives us a clear insight into God's divine or-
    der, that we owe the Gospel message "to the Jew
    first" regardless of whether he will hear or will not
    hear. I heard a good answer given by a banker to
    a Christian brother who resented the doctrine of
    "to the Jew first." This banker simply turned to him
    and asked, "In what age are we living now?" The
    other answered immediately, "In the church age, of
    course." The next question the banker asked was,
    "In what age did Paul write Romans 1:16?" The
    other answered, "In the church age." "Then there
    you have your answer," said the banker, "for God
    never changes His plans in any given dispensation;
    whatever was true in the days when Paul wrote the
    Epistle to the Romans, is just as true this very mo-
    ment, for it is one and the same dispensation."
        You quote Romans 10:12, "For there is no dif-
    ference between the Jew and the Greek: for the
    same Lord over all is rich unto all that call upon

Him"; but are you not misapplying Scripture? Paul is here speaking specifically concerning the method by which a person becomes a child of God in the present age of election; by that method, which is through individual faith in the Lord Jesus Christ, the same God is rich unto all that call upon Him; furthermore this same teaching is given later on in the epistle when it has to do with the church; in the church there is neither Jew nor Greek, we are all one in Christ. If you and I are members of the same church body, we are both children of God and there is not the slightest preference to be given to me because I am a Jewish Christian; we are both one in Christ. But the Lord does make a very clear distinction as to the peoples outside of the church, as you will notice in 1 Corinthians 10:32, "Give none offence, neither to the Jews, nor to the Gentiles, nor to the church of God." Here we have clearly stated that there are three classes of peoples in the world, Jews, Gentiles and Christians.

The Christian is given instructions by God how to bring the message of His salvation to the world. Just imagine that the church stands by herself on the mountain top and sees below her the huge masses of peoples; the church, counting herself out from the world, will see only two classes, Jews and Gentiles. Now the Lord's instruction to the church is to evangelize the whole world, but she must do it by giving the Gospel "to the Jew first" and then to the Gentile. It does not mean that the Jew is better than the Gentile, nor that the Jew even has preference over the Gentile, it simply means that it is God's order. Perhaps I can illustrate it more clearly by referring to the making of a fire in the kitchen stove: We know that the proper *order* for making a fire is first to put in the grate some paper, and on top of the paper some light pieces of wood, then a little heavier wood, and then finally coal. This method will produce a fire. But supposing that one were to say, "I do not like this order, putting the paper in first. I think I will put the coal in first, and then the wood and then the paper." You can readily see that there would be no permanent fire built on that basis. At the same time nobody claims that the paper is better than the coal, it simply has to be put into the grate *first* and it has to serve its purpose first. The same truth applies to the question of "To the Jew first." There is a peculiar function which the Lord wants the Jew to perform and that is why He has given the command "To the Jew first." That the church has refused to obey this command for these last two thousand years is a matter of serious loss to herself and of incalculable grief to our Lord Jesus Christ.

To Paul was revealed a glimpse of the importance of this doctrine; so important indeed did he realize it to be, that he was impelled to say in Romans 9:1, 3, "I say the truth in Christ, I lie not, my conscience also bearing me witness in the Holy Ghost . . . I could wish that myself were accursed from Christ for my brethren." When Paul calls upon the things most sacred in life with which to enforce the teaching as to the importance of Jewish evangelization, it is surely sufficient reason for us in these days to follow his example, for as he himself says, this revelation was given to him by God Himself, and is not merely a matter of patriotism.

Finally, I have asked many objectors to this doctrine of "To the Jew first," among them ministers of wide knowledge, to show me a single passage in the Bible which definitely cancels the instruction that the Gospel should be given "to the Jew first." I have never found one person who gave me a satisfactory answer to this question. It surely is reasonable to expect that when God gives space in the Bible to such a positive phrase as "to the Jew first" He would give equal space to an equally positive canceling; but all such contrary instruction is lacking, and in the face of this lack I am satisfied in my own mind, and there are thousands of earnest Christians who are likewise satisfied, that the divine method of missions is today as it was two thousand years ago, "to the Jew first." It will not do to argue that the Jews had the Gospel first, for that argument is specious; I can counter such argument by saying that the Gentiles also had the Gospel, therefore we ought not to go to the Gentiles either. The only logical and fair conclusion is that we owe the Gospel to the Jew first here in our generation; God will not excuse us from our obligation now in the present day and age simply because we point to an incident two thousand years ago when some Jews in some particular town through some particular apostle did have the Gospel "to the Jew first." That does not help to bring salvation to the Jew of today. The whole summing up of the matter is, simply, that in every generation the church must give the Gospel to the whole world, but in that particular order "to the Jew first," and then to the Gentile; and then keep repeating this over and over again in each succeeding generation.[21]

To summarize Dr. Cohn's views, he clearly rejected a purely historical interpretation of the "to the Jew first" phrase. He believed that the phrase of Romans 1:16 should be understood in the same way as the phrase in Romans 2:9–10, meaning it is an ongoing principle. By way of application, Dr. Cohn applied it in two specific ways. First, he applied it to evangelism in that the gospel should be presented to the Jew first. Second, he applied it in the realm of finances in that people should consider supporting a Jewish mission first, and at least the first offering in January of each year should go to a Jewish ministry.

A Dispensational View

One of the functions of the local assembly is to carry out the Great Commission of Matthew 28:18–20:

> And Jesus came to them and spake unto them,
> saying, All authority hath been given unto me in
> heaven and on earth. Go ye therefore, and make
> disciples of all the nations, baptizing them into the
> name of the Father and of the Son and of the Holy
> Spirit: teaching them to observe all things whatso-
> ever I commanded you: and lo, I am with you al-
> ways, even unto the end of the world.

The methodology by which this is to be carried out is a matter
of procedure, and the procedure is stated in Romans 1:16:

> For I am not ashamed of the gospel: for it is the
> power of God unto salvation to every one that be-
> lieveth; to the Jew first, and also to the Greek.

The gospel is the power of God, and the proper procedure is
for it to go to the Jew first. The governing verb, *is*, is in the present tense, which emphasizes continuous action and controls both
clauses: the gospel *is* the power of God and the gospel *is* to the Jew
first. To interpret this verse historically to mean that the gospel was
to the Jew first in the sense that it came to them first and that this
is no longer the case, or that it was only true during the apostolic
period, is also to say that the gospel was the power of God, but it
is no longer that. Consistent exegesis would demand that if the
gospel is always the power of God to save, then it is always to the
Jew first.

The Greek word that Paul used for the English word *first* is *proton*, the neuter form of *protos*. Among the lexicons, Thayer[22] notes
that the Septuagint uses *protos* for both the Hebrew רִאשׁוֹן (*rishon*),
meaning "first," as well as for אֶחָד (*echad*), meaning "one." He then
gives *protos* three categories of meaning. The primary category is
"first either in time or place, in any succession of things or of persons." The secondary meaning is "first in rank, influence, honor;
chief; principal." The third category is "first, at the first, in order of
time." It is in this category that Thayer places Romans 1:16. Arndt
and Gingrich[23] state that *protos* means "first," which includes "*a.* of
time first, earliest, earlier . . . *b.* of number or sequence . . . *c.* of rank
or degree first, foremost, most important, most prominent . . . *d.* of

space outer, anterior." They put the neuter form, *proton,* in a separate category, giving it the meaning first, "*a.* of time first, in the first place, before, earlier, to begin with . . . *b.* of sequence in enumerations . . . *c.* of degree in the first place, above all, especially . . ." and it is in the last category that they place Romans 1:16.

Jim Sibley makes the following observation:[24]

> Clarifying the Meaning of the Verse: "First"
> The standard Greek Lexicon says of the word translated "first" in this verse, ". . . degree *in the first place, above all, especially.*"[25] So, Paul is not using "first" with reference to time as much as to priority. He uses the same word in the same sense two additional times in Romans 2:9–10. The word is also used in Matthew 6:33 and in Acts 3:26.
>
> Clarifying the Meaning of the Verse: Present Tense
> The precise use of the present tense in Romans 1:16 is also very significant. There is a specialized use of the present tense,[26] both in Greek and in English, when expressing a universal truth. For example, when we say, "Honesty *is* the best policy," we mean to say that it is *always* the best policy. When Paul says "the gospel *is* the power of God unto salvation for all who believe; especially for the Jew, and also for the Gentile," he is stating a universal truth. If we wanted to bring out these two clarifications based on the meaning of "first" and the significance of the present tense in this verse, we might say, "*As long as* the gospel is the power of God unto salvation, *it is especially so* for the Jewish people, and also for the gentiles."[27]

In summary, then, *proton* has the meaning of "first," and this includes "first in time, in place, in order, and in importance." Applying this verse to the Great Commission, the gospel, wherever and by whatever means it goes out from the local church, must go to the Jew first. This is the biblical procedure for evangelism regardless of the method (radio, television, street meetings, literature, mass evangelism, door-to-door, etc.). Since most believers and local assemblies participate in the Great Commission mainly through monetary giving, this would require giving *to the Jew first*. This is true of the individual believer as well as of the local assembly in their missions budget (Rom. 15:25–27). What is true of the local church is also true of the missionary in the field. He must first take the gospel to any Jews who may be in the field where he is working. Regardless of his particular place of calling, his obligation is to seek out the Jews and present them with the gospel. Where there is already a command, no special leading is necessary.

Many missionaries may object, but fortunately there is a biblical and an apostolic example in Paul, although he was not called to the Jews:

> But I speak to you that are Gentiles. Inasmuch then as I am an apostle of Gentiles, I glorify my ministry; if by any means I may provoke to jealousy them that are my flesh, and may save some of them. (Rom. 11:13–14)

On this point, his ministry was different from Peter's:

> . . . but contrariwise, when they saw that I had been intrusted with the gospel of the uncircumcision, even as Peter with the gospel of the circumcision for he that wrought for Peter unto the apostleship of the circumcision wrought for me also unto the Gentiles; and when they perceived the grace that was given unto me, James and Cephas and John, they who were reputed to be pillars, gave to me and Barnabas the right hands of fellowship, that we should go unto the Gentiles, and they unto the circumcision. (Gal. 2:7–9)

Thus, there are two basic missions: they are not home and foreign missions, but are Jewish and Gentile missions. Hence, there was an apostleship of the circumcision and an apostleship of the uncircumcision. But even the Apostle to the Gentiles always went to the Jew first.

Only if Romans 1:16 is understood in this way can one better understand Paul's actions in the book of Acts. While one must be careful not to develop theology from historical books like the book of Acts, historical books can be used to illustrate doctrine. The doctrinal statement of Romans 1:16 is that the gospel is to the Jew first, and also to the Greek. The book of Acts contains numerous illustrations of that doctrinal point.

The beginning of his mission to the Gentiles is found in Acts 13:2–3:

> And as they ministered to the Lord, and fasted, the Holy Spirit said, Separate me Barnabas and Saul for the work whereunto I have called them. Then, when they had fasted and prayed and laid their hands on them, they sent them away.

But Paul proceeds to the Jew first, as in Acts 13:4–5 and 14:

> So they, being sent forth by the Holy Spirit, went down to Seleucia; and from thence they sailed to Cyprus. And when they were at Salamis, they proclaimed the word of God in the synagogues of the Jews: and they had also John as their attendant. (13:4–5)

> But they, passing through from Perga, came to Antioch of Pisidia; and they went into the synagogue on the sabbath day, and sat down. (13:14)

After presenting the gospel to the church of Antioch, and having a second opportunity to do so, and after its rejection by the majority of the Jewish population of Antioch of Pisidia, Paul and Barnabas state the following in Acts 13:46:

> And Paul and Barnabas spake out boldly, and said, It was necessary that the word of God should first [πρῶτον] be spoken to you. . . .

The key phrase that should not be missed is, "It was necessary that the word of God should first be spoken to you." This was not a matter of preference, but of necessity. The question to be asked is, *What kind of necessity was it that the gospel be first presented to the Jews?* It would not be a historical necessity simply because it would not fit this passage. The historical presentation of "to the Jew first" would only have been an *option* on Paul's part, not a *necessity*. This is best interpreted as a theological necessity in light of Romans 1:16. Thus, it was a doctrinal, theological necessity that the gospel be presented to the Jews of Antioch of Pisidia first, and then Paul could move on to the Gentiles as he does in this verse. As the following verses in Acts 14:1 and 16:1–13 show, however, once he left Antioch of Pisidia, he again went back to the Jew first:

> And it came to pass in Iconium that they entered together into the synagogue of the Jews, and so spake that a great multitude both of Jews and of Greeks believed. (14:1)

> Setting sail therefore from Troas, we made a straight course to Samothrace, and the day following to Neapolis; and from thence to Philippi, which is a city of Macedonia, the first of the district, a Roman colony: and we were in this city tarrying certain days. And on the sabbath day we went forth without the gate by a river side, where we supposed there was a place of prayer; and we sat down, and spake unto the women that were come together. (16:11–13)

Acts 16:11–13 is a good example of how carefully Paul followed the principle of Romans 1:16. This being a Sabbath prayer meeting means that it was a Jewish prayer meeting. Normally, Paul would go immediately to the synagogue, but could not do so in Philippi for the Jewish community in that town was too small to finance a synagogue. By Jewish tradition, if the Jewish community was too small to finance a synagogue, Jews were to congregate by a body of water for the Sabbath service. Paul, knowing this, waited until the Sabbath before he preached elsewhere because he knew that the gospel must go out to the Jew first. There, he found a little Jewish group in order to preach the gospel to them.

Now when they had passed through Amphipolis and Apolonia, they came to Thessalonica, where was a synagogue of the Jews: and Paul, *as his custom was*, went in unto them, and for three sabbath days reasoned with them from the Scriptures. (17:1–2, emphasis added)

And the brethren immediately sent away Paul and Silas by night unto Berea: who when they were come thither went into the synagogue of the Jews. (17:10)

Now while Paul waited for them at Athens, his spirit was provoked within him as he beheld the city full of idols. So he reasoned in the synagogue with Jews and the devout persons, and in the marketplace every day with them that met him. (17:16–17)

Acts 17:16–17 is another good example for showing exactly Paul's procedure. He came to Athens and saw the city given over to idolatry, and he was provoked to preach to those who worshiped these idols. It was not the Jews who worshiped the idols, because idolatry largely ceased to be a Jewish problem with the Babylonian captivity. Rather, the Gentiles worshiped these idols, and to these Gentiles Paul was provoked to preach. The principle of Romans 1:16, however, had to stand. According to verse 17, *so*, that is, for that reason, he went to the Jew first (v. 17), and then he went to the Gentiles (v. 18).

After these things he departed from Athens, and came to Corinth. . . . And he reasoned in the synagogue every sabbath, and persuaded Jews and Greeks. (18:1, 4)

And they came to Ephesus, and he left them there: but he himself entered into the synagogue, and reasoned with the Jews. (18:19)

And it came to pass, that, while Apollos was at Corinth, Paul having passed through the upper

country came to Ephesus, and found certain disciples: . . . And he entered into the synagogue, and
spake boldly for the space of three months, reasoning and persuading as to the things concerning the
kingdom of God (19:1, 8)

And when we entered into Rome, Paul was suffered
to abide by himself with the soldier that guarded
him. And it came to pass, that after three days he
called together those that were the chief of the
Jews: and when they were come together, he said
unto them, I, brethren, though I had done nothing
against the people, or the customs of our fathers,
yet was delivered prisoner from Jerusalem into the
hands of the Romans: . . . (28:16–17)

In Acts 28:16–17, Paul was a prisoner and could not go to the
synagogue of Rome. He, therefore, called the Jewish leaders of Rome
to his prison in order to proclaim the gospel to them first.

To the very end of the book of Acts, Paul is presenting the gospel to the Jew first. Even after returning to a city where he had already established a church, he first went to the Jews. Everywhere in
the book of Acts, the Apostle to the Gentiles, as he went out to the
Gentiles, always went to the Jew first. That is because of the doctrinal statement of Romans 1:16. The gospel, whenever it goes out and
by whatever means it goes out, is to go to the Jew first. This applies
both to active and passive evangelism. Active evangelism entails
persons' doing the work of evangelists; as they go out evangelizing,
they are to go to the Jew first. These examples in the book of Acts
are illustrations of active evangelism. The principle also holds in
passive evangelism, which is supporting those who do the work of
evangelism. An example of such is found in Romans 15:25–27:

. . . but now, I say, I go unto Jerusalem, ministering
unto the saints. For it hath been the good pleasure
of Macedonia and Achaia to make a certain contribution for the poor among the saints that are at
Jerusalem. Yea, it hath been their good pleasure;
and their debtors they are. For if the Gentiles have

been made partakers of their spiritual things, they owe it to them also to minister unto them in carnal [material] things.

The collection of funds by Gentile believers for the church of Jerusalem was not due merely to "Christian charity." Gentile believers are partaking of Jewish spiritual blessings. This has put Gentiles into debt. One means of paying this debt is by sharing with Jewish ministries materially.

Sibley makes the following notation:

> Another important observation regarding to this verse is that Paul is here speaking about *the nature of the gospel*, rather than setting forth an evangelistic methodology, per se. We cannot but conclude that the nature of the gospel is such that it is particularly and uniquely relevant to the Jewish people.
>
> In the New Testament, there are only two kinds of missions—not home missions and foreign missions, but Jewish missions and Gentile missions. A very small percentage of Christians have been called to Jewish missions, while most Christians live and serve primarily among Gentiles. This is as it should be. Jewish ministry is in no way superior to Gentile ministry. If God has called you to a ministry to Gentiles, who could possibly object? But in that case, you would want to model your ministry after that of the Apostle to the Gentiles, Paul of Tarsus.
>
> In fact, when we look at the practice of Paul in the Book of Acts, we see the outworking of the principle he stated in Romans 1:16. While Paul speaks of the nature of the gospel in Romans 1:16, he shows us how this understanding of the gospel affects his evangelistic procedure in the Book of Acts. In Romans, he emphasized the "first" was first in priority, but in Acts, we see that since Jewish evangelism was first in priority, it became his first order of business in terms of chronological sequence.
>
> Since Romans 1:16 is prescriptive, we should

make Jewish evangelism our priority today. However, since Paul's practice in the Book of Acts is descriptive, it may or may not be essential to make Jewish evangelism the first thing one should do when entering a new city or area. Nevertheless, our actions should still reflect the nature of the gospel, as revealed by the inspired Word of God. When Paul was in the areas where there was no Jewish population, he demonstrated the priority of Jewish evangelism by praying for their salvation (as in Romans 10:1) and by raising financial support for Jewish ministry (as in Romans 15:26–27).

God, Himself, chose the descendants of Abraham, Isaac, and Jacob—the Jewish people—to be set apart for His specific purposes in history. God's choice of Israel was to be a blessing, not only to Israel, but to the entire world. To understand (even partially) God's purposes should lead us to marvel at the wondrous ways of God (see Romans 11:33–36).[28]

Although the Scriptures are very clear about this procedure, it is nevertheless denied by many. A major argument used to refute this doctrine is based on Acts 28:25–28:

> And when they agreed not among themselves, they departed after that Paul had spoken one word, Well spake the Holy Spirit through Isaiah the prophet unto your fathers, saying, Go thou unto this people, and say, By hearing ye shall hear, and shall in no wise understand; And seeing ye shall see, and shall in no wise perceive: for this peoples heart is waxed gross, and their ears are dull of hearing, and their eyes they have closed; lest, haply they should perceive with their eyes, and hear with their ears, and understand with their heart, and should turn again, and I should heal them. Be it known therefore unto you, that this salvation of God is sent unto the Gentiles: they will also hear.

Because of these concluding words and Paul's declaration that the gospel will now go to the Gentiles, the passage is taken to mean that the gospel is no longer to the Jew first and that God has now changed his program of evangelism, superseding Romans 1:16. It is agreed that Romans was written before Acts, but this passage does not mean that the gospel is no longer to the Jew first or that God has changed his program of evangelism. The true meaning is to be found in comparison with two other passages, where these words had been spoken before:

> And the next sabbath almost the whole city was gathered together to hear the word of God. But when the Jews saw the multitudes, they were filled with jealousy, and contradicted the things which were spoken by Paul, and blasphemed. And Paul and Barnabas spake out boldly, and said, It was necessary that the word of God should first be spoken to you. Seeing ye thrust it from you, and judge yourselves unworthy of eternal life, lo, we turn to the Gentiles. For so hath the Lord commanded us, saying, I have set thee for a light of the Gentiles, that thou shouldest be for salvation unto the uttermost part of the earth. And as the Gentiles heard this, they were glad, and glorified the word of God: and as many as were ordained to eternal life believed. (Acts 13:44–48)

> But when Silas and Timothy came down from Macedonia, Paul was constrained by the word, testifying to the Jews that Jesus was the Christ. And when they opposed themselves and blasphemed, he shook out his raiment and said unto them, Your blood be upon your own heads; I am clean: from henceforth I will go unto the Gentiles. (Acts 18:5–6)

The true interpretation of Acts 28:25–28 is to be seen in these two passages, which show a local change and not an overall change in the program of evangelism. In the first passage, the Jews of Antioch of Pisidia rejected the gospel; so now in Antioch of Pisidia, Paul will go to the Gentiles. In the second passage the Jews of Corinth rejected the gospel; so now Paul will turn to the Gentiles of Corinth. But when he left both Antioch of Pisidia and Corinth for new territory, he went back, as related in chapters 14 and 19, to the Jew first, even after his declaration in the previous chapters that he would go to the Gentiles.

What is true of Antioch of Pisidia and Corinth is also true of Rome. The Jews of Rome had rejected the gospel, so Paul went to the Gentiles of Rome. Paul made no shift in the procedure of presenting the gospel. Acts 28 presents only a continuation of the procedure already in progress, that of presenting the gospel to the Jew first and then turning to the Gentiles. If Paul left Rome after two years (and I believe that he did), he continued the same practice; after leaving Rome, he went to the Jew first, as he had after leaving Antioch of Pisidia and Corinth.

In relation to missions, then, the gospel must be to the Jew first. This is not a matter of preference, but a matter of procedure. In the outworking of the Abrahamic covenant, the local church can appropriate certain blessings, for in giving the gospel to the Jew first, the church is blessing the Jews. The local church will, of course, always have certain blessings as long as the gospel is preached from the pulpit and the local assembly stands true to the fundamentals of the faith. Some blessings, however, are based on other conditions. The blessings of the Abrahamic covenant available to the local congregation are conditioned upon the congregation's blessing the Jews, by presenting the gospel to the Jew first. Then the local church can appropriate the blessings of the Abrahamic covenant, blessings that cannot be obtained any other way.

PART 3

MISSION

The mission of the church is its *praxis*—the practical outworking of its theology. Put another way, the mission of the church is the incarnational ministry of the Holy Spirit in its connection to the Great Commission.

The church's mission to the Jewish people carries enormous historical baggage. On the one hand, God's command to bring the gospel "to the Jew first" must be reckoned with as a priority that cannot be evaded. On the other hand, speaking in human terms, no people have earned the right to demand a "hands-off" policy. Yes, the Jewish people have been shamefully treated by those charged with the task of loving others and sharing the Messiah with them. Yet these realities do not change the ultimate calling of the gospel "to the Jew first."

Jewish missions in the new millennium, therefore, carries with it the burden of a doubly difficult task. The first is to find a context in which the gospel may once again be recognized as intelligible and compassionate to the broad spectrum of the Jewish community. The second task—in order to obtain even a hearing, let alone a trial, of the church's claims—is to overcome the obstacles that have so damaged the church's credibility. The gospel messenger must not regain a positive image, however, by relinquishing its message. Only by sharing the gospel with words and deeds of compassion, in the context of relationship, will the gospel be heard and received by Jewish listeners. The gospel that is shared must also be the unadulterated Jewish gospel as first delivered in its Jewish context, not a gospel with cultural or theological overlays of the past two millennia.

The articles in this section are the fruit of not only scholarship, but also of experience. This befits a topic that, more than any other, directly affects the lives and destinies of the humanity the gospel professes to love and deliver.

Chapter 11: "Lessons in Jewish Evangelism from the Past Century," by Mitch Glaser

Dr. Glaser's survey of Jewish missions in the past century places those missions in their social and political framework. He invites those of us who participate in modern missions to the Jews to learn from the creative strategies of those who came before as we meet the challenges of the twenty-first century. Dr. Glaser also calls upon the church to recommit itself to Jewish evangelism.

Chapter 12: "Jewish Evangelism in the New Millennium: The Missiological Dimension," by Arthur F. Glasser

Dr. Glasser examines Jesus' ministry of proclamation in the context of missiology, which he defines as "an inter-disciplinary branch of theology that involves all aspects of the human condition." In so doing, he stresses the uniqueness of Jewish missions and applies Jesus' own ministry to evangelism today.

Chapter 13: "The Ongoing Importance of Messianic Prophecy for Jewish Evangelism in the New Millennium," by Michael Rydelnik

Dr. Rydelnik builds a case to demonstrate the importance of Messianic prophecy to Jewish evangelism, arguing that it was crucial to Jesus of Nazareth, the apostles, the historic church, and modern Jewish missions. He also offers lessons for using Messianic prophecy in Jewish evangelism today.

Chapter 14: "One Way for Jews and Gentiles in the New Millennium," by Kai Kjær-Hansen

Dr. Kjær-Hansen explores the ramifications of the gospel proclamation for Jews and Gentiles, positing that if the gospel is not for the Jewish people, then it is also invalid for Gentiles. Along the way, he offers a historical overview and critique of two covenant theology.

Chapter 11

Lessons in Jewish Evangelism from the Past Century

MITCH GLASER

I remember when I first began the research for my dissertation. It was to be on the subject of missions to the Jews in Europe during the first half of the twentieth century. I started with the topic, "Missions to the Jews throughout the entire world during the entire century"! Yes, I was naive.

I thought I knew something about missions to the Jewish people, but I found that I knew very little. Jewish believers, missions to the Jews, and even Messianic congregations have a long history and a rich tradition. It's unfortunate, then, that very little of this exciting story of God's grace has been passed on to our post-Holocaust generation.

Eventually, I whittled down my study to "Missions to the Jews in continental Europe between 1890 and 1950." This was a more manageable topic for a few reasons. First, the greatest concentration of Jewish people to ever live in this century—almost 15 million—lived in continental Europe. The majority of mission efforts in the century were focused there. The major missions of the first half of the century were based there as well, and the majority of Jewish believers and missionaries to the Jewish people who ever lived were located there during that period of time. All that would change, however, after the Holocaust.

Certainly, the last fifty years and especially the last quarter century have been a period of growth in Jewish missions, especially in the United States. But even with all of the many Jewish people finding faith in Yeshua as Messiah these past three decades, pre-Holocaust levels of Jewish mission activity or pre-Holocaust numbers of Jewish believers have yet to be reached. If, then, we who are involved in today's missions to the Jews are to find sound advice, wise counsel, and helpful models for Jewish evangelism in the new millennium, we must look to this most fruitful period of our millennium—the first fifty years of the twentieth century.

The Last Millennium

We begin this study with a brief survey of Jewish missions prior to the twenty-first century. The development of missions to the Jews in the previous millennium is, in general, linked to the rise of the modern missionary movement. Alongside William Carey, Hudson Taylor, and many of the great missionary pioneers of the eighteenth and nineteenth centuries were missionaries to the Jews. It is difficult to identify any single, significant Jewish mission in the previous millennium, yet some mission efforts should be noted.

The work of German missionaries to the Jews, influenced by the Moravian movement and eighteenth-century Pietism, has recently been detailed in a dissertation by Christopher Clark, *The Politics of Conversion: Missionary Protestantism and the Jews in Prussia 1728–1941*.[1] Clark's work is based upon his primary resource material, once thought to have been lost to the Nazis but found in the archives of the Berlin Society for Promoting Christianity Among the Jews. Clark's findings are a good source of information about missions among German Jews prior to 1941, after which all missions were ordered closed by the government.

Pietist leaders August Hermann Francke, Philip Jakob Spiner, and Johann Heinrich Callenberg established the *Institutum Judaicum* at Halle. Established in 1728, this collaboration was more than a training institute. Callenberg not only trained missionaries, but also printed materials for Jewish evangelization and sent out missionaries to reach Jews. He had at least three full-time missionaries at most times, the majority of them being theological students.

They were well trained and were conversant both in Hebrew and Yiddish. Until the institute's demise following Callenberg's death in 1760, more than twenty missionaries served at least a year or two with him.[2] Other missions made efforts as well, but missionary work among the Jewish people was a rarity until the nineteenth century.

Reverend Joseph Samuel Christian Frey is considered the father of modern Jewish missions. A German Jew who accepted the Lord, Reverend Frey in 1809 started what is now known as the Church's Ministry Among the Jews (CMJ). This mission grew through the years, and by the turn of the century had hundreds of missionaries on its staff, serving in almost twenty nations around the globe.[3] Becoming Anglican in character, CMJ was joined by others, and by the turn of the century, missions to the Jews had originated from countries such as England, Scotland, Ireland, Germany, Finland, Denmark, Norway, Sweden, Holland, and others!

Missions to the Jews in North America were also initiated in the early nineteenth century—the earliest of which was also started by Frey. Various Lutheran synods, as well as Anglican/Episcopal, Presbyterians, and Methodist groups commissioned missionaries to the Jews. These denominational missions were joined by independent mission agencies such as the Chicago Hebrew Mission (1886), now AMFI, and the American Board of Missions to the Jews (1894), now called Chosen People Ministries. Dozens of missions to the Jews, in fact, existed by the turn of the twentieth century, with more than five hundred missionaries to the Jewish people serving throughout the world. The vast majority are, of course, no longer functioning.

The results of Jewish mission work in the nineteenth century was chronicled most effectively by Reverend J. F. de le Roi, missions historian and worker among the Jews in Holland.[4] Reverend de le Roi noted that there were more than two hundred thousand Jewish people who had come to know the Lord during the nineteenth century.

Many within the Jewish community simply discount these "conversions" as motivated by the desire for greater social acceptance and economic expediency. These criticisms, sometimes accepted uncritically by Jewish believers themselves, need to be reexamined. Evidence strongly suggests that many of those who embraced the gospel during the twentieth century did so out of pure religious conviction.

Lessons from the Past

We can derive many lessons from this period about the ways and means used by God to reach Jewish people with the gospel. We can emulate some of these lessons, while other lessons we can merely note and be aware of as we formulate our strategies.

Behind the scenes of mission activity, for example, was the hand of God. His guiding, orchestrating, and providentially weaving the tapestry of events would affect the receptivity of the Jewish people and, therefore, the strategy of the missionaries to the Jewish people. Thus, there is much to learn from the way in which the significant world events of the first half of the twentieth century had an impact on missions to the Jews. We cannot separate evangelism from its social, political, and economic context. We can safely assume that this will be true in this new millennium as well.

The Impact of World War I

The First World War wrought terrible circumstances upon innocent Jewish victims caught between ruthless, competing armies. Hundreds of thousands of Jewish people living in the battle zones of the First World War, particularly on the Eastern Front, were killed. The anti-Semitic tendencies of the soldiers afforded them the opportunity to conduct *pogroms* in the midst of their battles with the enemy.

Immigration, which intensified during this period, moved the Jewish population westward. Thus, the war had a great effect on missions to the Jews in Western Europe and the Americas, as these countries became the new home for thousands of new Jewish immigrants from the East. Missions in the West responded to the challenge of reaching these impoverished and more intensely religious Jews of Eastern Europe now immigrating in increasing numbers.[5]

World War I also created significant changes in geographic boundaries, which affected the Jewish community. The separation of Austria and Hungary, the establishment of Czechoslovakia and Yugoslavia, and the formation of the USSR all had a transforming impact on the Jewish populations of the region.[6]

The missions survived World War I, but required time to rebuild their ministries. They had to adapt to changes in national bound-aries, the immigration of Jewish people to new areas, and particu-larly the movement of Eastern European Jews to Western nations. Yet the impact of World War I on missions to the Jews was minimal compared to the next war, which would alter the face of missions to the Jews forever.

The Impact of the Russian Revolution

The combined numbers of Jews in Russia and Poland was more than ten million. Therefore, anything that affected these countries would greatly impact the Jewish community and missions to the Jews. Missionary work was never easy in these areas during the first half of the twentieth century, even under the czar in Russia. It was a closed country, both politically and religiously, and the Orthodox Church had a tremendous influence on the government. Thus, it was very difficult for the Mildmay Mission to the Jews (MMJ), for example, to establish missionary work in Russia. Instead, they hired *colporteurs* to sell Bibles in bookshops through a relationship with the National Bible Society. This turned out to be a fruitful ministry and was the only way the MMJ could operate in Russia.

The most accurate figures, however, suggest that there were no more than twenty missionaries to the Jews in all of the former Soviet Union at any given time during the century. This would be far less than the entire staffs of the Bucharest station, or even the Warsaw station of the CMJ. Russia, the Ukraine, Belorussia, and Bessarabia (which became part of Romania) had been hostile to-ward mission efforts throughout their history, but the creation of a Communist-atheist nation ended what little efforts were left.

During the post-Revolution war between White and Red Russia, hundreds of thousands of innocent Jewish people were killed sim-ply because they were in the proximity of the fighting. Since both White and Red Russians hated the Jews, they often conducted *po-groms* and killed Jewish people living in the fields of battle.[7]

Messianic congregations in Odessa and Kiev underwent diffi-cult times, then entirely ceased to exist. The congregational leaders of these works, Leon Rosenberg and Peter Goroditch, often com-plained of the hardships that communities experienced during this period. Many believers, like their national counterparts, died of starvation in the midst of the Communist takeover. Within a few years after the Revolution, missions to the Jews within Russia and the Ukraine came to a ruthless end.[8]

The Impact of World War II

It is difficult to describe the impact of World War II upon the Jewish people and, therefore, upon missions to the Jews. The entirety of Europe was the scene of the greatest devastation and destruction ever to overtake a Jewish community. By the end of the war, the Jewish populations of these countries were a mere remnant of what they had been prior to the Holocaust. The Jews of this region were reduced by more than six million persons, and the survivors had scattered throughout the West. Hundreds of thousands spent months and even years in displaced persons' camps, where missionaries did have a measure of a ministry to them.[9] But from there the Jewish people moved on to Israel, the Americas, and to nations spanning the globe.

World War II also wrought inestimable damage to Jewish missions. The war brought with it the destruction of Jewish communities in Eastern Europe, which is where most of the major Jewish missions focused their efforts during the first half of the twentieth century. The properties of CMJ in Poland and Romania were destroyed. Arnold Frank's hospital—a great work established by the Irish Presbyterian Church in Hamburg—as well as his vocational center and chapel were taken over by the German army near the end of the war and almost fully destroyed. Those missionaries who were not martyred had to flee for their lives. Entire Messianic congregations, like the one established by the martyred Isaac Feinstein in Jassy, Romania, were decimated.[10]

This destruction of the Messianic Jewish community in Europe had implications not only there, but worldwide as well, as so many of the missionaries and leaders among the Jewish believers had come from this region. Essentially, an entire generation of young leaders was killed either in the war or in the death camps.[11]

The Holocaust also caused the destruction of a certain invaluable type of Jewish believer and leader. Yiddish speakers who were steeped in the Talmud and rabbinic writings, once so common among the Jewish believers of Europe, became a rarity within a few short years. An entire generation of Messianic Jews was, in fact, wiped out in the concentration camps. This devastating loss greatly impacted missions to the Jews throughout the remainder of the century, as it would reduce the level of Jewish scholarship available within the Jewish missions community.

The death and destruction of the war and the Holocaust afforded opportunities, however, for the missionaries to the Jews. Demonstrating kindness, compassion, and even heroism, they were active in rescue and relief during this terrible time. The Swedish Israel Mission, for example, served as a center for helping Jewish people escape the Nazis. Between 1938 and 1940, thousands of Jewish people escaped the possibility of extermination because of the efforts of the Swedish mission and of other missions as well, especially in Vienna.[12]

The dedication of some of the missionaries serving in Europe, however, cost them their lives. The generation of missionaries who served so effectively in the first third of the century in Europe are examples to us all of faith and courage in the face of impending martyrdom. Missionaries like Isaac Feinstein and John Rottenberg, Bazyli Jocz and many others have now become part of the cloud of witnesses (see Heb. 12). That great throng shall always exemplify to future generations of missionaries the true meaning of taking up the cross and following the Messiah, irrespective of personal cost.

By the postwar period, all organized mission work to the Jews ceased entirely. Missions to the Jews had already become impossible in Russia and the Ukraine, but after the expansion of the USSR, Romania, Hungary, and the smaller countries of Europe where numbers of Jews remained became inaccessible.

The persecution of Jewish believers in Romania by the Communists ultimately led that community to settle in Israel. This group had a considerable impact upon the Jewish believing community of Haifa, in particular, where many of them immigrated.

The greatest hindrance to the gospel as a result of World War II was that the mission agencies were no longer able to operate in the USSR and its satellites. And so missions to the Jews in that part of the world ceased to exist until Perestroika.

Jewish Social Conditions and Receptivity to the Gospel

While effects of these major world events had an impact on missions to the Jews, several social and economic conditions of Europe also influenced the response of Jewish people to the gospel. The first is anti-Semitism. The state of the Jewish people, and missions to the Jews in particular, in the first half of the twentieth century cannot be understood without taking into consideration the effect of anti-Semitism upon European Jewry. As a result of anti-Semitism, conditions prior to the Holocaust were wretched for the Jewish people. This manifested itself in every sphere of life, from academic and professional quotas, to a lack of legal status, to outright attacks by Gentiles against Jews.

Yet the terrible social conditions caused by anti-Semitism resulted in many Jewish people turning to Jesus.[13] This is a mystery, as the blame for the anti-Semitism was often laid at the feet of Christianity. Yet somehow, perhaps through the testimony of the missionaries, thousands of Jewish people were able to discern the difference between those who *claimed* to be Christians and others who through their authenticity demonstrated they *were* Christians.

The Jewish community interpreted this phenomenon differently, claiming that those Jews who embraced Christianity did so to escape the conditions brought about by anti-Semitism. Perhaps this was true for some, but it is highly doubtful this assertion is true of the majority, as many of the Jewish people who found faith in Jesus also suffered as Jews. In a mysterious way, the evil of anti-Semitism actually drove many Jewish people to Jesus.

A second influence on Jewish receptivity to the gospel was the increase of secularization and assimilation. During the first half of the twentieth century, the effects of the Enlightenment continued to work their way through the Jewish communities of Europe.[14] Liberation from the ghettos of Europe presented Jewish people with ideological and spiritual choices. Communism, socialism, Zionism, Reform Judaism, Christianity, and secularism were now all options to embrace.

Secularization and assimilation did create a climate of greater receptivity to the gospel, as ties to the more traditional forms of Judaism were loosened. On the other hand, a diminishment in the traditional understanding of the Scriptures and of God rendered the Jewish community more challenging to reach. Assimilation itself did not lead Jewish people to become Christians, although it may have opened the minds of some to new ideas. Nor did becoming a Christian lead to assimilation, as many of the Jewish believers also formed Messianic congregations and identified as Jews.

Thus, believing in Jesus did not cause Jewish believers to forgo their Jewish identity. The Jewish believers, in fact, clearly maintained community ties, observed Jewish holidays, and identified as Jews. Further, it cannot be substantiated that they received any earthly benefit for accepting Jesus as their Messiah. If anything was to be demonstrated in this vein, it was that Jewish believers in Jesus tended to resist assimilation more than some other Jews, as they believed their identity was rooted in God and Scriptures and therefore not to be denied, but affirmed.

A third impact on Jewish receptivity to the gospel was immigration. One of the most profound responses of the Jewish communities to the severe economic and social conditions of Europe was to migrate in search of better conditions elsewhere. The immigrants usually migrated west—some as far as Germany. Many others migrated to England, Canada, the United States, Argentina, and other countries. Between 1880 and 1920, more than two million Jewish people, mostly from Russia and Poland (the Pale of Settlement), immigrated to the United States.

The history of missions to the Jews in the first half of the twentieth century is dominated by the role and response of Jewish immigrants and those who were committed to reaching these Jewish immigrants with the gospel. Immigrants are often more open to the gospel than others who remain in their own communities. This was true of the Jews as well. Many of the Jewish people whom Arnold Frank led to the Lord in Hamburg were Russian and Polish Jews who had immigrated to Hamburg, a port city, as they passed by on their way to North America. An effective, ongoing ministry was conducted by CMJ in Liverpool, as Jews from Eastern Europe were coming off the ships between the wars.

The immigration of the Russian and Polish Jews in particular allowed the missionaries to minister not only to the spiritual needs of these people, but to their physical needs as well. They did an effective job of establishing homes for travelers as well as vocational training centers for the new settlers. The missionaries were able to demonstrate Christian charity, establishing soup kitchens and administering relief to Jewish people at that time.

The missions in the United States, including Chosen People Ministries, grew through the influx of immigrants, who became the founders of missions as well as the majority of the workers.

The majority of the postwar leaders in Jewish work were those who heard the gospel in Europe and had survived the Holocaust.

Great missionary scholars like Jakób Jocz,[15] Rachmiel Frydland, and Victor Buksbazen of Poland produced a legacy of fruitful years of ministry in Europe. Rachmiel Frydland, who accepted salvation in Warsaw before the war, was typical of a breed of Holocaust hardened survivors: tough, gentle, patient, and scholarly. God significantly used Frydland in the post-Holocaust Messianic renewal movement that began in 1967.[16] Others, like Leon Rosenberg of Russia and Poland, began new mission organizations in America.

A Resurgence of Success Between the Wars

The widespread sowing of the gospel seed saw periodic seasons of harvest throughout the century, but nothing that could compare with the numbers of Jewish people who became believers in Jesus between the wars. This movement was well known and considered viable by the most distinguished and respected mission leaders of that time. In the early 1930s, in the article "Jews Become Christians," Reverend John Stewart Conning quoted Sir Leon Levison, president of the International Hebrew Christian Alliance, regarding the numbers of Jews who were coming to the Lord in the twentieth century:

> According to Levison's research, 97,000 Jews in Hungary alone accepted the Christian faith; in Vienna 17,000; in Poland 35,000; and in Bolshevik Russia 60,000 Jews became Christians. We also found Jews turning to Christ in Germany, Sweden and Denmark. Not a few have done likewise in Britain. In America, careful estimate places the number of Christians of the Jewish race at no less than 20,000.[17]

Therefore, the number of Jews who became Christians during the first third of the twentieth century may have been upward of 230,000—far more than the 224,000 Jews during the nineteenth century mentioned by Reverend J. F. de le Roi. These figures are staggering. Since they can be corroborated in report after report from various sources, including those of the Jewish community itself, one cannot but affirm the integrity of these figures. The

Jewish community attempts to discredit this movement by inter-posing ignoble motives upon those Jews who confessed Jesus as their Messiah and Lord. These attempts were to be expected and would continue throughout the century in every decade and in ev-ery land. Even Hugh Schonfeld, a prominent British Jewish author who at one time had been a professing Christian (but when he wrote the following had already rejected the gospel), wrote,

> Revolutions swept away ghettos as well as dynas-ties. For many Jews, the freedom to choose their own lifestyle led to atheistic Communism, and for others, to nominal Christianity; 97,000 joined the Church in Hungary; 17,000 in Austria; 35,000 in Poland; 60,000 in Russia; 20,000 in America.[18]

Finally, the International Review of Missions reported a decade later:

> The work of various denominations for the Jews is also having its effect. More than 100,000 Jews in Eastern Europe since the war have entered the Christian church. While political influences in these lands have doubtless played an important part in the conversions reported, due recognition must also be given to the preparatory work of Christian teachers and evangelists whose self-denying service opened a way for the public acknowledgment of a change of faith. In other lands, especially in the West, many Jews dissatisfied with Judaism are find-ing the answer to their deepest longings in the faith of Christ. In America, at least 20,000 Jews are now connected to various Christian churches.[19]

The obvious conclusion is that the number of Jewish people professing Jesus during this period was extraordinary.

The End of the Movement

As stated, the wholesale slaughter of Jewish people by the Nazis closed the chapter on missions to the Jews in Continental Europe.[20]

The rise of Communism brought its full demise.[21] Certainly there were some continued efforts, mostly among the survivors of the Holocaust, but the great movement of Jewish people who came to believe in Jesus had ended with the destruction of European Jewry.

What the Holocaust and Communism did not do, more liberal views of theology did. The major denominations generally lost interest in Jewish evangelism as strains of universalism and the dual covenant theory seeped into the teaching of many Christian groups. By the 1950s, missions to the Jews, although filled with enthusiasm over the establishment of Israel, was in a post-Holocaust decline, which would not be reversed until the turning to the Messiah of young, Jewish people during the "Jesus movement."

Factors of Success

We must ask the question, *What led to the success of Jewish missions efforts during the first fifty years of the century?* We have already determined that great world events, along with the social and political conditions experienced by the Jews of Europe, created a climate that caused many Jewish people to be open to the gospel. Yet as noted from the start, these factors were beyond the control of the missionaries and churches involved. All they could do was respond. But what did the missionaries do that would provide lessons for those of us who are concerned with Jewish evangelism today? This is the question we now turn to.

Missions to the Jews Supported by the Church
Were More Effective

During the first fifty years of the century, the state churches of Europe were more warmly evangelical and had a desire to win Jewish people to the Messiah. The missions from Great Britain, serving so faithfully in Eastern and Western Europe, were primarily Anglican[22] or part of the Church of Scotland.[23] Others originated from the Church of Ireland and the state churches of Norway, Sweden, Denmark, and Finland.

Many Jews, upon accepting Jesus, found a spiritual home in conventional Protestant churches. The Reformed Church of Hungary undoubtedly included more Jewish believers than did any of the Messianic congregations in Europe. Jewish believers also found warm fellowship in the Polish Reformed and Baptist churches, the Brethren churches of Czechoslovakia, and many others. Jewish believers were also educated for the ministry in Protestant seminaries.

Evangelicals today do not appreciate the influence and power a state church or major denomination can have when missionary programs are specifically directed toward the Jewish people. Jewish missions today is primarily the work of independent agencies and not mission agencies attached to national church bodies or major denominations. Strong church support is likely one reason why there were a greater number of missionaries to the Jews and more Jewish believers during the first half of this century. The national church bodies seemed to have far greater resources available to them to reach Jewish people than the independent groups have available today. Certainly our growing evangelical church bodies have a lot to offer in the evangelization of the Jewish people, yet there are few groups that maintain this emphasis.

Weaknesses did exist at times in the past. The state church mission structures in Jewish communities, for example, inadvertently sought to impose a British, Scandinavian, German, or Scottish culture upon the Jewish people. This imposition was sometimes counterproductive and lacked sensitivity. Yet the historical data shows that to accuse the national church bodies that conducted mission work among the Jews of ineffectiveness or cultural imperialism is unwarranted. Actually, it would be a great boon to Jewish missions today if larger denominations and national church bodies would once again take up the torch of missions to the Jews.

Missions to the Jews That Contextualized the Message Were More Effective

Missions that contextualized the gospel most effectively were the most successful. Many of the missionaries to the Jews during this period were Jewish believers themselves. Some of the Gentile leaders, such as J. H. Adeney, were quite knowledgeable about Jewish culture and history, and could even be considered authorities on Jewish life in Eastern Europe.[24] Adeney was particularly sensitive to the spiritual needs of Jewish people and provided a contextualized approach to Jewish nonbelievers. He offered the same approach, too, in the development of a discipleship program and worship for Jewish believers. His reports testify to this sensitivity, as it would have been a rare year when he did not have Jewish High Holiday services or a number of Passover celebrations.

The missionaries of this period also struggled to stay current with changes within the Jewish community. Both secularism and Zionism produced great challenges, which was reflected in the development of literature. As the century progressed, evangelistic literature was developed to reach both. The literature distributed for the secular and more assimilated Jews of Russia, Poland, Hungary, Germany, Austria, and France was quite different than that produced to reach the more religious Yiddish or Ladino speakers.

The answer regarding whether it is appropriate and effective for missions to the Jews to contextualize the gospel is clear. Those who did contextualize, irrespective of how they expressed themselves, were more effective in reaching the Jewish community and maintaining a testimony. Those who did not encourage a contextualized approach to evangelism were far less fruitful.

Missions to the Jews That Encouraged Jewish Identity Were More Effective

Missionaries to the Jews who affirmed the Jewish identity of Jewish believers seemed to be more successful. The Jewish holidays were celebrated as a very natural expression of identity and a valuable means to preserve Jewish life, heritage, and values. Mission reports were filled with descriptions of the ways in which the missionaries and believers celebrated the events of the Jewish calendar.

The debate continues today over how a Jewish believer in Jesus should maintain his or her Jewish identity and allegiances. But missions that in the past encouraged the ongoing lifestyle of the Jewish believers were far more productive over the course of the years.

Missions to the Jews That Started Messianic Congregations Were More Effective

Most missions to the Jews, whether independent or attached to a national church body, established Messianic congregations. These assemblies were of primarily Jewish believers in Jesus who worshiped within a Jewish context, their existence usually a signal of successful missionary work. The validity of starting Messianic congregations in Europe was not, in fact, debated. Congregational planting was part of a holistic approach to missions by missionaries to the Jews. These congregations, all quite different, were established to meet the needs of the Jewish believers and were, for many of the missionaries, one aspect of their attempt to contextualize the gospel for the Jewish people.

Numerous examples of these congregations were planted by both church related and independent congregations. Among those congregations was one outside of Bucharest led by Isaac Feinstein, who worked with the Norwegian Israel Mission; the congregation of Peter Goroditch in Kiev, who served with the Barbican Mission to the Jews; the congregation started by Leon Rosenberg in Odessa and Lodz, Poland; and congregations in Constantinople and Hungary. Arnold Frank established a congregation in Hamburg as part of the Church of Ireland, and the United Church of Scotland established congregations in Constantinople and Hungary. Planting Messianic congregations was consistent with the strategy of the missions in Israel and North Africa as well.

The congregations were also created to meet the challenge of helping Jewish believers maintain their Jewish identity and, in particular, to provide training for the children. The liturgy, language, and customs of these congregations varied, depending on the region, and the church or missions structure to which they were attached. The Warsaw congregation, for example, affiliated with London Jews Society, an independent Anglican mission, was somewhat "Anglican" in flavor. One would expect that they would have been "less Jewish" in their expression, but their services were in Yiddish. Their leaders were Jewish believers who were quite learned in the Talmud and other rabbinic Jewish traditions, and their services were sometimes more liturgical. The Scandinavian missions also tended to be very sensitive to Jewish believers. Magnes Solheim, who served in Romania, began two Messianic congregations. He led one himself in Bucharest and the other was led by Isaac Feinstein in Jassy. Solheim was beloved by the Jewish believers, eventually leading to Israel those who survived the Holocaust and the Communist aggression in Romania. Once there, he helped them resettle.

Lessons for the New Millennium

Many lessons can be learned, then, from the past millennium and, in particular, the first half of last century. These lessons might help missions and missionaries to the Jews become more effective in the future.

The Need for a Renewed Commitment by the Church to Jewish Missions

Missions to the Jews were most fruitful when and where the church supported their activities. This kind of support needs to be reemphasized around the world and particularly in North America, where our larger and more influential evangelical churches, missions, and denominations must renew their commitment to Jewish missions. Few denominations and world mission agencies today have any type of specific mission to the Jewish people, and there is no reason why this should be the case. Churches in North America support missions to the Muslims, Chinese, Hindu, university students, and a host of other people groups. Missions to the Jews today have become the great omission of the Great Commission described in Matthew 29:19–20. Why is it that most major missions, both independent and denominational, do not maintain work among the Jewish people? It is time for this to change.

Some concern for Jewish missions have emerged in recent years among Southern Baptists, Missouri Synod Lutherans, and the Assemblies of God. No group, however, has demonstrated the level of commitment to the Jewish people that was prevalent during the first half of the preceding century. Our evangelical leaders and churches must once again become persuaded of the truth of Romans 1:16, and deploy personnel and resources in fulfillment of this apostolic mission.

This renewed conviction for missions to the Jews will not happen, of course, in a vacuum. Messianic Jews and those in the Jewish missions community must cultivate the involvement of larger church bodies as well as that of individual local churches. Standing aloof in our public and personal identification with the greater body of the Messiah will do nothing but alienate those whom God has called to make the Jewish people jealous with the gospel (Rom. 11:11). Let us together seize the future of outreach among God's ancient people.

The Need for a Renewed Commitment to Faithfulness and Endurance

It has been shown that the gospel bears greater fruit when there has been long-term missionary activity. And whereas we cannot control the social and cultural conditions that in the past lead to greater receptivity—only God can—we can remain faithful in our proclamation, without which there will be no harvest. We must encourage one another to keep sowing the gospel seed even where there is great difficulty and hardness of heart. We cannot give up hope that the Lord will save the Orthodox, Hasidic, or the more unresponsive secular Jews of North America. We must keep preaching, even when there is little fruit.

We have not seen a harvest in Israel, although many Russian Jewish immigrants have accepted the Lord in cities from Haifa to Tel Aviv. It is a growing movement, but still on the periphery of the more secular and Orthodox Israeli core. Thus, we have yet to see the harvest described in Paul's words to the Roman believers, "And so all Israel will be saved" (Rom. 11:25–26 NIV). We must be faithful to preach the gospel in season and out of season so that one day, with great patience, a major harvest will come.

Patience and perseverance is also needed in areas like New York City and London, where there has not been a sizeable harvest among the Jewish people in recent decades. Yet we know that "faith comes by hearing, and hearing by the word of God" (Rom. 10:17 NKJV). Therefore, in light of the history and teaching of this verse, we must be faithful in our preaching through all circumstances.

Missionaries of the previous century persevered through unfathomable difficulties: two world wars, the rise of Bolshevism, the strangling influence of growing secularism, and the terrible conditions in Europe prior to the Holocaust. The cruelty perpetrated by anti-Semitism alone could have discouraged the missionaries to the point of their ceasing missionary endeavors. Yet the missionaries to the Jews continued their work, although the loss of property, funds, and young leadership was most devastating.

Today, there may be as many as 125,000 Jewish believers worldwide. That number is few compared to Hungary alone prior to World War II, when more than 90,000 Jewish people became believers.[25] Yet God is faithful and, according to the words of Paul in Romans 11:5, a remnant of Jewish people are prepared by God to receive his Son: "Even so then, at this present time there is a remnant according to the election of grace" (NKJV). We must continue on with enthusiasm, knowing that the Lord of the harvest will be faithful to his people and promises. A harvest will indeed come.

The Need for a Renewed Commitment to Contextualization

The growing Messianic congregational movement in North America is evidence of the importance of contextualizing the gospel. The modern Messianic movement is trying to envelop the gospel in Jewish thought and practice, which should not be difficult considering that the gospel is Jewish in origin. Some actually prefer the term *recontextualizing* the gospel, contending that the gospel was first preached in a Jewish context. The point is well taken.

And yet one must wonder how we will need to contextualize or recontextualize the gospel for the Jewish people of the new millennium. Consider, though, how missionaries to the Jews in the first half of the twentieth century did so. Who, after all, could have predicted the development of Reform or Conservative Judaism? Who would have predicted the challenges that would arise as a result of these fundamental changes in the structure of the Jewish religion? Who would have thought that there would be Jewish people who do not keep the Sabbath and who believe that the Law did not come down from Sinai but from man? Who could have predicted the degree of Jewish immigration in the twentieth century and the effect it would have on Jewish community life around the world? What seer among us would have been able to predict the Holocaust and the shifting of the Jewish communities of Europe? The Scriptures speak of a regathering of the Jewish people to the land of Israel and of the reconstitution of the national entity under the leadership of the Messiah. Yet who could have predicted the events of 1948 and the establishment of Israel as a nation?

How, then, will we respond to future trends? Most of what in North America is described as indigenous or contextualized, for example, is related primarily to a form of Ashkenazic Judaism that is fading. The roots of this cultural expression were cruelly cut off by the Holocaust, and we are living on memories of days gone by. There will be no replenishment for Ashkenazic Judaism. Thus, rest assured that Judaism and the religious expression of the Jewish people will change significantly in the next millennium—should the Lord tarry. If you doubt it, just read a new book titled *Generation J*,[26] or Alan Dershowitz's new book *The Vanishing American Jew*.[27]

How, too, will we respond to trends of increased intermarriage, increased secularization, and a decreasing population growth? We must stay abreast of shifting demographics as the missionaries of our previous generation did so well. We need more missionaries like Adeney, students of Jewish life and culture, who are able to predict changes in the Jewish community that will impact our strategies and methods.

Missionaries to the Jews in the past sought to discover new models for mission activity as immigration, the Holocaust, and the rise of Communism transformed the landscape of missions to the Jews. The majority of missionaries to the Jews in the first half of the century were based in Europe, and the majority in the second half are in North America. Where will the major forces of missionaries to the Jews be deployed in the next millennium? Based upon history, and primarily because of the nature of the Jewish community, those forces may well be deployed in yet another place.

The establishment of the nation of Israel, for example, might play a major role in this change. The Jewish population of Israel will keep growing, and this tiny nation must become the site of dominant mission activity in the future, surpassing the United States and all other countries in the Diaspora. What will be the implications of missions being based in Israel? Missionaries will need to learn Hebrew. Ways and means of support must be developed, since the national church bodies in Israel are generally young and still require support from the Diaspora.

We should also continue our attention to opportunities around the world in reaching Jewish immigrants. Any significant movement of a Jewish population warrants careful attention by missionaries who implement strategy for reaching Jewish immigrants for Jesus. Such attention and strategic implementation has proven successful in recent years among the Russian Jews, and we do not know who might be next. We must be ready to act when the time comes.

We don't know what the future holds; what we do know is that it will be changing. The Jewish community is changing in so many ways—culturally, ideologically, and geographically. We must contextualize with more thought and focus, making certain that our very contextualization does not date us. We must be flexible to meet the ongoing and changing needs of the Jewish community in the name of our Messiah. Missions to the Jews must be well informed of Jewish cultural and religious trends, and, by necessity, must be malleable in the implementation of strategy.

Conclusion: The Future of Missions to the Jews

How will missions to the Jews change in the days to come? These missions will need to better cooperate in evangelism, sharing materials and resources in the training of each other's missionaries. Stronger and more committed partnerships need to be developed between the various missions to the Jews, which are today mostly independent and larger church bodies. Such a partnership will demand flexibility from all of those involved and a willingness to sacrifice certain institutional goals for the sake of the kingdom of God.

We must also give way to a new generation of leaders. Many of them will be from among the Russian Jewish immigrants and the Israelis, as today's population of Jewish people and Messianic Jews grows in Israel. Today's leaders must select and train tomorrow's, empowering them in particular to discover their own financial and organizational resources to do the work of Jewish missions.

The development of Messianic congregations will also continue to increase around the world. Christianity grows person by person and community by community. This is no different for Jews as it is for Koreans, African Americans, Chinese, and many other ethnic groups. Messianic congregations are not an attempt to rebuild the wall of partition or separate Jews from their Gentile brothers and sisters—it is the natural course of fruitful evangelism among the Jewish people who started these congregations. Once again, we need to look back as we move forward. Language and cultural issues surrounding the growth of Russian Jewish congregations, the suburbanization of the Jewish communities in North America, and the growth of the Messianic movement in Israel all contribute to an increase in Messianic congregations. These congregations, though, will certainly not be exclusively Jewish, but a place where Jewish and Gentile believers can build a Messianic community through evangelistic efforts.

Communities of faith will spring up whether we "plant" them or not. Messianic congregations are not new at all and starting Jewish or Messianic congregations was, in fact, the intentional strategy of the major missions, denominational works, and national church bodies in the early twentieth century. These cultural, ideological, and geographic changes in the Jewish communities around the world will also increase the numbers of those believers' becoming part of local evangelical churches. These same changes will mean that more and more Gentile believers will be able to reach Jewish people with the gospel.

The Jewish ghettos of Europe are now gone for the foreseeable future. Therefore, training the church around the world in reaching Jewish people with the gospel is of the utmost importance. Such outreach must become a matter of strategic and intentional effort on the part of missions to the Jewish people, especially as these missions partner with major national church bodies.

Thus, as we embark on a new millennium, I have written this chapter with hope for a new day in missions to the Jews—a day marked by cooperation between Jew and Gentile, between church and mission, and between mission and mission. It is my prayer that missions to the Jews will not only return to the greatness enjoyed prior to the Holocaust, but surpass all expectations and dreams until the morning star dawns when we witness the fulfillment of Paul's words, "And so all Israel will be saved" (Rom. 11:26 NIV).

Chapter 12

Jewish Evangelism in the New Millennium

The Missiological Dimension

ARTHUR F. GLASSER

By now, readers of this current volume are doubtless quite con-vinced that the missionary mandate Jesus gave to his people to "make disciples of all nations" includes the Jewish people. This chapter approaches Jewish evangelism from the demanding per-spective of missiology.

What is missiology? Missiology refers to all that is involved in crossing frontiers to proclaim the gospel to the various peoples of the world. It is an interdisciplinary branch of theology that in-volves all aspects of the human condition: a people's ancestry and environment, their history and culture, religious heritage, and pos-sible sense of mission to outsiders. Particular attention is given in this chapter to the differences as well as the commonalities of the various people with whom this witness is to be shared. Our specific objective, however, is to review the basic missiological elements involved in encouraging Jewish people to respond to the one and only uncreated God, who acted redemptively on their behalves through his Son, Jesus the Messiah, their coming King.

Mission to the Jewish People: Its Uniqueness

The Christian mission to the Jewish people is unique. It is especially so when encountering the realities of witnessing to Jews contrasted with all other frontier-crossing mission encounters in the world today. First, Judaism and Christianity are crowded with commonalities, which, paradoxically, greatly complicates the mission task. Second, Judaism—as well as other non-Christian religions—disagree with Christians about who Jesus was. At the same time, though, a third reality is that no other missionary task facing the church today is so advantaged by unexpected assistance, which God has granted to all Messianic Jews and Gentile Christians who seek to witness to the Jewish people. An important part of this advantage is the fourth reality—the evangelistic model of Jesus, the Originator of missions to the Jews. Let us begin with a brief review of these several realities.

First: Basic Commonalities of Jews and Christians

Both communities of faith—Jewish and Christian—acknowledge the same one, uncreated God. He is the God of creation (he created the heavens and the earth), of revelation (he discloses himself, and his will to his people), and of redemption (he delivers his people from their bondage to sin, Satan, and death). He is particularly the God of promise and of story (his purpose for Israel and all peoples will come to glorious consummation).

It follows, then, that both communities are agreed as to the unique authority of the Old Testament as the Word of God. Nor did Jesus ever question its divine authority or contradict it in the least. Hence, both are agreed that God—based upon his eternal purpose and without human consultation—made a succession of covenants with the Jewish people.[1]

First established was the *Abrahamic* covenant, through which God displayed his particular love for this one people. He called them into his service, set them apart from all other peoples, and gave them a particular land in the Middle East. Most central, he told them that his all-embracing purpose was that they were to be his means for blessing all the families of the earth (Gen. 12:1–3). Second came the *Mosaic* covenant, through which God revealed to Israel the essence of his holiness, the reality of their fallenness, and the consequent gulf separating himself from them. Even so, through grace he set before them the possibility of personal relationship with himself. He gave commandments defining their particular lifestyle and described the worship that alone would be acceptable to him. Third was the *Davidic* covenant, in which he promised Israel that a Son of David would achieve the world's redemption, become Israel's Messianic King, and be the means whereby a believing remnant would carry to completion the fundamental purpose of the Abrahamic covenant.

By his faithfulness to these three immutable covenants, the living God committed himself to exercise sovereign control over the direction of human history. He would bring everything to glorious consummation despite the sinfulness of human beings, the tragedy of Israel's repeated failure over the centuries, and the constant opposition of Satan. These two communities of faith—Jewish and Christian—are deeply persuaded that God will be faithful to all that he promised to Abraham, buttressed and amplified by these other two covenants. The key to everything would be the Messiah of Israel, the Redeemer and Savior of the world.

It has long been the practice of missions to the Jewish people to confine the task almost totally to showing how Jesus unambiguously fulfilled certain particular prophecies in the Old Testament concerning himself, the Messiah. Yet, of the total number of Messianic Jewish people, only a relatively small percentage has actually come to faith through this procedure. Perhaps this small number is due to the way in which Jews have been conditioned to use Scripture, making its study a meritorious duty but not perceiving that its primary function is to focus beyond itself to the Messiah and his total achievement of God's redemptive purpose in the earth (John 5:38–40).

Considering the emphasis of missions on prophecy, it is both surprising and significant that only after Jesus' resurrection from the dead do we find that he particularly and comprehensively stressed these Messianic prophecies. "O foolish men, and slow of heart to believe all that the prophets have spoken! Was it not necessary that the [Messiah] should suffer these things and enter into his glory?" Luke then summarizes, "Beginning with Moses and all the prophets, he interpreted to them in all the scriptures the things concerning himself" (24:25–27 RSV). The disciples reacted as though they were suddenly overtaken by a greatly enlarged understanding of the substance of the Hebrew Scriptures. They said to one another, "Did not our hearts burn within us while he talked to us on the road, while he opened to us the scriptures?" (v. 32). Later, Jesus enlarged this same instruction with all his disciples: "These are my words which I spoke to you, while I was still with you, that everything written about me in the law of Moses and the prophets and the psalms must be fulfilled" (v. 44).

On this occasion Luke comments, "He opened their minds to understand the scriptures" (v. 45). We should conclude from Luke's comment that as one's relation to Jesus is deepened through careful and consistent study of the Old Testament, there develops an increasing awareness of the full meaning of the redemptive purpose of God. Suffice it to say, then, generally speaking, all Christians should ponder the substance and context of all key Messianic passages from Genesis to Malachi. The occasion may arise, after all, for mentioning this one or that one in discussions with Jewish people.

It is common, though, that new believers, only after their having come to faith in Jesus as their Lord and Savior, find their subsequent study of the Old Testament increasingly opens their minds to its God-intended function—to bear witness to the Messiah. Indeed, nothing is so confirming to one's faith as to meet the Lord in surprising and often unexpected ways through pondering the Messianic promises scattered throughout the Pentateuch, the Prophets, and the Writings.

Thus, the focus of this chapter is *not* on the use of Messianic prophecies and their fulfillment in Jesus, but on describing a missiological approach to Jewish evangelism more in harmony with the total flow of God's universal promise to Abraham. With regard to this flow, I'm greatly indebted to Dr. Walter C. Kaiser Jr. for bringing to my attention a profound statement included in an address delivered at Princeton almost a century ago by Dr. Willis J. Beecher, a prominent biblical scholar in that day. Dr. Beecher's concern was to summarize the connection between the Old and New Testaments. After describing the prevailing note in both as "a multitude of specifications unfolding a single promise, the promise serving as a central religious doctrine," Dr. Beecher reduced this to the following biblical generalization: "God gave a promise to Abraham, and through him to all mankind, a promise eternally fulfilled and fulfilling in the history of Israel; and chiefly fulfilled in Jesus the Messiah, he being that which is principal in the history of Israel" (1905). We are all indebted to Walter Kaiser for his continuing service to the Messianic Jewish movement in our day, largely through his writings on Old Testament themes and particularly for his elaboration of Beecher's great statement in relation to Jewish evangelism in Kaiser's book *Toward an Old Testament Theology*.[2]

Second: Critical Disagreements over Jesus

Although the great issue dividing Judaism and Christianity is the identity of Jesus Christ, an unexpected complexity arises in the ways in which he is regarded. On the one hand, informed members in both communities are agreed that in his life and social conduct he exhibited moral truth "at its purest and best."[3] Let me repeat: the ethical and cultural dimensions of Jesus provoke no hostility, but rather admiration among informed members of both communities. Indeed, I know of no knowledgeable Jewish person who does not grant the depth and sanity of his moral teaching, and the manner in which he truly embodied it in his life. Wherever Jesus went he drew the crowds. Although he was primarily concerned to proclaim "the good news of the kingdom," he never omitted the least act of kindness to any in need. The poor, the disadvantaged, the sick, the dying, the leprous, the demonic, the lame, the blind— all were the objects of his love and care. And as for his Jewishness, no less a revered Jewish scholar than Rabbi Leo Baeck stated,

> In the ancient Gospel there stands before us a man with noble traits, who during tumultuous tension-filled days in the land of the Jews lived, helped, worked, endured and died, a man of the Jewish people, who walked in Jewish ways, in Jewish faith and hope. . . . We see in this ancient tradition a man before us who shows forth the form of Judaism in all the lines and features of his being in which the pure essence of Judaism is so authentically, so clearly revealed, a man who, as what he was, could have come forth only from the soil of Judaism, and it is only from this soil that his disciples and followers could have been recruited as they were.[4]

Yet, on the other hand, this same Jesus was rejected by the Jewish leaders and put to death through the compliance of the Romans. Why? Was it because of the jealousy and fear he engendered within the leaders of Jewry's religious and political establishments? Yes, to a degree. We read in the gospel of John that the judgment of the officials in the Sanhedrin was, "If we let him go on thus, every one will believe in him, and the Romans will come and destroy our holy place and our nation" (11:48 RSV). And in another place, "The Pharisees said to one another: 'You see that we can do nothing; look, the world has gone after him'" (John 12:19 RSV).

But more basic to his being rejected were the appalling and mind-stretching implications of the things Jesus frequently claimed about himself. His fellow Jews were offended by the assured authority with which he forgave certain people their sins. By mere command he delivered the demonized and raised the dead. On one occasion, while speaking to the people in Jerusalem, he said, "I keep on sending you prophets and wise men and scribes" (Matt. 23:34), and then went on to describe how they were rejected. When C. S. Lewis referred to this claim in one of his famous essays, he commented on the extraordinary nature of the remark:

> Quite suddenly, almost incidentally, he is claiming to be the power that all through the centuries is sending wise men and leaders into the world. . . . Sometimes the statements put forward the assumption that he, the speaker, is completely without sin or fault. . . . He says again, 'I am begotten of the One God, before Abraham was, I am,' and remember that the words 'I am' were in Hebrew. They were the name of God, which must not be spoken by any human being, the name which it was death to utter. . . . [He makes claims which] if not true, are those of a megalomaniac, compared with whom Hitler was the most sane and humble of men.[5]

On occasion, when Jesus noted the negative reaction of the people to something that he claimed, he supported its stark significance by performing a miracle to confirm his spoken authority. At first, the authorities regarded him as a troublesome Sabbath-breaker—a serious charge—but by these claims, they came to regard him as guilty of blasphemy, "the ultimate sin." At his trial he allowed himself to be put under oath by Caiaphas, the high priest: "Are you the [Messiah], the Son of the Blessed?" To this charge he replied without hesitation, "I am; and you will see the Son of man seated at the right hand of Power, and coming with the clouds of heaven" (Mark 14:61–62 RSV). It was such statements as these, coupled with his public teaching, that divided the Jewish people and evoked either their fear and hostility or their love and adoration.

Down through the centuries Jewish leaders have told their people that Jesus is not for Jews. Even so, a strange disquiet lingers in many a Jewish heart. In 1944 I was on a troopship crowded with Marines en route to the South Pacific conflict. One day a Jewish officer, noting my insignia as a chaplain, abruptly turned to me and suddenly asked, "Did Jesus ever confess to being the Messiah?" I naturally replied, "Oh sure, he said so several times." "Well, show me." I took out my pocket New Testament, turned to John 4, and pointed out the portion in which a Samaritan woman in the midst of a rather lengthy discussion with Jesus said, "I know that Messiah is coming . . . ; when he comes, he will show us all things." Jesus' reply to her was to the point: "I who speak to you am he" (vv. 25–26 RSV). The Jewish officer stared long at the passage, then abruptly disappeared in the crowd without a further word. I never saw him again.

Third: God's Unique Assistance to the Jewish Mission

God has provided unique and invaluable assistance to all those who seek to participate in missions to the Jewish people. Consider the following. First, we have in the four Gospels the model of Jesus as the missionary *par excellence*. We can draw from this record many helpful insights. We can reasonably imagine, for instance, the unique preparation he acquired beforehand for his ministry, and shape our lives by incorporating its details. We can profit from carefully studying the four Gospels for details of the three years that he devoted to seeking the awakening and spiritual renewal of his people. We can note particularly the emphases he made when he spoke to them. Finally, we find ourselves rejoicing when we realize that Jesus gave explicit summarization of the precise method he followed in his evangelistic work among individuals. He revealed this on the occasion in Acts 26:15–18 when he commissioned the apostle Paul to missionary service among Gentile peoples. Indeed, we cannot but conclude that its five elements are essential to all types of effective missionary service, whether among Jewish people or Gentiles.

Second, we have the gospel of John. This gospel is a polemic-styled record of details in Jesus' life and ministry written specifically for the Jewish people and containing as its stated purpose the following: "Now Jesus did many other signs in the presence of the disciples, which are not written in this book; but these are written that you may believe that Jesus is the [Messiah], the Son of God, and that believing you may have life in his name" (20:30–31 RSV). The prayerful and careful reading of this gospel has brought many Jewish people face-to-face with Jesus, and has resulted in their surrender to him in repentance and faith.

Third, God graciously provided spiritual enduement for his people that they might be effective in their witness to Jewish people. This becomes apparent when we turn to the opening chapter of Acts. In the forty-day interval between Jesus' resurrection and his ascension to heaven, he gave his disciples objective reality of his bodily resurrection, then followed this with detailed instruction on their missionary task, particularly its relation to the extension of the kingdom of God throughout the world. But he particularly stressed their forthcoming baptism in the Holy Spirit. Concerning this he said, "You shall receive power when the Holy Spirit has come upon you, and you shall be my witnesses in Jerusalem and in all Judea and Samaria and to the end of the earth" (1:8 RSV). The presence and empowerment of the Holy Spirit will make all the difference between effective and ineffective missionary service, as the subsequent chapters in Acts clearly indicate.[6]

Finally, Acts provides us with the early history of the establishment and extension of the Messianic community in Jerusalem and eventually in Rome. When the Holy Spirit revealed that Gentiles would also respond to the gospel (Acts 10), a meeting was convened by apostles and elders of the Messianic community in Jerusalem to discuss the significance of this revelation (Acts 15). With the Spirit's endorsement, from that time onward we find Messianic Jews welcoming Gentile believers into their congregations as equals in this growing movement. Acts also records the early persecutions of Messianic Jews, largely by leaders of the Jewish religious establishment, as well as continuing Jewish resistance to Jesus their Messiah.

Fourth: Jesus' Preparation for Jewish Mission

Once we accept Jesus as our model, it follows that the task of Jewish mission service begins with preparation of heart and mind beforehand, by studying all that was involved in his preparing himself for his personal mission to his people. This preparation is an ongoing task that continues throughout one's life of ministry. Even though a vast gulf separates us from the incarnate Son of God, we can derive practical help from reflecting on the elements in his earthly life that truly fitted him for missionary work.

When Jesus was around thirty years of age and began his ministry, we find him truly at home in the Hebrew Scriptures. He was also utterly loyal to the language and life of the synagogue, and thoroughly knowledgeable of the strengths and weaknesses of the popular Judaism of that day. Although Jesus was brought up in Nazareth of Galilee and not far from the Roman/Greek town of Sepphoris, scholars have searched in vain for any trace of Gentile thought in his essential Jewishness. The Hebrew Scriptures alone—the Law, the Prophets, and the Writings—shaped his thought and action. Besides all this, he was truly a member of his generation, fully aware of the needs and hopes of his countrymen. But he was also painfully troubled by their popular, although distorted, and growing Messianic expectations. He was indeed a student of the human heart.

We read in the Gospels that "the common people heard him gladly" (Mark 12:37 ASV), and can infer that Jesus must have been a superb, popular teacher. He doubtless did not become an expert communicator overnight, but rather made the most of every opportunity to develop this skill, possibly in caring for his widowed mother's children, although probably not in the local congregation that he frequented. Further, all of his teaching and preaching was contextualized in the sense that it was directed to people where they were in their thoughts and experience. He did not theorize or speculate. He had absolute confidence in the "good news" that he proclaimed, and shared it with gracious, although assured, authority. He *was* the personal embodiment of the truth he proclaimed. Without hesitation he spoke of himself as "the way, and the truth, and the life" (John 14:6 RSV). Without doubt, here is the great model for any person who would prepare for Jewish missionary service. Every aspect of his role as a teacher, especially his skill in answering controversial questions with questions, is worthy of reflection and emulation.

But his preparation was not merely mental and social. Spiritual preparation was equally of the sort that we do well to emulate. Consider his response to the preaching of John the Baptist and to the baptism that John administered. Not that Jesus had sins to confess or needed the spiritual benefits that accompanied this cleansing ritual. Actually, the Baptist could not quite understand why Jesus desired such close identification with the repentant segment of Jewry. To Jesus, however, John's baptism gave him occasion to seek divine approval for his readiness to undertake public ministry. When God confirmed, "Thou art my beloved son; with Thee I am well pleased," it was then that "the Holy Spirit descended upon him in bodily form, as a dove" (Luke 3:21–22 RSV). This confirmed to Jesus that spiritually he *was* ready to begin his ministry.[7] Even so, immediately thereafter, he fasted and prayed in the wilderness for forty days and found himself exposed not only to physical weakness but also to the Devil's repeated attempts to divert him from obedience to the will of God. "When the devil had ended every temptation," the text reads that "he departed" (Luke 4:13 RSV). This prolonged exposure to spiritual warfare and its triumphant outcome thus rounded off very well his preparation for what lay ahead.

So, then, the Messianic Jew or Gentile Christian who would evangelize the Jewish people needs to experience similarly all the reality arising from baptism with Messiah—buried with him in death to self, and raised with him to resurrection life—as well as gaining solid experience in fasting and prayer, along with spiritual conflict and victorious conquest. All these should be included in the maturing experience of the disciple who desires fruitfulness in ministry among the Jewish people. Happy is the person who can share with fellow believers the essence of what Jesus shared in the synagogue at Nazareth at the beginning of his glorious years of ministry. On that occasion he bore witness to having experienced the anointing by the Spirit for the work ahead (Luke 4:18–21 with Isaiah 61:1–2).

Jesus: His Missionary Method

How fortunate we are to have the inspired record of the manner in which Jesus actually witnessed to individuals during his three years of public ministry. Many studies have been made of the manner in which he called and trained twelve Jewish men with a view to their becoming key apostles in his purpose to seek the spiritual renewal of the nation. But this is not our present concern; what concerns us here is the manner in which he actually evangelized Jewish people. Its details are found in the Gospels. He summarized its basic elements when he commissioned the apostle Paul to missionary service. Drawing from his own ministry, Jesus stated that the task was to be carried out in five distinctly progressive steps: "Open their eyes, that they may turn from darkness to light and from the power of Satan to God, *that* they may receive the forgiveness of sins and a place among those who are sanctified by faith in me" (Acts 26:18 RSV). This is the sequence by which men and women, whether Jews or Gentiles, are brought into personal encounter with God and granted entrance into his kingdom. Its essential steps include conscious repentance toward him and the deliberate reception by faith of Jesus the Messiah as Lord and Savior. The end result is "the new birth," a matter of such supreme importance that he described it in detail to Nicodemus who was both "a ruler of the Jews" and "a teacher of Israel." Concerning this, Jesus was most emphatic: "Unless one is born anew, he cannot see the kingdom of God." He was most direct with Nicodemus: "You must be born anew" (John 3:1–15 RSV). Since all effective mission service is based on deliberate efforts to maintain this five-step sequence, let us examine these steps in turn.[8]

Step 1: "Open Their Eyes"—Help People Perceive Their Spiritual Need!

There are three forces that must work together to bring this about. First is the disciple of Jesus who makes the witness. Second is the "living and powerful" Scriptures, which provide us with a precise definition of gospel: "I delivered to you as of first importance what I also received, that [Messiah] died for our sins in accordance with the scriptures; that he was buried, that he was raised on the third day in accordance with the scriptures, and that he appeared to [Peter], then to the twelve" (1 Cor. 15:3–5 RSV). Finally is the Holy Spirit, who alone can bring a person to repentance and faith.

Because Jesus said that all people through their fallenness are blind to spiritual truth, we must not fail to recognize that spiritual conflict is involved in all evangelistic work. Hence, we should assume that all people are living in an almost hermetically sealed compartment of self-centeredness. Dale Carnegie used to say that when people are not engaged in their work, they usually spend about 95 percent of their time thinking about themselves.

We must also take seriously the efforts of Satan to make people unresponsive to the gospel. Jesus anticipated this in his parable: "How can one enter a strong man's house and plunder his goods, unless he first binds the strong man? Then indeed he may plunder his house" (Matt. 12:29 RSV). We dare not fail to take the full measure of Jesus' encounter with, and triumph over, Satan, culminating in Jesus' crucifixion and resurrection, and particularly his instructions on "binding" and "loosing" this "strong man" (16:16–19; 18:18). This will keep us from having only a casual regard for the dimensions of spiritual reality and satanic resistance when we pray. We shall claim by faith our Lord's victory over Satan when we pray to God for his solution to the almost insurmountable problem of reaching Jewish people with a positive initial contact that will open the door to genuine interaction.

John 4:7–42 records the account of Jesus bringing the blessing of God to the Samaritan people of a city called Sychar. It all began when he established interaction with a jaded, middle-aged woman at a local well. When first they met, she was completely wrapped up in herself, neither interested in him or his message. But very soon she began to change. The manner in which he dealt with her is very revealing and most instructive. At the outset, he had to build a bridge of love and understanding to her heart. She had to have confidence in him before she could become interested in his message. So he was friendly, respectful, and particularly determined to be a good listener. He knew that if he was not interested in what she might say in response to his opening words, he could not expect her to be interested in what he intended to share with her.

His opening words were, "Give me a drink" (John 4:7 RSV). She tried to put off this Jewish stranger, uttering a curt remark, reminding him of Jewish racial prejudice against Samaritans. But he completely ignored this jibe. Undaunted, he did not shift to a new theme but began to speak of "the gift of God" (v. 10) and of the possibility of her asking him for "water," although he added the interesting detail of "living water" (v. 10). She could not help but become curious. What did he mean? Was there something she was missing out on in life, something that was accessible to her through his assistance? All this heightened her curiosity and expectation, but not her understanding. She had to hear more. He, a gentle, winsome stranger, had truly opened her eyes, and a bridge of friendly communication was opening before her. She now faced him with stirrings of expectation.

How does all this apply to our establishing contact with Jewish people? One has only to secure a copy of *Witnessing to Jews: Practical Ways to Relate the Love of Jesus* by Moishe and Ceil Rosen.[9] Then, begin to read it! I've read my copy several times, and have scribbled notes over its pages. The Rosens describe in detail all sorts of excellent ways of awakening interest in Jewish people. They suggest a variety of opening lines, some specific questions, and even interest-provoking statements. All these are appropriate, and we can use them. And as for issues in regard to this new millennium, all one has to do is read any current Jewish publication like *The Jerusalem Post* to discover what worries most Jewish people when they think about the future of Israel in the days ahead, or about the future of Jewry in America. I find that carrying around a copy attracts curiosity, and readily provokes questions, provided, of course, that one is friendly and outgoing toward those who ask. But what comes next? The subject of Jesus must be brought into our interaction, but we soon find that most Jewish people are not interested in him. Everything about Jesus has long since been put behind them. They need to be turned around. This leads us to the second step.

Step 2: "Turn from Darkness to Light"—Face the Light of the World!

The problem is that Jewish people are facing the wrong way. They have been conditioned to look the wrong way when Jesus, the greatest living Jew, is mentioned. Although he claimed to be "the light of the world" (John 8:12 RSV), Jewish people seem content to ignore him even though he has revealed himself as particularly desirous of becoming their friend and personal Savior. He is the God of Israel, of the nations, and of all creation. And he has said, "He who follows me will not walk in darkness, but will have the light of life" (8:12 RSV). But all this is far from the conscious thought of Jews.

How then are we to turn Jewish people around and encourage them to face Jesus with an open mind? If you have ever attended a meeting in which Jewish people give their personal stories of how they became Messianic Jews—sincere followers of Jesus—you would be impressed with how few of their stories agree as to details. Very often, however, their stories include a friendly Gentile who became God's instrument in the process of opening their eyes and turning them around until they faced the reality of Jesus. Generally this involved a period of personal cultivation until trust and confidence developed between them. Along the way they were encouraged to read carefully the Gospel of John, and told to pray, "O God, if Jesus is the One I need, show this to me." Increasingly, this gospel fascinated them. They found themselves pausing again and again when they came upon Jesus' claims to be the "Bread of Life," or the "Light of the World," or the "Resurrection and the Life," or the "Good Shepherd," or the "Savior of the World," or the "Son of God," or the "Messiah of Israel," or the "Son of Man," or the "Way, the Truth, and the Life." These claims filled their minds with wonder, but in the end it was invariably the supreme fact of the redemptive gospel that brought them low before his loving presence and moved them to surrender to him in repentance and faith.

This supreme fact concerns an event—an execution—that took place in time—during a Jewish Passover celebration (33 c.e.)—and in space—at a hill called Golgotha, outside the city of Jerusalem. This event is confirmed by the nail prints in Jesus' hands and his feet, and by the mark of a Roman spear in his side. The whole of the gospel of John leads to this climax. His wounds speak of what he suffered for every one of us. During the last week of his earthly life, he said to those gathered around him, "Greater love has no man than this, that a man lay down his life for his friends. You are my friends" (John 15:13–14 rsv). And the more one faces the reality of his death, reads the gospel and prays, the more light floods the heart. The great prophecy of Isaiah becomes the confession of the heart: "All we like sheep have gone astray; we have turned every one to his own way; and the Lord has laid on him the iniquity of us all" (53:6 rsv). This is what his death means. Out of love for us, Jesus reached down and took to his innocence all our guilt and shame, and made it his own, receiving in himself the judgment we all deserved.

No wonder these Jewish believers then changed their heart attitude toward him. No wonder the desire grew in them to surrender to him and accept his rule over their lives. What other response could be given to such an invitation as the following: "My sheep hear my voice, and I know them, and they follow me; and I give them eternal life, and they shall never perish, and no man shall snatch them out of my hand. My Father, who has given them to me, is greater than all, and no one is able to snatch them out of the Father's hand. I and the Father are one" (John 10:27–30 RSV). It is the full realization of the personal meaning of the sacrifice—that Jesus died for our sins ("atonement," as the Levitical code defines it in the Sinaitic covenant)—that brings us to a sense of our utter unworthiness. And to think that he desires that we be his friends! Indeed, he rose from the dead to show us that newness of life is available to us if we but submit to his rule over our lives. Indeed, six times in the Gospels Jesus said that if any one would be his disciple and friend, he must first take up his cross. Only then, will one truly have the desire to respond to his invitation: *Follow me!* But what follows?

Step 3: "And from the Power of Satan to God"—Help People Change Allegiance!

Let us return to the account of our Lord dealing with the Samaritan woman. She has been drawn to him and is quite captivated by his promise: "Whoever drinks of the water that I shall give him will never thirst; the water that I shall give him will become in him a spring of water welling up to eternal life" (John 4:14 RSV). She does not fully understand what he is offering, but she wants it, and tells him so. Why, then, did he not immediately respond to her request? Something stood in the way. We must remember that the first word of his gospel is "Repent!" (Mark 1:15). For this reason he suddenly changes the subject and abruptly says to her, "Go, call your husband, and come here" (John 4:16 RSV). This unexpected response touches her heart and almost without reflection she candidly replies, "I have no husband" (v. 17). Jesus then commends her for her honesty and begins to detail the total marital disarray that has characterized her life. We readily sense his purpose. He wants to bless her, but first she needs to make an honest judgment of herself before him. No pride or face-saving can stand in the way. By responding in this fashion, she would be judging herself in his presence as unworthy of his love, but confessing that she needs him to replace whatever had been previously dominating her heart and life. In a very real sense, she dies to a self-centered, satanic-influenced existence and confesses that she wants him to cleanse her heart and to be the solitary occupant of its throne. Without this conscious transfer of authority from self to God, there would have been no grace for Jesus to extend to her.

In this account, the transfer of authority in her life seems almost automatic. But as we read the full story in John 4, we find that Jesus has to deal with a number of issues beforehand that troubles her as a Samaritan. In following him she would be making a break with basic elements in Samaritan religious thought that differed from Judaism. These elements came to the surface. She raised them one by one and he dealt with each one in turn. Among other things he told her that "Salvation is from the Jews," that the place of worship is unimportant, that acceptable worship must be "in spirit and truth," and that he was the Messiah (vv. 19–26). In the end, all her questions were answered.

It was then that the woman suddenly became aware of a new purpose in her life. The text says that she "left her water jar, and went away into the city, and said to the people, 'Come, see a man who told me all that I ever did. Can this be the [Messiah]?'" (vv. 28–29 rsv). The story has an exciting finish: "They went out of the city and were coming to him" (v. 30). First one by one, then in groups—the process continued until the whole city was aroused and went out to Jesus. The account (vv. 39–42) ends with many Samaritans saying, "We have heard for ourselves, and we know that [he] is indeed the Savior of the world." We can be sure that the city of Sychar was never the same after that!

All this reminds us of what might occur when we witness to Jewish people about Jesus. There is every possibility that—like the Samaritan woman—they will bring up all sorts of reasons why Jewish people should have nothing to do with Jesus and Christians. They may question how a man could become God. Or why Jewish people should listen to Christians, "whom everybody knows" have always been anti-Semitic. Or why the Christians and churches in Germany followed Hitler and actively endorsed the Holocaust, while churches all over the world were silent about his destruction of six million Jewish people. Or that Jesus couldn't have been the

Messiah, because the world is no different since he came. Add to that, when the true Messiah comes, he will bring peace and justice to the whole world, and so bless Israel that she will become the dominant nation in all the world.

Further, we must keep in mind that very often Jewish people resist the gospel even when it is presented in a loving and positive fashion. No person who witnesses to Jewish people has not been similarly disappointed, all of which reminds us that in the Gospels we find that Jesus often experienced this type of disappointment. When God created humans in his own image, he took a great risk. He gave them freedom of choice, the freedom to resist his love and disobey his will. Adam and Eve exercised this freedom, and sin entered the human race, with tragic consequences.

We do well to recall Jesus' encounter with a rich young ruler who came to him seeking a solution to his great need (Mark 10:17–22 RSV). This Jewish man asked Jesus, "What must I do to inherit eternal life?" Certainly he came to the right person and was sincerely concerned about a priority matter—the issue of eternal life. But Jesus had to test whether or not he was willing to accept God's control over his heart and life. He began by inquiring into the ruler's response to the law, and learned that he had obeyed the law from his youth. Jesus commended him for being a moral person. But this was neither the heart nor the end of Jesus' probing. The text states that "Jesus looking upon him loved him, and said to him: 'You lack one thing; go, sell what you have, and give to the poor, and you will have treasure in heaven; and come, follow me.'" But the man failed this test. He refused to accept Jesus' lordship. "He went away sorrowful; for he had great possessions." This story is repeated three times in the Gospels. It serves as a permanent reminder to us that evangelism, to be true to Scripture, must always raise the issue of turning the control of one's life over to Jesus. That is what repentance is all about. Without this turning and repentance, there is no possibility of receiving one of God's greatest gifts.

Step 4: "That They May Receive Forgiveness of Sins"—Enter the Life of Faith!

After repentance comes a conscious act of faith. This conscious act of faith marks the beginning of a life of faith. Jesus delights to grant forgiveness to the penitent. And yet the transfer of one's allegiance from self to God must take place before there is the possibility of deliberately receiving Jesus' forgiveness for all past sins. Only then follows the experience of moral cleansing and personal renewal, which Jesus is always ready to provide. Even so, those who turn their lives over to Jesus need to be assured that he has really forgiven them their sins. One of the joys of evangelism is that it grants one insight into the delight people experience when the reality of their inward assurance of personal salvation is experienced for the first time. But that realization involves a bit of probing.

At this point it is suggested that one bring the substance of a Bible passage, such as Colossians 1:13–14, into the discussion. The one who just professed to receive the Lord is asked to read and discuss its meaning. "[Jesus] has delivered us from the dominion of darkness and transferred us to the kingdom [or rule] of his beloved Son, in whom we have redemption, the forgiveness of sins" (RSV). This leads to a review of the many new things that Jesus grants to his followers: a new relationship, a new status, a new freedom, and a new set of responsibilities—all because sins have been forgiven. Then the key question is asked: "Has Jesus forgiven you your sins?" The typical reaction is a measure of uncertainty, some hesitation, and finally something like, "I guess he has forgiven me my sins." Then make the suggestion, "Well, if so, why don't you thank him? I'll begin with a brief prayer, and then you'll follow me. Yes?" It is in the new believer's offering to God his first prayer of thanksgiving that the heart is released. Joy overflows, and generally a lengthy prayer results! All unaided by you! Such delight!

Then again, some suggest that John 1:11–13 be used. This is the passage that begins with perhaps the most painful note of pathos in the Bible. Concerning Jesus, it states, "He came to his own homeland, yet his own people did not receive him. But to as many as did receive him, to those who put their trust in his person and power, he gave the right to become children of God, not because of bloodline, physical impulse or human intention, but because of God" (John 1:11–13 CJB). In the discussion that follows, the key question is, "What, then, are you . . . since you have just professed to receive Jesus as your Lord?" This time the hesitant reply is along the order of, "Well, I guess that I must be among the children of God." Again the suggestion, "Well, if that is so, why don't you thank him?" The result is invariably the same! Surprising joy and much gratitude!

Step 5: "A Place Among the Sanctified by Faith in Me"—Enter God's Community!

A further step of faith is to accept one's entrance into the family of God, beginning to take hold of its privileges and responsibilities. Jesus accomplished this by drawing people to himself, and then making them the members of his new community: "Fear not, little flock, for it is your Father's good pleasure to give you the kingdom," meaning, of course, the kingdom's fellowship, authority, and power (Luke 12:32 RSV). After his resurrection, Jesus greatly enlarged this dimension of the kingdom community by including the missionary mandate. Initially, he called for baptism as the essential initiatory rite into his body—the church—which consists of believing Jews and Gentiles. He also encourages members to begin to appropriate by grace the fullness of each one's "inheritance of the saints in light" (Col. 1:12 RSV).

It is significant that nowhere in Acts is there an account of any individual in which baptism is not immediately mentioned after his or her acceptance of Jesus. In our day there are many types of congregations defined by history, dogma, structure, and language. By God's grace, however, there are Messianic Jewish congregations and evangelical Gentile churches in which their priority is Jewish evangelism and into which Jewish believers are warmly received. Since there is no biblical validity for encouraging any form of "solitary religion," all new believers in Jesus should be directed toward those congregations that are committed—without qualification—to the historic biblical faith. Then, of course, follows the Great Commission and the positive activity of participating in the task still to be completed by the spiritual seed of Abraham: that "in you all the families of the earth will be blessed" (Gen. 12:3 NASB).

Conclusion

In this brief missiological discussion, this chapter has outlined the basic elements of Jewish evangelism. The essential elements that must be carried out involve (1) opening eyes that are blind, (2) turning people around to face Jesus as he is revealed in the Gospels, (3) enabling them with repentance toward God to surrender their lives to his control, (4) then by faith to receive his gift of forgiveness, and (5) enter the life, privileges, and obligations of a local congregation of the kingdom of God.

It goes without saying that for a Jewish person to respond to this call to follow Jesus, it may be at great personal cost. Concerning this, Jesus said, "He who loves father or mother more than me is not worthy of me; and he who loves son or daughter more than me is not worthy of me; and he who does not take his cross and follow me is not worthy of me. He who finds his life will lose it, and he who loses his life for my sake will find it" (Matt. 10:37–39 RSV). We cannot forgot that the same God, when he first spoke to Abraham when he was still Abram, used similar words: "Go from your country and your kindred and your father's house to the land that I will show you" (Gen. 12:1). If Abram had not obeyed, where would we all be now?

Chapter 13

The Ongoing Importance of Messianic Prophecy for Jewish Evangelism in the New Millennium

MICHAEL RYDELNIK

Messianic prophecy has always been crucial to Jewish evange-lism. As Jakob Jocz states, "The importance of the appeal to the Old Testament in discussions with Jews cannot be overestimated. It gave the Christian missionary the first point of contact, it created a mutual platform, and made it possible to point to the essential unity between the Old and the New Testaments."[1] Thus, it is not surprising that Messianic prophecy formed a central element in the church's efforts at reaching Jewish people with the gospel.

An unfortunate belief is common in some contemporary scholarly circles, however, that no clear Messianic idea existed in Israel until the postexilic period[2] or even generally until the second century B.C.[3] J. H. Charlesworth states, "I am convinced, Jewish messianology developed out of the crisis and hope of the non-Messianic Maccabean wars of the second century B.C.E."[4] This opinion would lead to the conclusion that Old Testament texts that have historically been interpreted as Messianic, even by the New Testament, should not be viewed as Messianic in their original intent. Thus, Juel views the apostolic Messianic identification of Old Testament texts as "a creative exegetical enterprise."[5]

This shift in scholarship has caused a difficulty for Jewish evangelism. If the Messianic hope is merely a postexilic scriptural phenomenon or, worse, if the Old Testament Scriptures are completely devoid of any Messianic hope, how can Jewish evangelists defend the messiahship of Jesus? Without direct Messianic prophecy, one of the essential arrows that Jesus and the apostles used to defend the messiahship of Jesus will be removed from the quiver of contemporary Jewish missions. Why should Jewish people, and for that matter, Gentiles, believe in Jesus if he is not, indeed, the Promised One.

The validity of direct Messianic prophecy, though, has been defended by various scholars.[6] Still, the goal of this chapter is not to defend the authenticity of Old Testament Messianic prophecy, but rather to demonstrate its importance to Jewish evangelism. My approach will be to show the importance of Messianic prophecy to Jesus the Messiah, the apostles, the historic church, and modern Jewish missions.

Messianic Prophecy Was Important to Jesus the Messiah

Jesus obviously considered himself to be the fulfillment of Messianic prophecy. His being so was essential to his self-disclosure to Jewish people. Thus, Messianic prophecy was crucial to Jesus in two primary ways. First, Jesus considered the central message of the Old Testament to be Messianic. Jesus revealed his view of Old Testament Messianic prophecy in two postresurrection encounters, the first recorded in Luke 24:25–27—teaching the two disciples on the Emmaus Road—and the second in Luke 24:44–46—teaching in the gathering of the eleven. By including those two occasions, it was Luke's intent to demonstrate that Jesus understood the Old Testament to point to the Messiah.

That Jesus believed the whole of the Old Testament predicted the Messiah is evident in his emphasis on the word "all" in both encounters. Jesus rebuked the men on the road to Emmaus for being slow to believe in *all* that the prophets spoke (ἐπὶ πᾶσιν οἷς ἐλάλησαν οἱ πρφῆται—Luke 24:25 NASB); he explained the Scriptures about the Messiah, beginning with Moses and *all* the prophets (πάντων τῶν προφητῶν—Luke 24:27); he interpreted the message about the Messiah in *all* the Scriptures (ἐν πάσαις ταῖς γραφαῖς— Luke 24:27); he affirmed that he had to fulfill *all* that was written about him in the Law, the Prophets, and the Writings (πάντα τὰ γεγραμμένα—Luke 24:44). This emphasis on "all" shows that Jesus saw the Messiah not merely in occasional isolated texts, but in all the Scriptures.[7] Ellison has correctly observed, based on this passage, "The whole Old Testament, and not merely an anthology of proof passages, was looked on as referring to Christ Jesus."[8]

From these encounters recorded in Luke 24, two corollary concepts become evident. First, Jesus believed the Messianic prophecies to be sufficiently clear that the two disciples on the Emmaus Road should have understood their meaning. He chided them for being "foolish men and slow of heart to believe in all that the prophets have spoken" (Luke 24:25 NASB)! The implication was that the disciples should have recognized the events of the crucifixion and the reports of the resurrection as fulfillments of Old Testament prophecy. Jesus did not say, however, "O poor men of faith, you could not understand what the prophets had spoken of me because they had not yet been given their full sense of meaning, [their *sensus plenior*] until this very moment as I am explaining them to you!" No, the prophecies were not so unintelligible that the disciples could be excused for their failure to understand.

It was not only in Luke 24 that Jesus affirmed the clarity of the Messianic prophecy. In John 5:45–47, for example, Jesus told the Jewish leaders who did not recognize him that Moses, upon whom they had set their hopes, would accuse them. If they truly had believed Moses, Jesus said, they would believe in him "for he wrote of me" (John 5:46). If Moses did not know that he was writing about the Messiah and the message was not clear, how could Moses' words indict their unbelief?

The second corollary concept evident from Luke 24 is Jesus' belief that spiritual insight was necessary to understand Messianic prophecy. "He opened their mind to understand the Scriptures" (Luke 24:45 NASB), demonstrating that divine enlightenment was essential to an accurate understanding of Messianic prophecy.[9] In addition to their diligent study of Messianic texts, the disciples could not understand Messianic prophecy without divine enablement.

The second primary way that Jesus demonstrated the importance of Messianic prophecy is that Jesus himself taught the apostles his Old Testament interpretive method. Since the Messiah himself taught the disciples how the Old Testament relates to the Messiah, states Ellison, "we can only interpret it reasonably as a claim that the church's use of the Old Testament was in fact based on and legitimized by the teaching of its Founder."[10] The apostles received their training in the hermeneutics of Messianic prophecy from the Messiah himself. The assertion that the apostolic use of the Old Testament was derived from their own creativity or simply from the rabbinic Midrashic method is not true. Liefield addresses the importance of this when he writes,

> With great clarity they show that the sufferings of Christ, as well as his glory, were predicted in the Old Testament and that all the Old Testament Scriptures are important. *They also show that the way the writers of the New Testament used the Old Testament had its origin, not in their own creativity, but in the post-resurrection teachings of Jesus,* of which this passage is a paradigm.[11]

Messianic prophecy was important, then, to Jesus. He saw the Old Testament as Messianic and himself as the fulfillment of those prophecies. Additionally, Messianic prophecy was vital enough to him that he taught his understanding of Messianic prophecy to his disciples. It is their perspective that will now be considered.

Messianic Prophecy Was Important to the Apostles

It was not only Jesus who affirmed the importance of Messianic prophecy. The apostles based their faith on it and made that message central to their proclamation in the book of Acts. The importance of Messianic prophecy to the apostles is seen first in their understanding of it and second in their use of it for Jewish evangelism.

First, as to their understanding of Messianic prophecy, the apostles believed that the Old Testament prophets did, indeed, understand that they were writing about the Messiah. Peter, leader of the apostles, spoke to this in two significant passages. The first, contained in Peter's sermon at Pentecost, is recorded by Luke in Acts 2:29–31. In that passage, having quoted Psalm 16:8–11 as a Messianic prophecy of the resurrection, Peter argued that David, writing as a prophet, had the Messiah in view and not himself. Peter asserted that David could not possibly have had himself in mind as the subject of Psalm 16 because David died and his flesh corrupted. Moreover, David was a prophet, who had confidence in God's oath (the Davidic covenant), so "looking ahead, he spoke concerning the resurrection of the Messiah, that He was neither abandoned to Hades, nor did His flesh see corruption" (Acts 2:31).

It is interesting, too, that Peter's perspective—that David was directly speaking of the Messiah—is in harmony with David's own understanding of his writings. In 2 Samuel 23:1–7, David's last words are recorded. The Septuagint rendering has a distinct Messianic focus. David's last words, as recorded in the Septuagint, claimed that as the man who was raised up by God, he gave prophetic oracles "concerning the Messiah of the God of Jacob, the delight of the songs of Israel" (2 Sam. 23:1).[12] Further, David claimed that the Spirit of the Lord spoke by him and through him (2 Sam. 23:2–3), David thereby recognizing his own role as a prophet. Then David described the righteous reign of the Messianic King, recognized his own failure ("for not so is my house with God"[13]), and declared his confidence in God to bring salvation because of the everlasting Davidic covenant (2 Sam. 23:3–5).

The parallels between Peter's and David's perspectives are significant. Both claimed that David's confidence was rooted in the Davidic covenant, that David's psalms spoke directly of the Messiah, and that David could write of the Messiah because he was a prophet. It is not surprising, then, that Peter would claim that the Messiah was the subject of Psalm 16 since David, the author of that psalm, also made that claim.

The second passage supporting the apostolic perspective that the prophets knew that they were writing about the Messiah is 1 Peter 1:10–12. Although, this passage is frequently cited as teaching that the prophets did not understand the Messianic significance of their words,[14] this is plainly not the meaning of these verses.

According to Kaiser, the interpretive crux is whether to translate the phrase εἰς τίνα ἢ ποῖον as "what person or time" (NASB) or "what time or circumstances."[15] Kaiser makes the case that it is a tautology for emphasis, with the resulting translation, "what time or circumstances."[16] Thus, the prophets searched for the time of fulfillment, but not the meaning of their own words. According to this view, the prophets knew they were writing about the sufferings and glories of the Messiah—but they did not know when he would come.

On the other hand, Grudem effectively argues, based on the normal use of τίς and ποῖος, that the phrase should be translated "what person or time."[17] Thus, the prophets searched for the identity of the Messiah and the time of his coming.

Regardless of the position taken, the passage still does not support the view that the prophets failed to understand that they wrote of Messiah. Kaiser states that according to 1 Peter 1:10–12, the prophets were aware of five facts in their prophecies:

> They knew they were predicting that: (1) the Messiah would come; (2) the Messiah would suffer; (3) the Messiah would be glorified (in kingly splendor); (4) the order of events 2 and 3 was that the suffering came first, and then the glorious period followed; and (5) this message had been revealed to the prophets not only for their own day, but also for a future generation such as the church of Peter's audience (v. 12).[18]

Kaiser's remarks are absolutely accurate except for his fifth point, which could be clarified as follows. Peter actually stated that the prophets served the future generations of the church with their words and not their own generation. Although the Messianic predictions had relevance to the original hearers, giving comfort and hope to those who looked forward in faith, their primary relevance was to the new covenant believers.[19]

The point is, regardless of which translation is chosen, "what time or circumstances" or the more probable "what person or time," the prophets still knew that they were predicting the sufferings and glory of the Messiah. As Reicke says, "The prophets of the Old Testament are here looked upon as having supernatural knowledge of the eschatological events, but still being obliged to discuss the problems of their historical fulfillment."[20] Although they knew that they wrote about the Messiah, they did not know when he would come or that Jesus of Nazareth would be the historical referent of their prophecies.

The apostolic conviction that the Old Testament was Messianic was not merely theoretical. It led directly to the second way Messianic prophecy was important for them, namely, the apostles proclaimed that Jesus of Nazareth was the fulfillment of Old Testament Messianic prophecy. That proclamation became, in fact, the backbone of their evangelistic practice with the Jewish people.

In the book of Acts, the central message of the apostles to the Jewish people was that Jesus was both Lord and Messiah (Acts 2:36). According to F. F. Bruce, the apostles substantiated their claim with two arguments, one from prophecy and the other from miracles. They proclaimed that "the prophetic scriptures which foretold Messiah's coming have been fulfilled by the ministry, suffering and triumph of Jesus, and the mighty works which he performed were so many 'signs' that in Him the Messianic age had arrived."[21] Both of these arguments were brought together in their proclamation of the resurrection of Jesus, which was both a mighty work of God and a direct fulfillment of Messianic prophecy.[22]

Further, the apostles used Messianic prophecy when preaching to Jewish people as recorded in the book of Acts.[23] Peter was the first to use Messianic prophecy in Jewish evangelism. At Pentecost in his first sermon, Peter, in fact, proved his central message with Messianic prophecy (Acts 2:22–36). He declared that Jesus of Nazareth had been raised from the dead in fulfillment of Psalm 16:8–11 and that he had ascended into heaven in fulfillment of Psalm 110:1.

In Peter's second sermon at Solomon's Colonnade after the healing of the lame man (Acts 3:11–26), he argued, "Now the things which God announced beforehand through the mouth of all his prophets that His Messiah was to suffer, He has thus fulfilled" (Acts 3:18). Having called on the crowd to believe in Jesus as the eschatological Prophet like Moses, foretold by Moses himself, Peter further claimed that "all the prophets from Samuel and those that followed him, as many as have spoken, they also announced these days" (Acts 3:24).

Later, when Peter made his defense before the Sanhedrin for healing the lame man, he cited Messianic prophecy to explain his position (Acts 4:8–12). He charged the council with rejecting Jesus in fulfillment of Psalm 118:22: "He is the stone which was rejected by you, the builders, which has become the headstone" (Acts 4:11).

Stephen also made mention of Messianic prophecy in his preaching. When he made his case before the Sanhedrin (Acts 7), Stephen's primary message was about Israel's long history of rebellion against God. Stephen's confidence in Messianic prophecy became evident, however, when he charged that the rebellious in the nation had killed the prophets "who had previously announced the coming of the Righteous One" (Acts 7:52).

Philip also used Messianic prophecy in evangelism. When the Ethiopian official (Acts 8:26–40), who apparently was a proselyte to Judaism, asked of whom does Isaiah speak in Isaiah 53, Philip answered that it was Jesus (Act 8:34–35). It is obvious, then, that Philip considered Jesus to be the fulfillment of that prophecy. The correspondence between the description of the Servant of Isaiah and the events surrounding Jesus' life, death, and resurrection was so convincing that the Ethiopian believed immediately and was baptized.

Paul was another apostle who used Messianic prophecy when preaching to Jewish people. In his sermon in the synagogue at Pisidian Antioch (Acts 13:16–41), he proclaimed that Jesus was the Savior whom God had sent to Israel in fulfillment of the Davidic covenant (Acts 13:23). Further, Paul claimed that even Jesus' rejection by the leadership of Israel was a fulfillment of the prophets' predictions: when they failed to recognize "the voices of the prophets which are read every Sabbath, they fulfilled these words by condemning Him" (Acts 13:27). Paul then maintained that God raised Jesus from the dead in fulfillment of Psalms 2:7 and 16:10 (Acts 13:33–37).

Paul's method in Pisidian Antioch was not unique. In Thessalonica, too, when he went to the synagogue, "he reasoned with them from the Scriptures, opening and placing before them that the Messiah had to suffer and rise again from the dead, and saying 'This Jesus whom I am proclaiming to you is the Messiah'" (Acts 17:1–3). Since preaching the risen Jesus in synagogues was Paul's custom, he followed the same procedure in Berea (Acts 17:10–15), although with greater success than in Thessalonica.

Before Agrippa and Festus, Paul maintained that his testimony about Jesus stated "nothing but what the Prophets and Moses said was going to take place" (Acts 26:22 NASB). This message remained the same at Rome while Paul was under house arrest. There, leaders from the Jewish community came to Paul and he tried "to persuade them concerning Jesus, from both the Law of Moses and from the Prophets" (Acts 28:23 NASB).

Apollos also had made his reputation as a Jewish evangelist through his use of Messianic prophecy. His effectiveness was rooted in his ability to convince Jews of Jesus' messiahship, "demonstrating by the Scriptures that Jesus was the [Messiah]" (Acts 18:28 NASB).

In discussing the apostles' use of Messianic prophecy, Dewart summarizes their method as follows: "In all this there was an appeal . . . to the things that had been foretold by the prophets and fulfilled by the events of the life and death of Jesus of Nazareth. It is evident that Peter and Paul had strong confidence in the evidential value of fulfilled prediction."[24]

The apostles' confidence was well founded, seen in the notable success they experienced. At Pentecost, three thousand Jewish people received Peter's word about Jesus as the fulfillment of prophecy (Acts 2:41). Among those who heard Peter's message on Messianic prophecy after the healing of the lame man, about five thousand men believed (Acts 4:4). Later on, "a great many of the priests became obedient to the faith" (Acts 6:7). Moreover, James was able to say to Paul, "You see brother how many myriads there are among the Jews of those who have believed" (Acts 21:20).

The apostles, then, consistently used Messianic prophecy in Jewish evangelism. They did so primarily because they were convinced of its veracity through the teaching they had received from Jesus himself (Luke 24:44–47). Further, the apostles used Messianic prophecy because they found it to be an effective method of Jewish evangelism.

To summarize thus far, Jesus saw himself as the direct fulfillment of the Old Testament Messianic hope. He taught this to the apostles, who in turn, declared their confidence in Jesus as the fulfillment of prophecy. Moreover, the apostles understood Jesus to be the primary object of the prophets' predictions and did not view his Messianic fulfillment in some secondary way. Therefore, they proclaimed Jesus as the direct fulfillment of Messianic prophecy to Jewish audiences. The teachings and practices of Jesus and his disciples partially affected in turn the way the historic church understood Messianic prophecy and proclaimed the messiahship of Jesus to Jewish people. To this subject we now turn.

Messianic Prophecy Was Important to the Historic Church

The church's historic record at convincing Jewish people of the messiahship of Jesus is tragically abysmal, filled with coercion, persecution, and even bloodshed.[25] Even so, there were some genuine attempts to communicate the message of the Messiah, even beyond the well-known *Dialogue with Trypho*, by Justin Martyr. A. Lukyn Williams[26] addresses these attempts when he writes,

> Everyone knows that Justin Martyr wrote in the middle of the second century a *Dialogue with Trypho*, a document purporting to give an account of his discussion with a Jew whom he met at Ephesus. . . . But most readers stop there, and many even suppose that Christians did little more by their writings to convince Jews of the truth until the beginning of the nineteenth century. The fact, of course, is that innumerable treatises were composed throughout the whole interval.[27]

Even a cursory reading of these documents would demonstrate that Messianic prediction and fulfillment provided a central apologetic in Jewish evangelism. Several of these significant works, in fact, demonstrate the importance of Messianic prophecy to Jewish evangelism throughout church history.

The Use of Messianic Prophecy in the Patristic Period

A major component of patristic apologetics involved their attempts to reach Jewish people with the gospel. A significant amount of literature arose in which Old Testament interpretation played a central role, continuing the debate that began in the New Testament period.

The church fathers generally advanced three arguments in their apologetic writings addressed to the Jewish people. First, they attempted to show from the Old Testament Scriptures that Jesus of Nazareth was, indeed, the promised Messiah. Second, they sought to show that the law of Moses had been abrogated by God with the onset of the new covenant. Third, they maintained that the Jewish people had lost their status as the people of God and that the church of the Gentiles had become the New Israel.[28] It is their first argument, however—that Jesus was the fulfillment of Messianic prophecy—that will be examined here.[29]

Testimonia

Rendel Harris has proposed that there existed a *Testimonia*, or a book of testimonies, containing a collection of texts from the Old Testament that testified to the messiahship of Jesus and to the veracity of Christianity. He suggested that this must have been an ancient apostolic work that predated the four Gospels but passed into obscurity.[30] According to Harris, it was designed for "teachers, and indeed for all who wished to answer objections made by Jews, and to win them to the true faith."[31]

The problem is, no direct evidence has been found for this *Book of Testimonies*. Thus Williams, as well as other scholars, considers the existence of one central *Book of Testimonies* to be a myth. Therefore, he has proposed that not one book, but in all probability several books, of testimonies were used by later authors to compile their own apologetic works for Jews.[32] These books of testimonies established the method "which produced catena after catena of texts from the Old Testament which were regarded as testimonies to Christ and Christianity."[33] Later church fathers most likely built on these books of testimonies to produce their own apologetic works. They used the verses and interpretations found in these books, which provided the foundation for the Messianic prophecy cited in apologetic works written for Jewish people.[34]

Dialogue with Trypho

Justin Martyr's *Dialogue with Trypho* is the earliest extant patristic document designed to evangelize the Jews.[35] This work regarding the merits and truth of Christianity is Justin's record of a two-day discussion he had with a Jewish philosopher named Trypho.

The tone of the *Dialogue* is courteous throughout and concludes with expressions of mutual respect and goodwill. Despite the friendly tone, some of Justin's assertions, such as the Jews as a nation are responsible for the death of Messiah,[36] remain quite inflammatory. As a result, Justin Martyr is sometimes labeled as anti-Jewish.

In his proof that Jesus is the Messiah, Justin utilized a simple prophecy and fulfillment scheme. According to Skarsaune, Justin's approach is to (a) cite a Messianic prophecy, (b) give a brief exposition, and (c) provide a fulfillment report. Justin's argument is that the Messianic testimonies do not fit Israel's earthly kings. Rather, they portray a King who would conquer Satan and his demons. Only Jesus, the second Adam, has accomplished this superhuman feat.[37]

The main discussions of Messianic prophecy are the Messiah's two advents, the Messiah's preexistence and divine nature, the coming of Elijah, the virgin birth, the Holy Spirit's descent at Jesus' baptism, the Messiah's humiliation in general, and his crucifixion and resurrection.[38]

Many of the passages that Justin cited provided valid argumentation for the messiahship of Jesus. He occasionally cited passages, though, that unfortunately could not sustain a Messianic interpretation. Justin argued, for example, that Joshua's circumcision with knives of stone (Josh. 5:2) "was a sign of that circumcision by which Jesus Christ himself has cut us off from idols made of stone and other materials."[39] The writer of the book of Joshua obviously did not have "circumcision of the heart" in view in this passage.

Then, too, Justin tended to interpret valid Messianic prophecies allegorically by giving them subjective and far-fetched meanings. In his discussion of Genesis 49:11, for example, Justin interpreted the donkey and the colt separately. According to him, the "donkey" (loading ass) represented the synagogue with the law of Moses, while the colt represented the Gentiles without the Law.[40] Moreover, he interpreted "the blood of grapes" in Genesis 49:11 as the blood that purified those who believed in Messiah. He also regarded the "garments" in this same text as referring to those who believed in Messiah.[41] Lai summarizes Justin's principle of interpreting prophecy as follows: "Since all prophecy was fulfilled in Christ, so every detail must be fulfilled. For instance, he maintained that Jesus must have tied the donkey to the grapevine though the Gospels do not report this point."[42]

Justin's misidentification of some Messianic passages and his allegorical interpretation of true Messianic prophecies substantially weakened much of his argument. These errors in exegesis conceivably increased Jewish resistance to his message.

Justin's selection of Messianic texts did, however, frequently reflect the same Messianic prophecies most often cited as such in the Talmud.[43] Thus, Justin seems to have deliberately chosen those texts that would establish common ground with Jewish readers and provide his most effective apologetic. Although a Jewish audience might have rejected Justin's identification of these prophecies with Jesus, they certainly would have recognized the texts he used as Messianic. Thus, Justin's *Dialogue* provides the earliest, post-New Testament apologetic use of Messianic prophecy for Jewish people.[44]

Tertullian: Adversus Judaeos

Tertullian's *Adversus Judaeos*, written about A.D. 200,[45] was designed to be an apologetic for Jewish people as well as to provide answers for Christians interacting with Jews.[46] The work has a two-pronged approach. First, the temporary nature of the Law is discussed in chapters 1–5. Second, in chapters 6–14, Tertullian discusses Messianic prophecy, demonstrating Jesus as its fulfillment.

The method Tertullian uses in the second section shows his reliance on Messianic prophecy as an apologetic, presenting the Messiah of the Old Testament in a topical format. Tertullian seems to have been successful in identifying several important Messianic prophecies. His presentation was often weakened, however, by his trying to make these texts say more than was intended, which, of course, was the interpretive method of his day. It seems that Tertullian required a more positive response from his Jewish readers than could reasonably be expected. Perhaps this was because of his lack of "any personal knowledge of his opponents and their religion."[47]

Aphrahat: Homilies

Aphrahat was a fourth century A.D. bishop who lived on the Persian side of the Tigris. Between A.D. 336–345, he wrote twenty-three homilies in Syriac.[48] The seventeenth homily was directed especially to the Jews. In it, he argued that the prophets foretold that Jesus was the Messiah and that they called him the Son of God. He supported his argument with the usual texts, Psalms 2:7; 110:3; Isaiah 9:6; 7:14; and Daniel 9:26.[49]

Williams assesses Aphrahat's work as being on a different level from that of other evangelistic materials for Jews in that time. He says of Aphrahat, "His piety and sweet reasonableness, together with his patent knowledge of his subject, places his writings among the most attractive in the whole of Christian polemical literature for the Jews."[50]

The Discussion of Archbishop Gregentius with the Jew Herban

This late fourth/early fifth century A.D. document purports to record a formal public discussion between a Christian and a Jew. In it, the Christian Gregentius—an Egyptian who became the Archbishop of Tephra in South Arabia—and Herban—a learned Jew of which nothing is known—discuss the validity of Christianity. It is the earliest record of a disputation in the presence of royalty.[51]

The discussion was fairly unstructured, covering a wide range of topics including the divinity of Messiah, the temporary nature of the Law, and the nature of the church as the true Israel.[52] Gregentius generally uses allegorical interpretation of the Old Testament to defend his position. He does, however, cite various legitimate Messianic prophecies, such as Genesis 49:10; Psalms 2:7; 16:10; 72; 110:1; and Isaiah 53.[53]

The record unfortunately concludes with a bizarre account of a supernatural appearance of Jesus the Messiah and with threats against those Jews who would not believe.[54] This work seems to carry all the weaknesses of ancient Jewish evangelistic treatises: a condescending tone, allegorical interpretation intermingled with literal, supernatural signs, and the threat of violence.

In the patristic period, the early church was not always adequately concerned with understanding the author's intent when studying Old Testament prophecy. The Fathers often cited passages out of context and occasionally found meanings not evenly remotely related to the text. As Williams summarizes, "the Fathers in general were quite content with the method of their Jewish predecessors, seeing in the Bible anything which could by any possibility be seen there."[55] In addition, they castigated the Jews for blindness when they could not accept the Fathers' far-fetched interpretations.

The Use of Messianic Prophecy in the Medieval Period

By the Middle Ages, the church had triumphed in Europe and began to use its authority to attempt to win Jews, sometimes by means of forced baptism and coercion. This led to widespread Jewish distrust of Christianity, as well as some "conversions" that were insincere.[56] Some churchmen, however, opposed coercion and sought to win Jewish people to faith in Jesus through reason and personal persuasion. The following section reviews the way these clerics used Messianic prophecy.

Isadore of Seville: Contra Judaeos

Isadore of Seville was a Spanish churchman from the late sixth to the early seventh century. Considered the most learned man of his time,[57] he rejected King Sisebut's coercive attempts at conversion of the Jews.[58] Thus Isadore wrote *Contra Judaeos* as a handbook for reaching Jewish people with the gospel. In this work, he argued that Jesus is the Messiah according to the Old Testament. Williams considers it "perhaps the ablest and most logical of all the early attempts to present Christ to the Jews."[59]

Isadore compiled, in logical fashion, an extensive list of Messianic prophecies. He used Messianic prophecy in three ways. First, he used passages that were widely understood as Messianic, such as Genesis 22:18; 49:10; 2 Samuel 7:12–16; Psalms 16:9–11; 22:16; 110:1; Isaiah 7:14; 9:6; 11:10; 53; Daniel 7:13; and Micah 5:2. Isadore was correct in regarding these passages as legitimate Messianic prophecies, and he used them in a straightforward way.

Isadore would on the other hand cite a genuine Messianic text, but unfortunately would then interpret it allegorically. The result was his seeing far more in the prophecy than was either textually or contextually tenable. When he discussed Isaiah 11:1, for example, he understood it to speak of the Messiah coming from the family of David, but then also contended that the prophecy spoke of the Virgin Mary.

Isadore also cited passages as Messianic that, in their context, could not reasonably be considered so. He adduced Habakkuk 3:3, for example, "God shall come from the South," as evidence that Messiah was to be born in Bethlehem (chapter 11). He also argued from Psalm 51:4—in which David says that God is justified when he judges—as evidence that Messiah would be judged (chapter 11). He took God's promise to Israel in Hosea 6:2, "He will revive us after two days; He will raise us up on the third day, that we may live before Him" (NASB), as evidence that Messiah would be raised from the dead on the third day (chapter 54).

Williams has stated that in *Contra Judaeos*, Isadore did his best and that his work became a storehouse from which many tracts for Jewish people were written, even down to the nineteenth century.[60] Isadore unfortunately weakened his case, however, by adding too much speculative material. His allegorical interpretations of passages that are both genuinely Messianic and not even Messianic discredited his accurate exegesis of genuinely Messianic passages. Jewish readers would reject the legitimate citations because the illegitimate ones were so patently wrong.

Even so, Isadore's work was far ahead of its time. By rejecting force and coercion and, instead, using Scripture, he demonstrated a more appropriate form of Jewish evangelism.

Gilbert Crispin: A Discussion of a Jew with a Christian Concerning the Christian Faith

Gilbert Crispin (1046–1117), Abbot of Westminster and a disciple of Anselm of Canterbury, left a record of a religious discussion he had with a Jewish acquaintance sometime before 1096. In the words of Werblowsky, it is "one of the genuine gems of mediaeval polemical literature."[61] The distinctives of Crispin's work is the friendly attitudes of the disputants, the authenticity of the Jewish arguments, and the highly academic standard it displays.[62]

The structure of the dialogue was that the Jew would ask a brief question, which would be followed by a long response by Crispin. Perhaps when the event took place, the discussion was more evenly balanced. In the text, however, Crispin does most of the talking, and the primary subject is the biblical and exegetical evidence for the messiahship of Jesus.[63] Crispin and his friend discuss Genesis 49:10 and the time of Messiah's coming.[64] Other significant passages they discussed were Isaiah 2:2–4 and world peace,[65] Isaiah 7:14 and the virgin birth,[66] and Isaiah 53:1–10 and its relation to the sacrifice of Messiah.[67]

Throughout the discussions, Crispin insisted on favoring allegorical interpretation and rejecting literal interpretation. He argued, for example, that Ezekiel 44:2, "this gate shall be shut; it shall not be opened" (NASB), was a reference to the perpetual virginity of Mary. His Jewish disputant exclaimed "You do violence to Scripture. . . . Ezekiel refers to a gate, not a woman!" Crispin replied that the passage cannot be understood literally because God could not go through a gate.[68]

The most noteworthy aspect of Crispin's dialogue is its courteous tone. Throughout the discussion, the two disputants treat each other generously and fairly, without any hostile epithets as are commonly found in medieval polemical literature. Even at the conclusion, there is not a note of triumph. This is all the more remarkable since Crispin wrote on the eve of the first Crusade.[69] Despite the tone, it is unfortunate that Crispin did not realize that, with Jewish people, the allegorical interpretation as a form of proof was inadequate.

Petrus Alphonsi: The Dialogues of Peter and Moses

Another work that used Messianic prophecy in Jewish evangelism in the Middle Ages was written by Petrus Alphonsi (1062–1110), a Jewish believer in Jesus. After receiving baptism, Petrus wrote a polemical work for Jewish people, which was, in essence, a dialogue with himself. Called *The Dialogue of Peter and Moses*, Petrus wrote a series of twelve dialogues between himself, before and after faith in Messiah.[70] Funkenstein notes the sincerity of Alphonsi's faith because "his dialogue contains no defamation" of the Jewish people.[71]

In the *Dialogue*, Petrus makes the case for Christianity, arguing that Messiah came at the very time that had been foretold by the prophets. According to Williams, Petrus does not break new ground when using Messianic prophecy, citing the same texts found in almost all polemical materials.[72] The primary argument that Alphonsi used was hermeneutical. In the very first *Dialogue*, he argued that the prophets should be interpreted spiritually, meaning allegorically. Further, he asserted that his own Jewish nation had been led astray by interpreting them *carnaliter*, meaning literally.[73]

In this very same period, the great Jewish scholar Rashi used the Peshat (or literal) interpretation to rebut Christian interpretation of Messianic texts.[74] It would certainly have strengthened Petrus's case had he chosen to defend the messiahship of Jesus on the basis of literal interpretation.[75]

Raymond Martini: Pugio Fidei

Pugio Fidei (Dagger of Faith) by Raymond Martini (1225–84) marks the pinnacle of thirteenth-century literature designed to evangelize the Jews.[76] It was not designed for Jewish people directly; rather it was prepared as a technical manual for those who would serve as missionaries to Jews.[77] As such, it became the basis for many future works related to missions to the Jews.[78]

In the thirteenth century, missions to the Jews took a new approach, which is evident in *Pugio Fidei*.[79] The primary innovation was the use of the Jewish exegetical tradition to support the claim of Jesus' messiahship. This new strategy can be traced to Raymond Penyaforte (1176–1275), a leading Dominican, who sought to train other friars in Hebrew and rabbinic literature. This training, in turn, enabled them to use Midrashic and Talmudic sources to prove that the Messiah had truly come.[80]

One of the techniques Friar Raymond used was citing Messianic prophecy in conjunction with rabbinic literature. Williams states that Martini used the usual Old Testament texts to support his view.

> He brings forward the Seventy weeks of Daniel (Daniel 9:24–27), Gen. xlix. 10 . . . the image of Nebuchadnezzar (Daniel 2), and the Stone throwing it down at one stroke. Further, he tells us that Gen. iv. 25, Jer. xxxi. 22, Ps. ii. 7 are all made to refer to the Messiah in the Great Midrash by Moses ha-Darshan. . . . He then shows that Messiah was to come while the Second Temple was still standing, adducing Mal. iii. 1, 2, Ps. lxxxix. 36, Hagg. ii. 6–9 and other passages.[81]

Chazan has cited an extended discussion of Genesis 49:10 as found in *Pugio Fidei*,[82] in which Martini combined the use of Messianic prophecy with rabbinic materials.

Martini's *Pugio Fidei*, although exceptional for its extensive knowledge and use of rabbinic materials, suffered from two significant flaws. First, the tone was harsh, portraying the Jewish people in a vicious way. A second serious weakness was Martini's overreliance on rabbinic literature. Even as Nachmanides had argued, it is implausible to conclude that Talmudic rabbis believed that the Messiah had, indeed, come, but that they refused to accept him. In the words of Chazan, "The notion that authoritative Jewish texts in fact bore Christological implications to which the Jews had over many centuries been blind strained credulity."[83]

Even so, when Martini used Messianic prophecy accurately and in conjunction with rabbinic literature, he made a strong case for Jesus' messiahship. Further, his broad knowledge of Jewish sources and sophisticated argumentation made *Pugio Fidei* "the magnum opus of medieval Christian missionizing among the Jews."[84]

Nicolas de Lyra: Contra Judaeos

Nicholas de Lyra (1270–1340) of Normandy was a Franciscan friar and professor of religion at the University of Paris. He is considered one of the most able Christian Bible commentators of his time, as evidenced by his *Postilla litteralis super totam Bibliam*, a running commentary on the whole Bible. He was so highly influenced by the Jewish master commentator, Rashi, that he has been called, perhaps unfairly, "Rashi's Ape."[85]

De Lyra's commentaries were significant in that they attempted to explicate the literal sense of Scripture. He wrote, "In like manner, I intend, for making clear the literal sense, to introduce not only the statements of the Catholic doctors, but also of the Hebrews, especially of Rabbi Salomon,[86] who among the Hebrew doctors has spoken most reasonably."[87]

Besides his commentaries, de Lyra wrote *Contra Judaeos* (Against the Jews), aimed to demonstrate that Jesus was the promised Messiah and that he was both God and man. Even his commentaries had an apologetic aspect to them. Cohen quotes de Lyra's biographer, Henri Labrosse, as saying, "To convince the Jews [of the truth of Christianity]—that is his constant preoccupation, the constant and definite goal of all his work."[88]

Contra Judaeos was written in 1309 after de Lyra participated in an academic disputation on the deity and messiahship of Jesus, held at the University of Paris. It was revised between 1331 and 1334.[89] Hailperin gives a helpful insight into de Lyra's apologetic works. While other such materials could be characterized as unscholarly and offensive, de Lyra's are

> . . . noteworthy for the moderation of the polemic and for the power of the argument. . . . It is no exaggeration to say that de Lyra is serious, loyal, courteous, positive, and truly scientific. A careful reading of his works leaves one with the conviction that Nicolas de Lyra was not only a person of great scholarship, but also a man of integrity. The present writer has found that all of de Lyra's excerpts of the Hebrew materials are an accurate and faithful transcription of the Jewish commentators.[90]

Not only is de Lyra's tone uncommon, but his mode of argumentation is distinctive. He sets out to demonstrate through the literal interpretation of Messianic prophecy that Jesus is the Messiah. In demonstrating the Messianic interpretation of Psalm 2, for example, he wrote, "Proof, however, is not valid from the mystic sense, but from the literal only . . . one ought to say that the Psalm is understood of Christ *ad litteram* [literally]." Additionally, he wrote, "But no proofs are evidence except out of the literal sense, as was said above. And thus it is evident according to the learned men, converted from Judaism, that Psalm is understood as referring to Christ *ad litteram*."[91]

Following earlier Jewish interpretations, Nicholas sought to demonstrate that the literal sense of various traditional Messianic passages proved that they were, indeed, Messianic prophecies. Some key passages that he discussed were Genesis 49:10[92]; Numbers 24:17–19[93]; Psalms 2; 45; 110[94]; Psalm 72[95]; Isaiah 7:14[96]; 52:13–53:12[97]; Zechariah 9:9–10.[98]

De Lyra also allowed for a double sense of certain passages. In these cases, the human author may have meant one thing and the divine author another. In 1 Chronicles 17, for example, de Lyra believed that the human author was referring to Solomon, whereas, the Holy Spirit was referring to the Messiah.[99]

De Lyra's Jewish apologetics had a notable impact. Whereas Raymond Martini's *Pugio Fidei* was massive and required considerable knowledge of Hebrew to use, de Lyra's *Contra Judaeos* was brief, concise, and far more usable. Perhaps this utility is the reason there are only seven extant manuscripts of *Pugio Fidei* but over eighty of *Contra Judaeos*.[100] Moreover, no Jewish counterapologetic admits to direct acquaintance with *Pugio Fidei*, but several Jewish authors mention de Lyra's work and felt it necessary to respond to it.[101]

Nicholas de Lyra should be noted for raising the level of apologetics for Jewish people in several ways. First, his tone was both respectful and cordial. Further, his friendly attitude was joined with careful scholarship, thorough knowledge of Hebrew and rabbinic sources, and a literal hermeneutic. It is not surprising, then, that Nicholas's work was viewed as demanding rebuttal by Jewish scholars, since the strategy he employed had the potential of influencing Jewish people more than any previous work.

Abner of Burgos

In the year 1295, Abner of Burgos (1270–1348), a brilliant young Jewish scholar and physician, was called to treat many Jews who had seen strange visions of the cross. So shook was he by the reports of these visions that he prayed that God would give him wisdom for dealing with them. According to his account, he also received a vision in a dream, in which it was explained that the Jewish people's suffering was caused by their rejection of their true Teacher of righteousness. For twenty-five years he wrestled with this idea. Finally, in the year 1321, in a Hebrew book titled *The Wars of the Lord,* Abner announced his acceptance of Christianity. He was baptized and became known as Maestre Alfonso de Valladolid.

Abner wrote many books and pamphlets, always in Hebrew, designed to win his Jewish brethren to faith in Jesus. His major work was titled *Moreh Zedek* (Teacher of Righteousness), which has been preserved in a Spanish translation.[102] According to Baer, Abner was convinced of the truth of Christianity "by the tribulations of his people and the . . . misinterpretation of its Messianic prophecies."[103]

The bulk of Abner's apologetics revolved around theological argumentation and interaction with rabbinic texts. Even so, he did root his contentions in the Old Testament. When Abner used Messianic prophecy, he was quite traditional in his interpretations.

He cited Malachi 3:1, for example, as a direct reference to the Messiah.[104] As was common at that time, Abner also "spiritualized" in his interpretation of Messianic prophecy.

Although Baer recognizes that Abner "remained a Jew at heart,"[105] he states that Abner also was responsible for some anti-Jewish actions in Spain.[106] Williams, too, points out, "It is to be regretted that Abner-Alphonso allowed himself to accuse his former co-religionists of reciting in their synagogue services a prayer against the Christians, and thus to lead the King of Castile (Alphonso VI) to publish an edict forbidding the Jews to use it."[107]

Despite these shortcomings, Baer recognized Abner's significance: "The apostate Abner of Burgos exceeded in intrinsic merit and in the depth of his influence all the polemical opponents of the Jews during the Middle Ages."[108]

Paul of Burgos

Paul of Burgos (1350–1435) was born Solomon Ha-Levi in the city of Burgos. In the writings of Isaac ben Sheshet and Abarbanel, Paul was recognized as a noted rabbi, as well as for scholarship, piety, and wisdom.[109] At the age of forty, after studying Messianic prophecy—particularly Jeremiah 31:31–34,[110] the Pauline Epistles, and Aquinas's *De Legibus*[111]—Solomon became a Christian, adopting the name Paul de Santa Maria. His mother and two brothers were baptized with him, but his wife did not become a Christian until some time later.[112] He studied theology in Paris, receiving a doctorate, after which "he became Archdeacon of Trevino, Bishop of Cartagena in 1402, Keeper of the Royal Seal in 1406, and Archbishop of Burgos in 1415, holding office until 1435, when he was succeeded by his son Alphonso."[113]

Shortly after his baptism, Paul wrote to Joseph Orabuena "that he had come to the conclusion that the Messianic prophecies had been fulfilled in Jesus of Nazareth."[114] This perspective on Messianic prophecy much later became the foundation for his most significant polemical work. Not forgetting his own Jewish roots,[115] he wrote *Scrutinium Scripturarum* (Search the Scriptures) as an evangelistic book for Jews. Basing the title on John 5:39, Paul wrote that for Jewish people to come to the knowledge of Messiah required their diligent study of the Scriptures. He supported his arguments by using other authoritative Jewish sources, such as the Talmud, to confirm the truth of the interpretations, and most importantly, to interpret the Scriptures literally and not mystically.[116] This last requirement is so essential to Paul's work that Preus says that in Paul of Burgos "one meets . . . a repeated and passionate insistence on the primacy and hegemony of the *sensus litteralis*," and that "only from the literal sense can argument be made."[117]

In fact, Paul of Burgos's view of direct and literal Messianic prophecy was that the Old Testament spoke directly of Messiah.[118] He did not read the Old Testament through the New, but rather he saw the Old Testament as Messianic in and of itself. He argued that Psalm 2, for example, is Messianic, not only because Paul the apostle regarded it so, but because David, the writer, intended it to be understood that way.[119] Burgos defended his view of Messianic prophecy as follows:

> I dare to say to you . . . search all the holy Gospels of God, and you will not find that Christ appealed to any authority of the Holy Scriptures—either when he was instructing his disciples, or when he was contradicting the Jews, or even when the devil was tempting him—except as understood under the literal sense.[120]

According to Paul of Burgos, the Jewish failure to recognize Jesus was not because they interpreted literally what should have been interpreted mystically. Rather, they did not recognize him because of their "false understanding of the literal sense."[121]

The result of Paul of Burgos's labors was his seeing many Jews come to faith in Messiah.[122] Among those whom Paul played a part in convincing to accept Jesus as Messiah was Joshua Halorki, a prominent Jewish physician and scientist.[123] Paul's fruitfulness was likely a result of his ability to interact with Jewish arguments, using a literal hermeneutic supported by his significant knowledge of Jewish sources. Overall, Paul of Burgos made a notable contribution to the cause of Jewish evangelism through his literal interpretation of Messianic prophecy.

It is commonly thought that during the Middle Ages there were no genuine efforts to evangelize Jewish people, nor were there authentic Jewish believers. The survey above demonstrates that the medieval church did, indeed, remember its responsibility to convince Jews of Jesus' messiahship, albeit too often with harsh methods and hostile attitudes. Moreover, some Jews genuinely accepted Jesus as the true Messiah.[124] Their faith unfortunately caused them to be cut off from the rest of the Jewish community. These Jewish believers continued, however, in their attempts to convince other Jews to believe in Jesus.[125]

Although in no way seeking to excuse the coercive and hostile methods used in this era, this section has demonstrated that the central argument between Jews and Christians related to Messianic prophecy. Moreover, it has also shown that Christians used both allegorical and literal hermeneutics to interpret Messianic prophecy. The literal, however, made it more difficult for Jewish polemicists to form rebuttals to Christians. Recognizing the greater efficacy of literal interpretation affected the approach taken in modern Jewish missions.

Messianic Prophecy Was Important to Modern Jewish Missions

The modern age produced a significant change in Jewish evangelism as compared to the medieval period. Jocz cites four important differences between the earlier missionary work of the church and modern evangelical missions.[126] First, in the modern period, the church had a more positive attitude toward the Jewish people and a greater understanding of Judaism. This was an outgrowth of the church's having abandoned the view that Israel was utterly rejected by God, and their adopting instead an eschatological hope for Israel.

A second difference in the modern period was the forsaking of all forms of coercion from the missionary enterprise, and instead adopting friendly relationships as the means of evangelism. The German Lutheran Pietist Philipp Jacob Spener (1635–1705) was the great pioneer in this regard.

A third change was that, rather than simply requiring conformity to the dogmas of the church, as had been the case in the past, modern evangelism emphasized personal religious experience. This was a direct result of modern Jewish missions being an outgrowth of religious revivals, such as Methodism in England and Pietism in Germany.

Fourth and finally, the modern church increasingly recognized that Jewish followers of Jesus should not be separated from the rest of the Jewish people. Whereas in the Middle Ages, Jews who believed in Jesus were required to break with their ethnic heritage, modern Jewish missions encouraged Jewish believers to maintain a Jewish identity. Jocz quotes Gustav Dalman in this regard:

> We have not to Germanize or to Anglicize but only to Christianize them. . . . Jewish missionaries are called upon to endeavour to preach the gospel in as Jewish a shape as its essence permits, and so to respect the peculiarity of the Jewish nation. . . . At all events, let us not help to kill the spirit of Jewish nationality by our missions![127]

These differences in missionary approach produced a significant change in the use of Messianic prophecy. If coercion was out, then convincing was in—and this required an even greater emphasis on using Messianic prophecy. Moreover, the greater adherence to literal interpretation, as evident in the eschatological expectations for literal, ethnic Israel, was also manifested in interpreting Messianic texts. Thus, apologetic literature for Jewish people became far more gentle and accurate. Although there have been many works devoted to Messianic prophecy in the modern era of Jewish missions, the following will address only a selection of the more significant apologetic writers in the field of Jewish evangelism.[128]

Alexander McCaul

The most significant event in the rise of modern missions to the Jews[129] was the establishment of the London Society for Promoting Christianity Among the Jews.[130] This agency established stations all over the world and had a profound impact on all future Jewish missions. Many hardworking and scholarly missionaries served with this agency, including the Gentile scholar of Hebrew and Talmud, Alexander McCaul.[131]

McCaul's works included *Lectures on the Messiahship of Jesus*, which sought to demonstrate Jesus' messiahship through literal and grammatical interpretation of Messianic prophecy. Although not written directly for Jewish inquirers, it reflects McCaul's interactions with Jewish people and was used for training missionaries to the Jews. In the appendix of the book, McCaul gives an excellent survey of crucial Messianic prophecies, showing their literal and direct fulfillment in Jesus. Among the prophecies that McCaul interprets as directly and literally Messianic are Genesis 3:15; 49:10; Deuteronomy 18:15–19; Psalms 2; 16; 22:16; 40:7–8; 68:19; 69; 72; 89; 110; Isaiah 7:14; 9:6; 52:13–53:12.[132] The outstanding nature of McCaul's work is a result of his careful attention to Hebrew grammar and lexicography, as well as his interaction with both Talmudic literature and medieval Jewish commentators. McCaul's volume was used by numerous missionaries to the Jewish people, including David Baron.[133] It is so helpful that modern missionaries to the Jewish people and Jewish inquirers could, in fact, still find value in consulting this work.

Franz Delitzsch

Missions to the Jews in Germany ceased as rationalism swept through that nation at the end of the eighteenth century.[134] Old Testament scholar Franz Delitzsch, however, from 1839 onward played a most significant role in revitalizing Jewish missions. He organized and unified various mission agencies, translated the New Testament into Hebrew, and most importantly, in 1880 he reestablished the Institutum Judaicum in Leipzig, which had formerly flourished at Halle.[135]

As part of his teaching at the Institutum Judaicum, Delitzsch delivered lectures on Messianic prophecy, which he committed to writing in 1890. This work, titled *Messianic Prophecy in Historical Succession* (1891), has been a standard text on the subject and used by numerous missionaries to the Jews. Although written to train Christians, Delitzsch acknowledged that he also had a Jewish audience in mind: "How much we should rejoice, if we could also secure the sympathy of those belonging to the Jewish confession who are seeking after the truth."[136]

Delitzsch adopted a developmental view of the Messianic hope that saw Messianic prophecy as the historical outcome of the progress of redemption, but also allowed for isolated Messianic predictions. In writing his work, he sought to use literary and historical criticism while allowing for the supernatural aspect of prophecy. His goal was to produce a presentation that would "be more thoroughly revised, more exact, more many sided, in many respects different, from that which was usual in earlier centuries, and which has been handed down even to the later missionary literature."[137] In other words, Delitzsch wanted to produce an argument for the messiahship of Jesus that would abandon the fanciful interpretations of other Messianic apologetics and instead be based on a more literal interpretive position.

Delitzsch affirmed the direct nature of the following prophecies: Genesis 3:15; 49:10; Numbers 24:15–19; Deuteronomy 18:15–19; Psalms 2; 45; 110; Isaiah 7:14; 9:6; 11:1–10; 42:1–9; 49:1–7; 50:4–11; 52:13–53:12. It is correct to affirm that Delitzsch's book elevated the apologetic use of Messianic prophecy because of his careful attention to the biblical text and his knowledgeable interaction with Jewish sources. These strengths were offset by his desire to treat the prophecies according to their chronological unfolding, which resulted in considerable hopping around the Bible without regard for the literary context of the given texts. Even so, this book became a standard Jewish missionary textbook because of its many strengths, and it is still in use today.

David Baron

David Baron (1855–1926) was raised in an Orthodox Jewish home and became a believer in Jesus at age twenty-three. He was a missionary to the Jewish people and in 1893 cofounded the Hebrew Christian Testimony to Israel, which was unique in that it employed only Jewish believers as missionaries.[138] The aim of this mission was to be a testimony "of Jews to Jews." Baron once wrote,

> What we continually press upon the Jews is that we believe in Christ, the Son of Man and the Son of God, *not in spite of, but because we are Jews*, that Jesus is the Divine King of our people, the sum and substance of our Scriptures, the fulfiller of our law and our prophets, and the embodiment of all the promises of our covenant God.[139]

Baron's missionary strategy was to have Jewish believers witness to the Jewish people, presenting Jesus as the fulfillment of Messianic prophecy. Therefore, Baron had two objectives in mind as he wrote on Messianic prophecy—to win Jewish people to faith in Jesus and to instruct Gentile Christians in Jewish evangelism. His three famous works are *Rays of Messiah's Glory* (1886),[140] *Types, Psalms and Prophecies* (1906),[141] and *The Servant of Jehovah* (1922).[142] In each of these, Baron sought to establish the messiahship of Jesus through normal interpretation of Messianic texts, as well as interaction with rabbinic commentators.

In these three works, Baron treats various Messianic prophecies to demonstrate that they are direct predictions fulfilled by Jesus of Nazareth. Some of these include Genesis 3:15; 49:10; Deuteronomy 18:15–19; 2 Samuel 23:5; Psalms 22:16; 45; 72; 89:36; 110; Isaiah 4:2; 7:14; 11:10; 49:5–7; 50:4–11; 52:13–53:12; Jeremiah 23:5–6; Daniel 9:24–27; Micah 5:2–4; Haggai 2:7–9; Zechariah 3:8; 6:12–13; 9:9; 10:4; 11:4–14; 12:10; 13:7.

In summary, David Baron combined excellent scholarship, sound hermeneutics, missionary zeal, and a gentle spirit. His work provided a persuasive argument that Messiah has already come, and his name is Jesus of Nazareth. It is no wonder that his books, despite their dated language and research, remain excellent tools for Jewish missions today.

A. Lukyn Williams

A. Lukyn Williams, onetime Hebrew scholar at Cambridge University, has been a great apologist for Jewish missions in England. In addition to writing *Adversus Judaeos* (1935),[143] which surveyed Christian apologetics for Jewish people from the patristic period until the Renaissance, he also wrote a Christian apologetic for Jewish people, *A Manual of Christian Evidences for Jewish People* (1911).[144] This was written in response to Isaac of Troki's *Chizzuk Emunah* (*Faith Strengthened*),[145] a sixteenth-century Karaite work that attempted to refute the claims of Messiah.

R. Isaac's book was written in two parts, the first being an attempt to refute the divinity of Jesus and to show that Jesus was not the predicted Messiah of the Old Testament. In the second part, Troki attempts to critique the New Testament, and particularly to identify its inconsistencies and contradictions. In Williams's two-volume response, he first addresses the objections Troki raised regarding Messianic prophecy, and in the second volume, he seeks to answer Troki's objections to the New Testament.

This current discussion is limited to Williams's first volume since it pertains to the apologetic use of Messianic prophecy. Williams states that it is for "Orthodox Jews, diverse though they are in degrees of western culture and of Jewish practice, that the following pages are written."[146] He further states that his "one aim has been to set forth before his readers arguments for Christianity from the point of view of sound modern scholarship."[147]

Williams uses careful scholarship and a literal hermeneutic to refute Isaac of Troki, point by point. The key passages that he includes are Genesis 3:15; 49:10; Psalm 110; Isaiah 7:14; 9:6–7; 52:13–53:12; Micah 5:2; and Zechariah 9:9; 12:10.

In a number of places, Williams either does not take a position or concedes the point to Troki. While stating, for example, that Troki is assuredly wrong in his interpretation of Daniel 9:25–27, Williams himself is dissatisfied with all interpretations of this passage so he refuses to discuss it.[148] Additionally, he concedes that Troki is correct that in Daniel 7:13 "the one like unto the son of man" is probably the people of Israel and not the Messiah.[149]

Generally speaking, Williams's response to Isaac of Troki is excellent. He is careful in his exegesis, knowledgeable in Hebrew and rabbinic commentators, and quite respectful in tone. Since virtually all modern Jewish anti-Christian polemics are based on Troki, Williams's book has enduring value as a response to common Jewish exegetical objections to Jesus as the fulfillment of Messianic prophecy. This book is unfortunately no longer in print even though it is an excellent resource for both Jewish seekers and those trying to reach them with the gospel.

The preceding section has surveyed selected modern apologists for Jewish people who have used Messianic prophecy in their evangelistic witness. It has shown that in the modern period a vast improvement took place in the use of Messianic prophecy. This improvement was the result of greater reliance on literal hermeneutics coupled with greater sensitivity to, and regard for, the Jewish people.

Throughout history, Messianic prophecy has been crucial to Jewish evangelism. It was used by the apostles, the church fathers, medieval Christian scholars, and modern missionaries to the Jews. The purpose of this chapter has been to demonstrate this vital importance of Messianic prophecy to Jewish evangelism.

It is imperative, then, to learn three essential lessons from the foregoing.

First, with regard to tone, Messianic prophecy should always and only be presented in a respectful and sensitive fashion toward Jewish people. The patristic and medieval church frequently castigated Jewish people for their blindness in failing to see Jesus predicted in Messianic prophecy. Some churchmen even asserted that the Jews understood that Jesus was the promised Messiah but refused to acknowledge him out of stubbornness. These attitudes were manifestly uncharitable and decidedly ineffective.

As the modern church grew in its positive regard for the Jewish people, so the tone of its polemic improved from reproach to respect. This would explain, in part, the greater success of modern Jewish missions. Those who engage in Jewish gospel outreach today need to use Messianic prophecy without recrimination, especially when speaking to Jewish people who remain unable to see or understand the Christian perspective regarding Jesus.

Second, with regard to interpretation, Messianic prophecy should be included in gospel witness only when backed by sound exegesis.[150] In the past, many alleged Messianic proof texts were ripped from their literary context and frequently used incorrectly. Passages that had nothing to do with Messianic prophecy were sometimes spiritualized to fit with the gospel narratives. On the other hand, expositors at times used a wooden literal approach to Old Testament passages. Still other apologists used unwise methodology in arguing from translations rather than from the Hebrew text.

To be effective in presenting Messianic prophecy, would-be evangelists should use sound interpretive principles. It is essential to use whenever possible the Hebrew Scriptures as the basis for discussion. Messianic prophecies should be examined in light of their literary context. Normal hermeneutics must be followed, avoiding the extremes of questionable allegorizing or unwarranted wooden literalism. This more normal interpretation will guard against the accusation that both the New Testament and Christians misuse the Jewish Bible in their efforts to find Jesus in its prophecies.

Third, with regard to strategy, it is essential to interact with Jewish sources when examining Messianic prophecy. Too often, those who present Messianic prophecy are unaware of the arguments a knowledgeable Jewish person would use in response to the presentation of Messianic prophecy. Thus, the contemporary Jewish evangelist who seeks to use Messianic prophecy must be aware of how these passages were understood by Talmudic and Midrashic authorities[151] and the medieval Jewish commentators, and how they are explained by modern anti-Christian polemicists.[152] Only then can the evangelist effectively answer the objections that will be raised to seeing Jesus in the Hebrew Scripture. Knowing traditional Jewish sources and current Jewish interpretations are vital aids to communicating Messianic prophecy correctly to contemporary Jewish people.

Conclusion

Messianic prophecy remains the vital link in effective Jewish evangelism today. Messianic prophecy was crucial to Jesus of Nazareth, the apostles, the historic church, and modern Jewish missions. Regardless of the terrible abuses of Messianic prophecy in the past, its correct use still constitutes a crucial dimension of effective Jewish evangelism today. Its importance is captured by Jakob Jocz:

> The Hebrew Scriptures are still of fundamental importance in the proclamation of the Christian message. Without them Christianity is inexplicable. However much our exegetical methods have changed, the appeal to the Old Testament is still an essential part of Christian evidences.[153]

Indeed, the effective use of Messianic prophecy remains critical to all successful Jewish evangelism.

Chapter 14

One Way for Jews and Gentiles in the New Millennium

KAI KJÆR-HANSEN

The subject for this chapter, *One Way for Jews and Gentiles in the New Millennium,* puts Jews and Gentiles to the test. It reveals what Jews and we Christians think about our faith in Jesus—and about Jesus and his work of salvation. If we dare say today that *all* people need Jesus for salvation—and say it with the humility that the Christian church's tragic history toward the Jewish people requires of us—it means that we, at the beginning of the third millennium, identify with the first Jesus-believing Jews. If we dare not say it, then it means we distance ourselves from the first believers—and also from Jewish believers in Jesus of our day. And if we dare not say that salvation is exclusively bound up with Jesus, then what do we have that we can bring to Jews or Gentiles in the third millennium? And if the message of salvation in Jesus is not for Jews today, why should it be for Gentiles today when, according to the first Jesus-believers, it was a message that was first presented to Jews?

These introductory comments and rhetorical questions have already indicated what direction this chapter is going to take. In the world of faith, however, the ultimate issues of God are not subject to *proof*. They are something we can witness about, and which can be rejected or received in faith. If this chapter contains a hidden agenda, it is not to *prove* that faith in Jesus is *the* truth and *the* way for Jews and Gentiles, nor is it to give a testimony of my own faith—although I neither deny the former nor am ashamed of the latter. The purpose is a more limited one—namely, to show that if the New Testament still has a word about determining what the gospel is—and for whom it is relevant—it must include Jews. Or phrased in a different manner, *If the gospel is not, or no longer is, for Jews, then it is also not, or no longer is, good news for Gentiles*. The relevance of the gospel for non-Jews depends on its relevance for Jews. This affirmation is diametrically opposed to the assertions of the so-called two covenant theology; indeed, it is the antithesis of it.

If the uniqueness of Jesus the Messiah changes with the turn of one hour into another—or with one millennium into another—then he is not unique, nor has he ever been unique. In relation to the gospel, then, when all is said and done, the turn of a millennium is a rather trivial thing.

Millennium or Not . . .

The turn of a millennium has no major theological significance. Nor did passing from the second to the third millennium create any great disasters. Calendars, which tell us when we go from one millennium to another, are man-made things. Nothing made by humans, though, can change God's plans or change what the gospel is, or for whom it is. If the transition to a new millennium can be used to talk about Jesus and to invite people into fellowship with the crucified and risen Messiah, then Jewish believers in Jesus and the Christian church should use the man-made calendar.

In relation to the new millennium, however, what has so far appeared in the Israeli press about Christians and the Christian faith makes rather depressing reading. The Israeli press alone, however, is not responsible for rash claims. To blame are also those Jewish and Gentile believers in Jesus who have a regrettable strong focus on, and have added their own speculations about, the "future" Messiah or Israel's eschatological role in salvation history. The message in the *Jerusalem Report*, for example, has been, "Jesus will return sometime around the year 2000"; or, "Based on the words of the prophets of Israel I believe that [the Mideast] peace process will lead to the most devastating war Israel has ever known. After that war, the longed-for Messiah will come"; or, "Netanyahu is indeed, as his name states, the gift of God." Or as a headline in the *Jerusalem Post*, 1 January 1999, stated, "Preparing for the false prophet," with the following subtitle, "Some of the millions of Christian pilgrims drawn to visit Jerusalem in the year 2000 will find themselves in the capital's psychiatric center . . ."[1]

And much more speculation of this dubious nature could be mentioned. But suppose someone had been quoted in the Israeli press, at the beginning of the new millennium, as saying, "Jewish believers in Jesus and the Christian church are still convinced that the Jew Jesus came to save his people from their sins"! That is sensational news—but hardly sensationalism. In terms of theology and salvation history, the new millennium didn't change our being at the same point on God's time line as were the first believers in Jesus. The death of Jesus and the day of Pentecost are events of the *past*; the return of Jesus is still in the *future*—be it the near or the distant future. Thus, whether a group of people accepted Jesus as Messiah at Pentecost, or recognized him one minute ago, both groups are at the midpoint of salvation history, because the decisive midpoint of salvation history lies in the past.[2]

Further, according to the New Testament, it is the suffering Messiah of the past who is going to be the Messiah of the future—not the other way round! That's why the above news reports are so depressing. It is a sad thing if and when, here in the third millennium, Christians and Jewish believers in Jesus present the "future" Messiah and the second coming of the Messiah in such a way that the "past" and what the Messiah did in the past are no longer the focal point.

Joseph Rabinowitz (1837–1899), one of the great personalities in the history of the Messianic movement, reminds us about this very thing. Rabinowitz, a Russian Jew who had come to faith in the Messiah during a journey to Palestine in 1882, held public services for the Israelites of the new covenant in Kishinev, in what is now Moldavia, from the Christmas of 1884 until his death in 1899. It seems appropriate to this current subject to allow him to tell a parable. Certain Jews are famous for telling good stories. The Jew Jesus was like that. So, too, is the Jew Rabinowitz.

The Four Wheels: A Parable by Joseph Rabinowitz

A few foolish people driving in a four-wheeler happened to lose a wheel. Finding that the car moved along heavily, they looked about and found that a wheel was missing. One of the foolish men jumped down and ran forward in search of the missing wheel. To everyone he met he said, "We have lost a wheel. Have you seen a wheel? Have you found a wheel?" One wise man at last said, "You are looking in the wrong direction. Instead of looking in front for your wheel, you ought to look behind." That is exactly the great mistake the Jews have been making for centuries.

They have forgotten that in order to look forward aright, they must first look behind aright. The four wheels of Hebrew History may be said to be Abraham, Moses, David, and Jesus. The Jews by looking in front, instead of behind, have failed to find their fourth wheel.

Thank God, that "the Sons of the New Covenant" have found the Supreme Wheel—Jesus. Abraham, Moses and David are but beautiful types and symbols of Jesus. They were, and still are, the repositories of His energy; they were, and are still, moved and managed by Him, as truly as are the Cherubim and Seraphim. Thank God, we have found Yeshua Achinu, our Brother Jesus, our All, "who of God has been made unto us, wisdom, righteousness, sanctification, and redemption"; from whom alone we have found divine light, life, liberty, and love, for the great Here and the greater Hereafter. And now with bright eye and jubilant heart, we are looking forward to the pulsing splendours of His appearing.[3]

Rabinowitz really understood what it is all about. He does not fail to look ahead, to the glorious second coming of Messiah—for that is vital to New Testament faith. But he understands that the future is based on the past, and that the future Messiah is identical with the Messiah of the past. Therefore it is necessary to look behind, into the past, in order to understand *who* is the future Messiah.

Now, let us turn our attention to Franz Rosenzweig (1886–1929).

Franz Rosenzweig and Two Covenant Theology

Another modern Jew, Rosenzweig very nearly came to the same faith as Rabinowitz. Although he did not come to faith in Jesus, he continued to ascribe importance to Christianity—but only for Gentiles!

His reasoning might go something like this: Jesus says, according to John 14:6 (RSV), "I am the way, and the truth, and the life; no one comes to the Father, but by me." In Jesus' parable about the prodigal son, the father in the parable says to his eldest son, "Son, you are always with me, and all that is mine is yours" (Luke 15:31 RSV).

Franz Rosenzweig says, with an allusion to John 14:6 and Luke 15:31,

> We are wholly agreed as to what Christ and his church mean to the world: no one can reach the Father save through him.
>
> No one can reach the Father! But the situation is quite different for one who does not have to reach the Father because he is already with him. And this is true of the people of Israel (though not of individual Jews).[4]

Hardly any Jew before Franz Rosenzweig (1886–1929) ever spoke with such appreciation of Christianity and the Christian church. Rosenzweig had a positive attitude regarding the church's role in the world. Therefore he has been extremely influential in the development of the doctrine of the two covenants.[5]

The path Rosenzweig walked to arrive at his positive attitude to Christianity and the church's importance for non-Jews cannot but make a certain impression. A person who through his struggle with himself and his God at last finds himself in his own tradition— while retaining faith in his God—such a person commands our respect and sympathy. Rosenzweig is that man. His principal work, *The Star of Redemption*, which he began writing on army postal cards at the end of August 1918 on the Balkan Front, is the expression of a personal need and is not determined by "objective, theoretical speculations," as mentioned by N. N. Glatzer.[6]

It would be a premature conclusion, however, to assume that the work is devoid of "theoretical speculation." Raised in an assimilated Jewish home, Rosenzweig found his way back to his Jewish heritage, the heritage that he had only got a glimpse of in his adolescence through his grandfather Adam Rosenzweig. In 1905 Rosenzweig began studying at university, first medicine but from 1907 he also studied history, philosophy, and theology. In 1914 he finished his doctoral thesis, titled *Hegel und der Staat* (published in 1920). While at university he had thoroughgoing discussions about Judaism and Christianity with Eugen Rosenstock-Huessy, professor of law and sociology, and with his two cousins Hans and Rudolf Ehrenberg, who had both become Christians and who made a strong impression on Rosenzweig.

The result of these conversations was that Rosenzweig, in 1913, was convinced that he ought to be baptized. A conversation with Rosenstock had led him from his "relativistic position into a non-relativistic one."[7] But he declared that he could turn Christian only *"qua* Jew—not through the intermediate stage of paganism." Rosenzweig wrote to Rudolf Ehrenberg, "I considered this reservation purely personal, and you approved of it, remembering early Christianity." While talking to his mother, who realized that he planned to be baptized, he pointed to the New Testament that he held in his hand: "Mother, here is everything, here is the truth. There is only one way, Jesus."[8]

Rosenzweig's search for truth, however, did not end with baptism. On October 11, 1913, he celebrated Yom Kippur in a small synagogue in Berlin. What was supposed to have been a farewell to Judaism became the inauguration of a new life for him *as a Jew*. The service on the Day of Atonement revolutionized his life, or, in the words of N. N. Glatzer, "What that day conveyed to him was that, essential as a mediator may be in the Christian experience, the Jews stand in no need of a mediator. God is near to a man and desires his undeviated devotion."[9] Franz Rosenzweig, the "near-believer" became "a traditional Jew," as Louis Goldberg puts it.[10] On October 23, 1913, he wrote to his mother, "I seem to have found the way back about which I had tortured myself in vain and pondered for almost three months."[11] On October 31 of the same year, he wrote to his cousin Rudolf, after acknowledging that the non-Jew cannot reach the Father save through Jesus, that "the situation is quite different for one who does not have to reach the Father because he is already with him. . . . Chosen by its Father, the people of Israel gazes fixedly across the world and history, over to that last, most distant time when the Father, the One and Only, will be 'all in all.' Then, when Christ ceases to be the Lord, Israel will cease to be the chosen people. On this day, God will lose the name by which only Israel calls him; God will then no longer be 'its' God."[12] In this letter he also wrote that he was not going to be baptized: "After prolonged, and I believe thorough, self-examination, I have reversed my decision. It no longer seems necessary to me, and therefore, being what I am, no longer possible. I will remain a Jew."[13]

By birth Franz Rosenzweig *was* a Jew. He did not *become* a Jew. But he became aware of what he already was, namely, a Jew. Judaism was no longer an anachronism. Like other religious philosophers, however—Jewish as well as Christian—Rosenzweig is difficult to put a label on. In the *Star of Redemption*, his magnum opus, he focuses on three major subjects: creation, revelation, and redemption. He is, in Phillip Sigal's words, "non-orthodox in style, existentialist in philosophy and immersed in romanticism." Add to this that he also "rejected historicism."[14] N. N. Glatzer calls him "one of the most undogmatic thinkers of his time,"[15] which makes it close to impossible on a few pages to assess Rosenzweig as a religious philosopher.

But the following can be said about the matter that is relevant in this context: for Rosenzweig, the difference between Jews and non-Jews is that the Jew, because he is a descendant of Abraham, does not need to be reborn, which non-Jews need to. The Jew is born a Jew. It is different with the pagans. When a non-Jew receives Jesus, he is reborn. "A Christian is made, not born." As for the Jew, "the individual is born a Jew. He no longer needs to become one in some decisive moment of his individual life."[16] The fundamental difference between Jewish and Christian is that "the Christian is by nature or at least by birth—a pagan; the Jew, however, is a Jew."[17] A Jew is born into the faith community that was instituted between God and Israel on Sinai, it is a natural phenomenon; in contrast, pagans have to undergo a rebirth.

In the words of Frank Ephraim Talmage, "Judaism is the Life—the faith that was with the Father at the beginning—while Christianity is the way toward the Father of those who are not yet with him. Judaism is the fire, Christianity the rays."[18] The fire, Judaism, is already with God, the Father; Judaism is at the goal, not on the way, as Christianity is. Therefore Judaism does not need a salvation history.[19] "Whether Christ is more than an idea—no Christian can know it. But that Israel is more than an idea, that he knows, that he sees. For we live. We are eternal, not as an idea may be eternal: if we are eternal, it is in full reality."[20]

As complementary entities, Judaism as well as Christianity have a God-willed function in the world. Rosenzweig has the following to say about this:

> Before God, then, the Jew and Christian both labor at the same task. He cannot dispense with either. He has set enmity between the two for all time, and withal has most intimately bound each to each. To us [Jews] he gave eternal life by kindling the fire of the Star of his truth in our hearts. Them [the Christians] he set on the eternal way by causing them to pursue the rays of that Star of his truth for all time unto the eternal end.[21]

In the same passage Rosenzweig goes on to say, "The truth, the whole truth, thus belongs neither to them [the Christians] nor to us." But this does not challenge his position that Judaism is superior to Christianity, as the star is primary in relation to the rays. The Christians "are in any event already destined for all time to see what is illuminated, and not the light."[22] But exactly Christianity's inherent "paganism"[23] qualifies the Christian to convert the pagans. "The Christian credo had to accommodate itself to a pagan impulse in order to win over the pagans, and this impulse is quenched by the worship of God in the Spirit and the truth, by the promise that Spirit would lead Christendom."[24] While Judaism does not need to missionize—it only needs to be, and is already a testimony of God through its very being—it is a different matter with Christianity. "Christianity must proselytize."[25]

But to Rosenzweig, Christianity holds no decisive message for Jews. Jewish Christians have only a historical claim as an early church phenomenon and a dogmatic claim in Christian eschatology—in the first case as an anachronism, he says, and in the last as a paradox.[26]

The Ring of "Good News"

What, though, is the theological foundation of the view that the gospel of and by Jesus is for non-Jews *only*? And is it possible to maintain the New Testament's view of Jesus if two covenant theology is recognized?

That is the very heart of the matter!

It is true that, for many, the doctrine of the two covenants has the ring of "Good News." At long last a solution has been found to the difficult relationship between Judaism and Christianity. Both religions are equal (that is the way the matter is often portrayed); both have the same claim; both are willed by the same God, and both have a divine mission in the world. Therefore it is not for them to compete about "souls," which is the reason why the church's mission among Jews can stop. The Christian church need no longer have a bad conscience because it has failed to bring the gospel to the Jews so that they would believe in Jesus. The church has been released from what it used to believe was its obligation. And this has happened, not through something negative—a prohibition—but thanks to what seems a positive theological argument. And if it is possible to talk about superiority here, it is no longer the question of the superiority of Christianity over Judaism but, on the contrary, the superiority of Judaism over Christianity.

It is not difficult to understand why a great many Jews subscribe to the idea of a double covenant—the "second" covenant does not really challenge their position. Nor is it very difficult to understand why liberal and radical Christian theologians support this view, considering how they have reduced and transformed Jesus in relation to the New Testament.[27] It is remarkable, however, and nothing less than a contradiction in terms, that this theory has gained advocates among evangelical Christians. Although most Jews state that they do not missionize and that they do not have a need to missionize among non-Jews, they have nevertheless succeeded to a certain degree in convincing many Christians that Jews have their own covenant with God, which for them makes belief in Jesus unnecessary. That convincing is also a kind of "mission."

Unlike some Jews who do not recognize the Christian church's right to missionize Jews, I fully recognize the right of Jews to influence Christians and fight for what they are convinced is the truth. To fight for the "truth" with arguments is, after all, a human right. I'm even impressed with the efficiency achieved by Jews in the Jewish-Christian dialogue when it comes to asserting that Jews have no need for faith in Jesus. Seen against that background, it is no wonder that Jews who are involved in this dialogue urge Christians to give their testimony only within the framework of the Jewish-Christian dialogue.[28] So far, what testimony there may have been within that framework has proved a relatively harmless affair for Jews.

Historical and Exegetical Absurdities

As stated, it is within human rights to fight for truth by using arguments. It is impossible, though, to prevent people from reinterpreting historical texts to mean something other than their original intent. If the arguers do reinterpret in obvious conflict with the original intent, however, their admitting so would be welcomed—and would increase the degree with which the arguers are taken seriously. When philosophers and theologians make the leap away from the obvious historical meaning of a text, they must be prepared to meet with criticism—whether they are Jews or Christians.

Following are a few examples of the frivolous play, from a historical and exegetical standpoint, with New Testament words.

John 14:6

Frank Ephraim Talmage argues that "Rosenzweig tried to abandon the apologetic approach and establish a co-relationship with Christianity which would affirm the necessity of each."[29] When the Star of Redemption is compared, for example, to earlier Jewish apologetics and polemics, then Talmage is right. But it does not change the fact that Rosenzweig's thinking is apologetic. Arnulf H. Baumann rightly observed that Rosenzweig's argument "serves to refute the traditional Christian claim to absolute truth." Baumann refers to Rosenzweig's use of John 14:6 as "a way of saying, 'Leave us alone with your claims to ultimate truth. Leave us in peace.'"[30]

Rosenzweig's use of John 14:6 shows that in his approach he has not completely abandoned a *way* of thinking and arguing that has parallels in traditional polemics—Jewish as well as Christian.

It can hardly be denied that Rosenzweig uses the words from the gospel of John contrary to their original meaning. Jesus' words, "No one comes to the Father, but by me," were addressed *to* Jews. So when Rosenzweig takes the words to refer unambiguously to non-Jews, it is a historical and exegetical absurdity. Only if Rosenzweig's use of these words is seen in the light of an apologetic context may it be argued that it bears the hallmark of "near-genius," as Shemaryahu Talmon characterizes it.[31] Talmon quite rightly asserts, however, that Rosenzweig is contradicted by the first half of the verse, "I am the way, and the truth, and the life," since the point of this verse is that eternal life can now be received through faith in Jesus. According to the gospel of John, this verse speaks of the redemption that Rosenzweig claims belongs to Judaism.[32]

Luke 15:31

In the Rosenzweig quotation above is an allusion to the parable of the prodigal son or, as Joachim Jeremias prefers to call it, the parable of the father's love (Luke 15:11–32). In the parable the father says to the elder son, who does not want to take part in the celebratory homecoming for the younger son, "Son, you are always with me, and all that is mine is yours."

Rosenzweig and others use the quotation to say that Jews do not need Jesus in order to reach the Father; they are already with the Father. The parable may be identified as an apologetic parable "in which Jesus justifies his table companionship with sinners against his critics," as Joachim Jeremias says.[33] In the Luke context, Jesus' critics are the Pharisees and the scribes (Luke 15:2). And the sinners and tax collectors are—like the Pharisees and the scribes—*Jews*. On the basis of just this one observation, it is absurd to use Luke 15:31 as an argument for the view that Jews, without accepting Jesus' teaching, are with the Father.

The parable has a double climax: it describes not only the return of the younger son but also the protest of the elder brother. While the point is to defend that the gospel is for sinners—Jewish sinners—the second is an invitation to some leaders—Jewish leaders—to abandon their resistance to the gospel.[34] This invitation contains a criticism of them because they cannot rejoice when the "big" sinners accept the love of God, which Jesus proclaimed. The parable has an abrupt end. "Sadly," Robert L. Lindsey says, "the parable ends without our knowing whether the father is going to convince the elder brother to join the merrymaking or not."[35]

The double climax of the parable does not, however, speak for, but rather against, a dual covenant theology. Let us suppose that the younger son does not merely represent sinners and tax collectors in Jesus' day but, in an anticipatory way, includes future generations of non-Jews who accept the gospel. We shall still do violence to the parable by isolating one verse, then use it to contradict the information given in the immediate context and also the context of the totality of Jesus' teaching.

Quite apart from that, modern research of the parables has seriously challenged the allegorical interpretation of the parables of Jesus. For centuries allegorical interpretation has been very popular, not least because it allowed the possibility for readers to inject their own subjective, profound ideas into single words. It is the main point—or as here—the two main points of the parable that require our attention.

Kenneth E. Bailey captures the meaning well when he says this, among other things:

> The older son then insults his father publicly and demonstrates himself to be as "lost" as his brother was in the far country. The father extends the same love in humiliation, but no confession and repentance result. Rather, the older son launches a bitter tirade against the father. The parable closes with a final appeal for reconciliation. Both sons are seen as rebels needing a visible demonstration of love to win them from servanthood to sonship.[36]

The main issue is very clear. Jesus, the narrator of the parable, is a Jew, and both those whom he defends and those whom he criticizes through the parable are Jews. The message Jesus brings is for both "big" and "small" sinners, and consequently also for the Jewish leaders. From an exegetical point of view, it is therefore absurd when Luke 15:31 is used to argue—as does Roy Eckardt, among others[37]—that Israel, interpreted as the elder son in the parable, belongs to the father's house and is on God's way and in God's will.

"To Save Those Who Are Eagerly Waiting for Him"

Franz Rosenzweig's statement that "whether Jesus is Messiah will be shown when the Messiah comes"[38] is sometimes transformed into the popular idea that the second coming of Jesus will be the first coming of the Messiah for the Jews. Even the esteemed scholar David Flusser can say, "I do not think many Jews would object if the messiah when he came again was the Jew Jesus."[39]

And Hans Ucko—executive secretary for Christian-Jewish Relations, New Religious Movements, and Marxism in the World Council of Churches' Office on Inter-religious Relations—writes,

> Jews and Christians, though in different ways, are both waiting for the Messiah to come. Christians are expecting the Christ, the "Lord himself with a cry of command, with the archangel's call and with the sound of God's trumpet, [to] descend from heaven" (1 Thess. 4:16). Jews are waiting for the Messiah and the Messianic kingdom. There is a story about a Jew and a Christian engaged in heated discussion. All of a sudden someone comes in and says: "We hear that the Messiah is coming." They run to the place where the Messiah is to appear. And there he is. They both go up to him and ask: "Is this your first or second visit?" The Messiah responds: "No comment."
>
> The story doesn't end there. It goes on to say: "Perhaps now you will understand the true meaning of the Messiah: messianism is the quality of life that we live together along the way."[40]

And yet the whole idea—that be he Jesus or not, his return will be the first coming for the Jews—is an absurd one from not only a New Testament point of view but also from a traditional Jewish point of view. According to the New Testament, the same Jesus who went into heaven will come again—from heaven; according to the post-Maimonides way of thinking about the Messiah, he will be a man among men, who does *not* come from heaven. The comparison reveals the important difference between the New Testament doctrine of Jesus' supernatural second coming from heaven and the traditional Jewish expectation that the Messiah is a human being of this world.

The Exegetical and Historical Difficulty Admitted

Hans-Joachim Schoeps, one spokesman for two covenant theology, admits its exegetical and historical difficulties in relation to the New Testament. "The New Testament is glad tidings only for the nations of the world," says Schoeps, "and the latter bear witness to it in the polyphony of the Christian churches and communities centred in Christ." Schoeps poses the question, wondering "how far Christian dogmatics may be ready to grant the existence of an absolute revelation apart from its own, such as would except Israel from the sphere of its saving proclamation." He formulates the difficulties of such without beating about the bush: the issue is complicated, he admits, by, among other things, "the fact that Jesus' original sense of mission was directed toward His own people." Schoeps's own answer to this is, "However, the continued existence of Israel almost 2,000 years *post Christum natum*, still undisturbed in its consciousness of being God's covenant people, is testimony that the old covenant has not been abrogated, that as the covenant of Israel it continues to exist alongside the wider human covenant of the Christian Church." Schoeps describes the problems in a disarmingly honest way:

> We stand in obvious opposition to the view of history outlined by Paul. But we have taken into account the possibility that Paul falsely interpreted the will of God, that his understanding of saving history was a subjective judgment and an objective error. Although his view became official church teaching, the question of revision of this might now be raised, one result of which would be to correct the church's judgment on Israel in such a way as would involve the abandonment of the church's mission to the Jews. For to speak of the blinding and hardening of the Jews was a mistake, which might even now be rectified.[41]

Questions That Have to Be Asked

Schoeps thinks that to speak of the blinding and hardening of the Jews was a mistake. As a Gentile, I feel tempted to say, "Is, then, speaking of the blinding and hardening of the *non*-Jews—which the New Testament also does—a mistake, which might even now be rectified?" The response demonstrated by the two groups hangs together.

Schoeps does concede that Jesus addressed his message to his own people. For Schoeps to oppose that view would also be a hopeless affair. Historically speaking, Christianity was a Jewish phenomenon: the "where" of revelation was Israel; the "from whom" was the God of the Jews; the first "to whom" was the Jews; the main character of revelation was the Jew Jesus. The entire framework of the message and the conceptual universe of the New Testament is Jewish.

Further, it was to Jews that Jesus said, "Repent, for the kingdom of heaven is at hand" (Matt. 4:17 RSV). There are relatively few examples in the New Testament of Jesus addressing non-Jews, but those that do exist are the exceptions that prove the rule—namely, the primary addressees were Jews. The mission of Jesus was mission to Israel, although it had far-reaching consequences for Gentiles in terms of theology and salvation history.

The mission of the apostles, too, and of Paul was also a mission to Jews *and* Gentiles. It is not possible to question the historicity of this. It is true that Schoeps recommends that people take into account the possibility that Paul falsely interpreted the will of God concerning the relevance of the gospel for Israel, that, as cited above, "[Paul's] understanding of saving history was a subjective judgement and an objective error." If we as Christians consider that a possibility in Paul's case, we are forced to conclude that the same possibility exists in Jesus' case, namely, that *Jesus'* understanding of salvation history was a subjective judgment and an objective error. And such a person was to bring glad tidings—to the nations! To maintain something like that is, in a New Testament perspective, theologically untenable. The crux of the matter is, "Is it at all possible to speak of glad tidings for Gentiles if these are not glad tidings also for Jews?"

The answer is simple: in a New Testament perspective, the relevance of the gospel for non-Jews is derived from its relevance for Jews. The relevance of the gospel for non-Jews *depends* on its relevance for Jews. For the first Jewish believers in Jesus, there is no gospel at all if the gospel does not first apply to them.

Based on reason, then, it may be declared at the outset of the third millennium, the gospel is neither for Jews nor for non-Jews. But to declare that the gospel, which Jesus first proclaimed for Jews, no longer applies to Jews while it should still apply to Gentiles—that is an untenable position approaching theological nonsense. Salvation for both Jews and Gentiles hangs together. The first believers in Jesus were not, after all, talking about a new God but about the God of Israel, who has revealed himself in a new way in Jesus and thereby fulfilled what he had earlier promised to Israel through the prophets. These first believers say, referring to the resurrection of Jesus, "Let all the house of Israel therefore know assuredly that God has made him both Lord and Messiah" (Acts 2:36 RSV). They speak as brothers to brothers about God's Anointed One—Jesus—who was going to suffer (Acts 3:18). They challenge their Jewish brothers to repent, "that your sins may be blotted out" (Acts 3:19 RSV). They know that they live in the Messianic age, and they have the courage to tell their Jewish brothers that as Jews they are going to effect their own exclusion from the fellowship of the people of God if they do not believe in Jesus Messiah (Acts 3:23). And not only that, if their brothers do not repent and believe in Jesus Messiah, they will not fulfil the prophecy that "all the families of the earth" will be included in the fellowship of the people of God.

For the apostle Peter—in Solomon's Portico—all the preceding elements of revelation hang together. There is good news for Gentiles in God's covenant with Abraham (Gen. 12:3). Peter invites his Jewish audience to realize God's promise to Abraham. The precondition has been fulfilled: God has sent his Messiah *to Israel.* "Will you take part in the realization of God's promise to Abraham," Peter asks, "so that *Gentiles* may partake in the promised blessing?" (Acts 3:25). The underlying idea is that, as a *Jew* and through faith in Jesus, Jews share in the blessing from Israel's God and thereby help make it possible for Gentiles to share in the blessing of God's covenant with Abraham.

The Jew in Peter's train of thought is closely reasoned. Therefore he can say to fellow Jews about the Jew Jesus, "And there is salvation in no one else, for there is no other name under heaven given among men by which we must be saved" (Acts 4:12 RSV). For Peter and the other Jewish believers, it is out of the question that Jesus should have any relevance for the Gentile world if he was not crucially relevant for the Jewish world.

In this new millennium, Jewish believers in Jesus, as well as the Gentile Christian church, should dare to say that which was said by Jewish believers in the first century. For if it is said that Jews do not need Jesus for salvation, it is also said, theologically speaking, that non-Jews do not need him, either.

If Jesus is not the way for Jews, he is not the way for Gentiles, either.

The Jewish Reaction

The change of the millennium does not usher in any radical change, theological or otherwise. It is to be expected, then, that advocates for the Jewish community will in the third millennium accuse Christians who believe that Jesus is the way—also for Jews—of being anti-Semites. Such was accused at the end of the second millennium.

Reactions to "The Willowbank Declaration on the Gospel and the Jewish People" were prompt.[42] In this document these words by Paul were quoted: "The gospel is the power of salvation, to everyone who believes, to the Jew first and also the Greek" (see Rom. 1:16). In an interview, Rabbi A. James Rudin, national director of Inter-Religious Affairs for the American Jewish Committee, called the declaration a "blueprint for spiritual genocide that is shot through with the ancient Christian 'teaching of contempt' for Jews and Judaism."[43] Elsewhere Rudin refers to the declaration as "wrong-headed" and "arrogant."[44] Rabbi Alexander Schindler, president of the Union of American Hebrew Congregations, describes the declaration as "retrograde and primitive."[45] In an article titled "Jewish Leaders Call on Evangelicals to Repudiate Their Conversion Goals," Schindler is quoted as labelling the declaration "a desperate attempt to stop the clock of progress in inter-religious relations." Rudin calls the declaration "the worst kind of Christian religious imperialism."[46]

And the resolution that the Southern Baptist Convention, USA, passed in the summer of 1996 (which did not contain anything new—only that Jews need the gospel) is characterized, in the magazine *Christians and Israel,* as being "clearly not in the spirit of our time: the spirit of interfaith respect, cooperation and dialogue." And it goes on to say, "Implicitly or explicitly, it has been recognized in enlightened Christian circles that dialogue and evangelization cannot peacefully coexist."[47]

To this reaction, Jewish believers in Jesus and Gentile Christians must be allowed to insist that the question of whether or not Jews need Jesus for salvation is *not* something the Gentile Christian church has invented. In the New Testament message, exclusivity is attached to Jesus the Jew. It is not possible to remove this exclusivity without at the same time violating the Christian message. Christians who feel committed to the New Testament message have a clear right to go on believing that Jesus is the Messiah for Jews as well as for non-Jews. And they have the same clear right to *repeat* the exclusivity that was expressed by one of the first Jesus-believing Jews, namely, the apostle Peter, who, facing the Jewish council in Jerusalem, asserted that there is salvation in no other name under heaven but the name of Jesus (Acts 4:12). For those who share this conviction, it means a commitment to take the gospel back to the Jewish people.

This attitude cannot under any circumstances be described as un-Jewish. That Jesus is the Messiah is something Gentiles have learned from Jews. That the God of Israel, when he reveals himself, means what he says is something Gentiles have learned from Jews. That there is such a thing as truth—distinct from relativism—is something Gentiles have learned from Jews. That the gospel is for Jews is not a Gentile or a Gentile-Christian invention, but a Jewish conviction delivered to us by the first Jesus-believing Jews. That there is salvation only in the name of Jesus is something said to fellow Jews by the first Jesus-believing Jews.

Much could be said about the way Christian theology has led to negative relationships between Jews and Christians. Much more could be said about the poor way the Christian church has treated the Jewish people over the centuries. One thing that cannot be said, however, is that it is "un-Jewish" to tell Jews about the Jew Jesus. That to do so is "un-Jewish" has been repeated so often that some have come to believe it. Jewish theologians have long accused Christian theologians of not paying sufficient attention to the Jewish roots of the Christian faith. Or they have been able to maintain, with some right, that Christians have transferred all the good promises in the Hebrew Bible (the Old Testament) to the Christian church while they have left all the curses to Israel.

The antithesis to two covenant theology, which is outlined above, implies that the gospel is for Israel *first*. The gospel *is* good news for Israel. Against this background it is difficult to take seriously the Jewish accusation of anti-Semitism when Jewish believers in Jesus, and the Gentile Christian church, continue to say that Jesus is the way also for Jews. For when that is said, the Jewish nature of the gospel is really taken seriously.

That Jews need Jesus for salvation is not something the Gentile Christian church has made up. Jews are responsible for that statement. And at the beginning of the third millennium, Gentile believers in Jesus are grateful to those Jews—Jesus-believing Jews—for that statement. But when Gentile believers say that Jesus is the only way to God for all—Jews as well as Gentiles—we are touching a tender spot. For non-Christian Gentiles as well as Jews, Joseph Rabinowitz has a comment on the reaction from Jewish people who are touched on the tender spot.

Joseph's Misfortune

The misfortune of my people has always been on my heart. I have also tried various remedies to relieve it, but all has been in vain.

When a doctor comes to a patient, he first has to question the patient closely before he can prescribe a remedy for the disease. He feels the pulse, presses here and there, asking all the time, "Does it hurt here?" "Is there pressure there?" "Have you pain here?" But not until the doctor touches the tender spot, does a really clear answer come from the patient. The pain squeezes the words from him, "Don't press so hard, it hurts!"

That was my experience when I concerned myself with my people's sufferings. I have in vain pressed various places. As I was not striking the tender spot, there was hardly any answer.

If I said, "The Talmud and all the rabbinical extraneous matter do not come, as is claimed, from Sinai, but they are human matters full of wisdom and unwisdom," then these words made little impression upon my people.

If I said, "Nor does the Tanakh (the Old Testament) contain anything other than human words, unproven stories, and unbelievable miracles," then all the time I remained the respected Rabinowitz; that did not cause my people any pain either.

My people remained calm when I placed Moses on an equal footing with the conjurors of our day; it did not hurt them when I called the same Moses an impostor. Indeed, I might even deny God without my people uttering a single sound of pain.

But when I returned from the Holy Land with the glad news, Jesus is our brother, then I struck the tender spot. A scream of pain could be heard and resounded from all sides, "Do not press, do not touch that, it hurts!"

Well, it does hurt: But you must know, my people, that that is indeed your illness; you lack nothing but your brother Jesus. Your illness consists precisely in your not having him. Receive him and you will be healed of all your sufferings.[48]

Notes

Introduction

1. Walter Bauer, *A Greek-English Lexicon of the New Testament and Other Early Christian Literature*, trans. and rev. W. F. Arndt and F. W. Gingrich, 2d rev. F. W. Gingrich and F. W. Danker (Chicago: University of Chicago Press, 1979), 726; Wilhelm Michaelis, "*proton*," in *Theological Dictionary of the New Testament*, ed. Gerhard Kittel and Gerhard Friedrich, trans. and ed. Geoffrey W. Bromiley (Grand Rapids: Eerdmans, 1968), 6:869.
2. So C. E. B. Cranfield, *The Epistle to the Romans*, International Critical Commentary (Edinburgh: T & T Clark, 1975), 1:90–91; John Murray, *The Epistle to the Romans*, The New International Commentary on the New Testament (Grand Rapids: Eerdmans, 1968), 28; Douglas J. Moo, *The Epistle to the Romans*, The New International Commentary on the New Testament (Grand Rapids: Eerdmans, 1996), 69; James D. G. Dunn, *Romans 1–8*, Word Biblical Commentary (Dallas: Word, 1988), 40; and Thomas R. Schreiner, *Romans*, Baker Exegetical Commentary on the New Testament (Grand Rapids: Baker, 1998), 62.
3. See Ernst Käsemann, *Commentary on Romans*, trans. and ed. Geoffrey Bromiley (Grand Rapids: Eerdmans, 1980), 23; and William R. Newell, *Romans Verse by Verse* (Chicago: Moody, 1938), 22.
4. For a helpful discussion of this subject, see the essay by Wayne A. Brindle, "'To the Jew First': Rhetoric, Strategy, History, or Theology?" *Bibliotheca sacra* 159 (2002): 221–33.

Chapter 1: "For the Jew First"

1. His statements in Romans 11:25–27 are based upon the coming of the Redeemer from Zion, in whom God's promises have been fulfilled. As Israel's Messiah, Jesus embodies the salvation of the nation. The entrance of the Gentiles into salvation follows this proleptic salvation of Israel.
2. I have explored this theme at greater length in *Christ, Our Righteousness: Paul's Theology of Justification*, ed. D. A. Carson (Downers Grove, IL: InterVarsity, 2001). See now especially Sigurd Grindheim, *The Crux of Election: Paul's Critique of the Jewish Confidence in the Election of Israel*, Wissenschaftliche Untersuchungen Zum Neuen Testament 2.202 (Tübingen: Mohr Siebeck, 2005).
3. On this theme see Noel S. Rabinowitz, "Remnant and Restoration as a

Paradigm of Matthew's Theology of Israel" (Ph.D. diss., The Southern Baptist Theological Seminary, Louisville, KY, 2004).

4. Paul's strong words in 1 Thessalonians 2:16 ("wrath has come upon them ultimately") should be understood in this framework even if εἰ τέλό should not be read temporally.

5. On this theme in Romans 9–11, see especially Richard H. Bell, *The Irrevocable Call of God: An Inquiry into Paul's Theology of Israel*, Wissenschaftliche Untersuchungen Zum Neuen Testament 184 (Tübingen: Mohr Siebeck, 2005); and idem, *Provoked to Jealousy: The Origin and Purpose of the Jealousy Motif in Romans 9–11*, Wissenschaft liche Untersuchungen Zum Neuen Testament 2.63 (Tübingen: Mohr Siebeck, 1994). Against Bell, however, it is more than doubtful that Paul expected the salvation of every last member of the Jewish race through faith in the appearing Christ. Among other things, in that case his lament over Israel's failure hardly makes sense.

6. On this topic see Craig Evans, *To See and Not Perceive: Isaiah 6:9–10 in Early Jewish and Christian Interpretation*, Journal for the Study of the Old Testament: Supplement Series 64 (Sheffield: JSOT, 1989).

7. Following the biblical texts, he shifts from λαός (Hos. 1:10) to ἔθνός (Deut. 32:21).

Chapter 2: Jewish Evangelism in the New Millennium in Light of Israel's Future (Romans 9–11)

1. This expression is from Mark D. Nanos, *The Mystery of Romans: The Jewish Context of Paul's Letters* (Minneapolis, MN: Augsburg Fortress, 1996), 239–47.

2. Acts 17:1–2: "When they had passed through Amphipolis and Apollonia, they came to Thessalonica, where there was a Jewish synagogue. As his custom was, Paul went into the synagogue, and on three Sabbath days he reasoned with them from the Scriptures" (NIV).

3. Geoffrey Chapman, *The Documents of Vatican II* (London: n.p., 1966), 24–26, as cited in D. B. W. Robinson, "The Salvation of Israel in Romans 9–11," *Reformed Theological Review* 26 (1967): 81. Robinson also alerted me to several of the sources that follow from the church documents.

4. Joint Commission on Church Union, *The Church: Its Nature, Function and Ordering* (Melbourne: Joint Board of Christian Education, 1964), 12ff.

5. Hendrikus Berkhof, *Christ the Meaning of History*, trans. Lambertus Buurman, Dutch 4th ed. (Richmond, VA: John Knox Press, 1966), 141.

6. I have developed the continuity theme of the promise-plan of God between the two testaments in my books *Toward an Old Testament Theology* (Grand Rapids: Zondervan, 1978) and *The Christian and the "Old" Testament* (Pasadena, CA: William Carey Press, 1999).

7. Anthony A. Hoekema, *The Bible and the Future* (Grand Rapids: Eerdmans, 1979), 142.

8. C. F. D. Moule, The Birth of the New Testament (London: Adam and Charles Black, 1962), 46.

9. This fine point is made by Robinson, "The Salvation of Israel in Romans 9–11," 89. Robinson notes that this equation is sometimes made by theologians, but Paul never makes it.

10. For further details, see Walter C. Kaiser Jr., "Israel as the People of God," in *The People of God: Essays on the Believer's Church*, dedicated to James Leo Garrett Jr. (Nashville: Broadman, 1991), 99–108.

11. The most extensive treatment of the olive tree is found in A. G. Baxter and J. A. Ziesler, "Paul and Arboriculture: Romans 11:17–24," *Journal for the Study of the New Testament* 24 (1985): 25–32.

12. W. D. Davies, "Paul and the Gentiles: A Suggestion Concerning Romans 11:13–24," in *Jewish and Pauline Studies* (Philadelphia: Fortress, 1984), 153–63, esp. 155.

13. Nanos, *The Mystery of Romans*, 261.

14. Bruce W. Longenecker, *Eschatology and the Covenant: A Comparison of 4 Ezra and Romans 1–11* (Sheffield, UK: Journal for the Study of the New Testament, 1991), 261.

15. Nanos, *The Mystery of Romans*, 274.

16. Hoekema, *The Bible and the Future*, 144–45.

17. Walter C. Kaiser Jr., "The Old Promise and the New Covenant," *Journal of the Evangelical Theological Society* 15 (1972): 11–23.

18. John Murray, *The Epistle to the Romans*, 2 vols. (Grand Rapids: Eerdmans, 1965), 2:99–100.

19. Peter Richardson, *Israel in the Apostolic Church* (Cambridge: Cambridge University Press, 1969), 205–6.

20. James D. G. Dunn, *Romans 9–16*, Word Biblical Commentary (Dallas: Word, 1988), 38B:681. See, for example, 1 Samuel 25:1; 1 Kings 12:1; 2 Chronicles 12:1; Daniel 9:11, etc.

21. Willis J. Beecher, *The Prophets and the Promise* (Grand Rapids: Baker, 1970), 383. See also Walter C. Kaiser Jr. "The Land of Israel and the Future Return (Zechariah 10:6–12)," in *Israel: The Land and the People*, ed. H. Wayne House (Grand Rapids: Kregel, 1998), 168–85.

Chapter 3: The Book of Acts and Jewish Evangelism

1. Stephen's speech in Acts 7 goes through a long overview of Israel's history but does not get to Jesus in any detail.

2. The Jewish work of *Jubilees* 1:1–2 places the celebration of the giving of the Law on Pentecost on the sixteenth day of the third month. The third month also is when Pentecost is celebrated. It comes fifty days after the Feast of Unleavened Bread. The number of days is the source for the name Pentecost. This association between Law and Pentecost may not have been absolutely firm or unanimous at this time, but it was "in the air." See Max Turner, "Power from on High: The Spirit in Israel's Restoration and Witness in Luke–Acts," *Journal of Pentecostal Theology*, supplement series 9 (Sheffield: Sheffield Academic Press, 1996), 280–82. Possibly 2 Chronicles 15:10–12 points to this association as well, where it was in the third month that the renewal of covenant was celebrated. The targums to Exodus 19:1 also set the day of the giving of the Law as fifty days after Passover. In Judaism, Passover was sometimes referred to as both Passover and Unleavened

Bread since they came one right after the other. Josephus *Antiquities* 3.249; 14.21.

3. *The Testament of Levi* presents Messiah as "Renewer of the Law" (chap. 16) and "prophet of the Highest" (8:15), although some think chapter 16 has been reworked by Christian interpolators. See James H. Charlesworth, *Old Testament Pseudepigrapha* (New York: Doubleday, 1983), 1:794n. 16a. More importantly, Deuteronomy 18:15 shows up in the Messianic testimonia text collection of Qumran (4Q175). The Samaritans used Deuteronomy 18:15 to speak of the *Taheb*, "the one to come," and saw him as a great teacher. This hope was added to the Samaritan rendering of the tenth commandment in their version of the Pentateuch.

4. In all likelihood, the audience would have read the psalm as being about David because of the numerous first person references it contains and because David was its author. Peter argues that, whatever the psalm means, it cannot ultimately be about David, because he was not the beneficiary of the promise not to see corruption (at least read in its most literal sense). The hermeneutics of the use of this psalm are complex. For details, see Darrell L. Bock, "Proclamation from Prophecy and Pattern: Lucan Old Testament Christology," *Journal for the Study of the New Testament*, supplement series 12 (Sheffield: Sheffield Academic Press, 1987), 169–81.

5. The Mishnaic text reads, "He came out [of the Most Holy Place], going along the way he had gone in. And he said a short prayer in the outer area. He did not prolong his prayer, so as to frighten the people."

6. In 1 Enoch 14, Enoch is brought into God's presence to see what God will do. First Enoch 46 describes the Son of Man in the context of his presence in heaven. In 1 Enoch 49, he stands in the Lord of the Spirits' presence (= God). In 1 Enoch 51:3, he is said to "sit on my throne" as he exercises judgment, while in 61:8 he performs that judgment from the "throne of Glory" (also 62:3, 8–9; 69:29).

Chapter 4: Jesus' Denunciation of the Jewish Leaders in Matthew 23, and Witness to Religious Jews Today

1. W. Davies and D. Allison, *The Gospel According to Saint Matthew*, International Critical Commentary (Edinburgh: T & T Clark, 1997), 3:260–61.

2. D. Gushee, "All Things Jewish," *Books and Culture* (November–December 2000): 6.

3. I have argued that Matthew 21:33–45 speaks not of the supersession of Israel by the Gentile church but of the replacement of the current Jewish leaders by Jesus' disciples, in "Matt. 21:33–46 and the Future of Israel," in *Bibliotheca Sacra* 159 (2002).

4. S. Sandmel, *Anti-Semitism in the New Testament?* (Philadelphia: Fortress, 1978), 68.

5. The KJV presents eight woes, but if 23:14 is textually dubious, there are seven. For this view, see B. Metzger, *A Textual Commentary on the Greek New Testament*, 2d ed. (Stuttgart: Deutsche Bibelgesellschaft, 1994),

50. But whatever its textual authenticity, 23:14 seems to echo such prophetic texts as Isaiah 1:23; 5:8.

6. L. Johnson, "The New Testament's Anti-Jewish Slander and the Conventions of Ancient Polemic," *Journal of Biblical Literature* 108 (1989): 419–41; and A. Saldarini, "Delegitimation of Leaders in Matthew 23," *Catholic Biblical Quarterly* 54 (1992): 659–80.

7. Scholars who take this view include D. Harrington, *The Gospel of Matthew* (Collegeville, MN: Liturgical, 1991), 303–5; J. Andrew Overman, *Church and Community in Crisis* (Valley Forge, PA: Trinity Press, 1996), 302–4; idem, *Matthew's Gospel and Formative Judaism: The Social World of the Matthean Community* (Minneapolis, MN: Fortress, 1990), 148–49, 151; A. Saldarini, *Matthew's Christian-Jewish Community* (Chicago: University of Chicago, 1994), 59–63; and D. Sim, *The Gospel of Matthew and Christian Judaism* (Edinburgh: T & T Clark, 1999), 148–49.

8. In light of the contextual stress on Jesus' disputes with the Jewish leaders, it is likely that Jesus' cursing of the fig tree (21:18–22) is an acted parable of judgment on the fruitless temple leaders, not on the nation as a whole. See Davies and Allison, *Gospel According to Saint Matthew*, 3:153–54; and R. Gundry, *Matthew: A Commentary on His Handbook for a Mixed Church Under Persecution*, 2d ed. (Grand Rapids: Eerdmans, 1994), 416.

9. Although some take 23:39 as stressing only the certainty of judgment, the image of the mother hen gathering her chicks (23:37) speaks of compassion, not rejection. Rather, there is hope of salvation if only Israel will acknowledge Jesus to be her Messiah. Israel has sinned in rejecting Jesus, and there will be punishment for that sin. But here, as throughout biblical history, repentance after sin and judgment brings grace and redemption. See the discussion in Davies and Allison, *Gospel According to Saint Matthew*, 3.323–24.

10. Ibid., 3.285.

11. It is not certain whether this should be understood as efforts to convert Gentiles to Judaism or as efforts to convert Jews to Pharisaism. Possibly both are in view. S. McKnight concludes that the Pharisees did not actively pursue new converts from among the Gentiles, but that they urged "God-fearing" Gentiles (cf. Acts 10:2, 22, 35; 13:16, 26, 43, 50; 16:14; 17:4, 17; 18:7) to become full converts to Judaism and to observe the Pharisaic *halakhah*. See S. McKnight's *A Light Among the Gentiles* (Minneapolis, MN: Fortress, 1991), 106–8.

12. Cf. *b. Rosh Hashanna* 17a; *Berachot* 10a.

13. It is well known that *halakhah* on oaths and vows was very important in second temple Judaism. *See m. Nedarim* and CD 15.

14. Davies and Allison (*Gospel According to Saint Matthew*, 3:296–99) are probably correct, against many commentators, that Jesus is not disputing existing Pharisaic tradition here but is simply using the washing of tableware metaphorically. Pharisaic fastidiousness about such matters renders the metaphor fitting, but Jesus is not attacking that fastidiousness *per se*.

15. Examples of this common Semitic idiom include Numbers 17:25;

Deuteronomy 3:18; 13:14; Judges 18:2; 21:10; 1 Samuel 14:52; 18:17; 2 Samuel 2:7; 3:34; 1 Kings 1:52; 2 Kings 2:16; 2 Chronicles 17:7; Job 28:8; 41:26; Jeremiah 48:45; and Hosea 10:9.

16. E.g., see the onomatopoeic interjection in Isaiah 5:8, 11, 18, 20, 21, 22; 10:1; Amos 5:18; 6:1, 4; Habakkuk 2:9, 12, 15, 19; and Zechariah 11:17.

17. R. Clements, "Woe," in *Anchor Bible Dictionary*, ed. D. Freedman (New York: Doubleday, 1992), 6.945–46.

18. E.g., Matthew 23:13, 15, 16, 23, 25, 27, 29; and parallels in Luke; Luke 6:24–26; Revelation 18:10, 16, 19.

19. Note especially 4Q169 f3–4ii:1 (on Nah. 3:1); 4Q179 f1i:4, ii:1 (apocryphal lamentations for Jerusalem). See also 1QpHab 10:5, 11:2, 12:14; 4Q162 2:2; 4Q185 f1–2i:9; 4Q511 f63iii:5. 1QS 2:5–9 and 4Q286 ii.2–12 use different terms, *arur* (accursed) and *z'um* (damned).

20. E.g., *b. Berachot* 3a, 24b, 33a, 61a; *Shabbat* 10a; *Pesachim* 65a, 87b; *Yoma* 72b, 86a; *Sanhedrin* 7b.

21. W. Bauer, F. W. Danker, W. F. Arndt, and F. W. Gingrich, *Greek-English Lexicon of the New Testament and Other Early Christian Literature*, 3d ed. (Chicago: University of Chicago Press, 1999), 338; but for examples in postbiblical Jewish literature of this word connoting insincerity or hypocrisy, see M. Jastrow, *Dictionary of the Targumim, Talmud Bavli, Yerushalmi, and Midrashic Literature* (New York: Judaica, 1971), 484–85.

22. R. Smith, "Hypocrite," in *Dictionary of Jesus and the Gospels*, ed. J. Green et al. (Downers Grove, IL: InterVarsity, 1992), 353.

23. J. Charlesworth, ed., *The Old Testament Pseudepigrapha*, 2 vols. (Garden City, NY: Doubleday, 1985), 2.640–42, 655–56.

24. The Talmudic discussions of seven types of Pharisees, of whom only the one who acted out of love was approved, is illuminating. See *y. Berachot* 14b and *Sotah* 20c and *b. Sotah* 22b. The "shoulder Pharisee," who conspicuously carries his good deeds on his shoulder so that people can see them, is particularly relevant to the charge of hypocrisy in Matthew 23. See also *b. Sotah* 41b and 42a, which affirm respectively that hypocrites will go to hell and never see the *Shechinah*.

25. 11Q19, the Temple Scroll from Qumran, clearly expresses this "deuteronomistic" theology in column 59, 2–13.

26. The motif of sin coming to its full measure is found in Genesis 15:16. Cf. *Jubilees* 14:16 and 1 Thessalonians 2:16.

27. Stephen, Paul, and the author of Hebrews also reflect on Israel's sad history of rejecting its own prophets (Acts 7:52; 1 Thess. 2:14–16; Heb. 11:32–38).

28. *Midrash Tanchuma Yelamdenu* on Leviticus 4:1; *Qohelet Rabbah* 3:16; 10:4; Targum Lam 2:20; *y. Taanit* 69a; *b. Gittin* 57b, and *Sanhedrin* 96b.

29. As does F. Beare, *The Gospel According to Matthew* (San Francisco: Harper, 1981), 447. Beare, with many others, views Matthew 23 as a "masterpiece of vituperation" (452), which does not reflect the historical Jesus but the fierce controversies between the church and formative Judaism after the 70 C.E. destruction of the temple.

Chapter 5: The Message of the Prophets and Jewish Evangelism

1. In this article, the English translations are from *The New International Version* unless otherwise noted. All emphases in Scripture quotations are added by the author.

2. The term *Holy Spirit* does not actually occur in this passage, but we know that "the Spirit" (vv. 17, 25–26) here is the Spirit of the Lord, since Moses wished "that the LORD would put his Spirit" on all the people of Israel (v. 29; see more on this presently).

    The term *Holy Spirit* occurs only three times in the Hebrew Bible: Psalm 51:11[13] and Isaiah 63:10–11. The expression in these three passages is literally "the Spirit of Holiness" (רוּחַ קֹדֶשׁ, *rûah qōdeš*; the LXX renders it "Holy Spirit," using the same Greek words as the New Testament). On Psalm 51:11[13], see footnote 3 below. Isaiah 63:9–10 refers to Israel's grieving of the Holy Spirit, whom the Lord had put in their midst in the days of Moses. Isaiah 63:14 identifies this "Holy Spirit" with "the Spirit of the LORD." The latter expression and its interchangeable counterpart "the Spirit of God" (cf., e.g., 1 Sam. 10:6 with 10:10) occur a total of ninety-four times in the Hebrew Bible, if one includes instances where "the Spirit" clearly refers to "the Spirit of the LORD/God" in the context.

    In the Jewish tradition, the Holy Spirit referred to in the Hebrew Bible is not, of course, taken to be the third person of the Trinity, so in such passages the Hebrew word is written "spirit," not capitalized. See, for example, Jacob Milgrom, *The JPS Torah Commentary: Numbers* (Philadelphia: Jewish Publication Society, 1990), 87, where Numbers 11:17 is rendered "I will draw upon the spirit that is upon you," and page 90 where Moses' statement in verse 29 is translated, ". . . that the LORD put His spirit upon them!" See also Milgrom's excursus on ecstatic prophecy and the spirit on pages 380–83. In general, the Jewish view is that "the spirit of God referred to in the Bible alludes to His energy (Isaiah 40:13; Zechariah 4:6)." Israel Abrahams, "God in the Bible," *Encyclopedia Judaica*, ed. Cecil Roth (Jerusalem: Keter Publishing House, 1971), 7:643.

3. The juxtaposition of these verses calls to mind Psalm 51:11[13], where David writes, "Do not cast me from your presence or *take your Holy Spirit from me.*" Most likely, David's fear is that what had happened to Saul in 1 Samuel 16:14 would happen to him as well. As Saul's minstrel, David himself had witnessed the effect this "evil spirit" had on Saul (1 Sam. 16:15–23; 18:10–11, etc.). See the remarks in Robert P. Gordon, *I & II Samuel: A Commentary* (Grand Rapids: Zondervan, 1986), 152.

4. The commentaries are divided on how they understand this expression. Some take primarily a psychological view of the problem. They argue that this is simply a matter of mental illness. According to this view, the ancients conceived of such things as divine impositions because of their limited understanding of human psychopathology. See, for example, S. Goldman, *Samuel*, Soncino Books of the Bible (London: Soncino, 1951), 96; Peter R. Ackroyd, *The First Book of Samuel*, The Cambridge Bible Commentary (Cambridge: Cambridge University Press, 1971), 134–35.

Others take a primarily theological view of the matter. The "evil spirit" was, in fact, sent directly by God to inflict him with periodic fits of paranoia and rage. See, for example, Hans W. Hertzberg, *I & II Samuel: A Commentary*, The Old Testament Library (Philadelphia: Westminster Press, 1964), 140–41; and P. Kyle McCarter Jr., *1 Samuel*, Anchor Bible (Garden City, NY: Doubleday, 1980), 280–81.

The latter does, indeed, seem to be the view of the text, but it is not without its own theological problems. See the discussion presently, and the well-balanced remarks in C. F. Keil and F. Delitzsch, *The Books of Samuel* (repr., Grand Rapids: Eerdmans, 1950), 170; Gordon, *I & II Samuel*, 152; and Joyce G. Baldwin, *1 and 2 Samuel*, The Tyndale Old Testament Commentaries (Downers Grove, IL: InterVarsity Press, 1988), 122–23.

5. According to the Babylonian Talmud *Yoma* 9b, "After the later prophets Haggai, Zechariah, and Malachi had died, the Holy Spirit departed from Israel, but they still availed themselves of the *Bath Qol*." See Rabbi Dr. I. Epstein, ed., *The Babylonian Talmud: Seder Mo'ed, Yoma* (New York: Rebecca Bennet Publications, 1959), 1:41, for the English translation, and for the original language of the Talmud, see the corresponding page in the same volume.

"Holy Spirit" is capitalized in the Epstein edition cited here. The actual Hebrew expression is רוּחַ קֹדֶשׁ (*rûah qōdeš*), which means literally "the Spirit of Holiness" (see footnote 2 above for the occurrences of this term in the Hebrew Bible). The term *Bath Qol* means literally "a daughter of voice (or 'sound')," and may refer to an "echo" or "reverberating sound." Here it refers to the "divine voice" that continued (to echo) in Israel even after the Holy Spirit had departed from Israel at the passing of Malachi.

For helpful remarks on "the quenched Spirit" tradition of the intertestamental period, see Gordon D. Fee, *God's Empowering Presence: The Holy Spirit and the Letters of Paul* (Peabody, MA: Hendricksen, 1994), 913–15.

6. For a more extensive discussion of some of the points made here and on the following pages, see Richard E. Averbeck, "The Holy Spirit in the Hebrew Bible and Its Connections to the New Testament," in *Who's Afraid of the Holy Spirit? An Investigation into the Ministry of the Spirit of God Today*, ed. Daniel B. Wallace and M. James Sawyer (Dallas, TX: Biblical Studies Press, 2005), 15–36.

7. The best treatment of this subject known to me is Gary Fredricks, "Rethinking the Role of the Holy Spirit in the Lives of Old Testament Believers," *Trinity Journal* 9 NS (1988): 81–104. He isolates three main categories of ministry of the Holy Spirit in the believer's life: power for salvation (i.e., the regenerating work of the Holy Spirit), power for living (i.e., the work of the Holy Spirit in the ongoing sanctification of the believer), and power for service (i.e., empowerment for ministry in the kingdom of God). Fredricks argues that all true Old Testament believers held the first and second in common with us as New Testament believers, but the third was restricted in the Old Testament to those who were called and empowered for specific ministries, one

of which was prophetic ministry. The Hebrew Bible often signifies the latter by referring to the Holy Spirit's coming "upon" a person or a group of people (see, e.g., the citations and discussions of Num. 11:17, 25–29 and 1 Sam. 10:6–10 above).

Fredricks's basic arguments are sound, and he responds well to many of the passages and theological constructs that some have used to object to such a view. One major problem he struggles with and is unable to resolve satisfactorily is that the Hebrew Bible never actually refers to the indwelling of the Holy Spirit in the lives of believers. This is, of course, a serious obstacle to his argument for the regeneration and permanent sanctifying empowerment of the Holy Spirit in the life of all Old Testament believers.

Although I cannot develop the point fully here, I believe there is an answer to this dilemma. Probably the best way to understand the Old Testament silence in this regard is that in the Old Testament world God actually resided in the sanctuary, whether it be the tabernacle or, later, the temple (see, e.g., Exod. 25:8; 40:34–38; Lev. 16:2; 1 Kings 8:10–13). Since he dwelt there in a physically manifested form (i.e., the glory cloud), it would never have occurred to them to speak of the Holy Spirit "indwelling" the believer. The New Testament terminology of "indwelling" derives, in part at least, from the use of Old Testament tabernacle and temple terminology for the believer and the community of believers (see, e.g., 1 Cor. 3:16–17; 6:19–20; Eph. 2:19–22). This is a New Testament innovation in terminology and theological rationale based on the shift in the nature of the community of faith from the Old Testament nation of Israel to the New Testament church.

The fact that "indwelling" terminology is used for believers in the New Testament but not in the Old Testament merely reflects this shift in perspective. We do not argue that because the Old Testament itself never explicitly says that the Old Testament believer is saved by faith in Jesus Christ, therefore, they were saved in some other way. I would argue that, similarly, the basic ministry of the Holy Spirit to all Old Testament believers was essentially the same as that for New Testament believers, even if it was not explicitly spoken about in that way. We do not, after all, take the "indwelling" of the Holy Spirit in the New Testament believer literally in the sense of location. No one argues that one could cut open the body of the New Testament believer and find the Holy Spirit residing there.

8. The problems involved in the textual reading and interpretation of "in you" in this passage has been discussed in some detail in Fredricks, "Rethinking the Role of the Holy Spirit," 93–96.

9. See, for example, the explanations in William Hendriksen, *New Testament Commentary: Exposition of the Gospel According to John* (Grand Rapids: Baker, 1953), 134; B. F. Westcott, *The Gospel According to St. John* (repr., Grand Rapids: Eerdmans, 1971), 49–50; R. C. H. Lenski, *The Interpretation of St. John's Gospel* (Columbus, OH: Wartburg, 1942), 237–38; and Ernst Haenchen, *A Commentary on the Gospel of John Chapters 1–6* (Philadelphia: Fortress, 1984), 200–201.

Haenchen makes the connection to Acts 19:1–7, where water

baptism in the name of Jesus, as opposed to the baptism of John, is treated as the natural lead into the baptism of the Holy Spirit. As John the Baptist himself put it, "He must become greater; I must become less" (John 4:30).

Lenski, in my opinion, overstates the importance of water baptism here. Jesus is emphasizing the baptism of the Holy Spirit, making the point that this is an overriding necessity for entrance into the kingdom of God. Jesus, in fact, rebukes Nicodemus for not knowing this already: "'You are Israel's teacher,' said Jesus, 'and do you not understand these things?'" (v. 10). Apparently, from Jesus' point of view, Nicodemus ought to have been able to discern more about the ministry of the Holy Spirit from the Old Testament than he had understood. Perhaps this should be taken as another argument for the broad based ministry of the Holy Spirit in the lives of Old Testament believers (see the discussion of this issue above and note 7 of this chapter).

10. Walter C. Kaiser Jr., "A Neglected Text in Bibliology Discussions: 1 Corinthians 2:6–16," *Westminster Theological Journal* 43 (Spring 1981): 310–19, argues that this passage is really about revelation and inspiration through Paul as an apostle rather than about illumination of the believer by the Holy Spirit through the revealed Word. I cannot deal with all the issues here, but in order to take this position, Kaiser must take the "we" in verses 6–16 to be the same as the "I" in verses 1–5. This is a serious problem. It seems that, in the context, the "we" refers to "mature" believers (v. 6) who are "spiritual" (vv. 15–16) as opposed to those who are "fleshly" (3:1ff.).

Chapter 6: The Future of Israel as a Theological Question

1. See Stephen G. Wilson, ed., *Anti-Judaism in Early Christianity*, vol. 2, *Separation and Polemic*, Studies in Christianity and Judaism, no. 2 (Waterloo, Ontario: Wilfrid Laurier University Press, 1986).
2. R. Kendall Soulen, *The God of Israel and Christian Theology* (Minneapolis, MN: Fortress, 1996), 30–34, 181n. 6.
3. Ibid., 12–56.
4. Peter Toon, *Puritans, the Millennium and the Future of Israel: Puritan Eschatology 1600 to 1660* (Cambridge: James Clarke, 1970), 23–26; and Christopher Hill, "Till the Conversion of the Jews," in *Millenarianism and Messianism in English Literature and Thought 1650–1800*, ed. Richard H. Popkin (Leiden: E. J. Brill, 1988), 12–36.
5. See Timothy P. Weber, *Living in the Shadow of the Second Coming: American Premillenialism, 1875–1925* (New York: Oxford University Press, 1979), 128–57; and also, David A. Rausch, *Zionism Within Early American Fundamentalism, 1878–1918: A Convergence of Two Traditions*, Texts and Studies in Religion, vol. 4 (New York: Edwin Mellen, 1979).
6. See, for example, Karl Barth, *Church Dogmatics*, vol. 2, *The Doctrine of God*, pt. 2, ed. G. W. Bromiley and T. F. Torrance, trans. G. W. Bromiley et al. (Edinburgh: T & T Clark, 1957), 195–305; C. E. B. Cranfield, *A Critical and Exegetical Commentary on the Epistle to the Romans*, 2 vols. (Edinburgh: T & T Clark, 1979), 2:445–592; Markus Barth, *The People of God* (Sheffield: JSOT Press, 1983); Peter Stuhlmacher, *Paul's Letter*

to the Romans: A Commentary, trans. Scott J. Hafemann (Louisville: Westminster/John Knox, 1994), 142–84; David E. Holweida, *Jesus and Israel: One Covenant or Two?* (Grand Rapids: Eerdmans, 1995), 147–76; J. Lanier Burns, "The Future of Ethnic Israel in Romans 11," in *Dispensationalism: Israel and the Church*, ed. C. Blaising and D. Bock (Grand Rapids: Zondervan, 1992), 188–229; S. Lewis Johnson Jr., "Evidence for Romans 9–11," in *A Case for Premillenialism: A New Consensus*, ed. D. K. Campbell and J. L. Townsend (Chicago: Moody, 1992), 199–223; and Harold W. Hoehner, "Israel in Romans 9–11," in *Israel: The Land and the People*, ed. H. Wayne House (Grand Rapids: Kregel, 1998), 145–67. Also see the collection of articles on the theme: "The Church and Israel (Romans 9–11)," in *Ex Auditu* 4 (1988).

7.   Cranfield, *Epistle to the Romans*, 2:448.

8.   Paul bases his argument for the salvation of all Israel on the promise of Isaiah 59:20–21. It should be noted that Isaiah follows this promise with an oracle on the return of divine favor to Zion, which concludes with the promise, "Then all your people will be righteous; they will possess the land forever. . . . That I may be glorified. . . . I, the Lord, will hasten it in its time" (cf. also Isa. 45:25).

9.   For example, see E. P. Sanders, *Jesus and Judaism* (Philadelphia: Fortress, 1985); N. T. Wright, *Jesus and the Victory of God*, Christian Origins and the Question of God, vol. 2 (Minneapolis, MN: Fortress, 1996); John P. Meier, *A Marginal Jew: Rethinking the Historical Jesus*, Anchor Bible Reference Library, 3 vols. (New York: Doubleday, 1991–); Ben F. Meyer, *The Aims of Jesus* (London: SCM, 1979); Scott McKnight, *A New Vision for Israel: The Teachings of Jesus in National Context* (Grand Rapids: Eerdmans, 1999); and Darrell L. Bock, *Jesus According to Scripture* (Grand Rapids: Baker, 2007).

10.   James Scott, "Jesus' Vision for the Restoration of Israel as the Basis for a Biblical Theology of the New Testament" (paper presented at the ninth annual meeting of the Wheaton Theology Conference, Wheaton, IL, April 6, 2000), audiocassette.

11.   McKnight, *New Vision for Israel*, 12–13, 39. On the presence of the kingdom, see 70–119.

12.   On the future coming of the kingdom, see ibid., 120–55.

13.   I develop the themes of the present inauguration and future coming of the kingdom of God and its focus on Israel in the teaching of Jesus and his apostles in C. Blaising and D. Bock, *Progressive Dispensationalism* (Wheaton: BridgePoint Books, 1993), 232–83.

14.   Two covenant theology is a general label for the consensus that has developed among the participants in and successors to the post-Holocaust Christian-Jewish dialogue. It should be noted, however, that not all the participants in the dialogue make use of the notion of "covenant" when setting forth their view of Judaism as a divinely sanctioned religion distinct from Christianity. Helpful overviews of this theological development can be found in Abraham J. Peck, ed., *Jews and Christians After the Holocaust* (Philadelphia: Fortress, 1982); John T. Pawlikowski, *Christ in Light of the Christian-Jewish Dialogue*, Studies in Judaism and Christianity (New York: Paulist, 1982); Peter

von der Osten-Sacken, *Christian-Jewish Dialogue: Theological Foundations* (Philadelphia: Fortress, 1986); James H. Charlesworth, Frank X. Blisard, and Jeffrey S. Siker, eds., *Jews and Christians: Exploring the Past, Present, and Future,* Shared Ground Among Jews and Christians: A Series of Explorations, vol. 1 (New York: Crossroad, 1990); Marvin Perry and Frederick M. Schweitzer, *Jewish-Christian Encounters over the Centuries: Symbiosis, Prejudice, Holocaust, Dialogue,* American University Studies, series 9: History, vol. 136 (New York: Peter Lang, 1994); and Eugene J. Fisher, ed., *Visions of the Other: Jewish and Christian Theologians Assess the Dialogue,* Studies in Judaism and Christianity: Exploration of Issues in the Contemporary Dialogue Between Christians and Jews (New York: Paulist, 1994).

15. See, for example, Donald A. Hagner, *The Jewish Reclamation of Jesus: An Analysis and Critique of the Modern Jewish Study of Jesus* (Grand Rapids: Zondervan, 1984); and David B. Holwerda, *Jesus and Israel: One Covenant or Two?* (Grand Rapids: Eerdmans, 1995).

16. Rosemary Ruether, *Faith and Fratricide: The Theological Roots of Anti-Semitism* (New York: Seabury, 1974), 246–51. See also, idem, "Christology and Jewish-Christian Relations," in *Jews and Christians After the Holocaust,* 25–38.

17. E. P. Sanders, *Paul and Palestinian Judaism: A Comparison of Patterns of Religion* (Philadelphia: Fortress, 1977), 75.

18. See Blaising and Bock, "The Fulfillment of the Biblical Covenants Through Jesus Christ," in *Progressive Dispensationalism,* 174–211.

19. Grant R. Osborne, *The Hermeneutical Spiral: A Comprehensive Introduction to Biblical Interpretation* (Downers Grove, IL: InterVarsity Press, 1991); Kevin Vanhoozer, *Is There a Meaning in This Text? The Bible, the Reader, and the Morality of Literary Knowledge* (Grand Rapids: Zondervan, 1998).

20. Walter Dumbrell, *Covenant and Creation* (London: Paternoster, 1997); John Sailhamer, *Introduction to Old Testament Theology: A Canonical Approach* (Grand Rapids: Zondervan, 1995); and idem, *The Pentateuch as Narrative: A Biblical Theological Commentary* (Grand Rapids: Zondervan, 1992).

21. Thomas Cahill, *The Gifts of the Jews* (New York: Doubleday, 1998).

22. Michael Wyschogrod, "Israel, Church, and Election," in *Brothers in Hope,* ed. John Oesterreicher (New York: Herder and Herder, 1970), 83; and idem, "Letter to a Friend," *Modern Theology* 11 (1995): 171.

23. A consensus exists on this point among many engaged in historical Jesus research. See the works cited in note 9 above.

24. On the disappearance of the varieties of Judaism after the crises of A.D. 70 and A.D. 135 and the rise of rabbinic Judaism vis-à-vis Christianity, see Marcel Simon, *Verus Israel: A Study of the Relations Between Christians and Jews in the Roman Empire, A.D. 135–425,* trans. H. McKeating, (repr., London: Littman Library of Jewish Civilization, 1986). Also see H. Shanks, ed., *Christianity and Rabbinic Judaism: A Parallel History of Their Origins and Early Development* (Washington, DC: Biblical Archaeology Society, 1992).

25. I develop the contrast between spiritual-vision eschatology and

new-creation eschatology along with implications for the question of millennialism in my essay, "Premillennialism," in *Three Views of the Millennium and Beyond*, ed. Darrell L. Bock (Grand Rapids: Zondervan, 1999), 160ff.

Chapter 7: The Holocaust and the Sacred Romance

1. Quoted in Eliezer L. Erhmann, ed., *Readings in Modern Jewish History: From the American Revolution to the Present* (New York: KTAV Publishing, 1977), 232.

2. Jacob Robinson, "Holocaust," in *Encyclopaedia Judaica*, 16 vols. (Jerusalem: Keter Publishing House Jerusalem, 1972), 8:831–32.

3. It must also be remembered that the institutional church had a long history of anti-Semitism that certainly paved the way for the Holocaust; for more on this, see Michael L. Brown, *Our Hands Are Stained with Blood: The Tragic Story of the "Church" and the Jewish People* (Shippensburg, PA: Destiny Image Publishers, 1992); A. Roy Eckardt, *Elder and Younger Brothers: The Encounter of Jews and Christians* (New York: Schocken Books, 1967); Edward H. Flannery, *The Anguish of the Jews: Twenty-three Centuries of Antisemitism*, rev. ed., A Stimulus Book (Mahwah, NJ: Paulist, 1985); Richard E. Gade, *A Historical Survey of Anti-Semitism* (Grand Rapids: Baker, 1981); Paul E. Grosser and Edwin G. Halperin, *The Causes and Effects of Anti-Semitism: The Dimensions of a Prejudice: An Analysis and Chronology of 1900 Years of Anti-Semitic Attitudes and Practices* (New York: Philosophical Library, 1978); William Nichols, *Christian Antisemitism: A History of Hate* (Northvale, NJ: Jason Aronson, 1993); David A. Rausch, *A Legacy of Hate: Why Christians Must Not Forget the Holocaust* (Chicago: Moody, 1984); and A. Lukyn Williams, *Adversus Judaeos: A Bird's-Eye View of Christian Apologiae Until the Renaissance* (London: Cambridge University Press, 1935).

4. For a detailed survey of the Jewish religious response to the Holocaust, see Barry R. Leventhal, "Theological Perspectives on the Holocaust" (Ph.D. dissertation, Dallas Theological Seminary, 1982), 14–102.

5. For more on Jewish identity and the Holocaust, see Barry R. Leventhal, "The Holocaust and Jewish Identity," in *Jewish Identity and Faith in Jesus*, ed. Kai Kjær-Hansen (Jerusalem: Caspari Center, 1996), 137–48.

6. Anne Frank, *The Diary of a Young Girl* (New York: Pocket Books, 1952), 186.

7. Azriel Eisenberg, ed., *Witness to the Holocaust* (New York: Pilgrim, 1981), 628.

8. Eli Wiesel, "Freedom of Conscience—A Jewish Commentary," *Journal of Ecumenical Studies* 14 (Fall 1977): 643.

9. Jakob Jocz, *The Jewish People and Jesus Christ After Auschwitz: A Study in the Controversy Between Church and Synagogue* (Grand Rapids: Baker, 1981), 23.

10. Seymour Cain, "The Question and the Answers After Auschwitz," *Judaism* 20 (Summer 1971): 263.

11. For the historical development of the dual covenant theory, see Jakob Jocz, *The Jewish People and Jesus Christ: The Relationship Between Church and Synagogue*, 3d ed. (Grand Rapids: Baker, 1979), 316–22; for a biblical

refutation of the dual covenant theory, see Louis Goldberg, *Are There Two Ways of Atonement? Confronting the Controversies* (Baltimore: Messianic Jewish Resources, 1992); Dan Gruber, *The Church and the Jews: The Biblical Relationship* (Hagerstown, MD: Serenity Books, 1997), 395–400.

12. For exegetical and theological evidence of the ongoing nature of Romans 1:16, "to the Jew first" (not merely historical or chronological priority), see Henry Alford, *The New Testament for English Readers* (Chicago: Moody, 1958), 848; C. E. B. Cranfield, *A Critical and Exegetical Commentary on the Epistle to the Romans*, 2 vols., International Critical Commentary (Edinburgh: T & T Clark, 1975), 1:90–91; Arnold G. Fruchtenbaum, *Hebrew Christianity: Its Theology, History, and Philosophy* (San Antonio, TX: Ariel Ministries, 1983), 99–105; idem, *Israelology: The Missing Link in Systematic Theology*, rev. ed. (Tustin, CA: Ariel Ministries, 1989, 1992), 725, 852–55, 923–24; Sanford C. Miles, *A Hebrew Christian Looks at Romans* (Grand Rapids: Dunham Publishing, 1968); John Murray, *The Epistle to the Romans: The English Text with Introduction, Exposition and Notes* (Grand Rapids: Eerdmans, 1959, 1965), 28; A. T. Robertson, *Word Pictures in the New Testament*, 6 vols. (Grand Rapids: Baker, 1931), 4:326; Joseph Shulam, with Hillary Le Cornu, *A Commentary on the Jewish Roots of Romans* (Baltimore: Lederer Messianic Jewish Publishers, 1997).

13. For a history of replacement theology, as well as a biblical refutation, see Fruchtenbaum, *Israelology*, passim; Derek C. White, *Replacement Theology: Its Origin, History, and Theology* (East Sussex, UK: n.p., 1997); S. Lewis Johnson, "Paul and 'The Israel of God': An Exegetical and Eschatological Case-Study," in *Essays in Honor of J. Dwight Pentecost*, ed. Stanley D. Toussaint and Charles H. Dyer (Chicago: Moody, 1986), 181–96; plus Gruber, *The Church and the Jews*, 333–56.

14. Unless otherwise indicated, all Scripture references are from the New American Standard Bible.

15. Emil L. Fackenheim, *Quest for Past and Future: Essays in Jewish Theology* (Boston: Beacon, 1970), 315.

16. Quoted in Alice L. Eckardt, "Rebel Against God," *Face to Face* 6 (Spring 1979): 18.

17. Quoted in Emil L. Fackenheim, Richard H. Popkin, George Steiner, and Eli Wiesel, "Jewish Values in the Post-Holocaust Future: A Symposium," *Judaism* 16 (Summer 1967): 298–99.

18. I am indebted to Search Ministries for these insights into the three barriers. For more on this, especially on the second barrier, see Ken Boa and Larry Moody, *I'm Glad You Asked* (Colorado Springs: Chariot Victor Publishing, 1982, 1994).

19. For Paul's exposition on true believers, both Jewish and Gentile, "provoking the Jews to jealousy," see Romans 11:11–14ff.

20. The Old Testament affirms this relational, Sacred Romance kind of evangelism approach toward Israel—it is God's own approach; cf. Genesis 12:3; Deuteronomy 32:10; Psalm 122:6–9; book of Hosea; Zechariah 2:8, and others.

21. Norman L. Geisler, *Baker Encyclopedia of Christian Apologetics*, Baker Reference Library (Grand Rapids: Baker, 1999), 37.

22. Among the better apologetic texts are the following: for the general field
     of apologetics, see Geisler, *Baker Encyclopedia of Christian Apologetics*;
     idem, *Christian Apologetics* (Grand Rapids: Baker, 1976); Norman L.
     Geisler and Peter Bocchino, *Unshakable Foundations* (Minneapolis,
     MN: Bethany House, 2001); Norman L. Geisler and Ronald M. Brooks,
     When Skeptics Ask (Wheaton: Victor Books, 1990); for an apologetic
     text written for youth, see Norman L. Geisler and Joseph Holden, *Living
     Loud: Defending Your Faith*, Truth Quest Books (Nashville: Broadman
     and Holman, 2001); further see Norman L. Geisler and Frank Turek,
     I Don't Have Enough Faith to Be an Atheist (Wheaton: Crossway Books,
     2004); Kenneth Boa and Larry Moody, *I'm Glad You Asked* (Wheaton:
     Victor Books, 1982); Kenneth Boa, *God, I Don't Understand* (Wheaton:
     Victor Books, 1975); Rick Cornish, *5 Minute Apologist: Maximum Truth
     in Minimum Time* (Colorado Springs: NavPress, 2005); William A.
     Dembski and Jay Wesley Richards, eds., *Unapologetic Apologetics: Meeting
     the Challenges of Theological Studies* (Downers Grove, IL: InterVarsity
     Press, 2001); Josh McDowell, *The New Evidence That Demands a Verdict*
     (Nashville: Thomas Nelson, 1999); and Dan Story, *Defending Your Faith*
     (Nashville: Thomas Nelson, 1992). For the specific apologetic area of
     the problem of evil and suffering, see Norman L. Geisler, *The Roots of
     Evil*, 2d ed., Christian Free University Curriculum (Dallas: Probe Books,
     1978, 1989); Henri Blocher, *Evil and the Cross*, trans. David G. Preston
     (Downers Grove, IL: InterVarsity Press, 1994); D. A. Carson, *How Long,
     O Lord: Reflections on Suffering and Evil* (Grand Rapids: Baker, 1990); C. S.
     Lewis, *The Problem of Pain* (New York: Collier Books/Macmillan, 1962);
     Alister E. McGrath, *Suffering and God* (Grand Rapids: Zondervan, 1992,
     1995); Hugh Sylvester, *Arguing with God: A Christian Examination of the
     Problem of Evil* (London: InterVarsity Press, 1971); John W. Wenham,
     The Enigma of Evil: Can We Believe in the Goodness of God? Academie
     Books (Grand Rapids: Zondervan, 1985), formerly published as *The
     Goodness of God* (London: InterVarsity Press, 1974); and Philip Yancey,
     Where Is God When It Hurts? (New York: Harper Paperbacks, 1977).
     For the specific area of Jewish apologetics, see Michael L. Brown,
     Answering Jewish Objections to Jesus: General and Historical Objections
     (Grand Rapids: Baker, 2000); idem, *Answering Jewish Objections to Jesus:
     Theological Objections* (Grand Rapids: Baker, 2000); and idem, *Answering
     Jewish Objections to Jesus: Messianic Prophecy Objections* (Grand Rapids:
     Baker, 2003); and Arnold G. Fruchtenbaum, *Jesus Was a Jew* (Tustin,
     CA: Ariel Ministries, 1974, 1981).
23. See Brent Curtis and John Eldredge, *The Sacred Romance: Drawing
     Closer to the Heart of God* (Nashville: Thomas Nelson, 1997); and John
     Eldredge, *The Journey of Desire: Searching for the Life We've Only Dreamed
     Of* (Nashville: Thomas Nelson, 2000).
24. Curtis and Eldredge, *The Sacred Romance*, 23.
25. For a recent piece addressing this particular apologetic task, see Barry R.
     Leventhal, "Holocaust Apologetics: Undoing the Death of God,"
     Christian Research Journal 28.4 (2005): 12–21.
26. Much historical documentation can be found about the thousands
     of Jews who came to a saving knowledge of the Lord Yeshua during

the Holocaust. From Jewish historical sources, see Eliezer Berkovits, *With God in Hell: Judaism in the Ghettos and Deathcamps* (New York: Sanhedrin, 1979), 12–14; Alexander Donet, *The Holocaust Kingdom: A Memoir* (New York: Holocaust Library, 1963), 28–31; Celia S. Heller, *On the Edge of Destruction: Jews of Poland Between the Two World Wars* (New York: Schocken Books, 1977), 183–209; and Léon Poliakov, *Harvest of Hate: The Nazi Program for the Destruction of the Jews of Europe* (New York: Holocaust Library, 1979), 296. From Jewish Christian historical sources, see Johanna-Ruth Dobschiner, *Selected to Live* (Old Tappan, NJ: Revell, 1973); Rachmiel Frydland, *When Being Jewish Was a Crime* (Nashville: Thomas Nelson, 1978); Jacob Gartenhaus, *Famous Hebrew Christians* (Grand Rapids: Baker, 1976), 25n. 2; Myrna Grant, *The Journey* (Wheaton: Tyndale, 1978); James C. Hefley, *The New Jews* (Wheaton: Tyndale, 1974), 57–67, 103–14; Arthur W. Kac, "Who Is a Jew?" in *The Messiahship of Jesus: Are Jews Changing Their Attitude Toward Jesus?* ed. Arthur W. Kac, rev. ed. (Grand Rapids: Baker, 1980, 1986), 141; Zola Levitt, *Meshumed!* (Chicago: Moody, 1979); Joel Marcus, *Jesus and the Holocaust: Reflections on Suffering and Hope* (New York: Doubleday, 1997); Jan Markell, *Angels in the Camp* (Wheaton: Tyndale, 1979); Elwood McQuaid, *Zvi* (West Collingwood, NJ: Spearhead, 1978); Naomi Rose Rothstein, *A Rose from the Ashes: The Rose Price Story* (San Francisco: Jews for Jesus, 2006); Ulrich Simon, *A Theology of Auschwitz: The Christian Faith and the Problem of Evil* (Atlanta: John Knox, 1967); Eliezer Urbach, with Edith S. Weigand, *Out of the Fury* (Charlotte, NC: Chosen People Ministries, 1987); and A. M. Weinberger, *I Escaped the Holocaust* (Alberta: Horizon House, 1978).
27. On God's "jealousy" over his covenant people Israel, see Exodus 20:5; 34:14; Numbers 25:11–13; Deuteronomy 4:24; 5:9; 6:15; 29:20; 32:16, 21; Joshua 24:19; 1 Kings 14:22; Psalms 78:58; 79:5; Ezekiel 8:1–5ff.; 16:35–42; 23:28–30; 36:5–6; Nahum 1:2; Zephaniah 1:14–18; and Zechariah 1:14; 8:2.
28. On Israel's covenant infidelity as portrayed in the imagery of an adulterous wife or a common prostitute, as well as God's Sacred Romance pursuit of her (as her jealous Husband), see Exodus 34:12–17; Leviticus 17:7; 20:1–7; Numbers 15:37–41; 25:1ff.; Deuteronomy 31:16–18; Judges 2:6–17ff.; 8:27–35; 1 Chronicles 5:23–26; 2 Chronicles 21:11–15ff.; Psalm 106:39; Isaiah 1:21; 54:5; 57:1–3ff.; Jeremiah 2:20ff.; 3:1–11, 19–20; 5:7–9; 9:2; 13:15–27; 23:9–14ff.; 31:32; Ezekiel 6:9–10; 16:1–63; 20:30; 23:1–49; Hosea 1:1–5:3ff.; 6:10; 7:1–4ff.; 9:1ff.; Micah 1:7ff.; Nahum 3:1–7.
29. For some of the best books arguing for the messiahship of Yeshua, see John Ankerberg, John Weldon, and Walter C. Kaiser Jr., *The Case for Jesus the Messiah* (Chattanooga: John Ankerberg Evangelistic Assoc., 1989); Brown, *Answering Jewish Objections to Jesus: Messianic Prophecy Objections*; Fruchtenbaum, *Jesus Was a Jew*; Arthur W. Kac, *The Messianic Hope: A Divine Solution for the Human Problem* (Grand Rapids: Baker, 1975); idem, ed., *The Messiahship of Jesus: Are Jews Changing Their Attitude Toward Jesus?*; and Walter C. Kaiser Jr., *The Messiah in the Old Testament*, Studies in Old Testament Biblical Theology (Grand Rapids:

Zondervan, 1995). In addition, see Barry R. Leventhal, "Why I Believe Jesus Is the Promised Messiah," in *Why I Am a Christian*, ed. Norman L. Geisler and Paul K. Hoffman (Grand Rapids: Baker, 2001), 205–21.

30. Of course there are other divine realities that the Holocaust has thrown into question—for example, the very existence of God. For more on a return to this divine reality, see Leventhal, "Holocaust Apologetics."

31. For a more detailed discussion on the Jewish Haskalah, see Yehuda Slutsky, "Haskalah," in *Encyclopaedia Judaica*, 16 vols. (Jerusalem: Keter Publishing House Jerusalem, 1972), 7:1433–52.

32. For an introductory discussion on the *yetzer-ha-tov* and the *yetzer-ha-ra* in Jewish religious thinking, see A. Cohen, *Everyman's Talmud*, A Classic Commentary (New York: E. P. Dutton, 1949), 54ff., 88–93, 119–20.

33. For the biblical teaching on man's total depravity, see Job 15:14; 25:4; Psalms 51:5; 58:3; Proverbs 22:15; Isaiah 59:1–2; 64:6; Jeremiah 17:9; Habakkuk 1:13; Matthew 15:1–20; Mark 7:1–23; Romans 1:14–32; 3:9–31; 6:1–23; Ephesians 2:1–3; and Titus 3:3.

34. Norman L. Geisler, *Systematic Theology*, vol. 3, *Sin, Salvation* (Minneapolis, MN: Bethany House, 2004), 146–47 (emphasis added).

35. Max Picard, *Hitler in Our Selves* (Hinsdale, IL: Henry Regnery, 1947).

36. Israel W. Charney, "Teaching the Violence of the Holocaust," *Jewish Education* 38 (March 1968): 23.

37. Daniel Polish, "Witnessing God After Auschwitz," in *Issues in the Jewish-Christian Dialogue: Jewish Perspectives on Covenant, Mission and Witness*, ed. Helga Croner and Leon Klenicki (New York: Paulist, 1979), 136.

38. Eugene B. Borowitz, *How Can a Jew Speak of Faith Today?* (Philadelphia: Westminster, 1969), 51.

39. Abba Eban, *My People: The Story of the Jews* (New York: Behrman House, 1978), 415.

40. Frederick Sontag, "The Holocaust God," *Encounter* 42 (Spring 1981): 163.

41. Morris Shapiro, "For Yom Hashoah," *Conservative Judaism* 28 (Spring 1974): 59.

42. Dennis Prager and Joseph Telushkin, *The Nine Questions People Ask About Judaism* (New York: Simon and Shuster, 1986), 35.

43. Michael Berenbaum, "Teach It to Our Children," *Sh'ma* (May 1, 1981): 100–101.

44. Quoted in Emil L. Fackenheim et al., "Jewish Values in the Post-Holocaust Future: A Symposium," 282; also see Eli Wiesel, *The Gates of the Forest*, trans. Frances Frenaye (New York: Avon Books, 1966), 192.

45. Eli Wiesel, "Telling the Truth," *Dimensions* 2 (Spring 1968): 10.

46. Bernard J. Bamberger, *The Search for Jewish Theology* (New York: Behrman House, 1978), 35. On this same note, see Jack Bemporad, "The Concept of Man After Auschwitz," in *Out of the Whirlwind*, ed. Albert H. Friedlander (New York: Schocken Books, 1976), 482–83, 485–87.

47. C. S. Lewis, *The Four Loves* (New York: Harcourt Brace Jovanovich, 1960), 144–45.

48. See note 33 above.
49. Carson, *How Long, O Lord?* 17.
50. Lewis M. Simons, "Genocide and the Science of Proof," *National Geographic* 209 (January 2006): 28.
51. McGrath, *Suffering and God*, 18.
52. Dietrich Bonhoeffer, *Ethics*, ed. Wayne Whitson Floyd Jr. (Minneapolis, MN: Fortress, 2005), 85–86.
53. For a detailed description of Israel's future tribulation period, see Stanley Ellisen and Charles H. Dyer, *Who Owns the Land? The Arab/Israeli Conflict*, rev. ed. (Wheaton: Tyndale, 1991, 2003); Fruchtenbaum, *Israelology*; idem, *The Footsteps of the Messiah*; Louis Goldberg, *Turbulence over the Middle East* (Neptune, NJ: Loizeaux Brothers, 1982); Michael Rydelnik, *Understanding the Arab-Israeli Conflict: What the Headlines Haven't Told You* (Chicago: Moody, 2004); Harold A. Sevener, *Israel's Glorious Future: The Prophecies and Promises of God Revealed* (Charlotte: Chosen People Ministries, 1996); Wilbur M. Smith, *Israeli/Arab Conflict and the Bible* (Glendale, CA: Regal Books, 1967); John F. Walvoord, *Armageddon, Oil and the Middle East Crisis*, rev. ed. (Grand Rapids: Zondervan, 1974, 1976, 1990); and idem, *Israel in Prophecy* (Grand Rapids: Zondervan, 1962).
54. For a detailed description of the doctrine of the remnant, see Leventhal, "Theological Perspectives on the Holocaust," 199–212; also, Fruchtenbaum, *Hebrew Christianity*, 30–33; on Israel's future remnant, see Fruchtenbaum, *Israelology*, 532–37, 777–80.
55. C. S. Lewis, *The Problem of Pain* (New York: Collier Books/Macmillan, 1962), 92–93, 95, 97.

Chapter 8: The Chosen People and Jewish Evangelism

1. A. J. Heschel's dissertation was published as *Die Prophetie* (Cracow: Polish Academy of Sciences, 1936). Nearly three decades later, he expanded the work and its central doctrine of "divine pathos," in *The Prophets*, 2 vols. (New York: Harper and Row, 1962).
2. "A Conversation with Abraham Joshua Heschel" (New York: National Broadcasting, 1973), transcript, 6.
3. Byron Sherwin, *Abraham Joshua Heschel*, Makers of Contemporary Theology (Atlanta: John Knox, 1979), 3. Samuel Dresner in his "Heschel the Man" summarized his friend as a *nasi*, a *shalem*, and a *zaddik*: a prince, a "complete" person, and a holy teacher respectively. John C. Merkle, ed., *Abraham Joshua Heschel: Exploring His Life and Thought* (New York: Macmillan, 1985), 3–25.
4. A. J. Heschel, *Israel: An Echo of Eternity* (New York: Farrar, Straus, and Giroux, 1969).
5. A. J. Heschel, "No Religion Is an Island," *Union Seminary Quarterly Review* 21.2 (January 1966): 117.
6. Heschel devotes an entire chapter of *Israel*, 139–44, to expose "the tendency to spiritualize the meaning of its words and to minimize its plain historical sense" that has "made many Christians incapable of understanding or empathy for what the Holy Land means to the Jewish people and to the authors of the Hebrew Bible, or for what the

people Israel means in the flesh, not just as a symbol or as a construct of theological speculation" (139).

7. Ibid., 46.
8. Ibid., 225.
9. A. J. Heschel, *The Wisdom of Heschel*, ed. Ruth Marcus Goodhill (New York: Farrar, Straus, and Giroux, 1975), 175.
10. Heschel, *Israel*, 100, 129.
11. Ibid., 100–101.
12. Ibid., 149, 127, 44.
13. Ibid., 44, cf. 121.
14. Ibid., 60–61.
15. Ibid., 173–89.
16. Ibid., 29, 195, 198–99.
17. Ibid., 129, 131.
18. A. J. Heschel, *Man's Quest for God* (New York: Charles Scribner's Sons, 1954), 109.
19. Heschel, *Israel*, 113, cf. 101, 138.
20. Ibid., 58, cf. 8, 20.
21. Heschel, "No Religion Is an Island," 117.
22. These statistics were reported in *USA Today*, October 2, 2000, 6D.
23. *Jewish News*, January 12, 2001.

Chapter 9: To the Jew First

1. Much thanks is owed to Ra McLaughlin, webmaster and editor for Third Millennium Ministries, for his editorial work with this manuscript.
2. The *Westminster Confession of Faith* with some modifications is the official doctrinal standard of many Reformed and Presbyterian denominations. It, therefore, adequately represents some of the central features of the Reformed theological system.
3. It should be noted that these and related topics appear in a number of important writings by Reformed theologians. See, for instance, Anthony A. Hoekema, *The Bible and the Future* (Grand Rapids: Eerdmans, 1979); David E. Holwerda, *Jesus and Israel: One Covenant or Two?* (Grand Rapids: Eerdmans, 1995); G. C. Berkouwer, *The Church* (Grand Rapids: Eerdmans, 1976); idem, *Faith and Sanctification* (Grand Rapids: Eerdmans, 1952); idem, *The Return of Christ* (Grand Rapids: Eerdmans, 1972); Iain H. Murray, *The Puritan Hope* (London: Banner of Truth Trust, 1971); and John Murray, *The Covenant of Grace* (London: Tyndale, 1954). Gospel ministry to non-Christian Jews has come under consideration in the declarations of Presbyterian churches in the United States in recent years.
4. For a summary of covenant in Reformed theology, see Geerhardus Vos, *Redemptive History and Biblical Interpretation: The Shorter Writings of Geerhardus Vos*, ed. Richard B. Gaffin Jr. (Phillipsburg, NJ: Presbyterian and Reformed, 1980), 234–67.
5. O. Palmer Robertson, *The Christ of the Covenants* (Phillipsburg, NJ: Presbyterian and Reformed, 1980), 201–27; Meredith G. Kline, *Treaty of the Great King* (Grand Rapids: Eerdmans, 1963); idem, *The Structure of Biblical Authority*, 2d ed. (Eugene, OR: Wipf and Stock,

1997); and idem, *Kingdom Prologue* (South Hamilton, MA: M. G. Kline, 1993).

6. *Westminster Confession of Faith* 7.3–7.6; 14.2; 17.2; 27.1; 28.1; *Westminster Larger Catechism* 30–36, 162; and *Westminster Shorter Catechism* 20, 94. In describing the covenant of grace, it should be noted that the viewpoint of the Westminster Assembly is a theological construct. It was not directly dependent on specific biblical passages or vocabulary of covenant. Instead, it summarized an assortment of biblical teachings on divine-human relations, much as the doctrine of the Trinity brought together into one doctrine many affirmations about the Godhead.

7. *Westminster Confession of Faith* 7.2; 19.1; and *Westminster Larger Catechism* 30.

8. *Westminster Larger Catechism* 20; and *Westminster Shorter Catechism* 12.

9. *Westminster Confession of Faith* 7.5.

10. Ibid. 7.6.

11. Ibid. 7.5.

12. Ibid.

13. Ibid.

14. John Calvin, *Commentaries on the Epistle of Paul the Apostle to the Romans* (Grand Rapids: Baker, 1993), 437.

15. Edmund P. Clowney, *The Church* (Downers Grove, IL: InterVarsity Press, 1995), 42–44; and Charles Hodge, *Systematic Theology* (Grand Rapids: Eerdmans, 1993), 3:548–52.

16. *Westminster Confession of Faith* 25.1.

17. Ibid. 25.2.

18. Cf. *London Baptist Confession* (1689) 26.2.

19. *Westminster Confession of Faith* 25.2.

20. Ibid. 25.5.

21. Ibid.

22. Ibid. 7.5; 20.1; 25.2.

23. *Formula of Concord*, Article 6.

24. Louis Berkhof, *Systematic Theology* (Grand Rapids: Eerdmans, 1966), 614–15; and Lewis W. Spitz and Wenzel Lohff, eds., *Discord, Dialogue, and Concord* (Philadelphia: Fortress, 1977), 93–94.

25. Calvin, *Commentaries on the Epistle of Paul the Apostle to the Romans*, 256.

26. John Calvin, *Institutes of the Christian Religion* (Philadelphia: Westminster, 1960), 2.7.4; 2.7.7.

27. The *Heidelberg Catechism* reflects Calvin's perspective when it sets the Ten Commandments under the rubric of "Of Gratitude" or "Of Thankfulness" (questions 92–115).

28. *Westminster Confession of Faith* 19.1.

29. Ibid. 19.2.

30. Ibid. 19.1. In this way, the Reformed perspective on Mosaic law is similar to rabbinical declarations of the eternality of Torah (see *Pirqe Abot* 1.2; 3.23—*Pirqe Abot* [Ethics of the Fathers] is an ancient document outlining the ethics of Judaism).

31. *Westminster Confession of Faith* 19.3.

32.   Ibid. 19.4.
33.   Ibid. 19.5.
34.   Ibid. 19.3.
35.   Ibid. 19.4.
36.   Ibid. 19.6.
37.   See William S. Barker and W. Robert Godfrey, eds., *Theonomy: A Reformed Critique* (Grand Rapids: Academie Books, 1990).
38.   Acts 2:46; 3:1; 5:21, 25, 42; 18:18; 21:20–26; 22:17; 23:4–5; 24:10–18; 25:8.
39.   Acts 10:1–11:18; Galatians 2:11–21; Ephesians 2:11–22.
40.   1 Corinthians 9:20–22; Galatians 2:11–21.
41.   John Calvin, *Commentary on the Book of the Prophet Isaiah* (Grand Rapids: Baker, 1993), 298–99; and idem, *Institutes of the Christian Religion*, 2.11.2, 451–52.
42.   Holwerda, *Jesus and Israel: One Covenant or Two?* 153–54, 168–75.
43.   See Hoekema, *The Bible and the Future*, 143–47; and Murray, *The Puritan Hope*, 48–49, 61–65.
44.   Murray, *The Puritan Hope*, 41.
45.   Hodge, *Systematic Theology*, 3:805. See similar sentiments in John Owen, *An Exposition of the Epistle to the Hebrews*, 2d ed. (Edinburgh: n.p., 1812), 1:443–44, 454–55; John Murray, *The Epistle to the Romans* (Grand Rapids: Eerdmans, 1984), 1:28, 2:xiv–xv, 2:76–101; Geerhardus Vos, *Biblical Theology: Old and New Testaments*, 10th printing (Grand Rapids: Eerdmans, 1948), 79; idem, *The Pauline Eschatology* (Grand Rapids: Baker, 1979), 88; idem, *Redemptive History and Biblical Interpretation*, 35; Jonathan Edwards, *The Works of Jonathan Edwards* (London: Banner of Truth Trust, 1975), 1:607; and Matthew Henry, *Matthew Henry's Commentary* (McLean, VA: MacDonald Publishing, n.d.), 6:448–53, as cited by CHAIM (see http://www.chaim.org under "Reformed Statements").
46.   Berkouwer, *The Return of Christ*, 323–58.
47.   Hoekema, *The Bible and the Future*.
48.   "Overture on Jewish Evangelism 20th General Assembly Presbyterian Church in America," cited *ver batim* from CHAIM at http://www .chaim.org under "Reformed Statements."

Chapter 10: To the Jew First in the New Millennium

1.   In this article, the English translations are from the *American Standard Bible* unless otherwise noted.
2.   Charles Hodge, *A Commentary on Romans* (1835; repr., Carlisle, PA: Banner of Truth Trust, 1975), 29–30.
3.   Ibid., 52.
4.   William G. T. Shedd, *A Critical and Doctrinal Commentary on the Epistle of St. Paul to the Romans* (1879; repr., Grand Rapids: Zondervan, 1967), 16.
5.   Ibid., 42.
6.   John Murray, *The Epistle to the Romans*, 2 vols. (Grand Rapids: Eerdmans, 1965), 1:28.

7.   Ibid.
8.   J. P. McBeth, *Exegetical and Practical Commentary on Romans* (Dallas: Crescendo Book Publications, 1937), 42–43.
9.   Ibid.
10.   F. F. Bruce, *The Epistle of Paul to the Romans* (Grand Rapids: Eerdmans, 1966), 78–79.
11.   Ibid., 90.
12.   Douglas J. Moo, *The Epistle to the Romans*, New International Commentary on the New Testament, ed. N. B. Stonehouse, F. F. Bruce, and G. D. Fee (Grand Rapids: Eerdmans, 1996), 68–69.
13.   Ibid.
14.   Alva J. McClain, *Romans: The Gospel of God's Grace* (Chicago: Moody, 1973), 58.
15.   Ibid.
16.   C. K. Barrett, *A Commentary on the Epistle to the Romans* (New York: Harper and Row, 1957), 29.
17.   Ibid.
18.   Sanford C. Mills, *A Hebrew Christian Looks at Romans* (Grand Rapids: Dunham, 1968), 37.
19.   Joseph Hoffman Cohn, *Beginning at Jerusalem* (New York: American Board of Missions to the Jews, 1948), 12.
20.   Ibid., 37.
21.   Ibid., 144–47.
22.   Joseph Henry Thayer, *Greek-English Lexicon of the New Testament* (Grand Rapids: Zondervan, 1963), 554–55.
23.   William F. Arndt and F. Wilbur Gingrich, *A Greek-English Lexicon of the New Testament* (Chicago: University of Chicago Press, 1957), 732–34 (italics in original).
24.   Jim R. Sibley, "Some Notes on Romans 1:16" (unpublished article), 1.
25.   Walter Baueret et al., *Greek-English Lexicon of the New Testament and Other Early Christian Literature*, 2d ed. (Chicago: University of Chicago Press, 1979), 726.
26.   Standard Greek grammars refer to this use of the present tense as "gnomic." Cf., e.g., James H. Moulton, *A Grammar of New Testament Greek*, 3d ed. (Edinburgh: T & T Clark, 1985), 3:63; C. F. D. Moule, *An Idiom Book of New Testament Greek*, 2d ed. (Cambridge: Cambridge University Press, 1959), 8; A. T. Robertson, *A Grammar of the Greek New Testament in the Light of Historical Research* (Nashville: Broadman, 1934), 866ff.; and Daniel B. Wallace, *Greek Grammar Beyond the Basics* (Grand Rapids: Zondervan, 1996), 523ff., though other grammarians may use other terminology. Cf., e.g., Stanley Porter's *Idioms of the Greek New Testament*, 2d ed. (Sheffield: Sheffield Academic, 1995), 33.
27.   Cf. Bent Noack's article, "Current and Backwater in the Epistle to the Romans," *Studia theologica* 19 (1965): 155–66. Cf., also, C. E. B. Cranfield, *The Epistle to the Romans*, International Critical Commentary, ed. J. A. Emerton and C. E. B. Cranfeld (Edinburgh: T & T Clark, 1979), 90–91; Moo, *Epistle to the Romans*, 68–69; Mark D. Nanos, *The Mystery of Romans* (Minneapolis, MN: Augsburg Fortress, 1996), 21–40; and

Thomas R. Schreiner, *Romans*, Baker Exegetical Commentary on the New Testament, ed. Moises Silva (Grand Rapids: Baker, 1998), 62.

28. Sibley, "Some Notes on Romans 1:16," 1–2.

Chapter 11: Lessons in Jewish Evangelism from the Past Century

1. Christopher Clark, *The Politics of Conversion: Missionary Protestantism and the Jews in Prussia 1728–1941* (Oxford: Clarendon, 1995).

2. Ibid.

3. See the study by William Thomas Gidney, *The History of the London Society for Promoting Christianity Amongst the Jews: From 1809 to 1908* (London: London Society for Promoting Christianity Amongst the Jews, 1908), microform; also see George Stevens, *Go Tell My Brethren: The Story of the London Jews Society from 1905–1959* (London: SPCK, 1960).

4. J. F. de le Roi, *Geschichte der Evangelischen Judenmission seit Entstehung des neureren Judentums* (Leipsic, Germany: n.p., 1899).

5. See Gidney, *The History of the London Society for Promoting Christianity Amongst the Jews.*

6. See Howard Morely Sachar, *The Course of Modern Jewish History* (New York: Dell, 1958).

7. The Jewish community in Russia was devastated by the war, yet the events between 1914 and 1917 were just a precursor to the extraordinary horrors that would take place during the Russian Revolution. According to a report in the MRW, the Jews experienced terrible persecution once again in the postwar revolutionary period. Actually, the renewal of pogroms had perhaps reached its most gruesome stage. See "The Ukraine Terror," *Missionary Review of the World* 33.12 (1921): 971. During the spring of 1919, when the Ukrainian army was retreating from the Red Army, which occupied Kiev, units of the Ukrainian army staged pogroms in Berditchev, Zhitomir, and various smaller towns. On February 15, 1919, these pogroms reached their height at the massacre of Proskurov where 1,700 Jews died within a few hours. During the years of 1920–1921, even while the Red Army had control of the Ukraine, independent Ukrainian units still managed to perpetrate their atrocities against the Jews, and in the town of Tetiev, 4,000 innocent Jews were put to death. *Encyclopaedia Judaica* (Jerusalem, 1972), 14:699.

8. For a detailed discussion of the events leading to the demise of Jewish missions in Russian, see Mitchell Leslie Glaser, "A Survey of Mission to the Jews in Continental Europe, 1908–1950" (Ph.D. diss., Fuller Theological Seminary, 1999), 69–97.

9. See, for example, the report of Henri Vincent, "Jewish Notes," *The Chosen People* 52.8 (1946): 18. Vincent wrote from Paris with a detailed description of the conditions and of their efforts to minister to the Jews of postwar Paris.

10. Richard Wurmbrand, *Christ on the Jewish Road* (London: Hodder and Stoughton, 1970), 33. Ester Feinstein's detailed and graphic

description of her husband's martyrdom was printed in *The Chosen People* magazine. See Ester Feinstein, "Jewish Notes," *The Chosen People* 53.1 (1947): 14.

11. See my discussion, "A Survey of Mission to the Jews in Continental Europe," 318ff.

12. See Allan R. Brockway, *For Love of the Jews: A Theological History of the IMCCAJ, 1927–1961* (Ph.D. diss., University of Birmingham, 1992).

13. For example, in 1933, Victor Buksbazen, a Hebrew Christian, was appointed head of the British Jews Society in Krakow, Poland. In one report to his society, Buksbazen suggested that the Jewish attitude toward Christ was notably changing in his time. He mentioned that the blind hatred of former days was disappearing, and he detected a growing consciousness among the Jews whom he met "that Jesus is one of their own, and not an outsider."

     Buksbazen almost seemed to believe that anti-Semitism was in some way driving the Jews to reconsider the Jewish Jesus as a friend of the Jews. Victor Buksbazen, "Our Mission Centres in Europe," *British Jews Society Annual Report* (London, 1934–35b): 45.

14. Regarding the assimilation of the Hungarian Jewish community, the *Encyclopedia Judaica* reported, "From the close of the 19th century, assimilation became widespread within Hungarian Jewry and there was an increase in 'apostasy,' especially among the upper classes." *Encyclopaedia Judaica*, 8:1088–89.

15. For a discussion of this important figure, see Arthur Glasser, "The Legacy of Jakób Jocz," *International Bulletin of Missionary Research* 17 (April 1993): 66–68, 70–71; idem, "Jakób Jocz, 1906–1983. 'To the Jew First': First Principle of Mission," in *Mission Legacies: Biographical Studies of Leaders of the Modern Missionary Movement*, ed. Gerald H. Anderson, Robert T. Coote, Norman A. Horner, and James M. Phillips (Maryknoll, NY: Orbis, 1994), 523–31.

16. Rachmiel Frydland records his remarkable story of conversion and survival in *Joy Cometh in the Morning* (self-published, n.d.); and idem, *When Being Jewish Was a Crime* (Nashville: Thomas Nelson, 1978).

17. See John Stuart Conning, "Jews Become Christians," *Missionary Review of the World* 40: 12 (1931): 905.

18. Hugh Joseph Schonfeld, *The History of Jewish Christianity from the First Century to the Twentieth Century* (London: Duckworth, 1936), 169–70.

19. *International Review of Missions*, 1930, 542–43.

20. Regarding the work of the London Jews Society, George Stevens writes, "During World War II, the mission premises were seriously damaged and the work was never able to begin again." Stevens, *Go Tell My Brethren*, 91. In his postwar memoirs, the great missionary statesman Arnold Frank recorded the story of the actual closing down of his ministry in Hamburg, Germany. See Arnold Frank, *What About the Jew: Pictures from the Gallery of My Memories* (Belfast, Ireland: Graham and Heslib, 1944).

21. See my discussion, "A Survey of Mission to the Jews in Continental Europe," 318ff.

22. For the work of the Anglican church among the Jewish people through

the auspices of the London Jews Society, see the volume by Stevens, *Go Tell My Brethren*, 1960.

23. For further reading regarding the Church of Scotland's role in Jewish missions, see David McDougall, *In Search of Israel: A Chronicle of the Jewish Missions of the Church of Scotland* (London: Nelson, 1941).

24. See J. H. Adeney, *The Jews of Eastern Europe* (New York: Macmillan, 1921).

25. See William O. McCagg, "Conversion in Hungary," in *Jewish Apostasy in the Modern World*, ed. Tod Endelman (New York: Holmes and Meier, 1987), 143. The veracity of these statistics is confirmed by the fact that these figures were compiled by the Jewish community, which sought to explain the large number of conversions to Christianity among Hungarian Jews.

26. Lisa Schiffman, *Generation J* (San Francisco: Harper, 1999).

27. Alan Dershowitz, *The Vanishing American Jew: In Search of Jewish Identity for the Next Century* (New York: Touchstone, 1997).

Chapter 12: Jewish Evangelism in the New Millennium

1. This paper was delivered at the "To the Jew First in the New Millennium" conference in 1999, and has been edited slightly for the purposes of this current volume. It was originally published, however, in three installments of the journal *Missionary Monthly*. See Arthur F. Glasser, "The Missiological Dimension: First of 3 Installments: Jewish Evangelism in the New Century," *Missionary Monthly* 104.1 (2000): 7–10; idem, "The Missiological Dimension: Second of 3 Installments: Jewish Evangelism in the New Century," *Missionary Monthly* 104.2 (2000): 11–14; and idem, "The Missiological Dimension: Third of 3 Installments: Jewish Evangelism in the New Century," *Missionary Monthly* 104.3 (2000): 10–13.

2. Walter C. Kaiser Jr., *Toward an Old Testament Theology* (Grand Rapids: Zondervan, 1978), 263.

3. C. S. Lewis, "What Are We to Make of Jesus Christ?" in *God in the Dock: Essays on Theology and Ethics*, ed. Walter Hooper (Grand Rapids: Eerdmans, 1970), 156.

4. Quotation cited by Leonard Swidler, Lewis John Eron, Gerard Sloyan, and Lester Dean, *Bursting the Bonds: A Jewish-Christian Dialogue on Jesus and Paul* (Maryknoll, NY: Orbis, 1990), 26.

5. Lewis, "What Are We to Make of Jesus Christ?" 157.

6. See Arthur F. Glasser with Charles E. Van Engen, Dean S. Gilliland, and Shawn B. Redford, *Announcing the Kingdom: The Story of God's Mission in the Bible* (Grand Rapids: Baker, 2003), 259–68.

7. Ibid., 184–85.

8. See Glasser, *Announcing the Kingdom*, 207–8.

9. Moishe Rosen and Ceil Rosen, *Witnessing to Jews: Practical Ways to Relate the Love of Jesus* (San Francisco: Jews for Jesus, 1999; repr., Chicago: Moody, 2002).

Chapter 13: The Ongoing Importance of Messianic Prophecy for Jewish Evangelism in the New Millennium

1. Jakob Jocz, *The Jewish People and Jesus Christ* (London: SPCK, 1949; repr., Grand Rapids: Baker, 1979), 207.

2. Sigmund Mowinckel, *He That Cometh*, trans. G. W. Anderson (Oxford: Blackwell, 1959), 17.

3. Joachim Becker, *Messianic Expectation in the Old Testament*, trans. David E. Green (Philadelphia: Fortress, 1977), 50, 87.

4. James H. Charlesworth, "From Messianology to Christology," in *The Messiah*, ed. James H. Charlesworth (Philadelphia: Fortress, 1992), 3.

5. Donald Juel, *Messianic Exegesis: Christological Interpretation of the Old Testament in Early Christianity* (Philadelphia: Fortress, 1988), 13.

6. See my article "Inner-biblical Perspectives on Messianic Prophecy," in *Mishkan* 27 (1997); as well as Walter Kaiser, *The Messiah in the Old Testament* (Grand Rapids: Zondervan, 1995); and John H. Sailhamer writes, "As part of the overall proposal for an approach to Old Testament theology offered in this book, we strongly urge the consideration of a return to the notion that the literal meaning of the Old Testament may, in fact, be linked to the Messianic hope of the pre-Christian, Israelite prophets" (*Introduction to Old Testament Theology: A Canonical Approach* [Grand Rapids: Zondervan, 1995], 154).

7. As A. T. Robertson said, "Jesus found himself in the Old Testament, a thing that some modern scholars do not seem to be able to do." A. T. Robertson, *The Gospel According to Luke*, vol. 2, *Word Pictures in the New Testament* (Nashville: Broadman, 1930), 294.

8. H. L. Ellison, *The Centrality of the Messianic Idea in the Old Testament* (London: Tyndale, 1957), 6.

9. For an excellent discussion of the spiritual dimensions of hermeneutics, see Gerhard Maier, *Biblical Hermeneutics*, trans. Robert W. Yarbrough (Wheaton: Crossway, 1994), 53–62.

10. Ellison, *The Centrality of the Messianic Idea in the Old Testament*, 5.

11. Walter Liefield, "Luke," in *The Expositor's Bible Commentary*, ed. Frank E. Gaebelein (Grand Rapids: Zondervan, 1984), 8:797–1059, esp. 1053 (emphasis mine). Jesus' hermeneutical perspective (that all the Old Testament pointed to the Messiah) is evident in Peter's evangelistic preaching to Jewish people. In his sermon at the portico of Solomon, recorded in Acts 3:11–26, he asserted that "all" the prophets pointed to the Messiah (Acts 3:18). Moreover, he maintained that the central message of the prophets was indeed eschatological and Messianic. He stated, "*All* the prophets who have spoken . . . announced these days" (Acts 3:24 NASB, emphasis added). This reflects Jesus' earlier emphasis on the word *all* (discussed above). It is apparent that Peter was only expressing what he previously learned from Jesus (Luke 24:44–46).

12. See Sailhamer, *Introduction to Old Testament Theology*, 221; and Michael A. Rydelnik, "The Promise of Messiah: Preparing a Course in Messianic Prophecy at the Bible College Level" (thesis, D. Miss., Trinity Evangelical Divinity School, Deerfield, IL, 1997), 32–33, for a discussion of the Septuagint reading of 2 Samuel 23:1.

13. Most English versions translate this as a question: "Is not my house

so with God?" (cf. NIV, NASB). However, the Hebrew does not have an interrogative h and the literal translation of the phrase כִּי־לֹאכֵן is "for not so."

14. James Smith, *What the Bible Teaches About the Promised Messiah* (Nashville: Thomas Nelson, 1993), 21; Roger Raymer, "First Peter," in *The Bible Knowledge Commentary: New Testament*, ed. John F. Walvoord and Roy B. Zuck (Wheaton: Scripture Press, 1983), 837–58, esp. 843; Edwin A. Blum, "First Peter," in *The Expositor's Bible Commentary*, ed. Frank E. Gaebelein (Grand Rapids: Zondervan, 1981), 12:207–54, esp. 222; and Peter H. Davids, *The First Epistle of Peter*, New International Commentary on the New Testament, ed. F. F. Bruce (Grand Rapids: Eerdmans, 1990), 61.

15. Walter C. Kaiser, *The Uses of the Old Testament in the New* (Chicago: Moody, 1985), 19.

16. Ibid., 19–20.

17. Wayne Grudem, *First Peter*, Tyndale New Testament Commentaries, ed. Leon Morris (Grand Rapids: Eerdmans, 1988), 74–75.

18. Kaiser, *The Uses of the Old Testament in the New*, 20.

19. Grudem, *First Peter*, 71.

20. Bo Reicke, *The Epistles of James, Peter, Jude*, Anchor Bible, ed. W. F. Albright and David Noel Freeman (New York: Doubleday, 1964), 37:80.

21. F. F. Bruce, *The Defense of the Gospel in the New Testament* (Grand Rapids: Eerdmans, 1959), 13–14.

22. Ibid., 14–15.

23. The apostles found that frequently their Jewish audiences were responsive to their Messianic message. This was, most probably, a result of the Jewish Messianic expectation evident during second temple times. Luke records that there were Jewish people "looking for the consolation of Israel" and "for the redemption of Jerusalem" (Luke 2:25, 38). It was the Old Testament Messianic prophecies that gave them this hope. For more on the pre-Christian use of Messianic prophecy, see Michael Green, *Evangelism in the Early Church* (Grand Rapids: Eerdmans, 1970), 78–111. For Jewish Messianic expectation, see Alfred Edersheim, *Life and Times of Jesus the Messiah*, reprint in 1 vol. (Grand Rapids: Eerdmans, 1971), 78–82, 160–79; and George Foot Moore, *Judaism in the First Centuries of the Christian Era* (repr., Boston: Harvard University Press, 1971), 2:323–76.

24. E. H. Dewart, *Jesus the Messiah in Prophecy and Fulfillment: A Review and Refutation of the Negative Theory of Messianic Prophecy* (Cincinnati: Cranston and Stowe; New York: Hunt and Eaton, 1891), 217–18. It is notable that Schoeps, who does not believe in Jesus as Messiah, recognizes that the events of Jesus' life and death fit the prophetic utterances. He explains this away as either the event being a fabrication inserted into the life of Jesus by the apostles to confirm the words of the prophets, or as deliberate actions on the part of Jesus, contrived to make it appear as if he were fulfilling prophecy. Hans Joachim Schoeps, *The Jewish-Christian Argument: A History of Theologies in Conflict*, trans. David E. Green (New York: Holt, Rhinehart, and Winston, 1961), 22.

Either way, he recognizes that the New Testament record agrees with the prophetic oracles about the Messiah.

25. See Edward Flannery, *The Anguish of the Jews*; and James Parkes, *The Conflict of the Church and the Synagogue* (Cleveland and New York: Meridian, 1961) for an overview of the tragic history.

26. The primary work surveying the history of apologetic materials for Jewish people from the second century A.D. until the Renaissance is A. Lukyn Williams, *Adversus Judaeos: A Bird's Eye View of Christian Apologiae Until the Renaissance* (New York: Cambridge, 1935). It addresses—at least in a cursory fashion for some works, and in a somewhat extended way for others—the materials that were used, in some way, for Jewish evangelism.

27. Williams, *Adversus Judaeos*, xv.

28. William Horbury, "Old Testament Interpretation in the Writings of the Church Fathers," in *Mikra: Text, Translation, Reading and Interpretation of the Hebrew Bible in Ancient Judaism and Early Christianity*, ed. M. J. Muldur and H. Sysling, Compendia Rerum Iudaicarum ad Novum Testamentum (Minneapolis, MN: Fortress, 1990), 727–87, esp. 740. It seems bizarre that the attempt to prove the messiahship of Jesus should cause the Fathers to falsify Jewish history and negate Jewish status as the chosen people. Parkes has said that the Fathers were "led on inescapably by the method of their own argumentation from the first legitimate assumption to the last and most extravagant fabrications." Parkes, *The Conflict of the Church and the Synagogue*, 96–97. How unfortunate that their proclamation of Jesus as Messiah included as an ancillary idea the denigration of the Jewish people.

29. What follows is a brief survey of the use of Messianic prophecy in the patristic and medieval church. For a more thorough analysis, see Rydelnik, *The Promise of Messiah*, 69–126.

30. J. Rendel Harris, *Testimonies* (Cambridge: Cambridge University Press, 1916), 1:23.

31. J. Rendel Harris, *Testimonies* (Cambridge: Cambridge University Press, 1920), 2:94.

32. Williams, *Adversus Judaeos*, 7.

33. Ibid., 12.

34. One such work is Cyprian's *Book of Testimonies*, written in response to a request by a wealthy layman named Quirinius. It is a collection of Old Testament passages without much interpretive discussion, which, according to Cyprian, established the truth of Jesus as the Messiah of Old Testament prophecy. Although it is a good, but late (mid-third century), example of a Testimonia book, it is not a work designed for Jewish evangelism. Jewish people are not mentioned in Quirinius's request or in Cyprian's reply. The book gives no evidence of any discussions with, or any knowledge of, Jews. Its purpose was to strengthen the faith of Gentile Christians by establishing the Old Testament basis of their faith. Hence, it will not be discussed in this chapter.

35. Justin Martyr, "Dialogue with Trypho," in *Writings of Saint Justin Martyr*, ed. and trans. Thomas B. Falls, which is in *The Fathers of the Church:*

A New Translation, ed. Ludwig Schopp (New York: Christian Heritage, 1948). Krauss dates it sometime after the Bar Cochba rebellion in A.D. 132–35 ("The Jews in the Works of the Church Fathers," *Jewish Quarterly Review* 5 [1893]: 123), whereas Williams puts it between A.D. 155–61 (*Adversus Judaeos*, 31).

36. Justin Martyr, "Dialogue with Trypho," 16.
37. Oskar Skarsaune, *The Proof from Prophecy: A Study in Justin Martyr's Proof-text Tradition: Text-type, Provenance, Theological Profile* (Leiden: E. J. Brill, 1987), 226–27.
38. Williams, *Adversus Judaeos*, 35.
39. Justin Martyr, "Dialogue with Trypho," 113.
40. Ibid., 53.
41. Ibid., 54.
42. Chien-Kuo Paul Lai, "Jacob's Blessing on Judah (Genesis 49:8–12) with the Hebrew Old Testament: A Study of In-textual, Inner-textual, and Inter-textual Interpretation" (Ph.D. diss., Trinity Evangelical Divinity School, Deerfield, IL, 1993), 85.
43. For example, Justin Martyr, "Dialogue with Trypho," cites Genesis 49:10; Isaiah 11:1–4; Psalm 72:15, 17; Zechariah 12:10–12. For a thorough discussion of the similarities between Justin's and Talmudic citations of Messianic prophecies, see Skarsaune, *The Proof from Prophecy*, 260–88.
44. Justin Martyr, "Dialogue with Trypho."
45. Williams, *Adversus Judaeos*, 43.
46. Marcel Simon, *Verus Israel*, trans. H. McKeating (London: Littman Library of Jewish Civilization, 1996), 136–39.
47. Williams, *Adversus Judaeos*, 52.
48. Ibid., 95.
49. Ibid., 100.
50. Ibid., 113.
51. Ibid., 141–42.
52. Ibid., 144–46.
53. Ibid., 143–44.
54. Ibid., 148–49.
55. Ibid., 63.
56. Jocz, *The Jewish People and Jesus Christ*, 79–96.
57. Williams, *Adversus Judaeos*, 216.
58. Ibid., 215.
59. Ibid., 217.
60. Ibid.
61. R. J. Zwi Werblowsky, "Crispin's Disputation," *Journal of Jewish Studies* 11 (1960): 69–77, esp. 69.
62. Ibid., 70; and Bernhard Blumenkranz, s.v. "Gilbert Crispin" in *Encyclopaedia Judaica*, ed. Cecil Roth (Jerusalem: Keter, 1971), n.p.
63. Ibid, 74.
64. Williams, *Adversus Judaeos*, 376.
65. Ibid., 377.
66. Ibid., 378–79.
67. Ibid., 379.

68. Ibid.
69. Werblowsky, "Crispin's Disputation," 70.
70. Blumenkranz, "Gilbert Crispin," n.p.
71. Amos Funkenstein, "Basic Types of Christian Anti-Jewish Polemic in the Later Middle Ages," *Viator* 2 (1971): 373–82, esp. 379.
72. Williams, *Adversus Judaeos*, 235.
73. Hugh J. Schonfield, *The History of Jewish Christianity* (London: Duckworth, 1936), 140; and Williams, *Adversus Judaeos*, 234.
74. Erwin I. J. Rosenthal, "Medieval Jewish Exegesis: Its Character and Significance," *Journal of Semitic Studies* 9 (Autumn 1964): 265–81, esp. 265–66.
75. Berger has pointed out that Jewish attempts to refute Christological interpretation of Messianic texts were through Peshat. He writes, "Jews argued that Christological explanations of individual verses could rarely withstand the scrutiny from the wider perspective of the passage as a whole, and they constantly cited adjoining verses to demonstrate this point." David Berger, *The Jewish-Christian Debate in the High Middle Ages: A Critical Edition of the Nizzahon Vetus* (1979; Northvale, NJ, and London: Aronson, 1996), 11–12.
76. For an outstanding analysis of thirteenth-century Roman Catholic missions to the Jews, see Robert Chazan, *Daggers of Faith: Thirteenth-century Missionizing and Jewish Response* (Berkeley: University of California Press, 1989).
77. Ibid., 116.
78. I have discovered a secondary citation of *Pugio Fidei* in Josh McDowell's discussion of Genesis 49:10 in *Evidence That Demands a Verdict* (San Bernadino, CA: Campus Crusade for Christ, 1972), 177. There he quotes M. M. Lemann, who cites the story of Rabbi Rachmon's words from *Pugio Fidei*.
79. See Chazan, *Daggers of Faith*, 167–85.
80. Funkenstein, "Basic Types of Christian Anti-Jewish Polemic in the Later Middle Ages," 381–82.
81. Williams, *Adversus Judaeos*, 252.
82. Chazan, *Daggers of Faith*, 120–26.
83. Ibid., 164.
84. Ibid., 115.
85. Eugene H. Merrill, "Rashi, Nicholas de Lyra, and Christian Exegesis," *Westminster Theological Journal* 38 (Fall 1975): 66–79, esp. 70–71. Herman Hailperin's book, *Rashi and the Christian Scholars*, has an excellent chapter on Nicholas de Lyra's use of the Bible and Jewish sources. Herman Hailperin, *Rashi and the Christian Scholars* (Pittsburgh: University of Pittsburgh Press, 1963), 137–246.
86. This is the name de Lyra used for Rashi.
87. Merrill, "Rashi, Nicholas de Lyra, and Christian Exegesis," 71.
88. Jeremy Cohen, *The Friars and the Jews* (Ithaca, NY: Cornell, 1982), 177.
89. Hailperin, *Rashi and the Christian Scholars*, 139–40.
90. Ibid., 140–41. Hailperin's positive appraisal of de Lyra is challenged by Cohen in his *Friars and the Jews*, 176–77. Since Cohen equates all

evangelism among Jews as "anti-Jewish," this explains his negative assessment of de Lyra.

91. Hailperin, *Rashi and the Christian Scholars*, 178.
92. Ibid., 157ff.
93. Ibid., 160–61.
94. Ibid., 177–83.
95. Ibid., 162.
96. Ibid., 163–67.
97. Ibid., 174–75.
98. Ibid.; Williams, *Adversus Judaeos*, 409–10.
99. James Samuel Preus, *From Shadow to Promise: Old Testament Interpretation from Augustine to Young Luther* (Cambridge: Belknap, 1969), 68.
100. Cohen, *The Friars and the Jews*, 190–91.
101. Ibid., 191.
102. Yitzhak Baer, *A History of the Jews in Christian Spain*, 2 vols., trans. Louis Schoffman (Philadelphia: JPS, 1961), 1:325–30.
103. Ibid., 1:330.
104. Ibid., 1:346.
105. Ibid., 1:334.
106. Ibid., 1:353–54.
107. Williams, *Adversus Judaeos*, 260.
108. Baer, *A History of the Jews in Christian Spain*, 1:339–40.
109. Schonfield, *The History of Jewish Christianity*, 156; and Baer, *A History of the Jews in Christian Spain*, 2:139–40.
110. Schonfield, *The History of Jewish Christianity*, 157.
111. Williams, *Adversus Judaeos*, 268.
112. Schonfield, *The History of Jewish Christianity*, 157; and Baer, *A History of the Jews in Christian Spain*, 2:140–42.
113. Williams, *Adversus Judaeos*, 268. Schonfield's biographical information on Paul (*The History of Jewish Christianity*, 156–62) is most sympathetic, whereas Baer (*A History of the Jews in Christian Spain*, 2:139–50) is harsh and critical, suspecting Paul of converting for financial and political gain (ibid., 2:144–45) and of fostering anti-Jewish measures at the royal court (ibid., 2:155). The difference in the presentations is no doubt a result of the two authors' different attitudes toward Jewish Christians. When Schonfield wrote his history, he identified himself as a Jewish Christian. On the other hand, Baer at no time seeks to conceal his antipathy for Jewish Christians. Even so, Baer does recognize Paul as one who wanted to retain some Jewish identity, classifying him as one who "wished to retain a foot in both doors" and as "the foremost converso" of that period (Baer, *A History of the Jews in Christian Spain*, 2:139). Norman Roth's recent book confirms Schonfield's biography, not Baer's. Norman Roth, *Conversos, Inquisition and the Expulsion of the Jews from Spain* (Madison: University of Wisconsin Press, 1995), 136–44.
114. Baer, *A History of the Jews in Christian Spain*, 143.
115. Jose Faur identifies Paul as a converso who actually considered himself hierarchically superior to Gentile Christians because of his Jewish heritage. In his dedication to his *Additiones ad postillam Magistri Lyra*

(1429), he reminded his son of their Jewish and priestly origin and exhorted him to continue in this tradition. Jose Faur, *In the Shadow of History: Jews and Conversos at the Dawn of Modernity* (Albany: State University of New York Press, 1992), 48.

116. Williams, *Adversus Judaeos*, 269.

117. Preus, *From Shadow to Promise*, 86.

118. Hailperin has understood Paul of Burgos as an opponent of de Lyra's literal method. Hailperin, *Rashi and the Christian Scholars*, 259. Preus explains that Hailperin has misread him because he failed to recognize "that the structure of Burgos' prologue is that of a scholastic *quaestio*, done in good Thomistic form." Thus, Hailperin takes the objections that Burgos would first state and then refute, as being Burgos's actual position. Preus, *From Shadow to Promise*, 86.

119. Preus, *From Shadow to Promise*, 88–89.

120. Ibid., 96.

121. Ibid., 97.

122. Schonfield, *The History of Jewish Christianity*, 157.

123. Baer, *A History of the Jews in Christian Spain*, 2:139, 171. Joshua Halorki had written to Solomon (Paul) challenging his friend's newfound faith. Unfortunately, very little of Solomon's extensive reply remains. Baer explains that it was "destroyed by Jewish copyists who saw no point in handing down the details of his theological views." Baer, *A History of the Jews in Christian Spain*, 2:148.

124. Norman Roth has recently argued that most of the conversos in Spain during the fourteenth and fifteenth centuries were not crypto-Jews, as commonly thought, but rather genuine Christians. He writes, "Curiously, it seems to be as difficult for some modern Christians as for Jewish historians to accept the simple fact, demonstrated here repeatedly, that the overwhelming majority of the Jews who converted did so because they sincerely believed in Christianity and just as sincerely were convinced of the falseness of the Jewish faith." Roth, *Conversos, Inquisition and the Expulsion of the Jews from Spain*, 133–34.

125. Ibid., 188–98; and Jocz, *The Jewish People and Jesus Christ*, 219–20.

126. Jocz, *The Jewish People and Jesus Christ*, 221–23.

127. Ibid., 395.

128. Although many works about Messianic prophecy are from the modern era, all were not devoted to using Messianic prophecy for Jewish evangelism. To read a literature review of modern era works on Messianic prophecy, see Rydelnik, *The Promise of Messiah*, 17–27.

129. German Lutheran Pietism had stimulated the beginnings of Protestant worldwide missionary outreach. It also was directly instrumental in launching the first organized evangelistic work among the Jewish people. Nikolaus Ludwig, later Count Von Zinzendorf (1700–1760), studied at Halle as a child. There, he was warmly influenced toward Jewish missions by the Pietists. As a result, the Moravian Church, through Zinzendorf's influence, was the first to establish a ministry to the Jews, which continued until Zinzendorf's death. A. E. Thompson, *A Century of Jewish Missions* (Chicago: Revell, 1902), 91–92. In 1728, at the University of Halle, a formal training school for Jewish missionaries

was established (Institutum Judaicum) where Deilitzsch later taught. The London Jews Society, however, was truly the first enduring modern Jewish mission with a worldwide impact.

130.   This agency was later known as "The London Jews Society," then "The British Jews Society," after World War II as "The Church's Mission to the Jews," and today as "The Church's Ministry Among the Jews." In the United States, it is currently known as "A Christian Ministry Among Jewish People."

131.   Thompson, *A Century of Jewish Missions*, 95–96.

132.   Alexander McCaul, *Lectures on the Messiahship of Jesus* (London: Unwin, n.d.), 139–88.

133.   David Baron, *Rays of Messiah's Glory* (London: Wheeler and Wheeler, 1886), 181–83.

134.   Thompson, *A Century of Jewish Missions*, 92.

135.   Ibid., 132–34.

136.   Franz Delitzsch, *Messianic Prophecies in Historical Succession*, trans. Samuel Ives Curtiss (Edinburgh: T & T Clark, 1891), 3.

137.   Ibid.

138.   For biographical information on David Baron, see E. Bendor Samuel, *David Baron and the Hebrew Christian Testimony to Israel* (London: Hebrew Christian Testimony, 1943); George Stevens, *Jewish Christian Leaders* (New York: Oliphant, 1966), 74–79; and Jacob Gartenhaus, *Famous Hebrew Christians* (Grand Rapids: Baker, 1979), 37–44.

139.   David Baron, *The Shepherd of Israel and His Scattered Flock* (London: Morgan and Scott, 1910), 130, emphasis his.

140.   Baron, *Rays of Messiah's Glory*, 1886.

141.   David Baron, *Types, Psalms, and Prophecies* (1906; New York: American Board of Missions to the Jews, 1948).

142.   David Baron, *The Servant of Jehovah* (London: Morgan and Scott, 1922).

143.   Williams, *Adversus Judaeos*.

144.   A. Lukyn Williams, *A Manual of Christian Evidences for Jewish People*, 2 vols. (New York: Cambridge, 1911).

145.   Troki, *Chizzuk Emunah*. This work was translated and published in recent times (1970) under the authorship of Isaac Troki and the English title, *Faith Strengthened*, trans. Moses Mocatta (New York: Hermon, 1970).

146.   Williams, *Adversus Judaeos*, viii.

147.   Ibid., ix.

148.   Ibid., 221–22.

149.   Ibid., 221. I disagree with Williams and take the Son of Man of Daniel 7 to be the Messiah.

150.   Sound exegesis is not characterized by adopting critical perspectives and thereby denying the validity of most, if not all, Messianic prophecies.

151.   That is not to say, as Pablo Christiani did, that the Talmudic authorities believed that Jesus was the Messiah but refused to acknowledge him. Rather, it is imperative to be aware of those passages that Talmudic authorities deemed Messianic but that are applied to others by Jewish authorities today.

152. There has been a proliferation of anti-Christian Jewish polemical materials in recent years. Some volumes that should be examined are Aryeh Kaplan, *The Real Messiah* (New York: Art Scroll, 1990); Samuel Levine, *You Take Jesus, I'll Take God*, rev. ed. (Los Angeles: Hamoroh, 1980); and Gerald Sigel, *The Jew and the Christian Missionary: A Jewish Response to Missionary Christianity* (New York: Ktav, 1981). Also, Rabbi Tovia Singer has produced a tape series titled *Let's Get Biblical*, audiotapes (Monsey, NY: Outreach Judaism, 1995) that is significant in its opposition to the Christian understanding of Messianic prophecy.

153. Jocz, *The Jewish People and Jesus Christ*, 208.

Chapter 14: One Way for Jews and Gentiles in the New Millennium

1. Gersom Gorenberg, "Warning! Millennium Ahead!" in *The Jerusalem Report*, February 19, 1998, 14–19. Cf. also "Inside the Mind of a Millennial Cult Leader," *The Jerusalem Report*, February 1, 1999, 12–15; and Judy Siegel-Itzkovich, "Preparing for the False Prophet," in *The Jerusalem Post*, January 1, 1999.

2. Cf. Oscar Cullmann, *Christ and Time: The Primitive Christian Conception of Time and History* (London: SCM, 1962), 81–93.

3. Kai Kjær-Hansen, *Joseph Rabinowitz and the Messianic Movement* (Grand Rapids: Eerdmans, 1995), 57–58.

4. Nahum N. Glatzer, ed., *Franz Rosenzweig: His Life and Thought* (New York: Schocken Books, 1953), 341.

5. See, e.g., Ronald H. Miller, *Dialogue and Disagreement: Franz Rosenzweig's Relevance to Contemporary Jewish-Christian Understanding* (Lanham, MD: University Press of America, 1989). Concerning criticism of two covenant theology from evangelical quarters, see Maurice G. Bowler, "Rosenzweig on Judaism and Christianity," *Mishkan* 11 (1989): 1–8; Arnulf H. Baumann, "The Two Ways/Two Covenants Theory," *Mishkan* 11 (1989): 36–43; and Mitch Glaser, "Critique of the Two Covenant Theory," *Mishkan* 11 (1989): 44–70. See also Louis Goldberg, *Are There Two Ways of Atonement?* (Baltimore: Lederer Publications, 1990); and Kai Kjær-Hansen, "The Problem of the Two-Covenant Theology," in *Mishkan* 21 (1994): 52–81.

6. Nahum N. Glatzer, introduction to *The Star of Redemption*, by Franz Rosenzweig (Boston: Beacon, 1972), x.

7. Glatzer, *Franz Rosenzweig*, 23–24.

8. Ibid., 25.

9. Nahum N. Glatzer, "Franz Rosenzweig," in *Great Twentieth Century Jewish Philosophers* (Washington, DC: B'nai B'erith Books, 1985), 162; cf. Goldberg, *Are There Two Ways of Atonement?* 7.

10. Goldberg, *Are Their Two Ways of Atonement?* 6.

11. Glatzer, *Franz Rosenzweig*, 27–28.

12. Ibid., 341

13. Ibid., 28.

14. Phillip Sigal, *Judaism: The Evolution of a Faith* (Grand Rapids: Eerdmans, 1988), 263.

15. Glatzer, *Franz Rosenzweig*, x.
16. Ibid., 27–28.
17. Ibid., 407.
18. Frank Ephraim Talmage, *Disputation and Dialogue* (New York: KTAV, 1975), 245.
19. Shemaryahu Talmon, "Das Verhältnis von Judentum und Christentum in Verständnis Franz Rosenzweigs," in *Offenbarung im Denken Franz Rosenzweig*, eds. R. Schaeffer, Bernhard Kasper, Shermaryahu Talmon, and Yehoshua Amir (Essen: Ludgerus, 1979), 133.
20. Rosenzweig, *The Star of Redemption*, 415.
21. Ibid., 415–16.
22. Ibid., 416.
23. Ibid., 350.
24. Ibid., 399.
25. Ibid., 341.
26. Edith Rosenzweig, ed., *Franz Rosenzweig/Briefe* (Berlin: Schocken Verlag, 1935), 553.
27. See Kjær-Hansen, "The Problem of the Two-Covenant Theology," 74–78.
28. See Yechiel Eckstein, *What You Should Know About Jews and Judaism* (Waco, TX: Word, 1984), 321.
29. Talmage, *Disputation and Dialogue*, 369.
30. Baumann, "The Two Ways/Two Covenants Theory," 37.
31. Talmon, "Das Verhältnis von Judentum und Christentum in Verständnis Franz Rosenzweigs," 135.
32. Ibid., 136.
33. Joachim Jeremias, *Rediscovering the Parables* (London: SCM, 1966), 104.
34. Ibid., 103
35. Robert L. Lindsey, "Dialogue or Mission or . . . ?" in *Let Jews and Arabs Hear His Voice*, ed. Ole Chr. M. Kvarme (Jerusalem: United Christian Council in Israel, 1981), 54.
36. Kenneth E. Bailey, *Poet and Peasant* (Grand Rapids: Eerdmans 1976), 206.
37. See Roy Eckardt, *Elder and Younger Brother* (New York: Schocken Books, 1973); and Rosemary Ruther, *Faith and Fratricide: The Theological Roots of Anti-Semitism* (New York: Seabury, 1974), 254–55.
38. Cf. David Berger, "Jewish-Christian Relations: A Jewish Perspective," *Journal of Ecumenical Studies* 20.1 (1983): 9.
39. Cf. Clemens Thoma, *A Christian Theology of Judaism* (New York: Paulist, 1980), 134; in David Flusser, "To What Extent Is Jesus a Question for the Jews?" *Concilium* 5.10 (1974): 71.
40. Hans Ucko, *Common Roots—New Horizons: Learning About Christian Faith from Dialogue with Jews* (Geneva: WCC Publications, 1994), 83–84.
41. Hans Joachim Schoeps, *Paul: The Theology of the Apostle in the Light of Jewish Religious History* (London: Lutterworth, 1961), 256–58.
42. "The Willowbank Declaration on the Gospel and the Jewish People," *Mishkan* 11 (1989): 71–84.

43. Darell Turner, "Evangelical Statement Stresses Importance of Witness to Jews," in *Religious News Service*, May 9, 1989.
44. Peter Steinfel, "Evangelical Group Urges Conversion of Jews," in *New York Times*, May 21, 1989.
45. "Ecumenical Debate: Preaching Jesus While Respecting Other Faiths," in *Los Angeles Times*, May 27, 1989.
46. In *Chicago Jewish Sentinel*, June 8, 1989. The references in notes 43, 44 and 45 above are available in Tuvya Zaretsky, "A Report: Response to the Willowbank Declaration," presented at the Lusanne Consultation on Jewish Evangelism meeting in St. Louis, March 15, 1990.
47. *Christian and Israel: A Quarterly Publications from Jerusalem* 5.4 (Autumn 1996): 1. This is published by the Association of Christians and Jews in Israel, Jerusalem.
48. Kjær-Hansen, *Joseph Rabinowitz and the Messianic Movement*, 235.